Scribe Publications
POZIÈRES

Scott Bennett was born in Bairnsdale, Victoria, in 1966, and holds an Executive Master of Business Administration from the Australian Graduate School of Management at the University of Sydney. Over the last ten years, he has worked for many of Australia's most recognised retail companies as a management consultant or an executive manager.

In 2003, he visited the Great War battlefields in France and Belgium to retrace the steps of his great-uncles, who had fought there. The experience led him to question the many 'truths' that have developed around the Anzac legend. The result was the writing of *Pozières*, which re-examines the battle of Pozières and the Anzac legend.

To my special girls: Alexandra, Isabella, and Amelia.
Thank you for your patience.

In loving memory of James 'Jim' Bennett

POZIÈRES
THE ANZAC STORY

Scott Bennett

SCRIBE
Melbourne

Scribe Publications Pty Ltd
18–20 Edward St, Brunswick, Victoria, Australia 3056
Email: info@scribepub.com.au

First published by Scribe 2011
This edition published 2012

Copyright © Scott Bennett 2011

All rights reserved. Without limiting the rights under copyright reserved above, no part of this publication may be reproduced, stored in or introduced into a retrieval system, or transmitted, in any form or by any means (electronic, mechanical, photocopying, recording or otherwise) without the prior written permission of the publisher of this book.

Typeset in Minion by the publishers.
Maps by Bruce Godden
Printed and bound in Australia by Griffin Press.

The paper this book is printed on is certified against the Forest Stewardship Council® Standards. Griffin Press holds FSC chain of custody certification SGS-COC-005088. FSC promotes environmentally responsible, socially beneficial and economically viable management of the world's forests.

National Library of Australia
Cataloguing-in-Publication data

Bennett, Scott, 1966-

Pozières: the Anzac story.

New ed.

9781921844836 (pbk.)

Includes bibliographical references and index.

1. Somme, 1st Battle of the, France, 1916. 2. World War, 1914-1918–Campaigns–France. 3. World War, 1914-1918–Participation, Australian.
4. Pozières (France)–History, Military.

940.4272

www.scribepublications.com.au

He died a hero's death,
They said,
When they came to tell me
My boy was dead;

But out in the street
A dead dog lies;
Flies in his mouth,
Ants in his eyes.

— Mary Gilmore, 'War'

Contents

Introduction	ix
1 The Road to Pozières	1
2 Foreboding	22
3 Fromelles	35
4 Lurid Clouds of War	43
5 Storming Pozières	54
6 Consolidation	69
7 The Pozières Ridge	94
8 The Price of Glory	117
9 Legge's Reckoning	131
10 Promised Land	143
11 Folly	173
12 *La Ferme du Mouquet*	188
13 Kicking in the Back Door	208
14 Second Stunt	222
15 Battering Ram	243
16 Graveyard or Glory	262
17 Aftermath	275
18 War-weariness	287
19 The Missing	303
Abbreviations	327
References	331
Notes	345
Acknowledgements	385
Index	387

Maps

1	The Allied and British Front Line in Northern France	2
2	The Somme District	9
3	The Battlefield Between 22 July and 5 September	55
4	2nd Division's Advance on OG lines	135
5	I Anzac Corps' Advance on Mouquet Farm, August to September 1916	195
6	4th Division's Advance on Mouquet Farm	263
7	The Gains of the Somme Offensive	285

I have chosen to reproduce all quotations from letters, diaries, and official sources exactly as they appear in the source documents, with no alteration to spelling, punctuation, or grammar. Ranks cited are those held at the time of the events being described in the text.

Introduction

> '*Many loved Truth, and lavished life's best oil*
> *Amid the dust of books to find her*'
> — James Russell Lowell, 'Commemoration Ode'

In July 1916, 24-year-old Private Arthur Foxcroft sat in the French staging village of Warloy, a needle and thread in hand, purposefully stitching away. Close by sat the other men of C Company, 4th Battalion, blokes like 'Bluey' Wilson and Paddy South, each concentrating hard, carefully threading a needle through a rough-cut square of flannel to affix it to the back of his coarse, pea-coloured tunic. These seemingly innocuous flannels, pink and frayed around the edges, could mean the difference between life and death in the coming battle — Foxcroft noted in his diary that they would enable artillery observers to identify the soldiers while they were charging.[1]

The roads nearby heaved with activity: columns of troops marched toward the front line while a slow procession of motorised field ambulances returned from the other direction, carrying broken men. Teams of horses, hauling ammunition limbers destined for the forward-supply dumps, stirred up clouds of dust as they went by. French peasants scattered about the fields, flaying their sickles at the sun-bleached hay, were ambivalent about the frenetic activity; for them, the war seemed just another force of nature to contend with, like floods, famine, or drought.[2]

Foxcroft was a world away from the little town of Gilgandra, New South Wales, where he had humped his swag in 1914, searching for work. He had taken a job as a farmhand, but it turned out to be backbreaking work. Soldiering, with a wage of 'six bob a day', had seemed a better proposition than battling against the severe drought that had baked the Outback dry. In August 1915, no doubt motivated by the widely reported exploits of the Australian troops on Gallipoli, he offered his services to the British Empire.

Just eleven months later, Foxcroft — who had spent the past week marching through the northern French countryside, through vast, ripening crops and scarlet poppies in full bloom — had been transformed into a soldier ready to fight, and possibly die, in the coming battle.

After finishing their needlework, the soldiers discarded all unnecessary kit. They would only carry the essentials into battle: a change of underclothing, a woollen blanket, a waterproof sheet, 120 rounds of small-arms ammunition, a rifle and bayonet, basic rations, a steel helmet, an entrenching tool, and a great overcoat.[3] Coloured armbands were allocated to those soldiers, such as runners and signallers, who had special functions to perform.[4]

Foxcroft's platoon officer, 23-year-old Second Lieutenant William Clemenger, checked the soldiers' kit: water bottles had to be positioned on the right hip; haversacks, just below the shoulder blades; ground sheets, in the small of the back; the entrenching tool moved to the front; and the ammunition bandoliers slung over the right shoulder.[5]

Just before dusk on 19 July 1916, C Company set off on the last leg of its march eastward, toward the sound of the distant, booming cannons, which shook the nearby houses. Foxcroft was one of about 60,000 soldiers of I Anzac Corps (ANZAC was the official acronym of the Australian and New Zealand Army Corps; members of the corps were informally known as Anzacs).⁶ The corps, composed of three all-Australian divisions, was converging upon a small parcel of land bordering the gloomy Somme river, where one million men were already locked in battle.⁷

Almost two years before I Anzac Corps began its journey eastward, the Great War — or the First World War, as it is known today — had erupted. Germany's armies, in a pre-emptive blow, swept through Belgium and into the rump of France in a desperate attempt to knock the country and its ally Britain out of the war before Russia could fully mobilise its massive force on the Eastern Front. The French armies managed to check the German advance a month later, in early September 1914, effectively ending the war of mobility. The combatants then entrenched themselves along a front line running from the North Sea down to the Swiss border. The Allies remained determined to break the deadlock, and on 1 July 1916 the French and British armies launched a massive offensive that became known as the Battle of the Somme. Yet by mid-July the 'Big Push' had stalled. The small farming village of Pozières was proving to be the impenetrable obstacle.⁸

Before the war, Pozières was a little-known village strung along the Bapaume road.⁹ However, Pozières's location, on the highest ridge of the Somme, meant that militarily it was valuable: it provided the Germans with a clear view across the surrounding valleys and into the British positions. If the British could expel the Germans from Pozières, they would snatch this critical advantage. Pozières also provided a potential backdoor route to capturing the German strongpoint of Thiepval, a once-beautiful village that had been dominated by a magnificent château and its surrounding wood, but the château had been destroyed and its ruins converted into a German-held fortress. After five bloody and unsuccessful attempts by British troops to take Pozières, the British high command assigned the unenviable task to the Anzacs.

Just after midnight on 23 July 1916, wave after wave of Anzac soldiers stormed the seemingly impregnable village. Over the next seven weeks they inched their way forward over shell-torn ground. When the corps was relieved on 3 September, it only had secured a few miles of shattered landscape — and at the frightful cost of 23,000 casualties. Yet despite their small gains and staggering losses, the Anzacs' efforts were widely celebrated. British historian Lyn Macdonald stated that as long as battles were remembered, the names of Pozières and the Anzacs would never be separated; British Expeditionary Force commander-in-chief General Sir Douglas Haig claimed that its capture would live in history; Australia's official war historian, Charles Bean, wrote that no acre in France was more richly steeped with Australian blood; and British poet laureate John Masefield believed that Pozières was as famous as Troy during those weeks in 1916.[10]

And yet, seeing Pozières today, I found it hard to believe that it was ever worth fighting and dying for. It's a blur of cottages barely noticeable while one travels along the Bapaume road to more-interesting places; it's no different from dozens of other villages dotted around the Somme countryside. There is nothing to suggest that it had any strategic importance back then, at least not enough to justify the masses of neatly tended cemeteries close by. I found myself asking why a labourer from Gilgandra — let alone 60,000 young Australian men — was thrown into conflict to capture such a minor prize. I couldn't help but question how a battle that resulted in such heavy casualties could be conceived as a victory.

To make sense of the events, I tried to connect with those men who had fought there, such as Foxcroft, by reading their fragile diaries and letters, held in libraries and museums. Their words reveal that they were excited and battle-hungry as they marched through the French countryside toward the Somme Valley. Yet their thoughts quickly turned from glory to survival once the battle erupted in all its chaos. In the trenches, they pondered simple yet crucial questions such as where they would sleep that night, whether the shelling would stop them from getting their day's rations, and when they would be relieved. They didn't mention valiant charges or glorious victories, but instead described how they cowered in shallow trenches, surrounded by bloated corpses, praying that the relentless German bombardments wouldn't bury them alive or kill them.

After escaping Pozières, they became sombre and reflective. They asked themselves why they had survived when others had not. They contemplated whether it would be better to have lived a life — any life, even one under German rule — than to have been subjected to the horrors of Pozières. Some wondered if God was really on their side.

Tellingly, their diaries cast doubt upon the many 'truths' that Australians have been fed about the Anzacs — a legend that has shaped our country's cultural identity. The embodiment of the legend, a bush-bred, square-jawed, and physically imposing man, does not feature in their diaries.[11] The fighting qualities that define an Anzac — an indifference to danger, nonchalance toward death, fierceness in battle, and natural competence as a leader — are rarely mentioned. Rather, they revealed that Australian officers were just as capable of sending their troops to slaughter in ill-conceived attacks as their British counterparts, and that most Australian soldiers were ordinary men who, at times, were understandably overcome with fear — sometimes deserting, refusing to go up to the front line, or running away once they got there. They reveal how Australian commanders grappled with a battle conducted on a scale never before experienced and how, after the war, many veterans struggled to live up to the suffocating Anzac legend.

But their diaries don't explain why the Pozières battle — a bloody and controversial military engagement on the Western Front — has been largely neglected by Australians while the Gallipoli campaign has etched itself upon the national psyche. Their diaries don't help us to understand why the numbers that turn out for the Gallipoli anniversary continue to swell while the Pozières anniversary passes without notice, or why Gallipoli has become a place of pilgrimage when there is little at Pozières to signify its importance to Australians.

In writing this book, I wanted to strip away the perceived 'truths' and to document the raw experiences of those individuals connected to the battle. I wanted to develop a deeper understanding of how the conflict touched its wide ensemble of characters — volunteer privates, career commanders, grieving mothers, war correspondents, veterans struggling to forget the battle, and future generations trying to make sense of it. How did the fight for Pozières change their lives, and what legacy did it leave upon their society?

This book is not primarily a military dissection of the Pozières battle; rather, the battle is the backdrop against which I've tried to explore the motivations and emotions of those involved. The key conflicts are laid out not to preserve the correct sequence of military events, but to give the reader a sense of how repetitive the attacks were, and how they gradually ground down the Australian soldiers' spirit and fighting capabilities. Nor is this book written in homage to those select few — one in 10,000 — awarded the empire's highest honour for valour, the Victoria Cross. To tell the story through their eyes would be like telling the story of Australia through the eyes of a lottery winner.

Nearly 7000 young Australians died at Pozières. After the battle, the curtains were drawn in thousands of homes across Australia. How did a mother like Hester Allen cope when told that her two sons would never return home? It was frowned upon to display emotions in public — Melbourne's *Argus* told its readers on 3 May 1915 that they must exhibit the self-control of a ruling race and not let their private sufferings dim their eyes to the glory of those injured or killed for the empire. 'No eyes can see us weep,' grieving mothers wrote in newspaper *in memoriam* notices on the anniversaries of their sons' deaths.[12] Hester had no grave at which to mourn — her sons' remains were never recovered. She wrote letters to their friends, officers, and the Red Cross, searching for answers, but few were ever proffered. Pozières resulted in thousands of Hester Allens.

In addition, almost 17,000 were wounded at Pozières. How does one 'recover' from a wound inflicted in a modern industrialised war?

What impact does a piece of jagged iron propelled at high velocity have upon human flesh, and the human mind? How did 23-year-old Private Roy Smith explain to his mother that his mangled leg had been amputated? And what of the thousands of soldiers who suffered from 'shell shock', the condition associated with the rise of industrialised warfare? Many felt ashamed that their 'nerves' had given way in battle. Proud men like schoolmaster Captain John Harris could not reconcile their bravery on one day with their lack of it on another. Some veterans felt too ashamed to march on Anzac Day.

The correspondents reporting on the battle rarely got close to the fighting. Yet when they did, they were often torn between their desire to report on the waste of human life and their duty to maintain morale back home. Official war correspondent Charles Bean exemplified those facing this dilemma. British prime minister David Lloyd George stated that if the correspondents reported the suffering of the Somme offensive truthfully, the public would stop the war in a day.[13] It was an ethical dilemma that each correspondent continually tried to navigate, and it often resulted in them recording 'public' and 'private' accounts of the war.

For politicians like prime minister William Morris Hughes, Pozières also posed a moral question. Although Hughes abhorred the deaths, it was a political reality that each fatality provided him with an additional bargaining chip when dealing with his British counterparts. By the war's end, Hughes could claim for Australia a seat at the Paris Peace Conference — an unthinkable possibility four years earlier. But the blood of 60,000 young Australians had paid for it. Did the political gains justify the lives lost at Pozières?

Australians closely monitored the Pozières battle through the newspapers. In July and August 1916, *The Sydney Morning Herald* published optimistic reports on the battle's progress, while the Melbourne *Herald* repeatedly reassured its readers that casualties were 'light', 'comfortably few', and 'less than expected'.[14] Then the butcher's bill came in, spilling over many pages. Between 2 August and 23 September, *The Herald* reported 21,000 casualties — Australia had incurred the same number of casualties in seven weeks as it had over each of the war's preceding two years. The escalating casualty lists pierced the public's resolve: people were shocked, and felt deceived. On 12 August 1916, the minister for defence publicly denied rumours that the government had deliberately tried to conceal the true extent of the casualties.[15] Cracks opened between the public and those once-trusted institutions — the British Empire, the government, the church, and the press — which were viewed as being in some way complicit in the slaughter. By October 1916, those cracks had widened into a chasm, culminating in the nation rejecting the government's plea to vote 'yes' in the conscription referendum.

Perhaps the shocking casualty lists contributed to the public's attitudes to Gallipoli and Pozières. If Gallipoli signified Australia's 'debut' on the world stage, Pozières laid bare the consequences of a small nation, still uncertain of its identity, participating in an international war. Gallipoli symbolised the nation's coming of age, while Pozières exposed the darker, uglier side of war. Gallipoli had a tinge of romanticism about it — young troops sailing to an ancient land where Achilles and Hector had gallantly fought over Troy — while Pozières represented industrialised warfare dominated by machine guns, barbed wire, and artillery. Pozières showed Australians the terrible cost of participating in a European war.

There is also a personal dimension for me in writing about Pozières: its consequences have reached across four generations of my family. When I was a teenager, my grandmother bequeathed to me a yellowed newspaper clipping; it read: 'Youngest AIF [Australian Imperial Force] soldier, enlisting at fourteen, lad fights at Pozières.'[16] It told the story of her older brother, Ernie Lee, and ignited my interest. I wanted to understand why that 14-year-old boy from Mossiface, Victoria, had felt compelled to enlist, and what he experienced at Pozières. I wanted to know what solace Ernie's mother, Mary Lee, drew from him being cloaked in the Anzac legend — did it dull the pain she felt after losing her other son, Jack, on the Western Front? What motivated my grandmother to cling to that clipping for 70 years and then pass it on to me? And why did I feel compelled, in 2003, to visit distant battlefields in order to better understand my great-uncles' experiences?

Other Australians, like me, are increasingly curious about the Great War, particularly the conflict on the Western Front. Recent books have lifted the shroud on neglected battles such as Fromelles, Mont St Quentin, Villers-Bretonneux, and Passchendaele; but only one, *Pozières 1916* by Peter Charlton, published over 20 years ago, has attempted to tell the Pozières story in full, although it clung to those popular visions of the Anzacs as fearless and brave, and British officers as the incompetent foils.

I hope that this book, told through the eyes of its many participants, will help us re-evaluate the long-neglected Pozières battle. Perhaps, after 95 years, we are ready to try to make sense of it.

CHAPTER ONE

The Road to Pozières

'The paths of glory lead but to the grave.'
— Thomas Gray, 'Elegy Written in a Country Churchyard'

In the unseasonably hot days of early August 1914, decades of pent-up nationalist fervour, rampant militarism, frenetic empire-building, petty royal jealousies, industrial rivalries, and colonialist ambition erupted into war upon the European continent. Within weeks, armies of Frenchmen — wearing ceremonial red trousers and blue coats, and blowing bugles — and Britons, dressed in grey-brown tunics and 'flat-top caps' and whistling marching tunes, marched off to war. Many clung to the hope of a speedy victory against the Germans.[1]

By late August, the shattered British and French armies were retreating in the wake of the Germans' pre-emptive and rapid advance through Belgium and France. In September, as the Germans pushed toward Paris, the French fought desperately, managing to check their enemy's advance near the river Marne. By late December 1914, the brief war of mobility had petered out into a stalemate, but not before the French had suffered almost one million casualties and the British Expeditionary Force had been largely destroyed. The illusion of a quick victory had evaporated, replaced by the bleak reality of a long and grinding struggle.

The draining stalemate persisted throughout 1915. The British and French armies' limited attempts to break through the solidified 500-mile front line, running from the North Sea to the Swiss border, failed miserably. But 1916 appeared to offer renewed hope: Italy entered the war on the Allies' side; Russia replenished its shattered army with new conscripts; France's wrecked army had been partially repaired; and Britain had recruited and trained the New Army, composed of citizen–soldiers. The enlivened Allies, according to Australia's official war correspondent, Charles Bean, were intent upon delivering 'an overwhelming concerted blow against Germany'.[2]

Map 1. The Allied and British Front Line in Northern France

In December 1915, the Allies had met at the French headquarters at Chantilly, agreeing to launch a simultaneous offensive against the Germans on three fronts in mid-1916. The French and British selected the region astride the Somme river as the location for their joint Western Front offensive, mainly because their armies, which each controlled discrete sectors — the British held the front line from Ypres in the far north to the Somme river in the south, while the French held from the Somme river to the Swiss border — intersected there.

In the same month that the Allies had met at Chantilly, the Mediterranean Expeditionary Force had abandoned Gallipoli, admitting defeat in their unsuccessful nine-month attempt to break the deadlock of the war by striking at Germany's supposedly unreliable ally, Turkey. The evacuating force included thousands of Anzacs who had been bloodied on the cragged slopes of what became known as Anzac Cove.

By January 1916, the Gallipoli Anzacs, along with other redirected troops, had arrived in Egypt, where Britain's secretary of state for war, Lord Horatio Kitchener, expected the Turkish forces 'to set the East in a blaze'.[3] As well as defending Egypt, the Anzac Corps would act as an 'Empire reserve', ready to assist in other operations, such as those planned for the Western Front.

According to Bean, tens of thousands of Australians and New Zealanders had also been inspired to enlist by the Gallipoli campaign, the first casualty lists, the sinking of the crowded passenger liner *Lusitania* by a German U-boat, and the realisation that the war hung in the balance.[4] The fresh troops flooded into Egypt in late 1915 and early 1916, providing British Lieutenant-General Sir William ('Birdie') Birdwood, who had temporary control of the Anzac Corps, and his Australian chief-of-staff, Brigadier-General Cyril Brudenell White, the opportunity to reorganise and expand from three Anzac divisions to six, and from one corps to two. Arthur Foxcroft was one of those fresh troops who arrived in Egypt in early 1916. Upon landing, he marvelled at the great mass of Anzacs already there: 'One would wonder where all the Australians came from; fine body of men,' he wrote in his diary.⁵

As the threat of the Turks attacking in the east gradually diminished, the likelihood of the Anzacs transferring to the Western Front increased. On 16 February 1916, the British commander-in-chief in the Middle East, General Sir Archibald Murray, told Birdie that I Anzac Corps (at that stage comprising the 1st and 2nd Australian divisions and a New Zealand division) had to be ready to sail within two weeks, while II Anzac Corps, under British commander General Sir Alexander Godley and comprising the 4th and 5th Australian divisions, would remain in Egypt until further notice. According to Foxcroft, by the time the 1st and 2nd Australian divisions began sailing for France on 13 March 1916, preparations down to the finest detail — including teaching Anzacs the importance of saluting French and British officers — had largely been completed.⁶

Charles Bean had shadowed the Australian soldiers since September 1914, when he accepted the position of being the country's sole war correspondent, and he accompanied I Anzac Corps on their voyage to France. Bean recognised that the Great War had the potential to reshape the world and, in the process, the young Australian nation, and that his official account would document this transformation. 'I want it to be the truest history that ever was written,' he stated in a letter to his parents.⁷

Bean knew that, as the chronicler of the truth, he had to be clean-living, conscientious, disciplined, above reproach, and scrupulously honest. A 36-year-old bachelor, he adhered to these values as a priest would to the vow of poverty.⁸ Yet, even though Bean searched for some form of 'absolute' truth, he still interpreted events rather subjectively. His main bias was toward the men he was chronicling: he believed that Australians represented the best of the British race and had inherent qualities, such as bravery and natural fighting instincts, which had been honed by their bush lifestyle and made them natural soldiers. Bean believed these men had learnt something of the art of soldiering by the time they were ten years old — how to sleep comfortably in any shelter, how to cook meat or bake flour, how to catch a horse, how to find their way across country by day or night, and how to persevere in tough conditions.[9] He thought that the Great War would provide the opportunity for Australians to prove the virtues of their unique bush ethos.

Bean's love affair with the Australian Outback had ignited when he visited the remote regions of western New South Wales in 1909 to write about the wool industry for *The Sydney Morning Herald*. He was impressed by the quiet determination of the stockmen, the boundary riders, and the station hands. Their adventurous spirit was a contrast to the Englishmen he had seen, who lived in industrialised cities and toiled away mindlessly in bleak factories. For Bean, Australia represented a new and exciting frontier, while Britain symbolised yesterday's world. In his mind, the hard men of Bourke, Broken Hill, and Gundagai would forge the new empire.

Bean's first flirtation with reporting the Australians' exploits had proven painful. His despatches had detailed their poor behaviour — such as drunkenness and indulging in practices that resulted in many contracting disease (Bean refused to mention 'venereal disease' by name in his despatches or diary) — when they first landed in Egypt in 1914, and had drawn a savage response. Soldiers and their families demanded to know why he had publicised the indiscretions of a few among many. Bean quickly found himself an outcast of the Australian Imperial Force, and he felt the estrangement deeply. In the early months of 1915, he often unfolded the offending article and reread it, dwelling on each word; he sought reassurance from officer friends that he had done the right thing in publishing it. 'My job is to tell the people of Australia the truth,' he continually reminded himself.[10]

Bean had decided that his personal diary, which he had kept since waving his father goodbye at Port Melbourne wharf on 21 October 1914, would become his chief personal record of the war.[11] His diary entries — he filled 286 volumes — were jotted down almost daily, irrespective of whether he was tired or half asleep.¹² He purposefully recorded whatever was on his mind, resulting in prose full of raw and unguarded opinions. As well as jotting diary entries, Bean, in his capacity as official war correspondent, continued to draft regular despatches for newspapers, which became one of Australia's main sources of news about the Anzacs. Bean would chronicle the Anzacs' exploits at Pozières in both his diary and official reports.

After the war, Bean drafted the *Official History of Australia in the War of 1914–18*, which recorded the efforts and experiences of his own country in the conflict. Scholar Graham Seal correctly noted in *Inventing Anzac* that 'Bean is everywhere' in the Great War landscape.¹³ His writings seemed to touch every part of Anzac, and eventually shaped how Australians perceived their soldiers' role in the conflict. This was especially true of Pozières: Bean filled nine diaries and drafted many despatches chronicling the Anzacs' exploits on the battlefield.

Fourth Battalion commander Lieutenant-Colonel Iven Mackay was part of the advance party at the port city of Marseilles, preparing for the arrival of the corps in France. The 33-year-old spent two weeks working between the docks and the railway stations, welcoming the troops, marching them through streets lined with French locals throwing rose petals and yelling, *'Vive les Australiens'*, and quickly pushing them north in cattle trucks marked '40 *hommes*, 8 *chevaux*'.¹⁴ Western Australian captain Geoffrey Drake-Brockman of the 2nd Field Company, Engineers, suspected the urgency to shift the troops north was due to the 'thousands of alluring prostitutes parading everywhere, dressed to entice', rather than military imperatives.¹⁵

The Australians were transferred by rail to Armentières, in French Flanders, about 130 miles north of Paris. Drake-Brockman remembered the journey across the undulating country, through miles of orchards filled with pink blossoms, recording in his autobiography that it was 'a magic carpet contrast to the Sahara'. Armentières, located in the British sector, was considered the 'nursery' section of the Western Front, where new troops could learn the skills of trench warfare in moderate safety, compared to other dangerous sectors such as Ypres in Belgium. Yet Drake-Brockman noted: 'Even in the "nursery" artillery fire was infinitely fiercer than at Gallipoli.'

Armentières was cold, damp, and dreary. 'A fortnight ago we were running around with very little clothing and swimming in the Canal. Now we cannot keep ourselves warm,' 7th Battalion medical orderly Albert Coates recorded in his diary.[16] Armentières was below sea level, so breastworks — above-ground trenches constructed with sandbags — had to be built to avoid the high watertable.

On 13 April, I Anzac Corps, which had been allocated to the Second British Army, took control of the front line, south-east of Armentières. 'Our first time in the trenches,' Arthur Foxcroft recorded in his diary in mid-April. 'Very cold.'[17]

I Anzac Corps' introduction to trench warfare in the nursery sector was relatively civilised. Nightly ration parties brought up food on the tramways, water was delivered by pipe, and London newspapers reached them within 48 hours of being printed. Platoons were provided with box respirators and trained on how to respond to poisonous gas, and they practised with the new, lightweight Lewis guns and trench mortars that were now attached to their battalions.[18] The Anzacs experienced heavy anti-aircraft fire for the first time. They stole their first glimpses of the Germans through their field glasses, and were surprised by the accuracy of the Germans' artillery, which had the knack of landing a shell at a busy intersection or directly on an Australian battery. 'Somebody in the landscape is clearly watching you all the time,' noted Bean.[19] Although the Australians did not realise it, the intermittent shelling they experienced at Armentières would be a precursor to the violent barrages of curtain fire they would constantly be exposed to on the Somme.

On 1 July, while the Anzacs familiarised themselves with life on the Western Front, the French and British launched their summer offensive, with around 18 divisions attacking along a 22-mile front in the Somme region.[20] The objectives of the offensive were three-fold: to break the German line; to grind the Germans down; and to relieve the pressure upon the French, further south at Verdun. On the first day of the offensive, the Allies' casualties were extraordinarily heavy, with little ground gained. The British troops, who had walked into a storm of steel, suffered 57,000 casualties — 19,000 killed outright or mortally wounded, 35,000 wounded, and 2000 taken prisoner. This day, years in the planning and moments in the execution, was the bloodiest in the British Empire's history. What haunted the British survivors most was the sheer hopelessness of their task: 'I could see a wall of German soldiers standing shoulder-to-shoulder right along the parapet of their front-line trench, waving us to come on,' remembered Private Ramage. Captain Alan Hanbury-Sparrow of the 8th British Division never forgot the sight of Germans standing well atop their trenches, firing and sniping at those men stranded in no-man's-land.[21]

Despite the carnage, the German line collapsed in some places; however, severe casualties and confusion prevented the British from exploiting these fleeting opportunities. It seemed that any hope of 'piercing the line' was evaporating. The British commander-in-chief, General Sir Douglas Haig, relied on Brigadier-General John Charteris, his chief-of-intelligence, for clues on how far the Germans were from collapse. Charteris, known as the 'principal's boy', told Haig that although the Germans had put up a first-class fight, their morale was low.[22]

It was decided that as long as there was a chance, a possibility, of a German collapse, the offensive would continue. The British had invested too much emotion, effort, and hope for it to be wound down without them having made any considerable gains. In addition, Britain's Allies, France and Russia, had shouldered the burden of the war for two years, and would never have allowed it. Both had chalked up one million dead soldiers by the end of 1915. Casualties like these were simply the price of membership to the Allied cause.

Over the next weeks, the Allies gradually edged forward, securing the first line of German trenches south of the Bapaume road, which bisected the battlefield, as well as the villages of Ovillers, La Boisselle, Fricourt, Mametz, and Montauban.

Before the offensive started, the French commander, General Joseph Joffre, had counselled Haig that he had to have adequate reserves if he was to continue the offensive beyond the initial thrust. On 30 June, Haig notified I Anzac Corps — which now comprised the 1st, 2nd, and the recently arrived 4th Australian divisions — that it had to be ready to transfer south to the Somme at a moment's notice. A week later, on 7 July, Birdie received orders from General Headquarters to shift the corps from Armentières to the Amiens area by 13 July.[23] 'We knew we were for it,' remarked Iven Mackay upon hearing the news.[24]

Transferring the corps from Armentières to the Somme was a huge logistical undertaking that required careful planning and management.

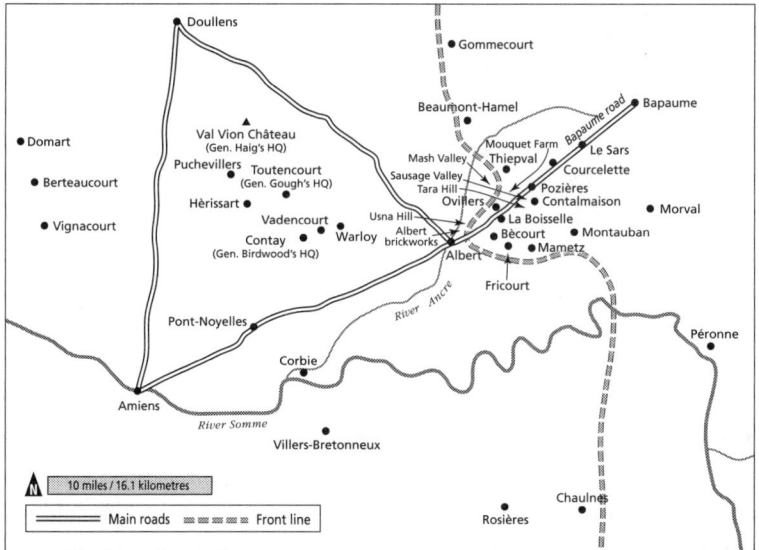

Map 2. The Somme District

The divisions would march from Armentières to the Flemish abbey-town of St Omer, and then travel by train to the Somme region, where they would march, stage by stage, toward the battlefront. Sixty thousand men — the population of a large city such as Ballarat or Toowoomba — had to be shifted 60 miles south in the space of a week. For every infantryman like Foxcroft — there were about 12,000 to a division — there was almost one other man in support: someone to bring ammunition and supplies forward; someone to bombard, machine-gun, and mortar the Germans; someone to dig the trenches they sheltered in; someone to carry and treat the wounded; someone to ferry messages back and forth; and someone to salvage the tons of derelict material left lying on the battlefield. Every possible contingency had to be catered for: people to care for their spiritual needs, arrange their weekly baths, pay their wages in French francs, interpret French, settle compensation claims made against them by the civilian population, entertain them when they were out of the line, and bury them. Billeting officers travelled ahead to arrange the nightly accommodation, farriers attended to the needs of thousands of transport horses, rolling cookers prepared tens of thousands of meals each day, mechanics maintained and repaired the fleet cars, quartermasters fitted the soldiers out, and clerks and orderlies followed in lorries with office furniture and stores for the new headquarters.[25] And when things went wrong, as they inevitably did — such as a cold meal, a late wages payment, or a night without billets — the men complained bitterly about their officers, who they referred to disparagingly as 'brass heads'.[26]

Despite the complexities, the transfer south was achieved without major incident. By 14 July, the three divisions were concentrated west of the Amiens–Doullens Road. The Anzacs immediately noticed that the French countryside was untouched by the war, and the weather was much more pleasant than in Armentières. The soldiers soaked up the warm sun, blue skies, and long hours of summer sunlight. The heat reminded them of Australia, but the land looked different: vast, rolling fields of green crops and freshly cut hay, not the brown, sunburnt expanse they were used to. 'This country is looking lovely now,' wrote Queenslander Sergeant Philip Browne. 'I often think that it is a perfect pity that all this grass that nothing eats couldn't be grown in Australia.'[27]

'The weather was warm and beautiful, all that could be desired,' recalled 37-year-old Collins Street tailor Corporal Arthur Thomas. 'The sight of our column winding its way through the undulating roads of France was awe inspiring.'[28]

Each division then marched eastward on its own separate route through different villages, many of which acted as staging locations, toward the battlefront. French liaison officer and sketch artist Paul Maze thought the columns of marching Australians presented a magnificent and cheerful sight. 'They passed swaying under their heavy haversacks and singing tunes,' he recorded in his autobiography, *A Frenchman in Khaki*. 'Battalion after battalion went by, impressing me with the fine physique of the men, all tanned by the Gallipoli sun.'[29]

Even though the columns of passing troops presented an impressive sight to observers, it was a taxing affair marching from one staging village to the next, day after day, under a blazing sun, in woollen khaki uniforms with full packs. The swaying poplar trees that lined the roads provided little shade, and by midday the soldiers' shirts and tunics were soaked through with sweat. According to the 4th Brigade Diary, the soldiers' feet, softened after months of inactivity and unaccustomed to the hard roads, became sore and blistered inside their English pattern boots.[30] By late afternoon, only the rhythm of their trampling feet maintained their forward momentum.[31]

The 1st Division marched eastward through to the village of Vignacourt while the 4th Division, one stage further back, passed through Domart and Berteaucourt. The 2nd Division marched through Amiens, the largest city on the Somme river. Conquering and vanquished armies had congregated around this 'little Paris' for over 2000 years — tribal Gauls had claimed it well before Christ was born, only to be kicked out by Julius Caesar and his Roman legions; William the Conqueror had assembled his invasion fleet nearby; and Henry V's army had passed close by before the Battle of Agincourt. The Anzacs, from isolated farms, small country towns, and burgeoning cities barely a century old, were awestruck by Amiens's magnificent gothic cathedral, built in the 13th century and reputed to house the severed head of John the Baptist.

Amiens seemed unaffected by the war. 'There was plenty of life stirring as we came to it and we were received with waves and smiles from the majority,' wrote Private Alfred Morrison.[32] But beneath the façade lurked the insidious signs of war: 'There were no young men, only old men and women and children and many widows and orphans,' recorded Albert Coates.[33] The officers discovered the reason for this absence whenever they sought billets from the French: 'Room, monsieur — yes, there is the room of my son who was killed at Argonne — of my husband who was killed at Verdun.'[34]

The Anzacs would soon be embroiled in the battle that might decide the greatest war of civilisation. Did this proposition excite them or, after the gruelling experience on Gallipoli, sicken them? News of the 'Big Push' along the Somme had been rippling through the corps since 1 July. Iven Mackay remembered soldiers asking: 'Are the Australians going to be given their chance at last?'[35] Captain John Harris, a schoolmaster at the Church of England Grammar School nestled in Sydney's beautiful north shore, recorded that there were few men who did not experience a sense of relief when the colonel announced to a full meeting: 'Gentlemen our period of training is over.'[36] While the soldiers had not been told why they were going south, most had guessed and were anxious, according to Geoffrey Drake-Brockman, to 'live up to the reputation established at Anzac'.[37]

The positive news coming from the other fronts buoyed the Anzacs. 'We have heard great yarns these last few days,' wrote Irish-born Gallipoli veteran Private Joe McSparron, 'about the crown prince being surrounded at Verdun and also about the Russians taking a lot of prisoners.'[38] The Anzacs passed British divisions who had been relieved from the front. 'They have been very successful and are all singing as they march along, every man wearing a German helmet,' recorded Corporal Apcar de Vine in his diary.[39]

The Anzacs were 'spoiling for action', as Harris put it, and hoped to emulate their feats. 'I hope the good old 5th leads the way,' wrote McSparron. 'A good many of them are seasoned warriors now as many of them have been in action at Gallipoli.'[40]

Charles Bean compared the feeling throughout the corps to that of a new boy joining a great school. One soldier broke down and wept when he sprained his ankle, realising that he wouldn't be continuing on to the Somme.[41]

Haig sensed the Anzacs' purposeful mood, writing in his diary: 'The men were looking splendid, fine physique, very hard and determined-looking. The Australians are mad keen to kill Germans and to start doing it at once!' Despite this eagerness, Haig counselled one brigadier to start quietly, 'because so many unfortunate occurrences had happened through being in too great a hurry to win this campaign!' He later confided in a letter to King George V that the Anzacs were undoubtedly a fine body of men, 'but their officers and leaders as a whole have a great deal to learn'.[42]

Mackay shared Haig's concerns. He believed that the Australians were seriously underprepared for the offensive. The instructors who had conducted their training had never occupied a fighting trench. In addition, soldiers were often diverted from critical training to perform mundane tasks such as digging trenches and shifting supplies.[43] The corps was badly short of periscopes and sniper scopes, and lacked magazines for the Lewis guns.

Even the Anzacs' Gallipoli experience offered little of value in terms of preparing for the Western Front. They were proud of their well-organised Gallipoli evacuation, but every general knew that battles weren't won by skilful withdrawals. The recent flood of raw recruits had diluted the core of experienced Gallipoli veterans. There was a chronic shortage of trained officers, so crotchety veterans of bygone wars had to be promoted to fill the vacancies.[44]

The troops were blissfully ignorant of what lay in store for them. Not even the most hardened Gallipoli veteran had experienced the volume of artillery and machine-gun fire that was decimating the British on the Somme. Instead, they talked excitedly of charging the Germans as if they were marching off to a 19th-century battle of sword and musket.

On 17 July, I Anzac Corps was notified that it had been allocated to General Sir Hubert Gough's Reserve Army, which was responsible for exploiting any breach made by General Sir Henry Rawlinson's Fourth Army. The following day, the corps was notified that its 1st Australian Division had been placed under the direct orders of the Reserve Army for special operations.[45]

That morning, the 1st Division commander, Major-General Harold 'Hooky' Walker — a diminutive man with receding red hair flecked with grey — was summoned to Gough's headquarters in Albert. 'I want you to go into the line and attack Pozières tomorrow night,' Gough told him.[46]

It was an astounding request, given that Birdie and I Anzac Corps staff had not yet arrived at their headquarters in the village of Contay and taken control of their sector. Gough had bypassed Birdie and put his orders to his subordinate.

Hooky, an astute officer, would have realised that attacking immediately would not have provided any time for reconnaissance. Although unafraid to question his commanders — he had clashed with Birdie over the plans for the Lone Pine attack on Gallipoli, which had resulted in many casualties for limited tactical gain — this order came from an army commander with two years' experience on the Western Front. Hooky would have been hesitant to question Gough's order to attack, and for good reason. Gough, after all, was the British army's rising star. His distinguished Irish family had military values coursing through its veins. His father, uncle, and younger brother had all won the British Empire's highest award for valour, the Victoria Cross. At 36, Gough had become the army's youngest ever lieutenant-general, and by the relatively young age of 46 he had commanded an army. According to Gary Sheffield and Dan Todman's study of Gough, he was considered a brilliant cavalryman with an optimistic spirit who partly owed his rapid rise through the ranks to Haig's patronage.[47] Clearly, the brilliant and well-connected Gough was not someone with whom to trifle.

Gough's insistence upon an immediate attack was based on orders received from his superior, Haig, who had instructed him to carry out methodical operations against Pozières with a view to capturing it with as little delay as possible. The word 'methodical' suggests taking the time required to prepare properly, but Gough believed that the Germans had to be kept off balance and that any breakthrough had to be exploited quickly. They could not allow the Germans to get their breath back, he reasoned.[48] He must have also understood that as the battle progressed and casualties mounted, nervous politicians would begin to pressure Haig to wind it down. Gough, given his nature, would focus on the words 'without delay' and in doing so would put Australian lives at unnecessary risk.

Why was Haig so intent upon capturing Pozières with as little delay as possible? On 1 July, Thiepval, the fortified village that sat on the same prominent ridge as Pozières but was 2000 yards to the north, had been a key objective. Although Rawlinson's Fourth Army troops had pushed either side of Thiepval, repeated frontal attacks had been unable to capture it. Rawlinson's troops did, however, make inroads south of Pozières. Rawlinson understood that if he captured Pozières he could, firstly, extend his hemmed-in northern flank and, secondly, attack Thiepval from the rear and, he hoped, capture it with fewer casualties. For this reason, Rawlinson told Haig on 13 July that 'Pozières was the key of the area'.[49] Haig, on considering the situation, had allocated I Anzac Corps to Gough's Reserve Army to capture the village and, in doing so, hopefully prise ajar the back door to Thiepval.

According to Bean's account, Hooky initially argued against the premature attack but then complied with Gough's order.[50] Perhaps Hooky was aware of the abrasive Gough's reputation for dealing ruthlessly with officers who lacked an offensive spirit. He probably also suspected that Birdie, always keen to avoid conflict and protect his own career, would not support him.

Hooky was a British regular soldier and had been with the Australians since Gallipoli. He'd originally been Birdie's chief-of-staff, but had swapped the job for brigade commands on Gallipoli, and then divisional command of the Australians. According to Charles Bean, Hooky, who enjoyed the finer things in life and spoke with a refined British accent, came to believe in and love his men. In turn, the Anzacs liked him. 'He was a good and friendly soldier,' remembered Drake-Brockman.[51] Hooky told Bean that he wouldn't change his command of the Australians for the world. Bean, in turn, believed 'Little Walker' was a man to whom the Anzacs 'owed something'.[52]

Hooky's work ethic and eye for detail were renowned throughout the division. A tireless worker, he often discussed pressing matters with officers at his headquarters late at night, between bouts of sleep and sometimes dressed only in his underwear. 'He did not look like a general,' Drake-Brockman recalled upon seeing him late one night stripped to a singlet and long woolly underpants, although he soon discovered that his instructions were 'lucid and to the point'.[53] So sharp was Hooky's memory for detail that, before arriving on the Somme, he had admonished his officers for being careless with government-issued boots, claiming accurately that of the 11,000 pairs supplied to the division, exactly 564 pairs had been abandoned.[54]

After failing to change Gough's mind, Hooky sent his meticulous chief-of-staff, 32-year-old Lieutenant-Colonel Thomas Blamey, to discuss the challenges of Pozières with the British units that had already attacked it. Two issues became clear. First, the distance between the British and German trenches was 600 yards, which would expose his advancing soldiers to prolonged and murderous artillery and machine-gun fire. Jumping-off trenches had to be dug closer to the Germans, and this would take time. Second, the attack's success depended on the division's artillery support, which would also take time to organise. Hooky was resigned to being pushed into an ill-prepared operation.[55]

Under pressure, Hooky continued preparations, but in the midst of these, on 19 July, Gough made a surprising about-face. Some of his staff saw the sense in delaying the attack and warned Birdie and White, who as yet had no responsibility on the battlefield, of the impending drama. Birdie, understandably keen to avoid the spate, sent White to argue the case for a delay. Gough relented, agreeing to postpone the attack until the night of 21 July.[56] Another delay of 24 hours was agreed to on 21 July itself, when White discovered that the planned artillery barrage hastily drawn up by three different 'staffs' (those of the Reserve Army, X British Corps, and the 1st Australian Division) would fall across the attacking troops.[57]

Hooky developed a simple plan to capture Pozières. He would attack from the south side of the Bapaume road on the moonless night of Sunday 23 July, just after midnight. The first objective was Pozières Trench, which protected the village; the second, the light railway that sat in front of the hedges on the outskirts of Pozières; the third, the portion of Pozières village south of the Bapaume road. If all three objectives were captured, the Australians would control one side of the village and, he hoped, the 48th British Division attacking north of the road the other side.

The 1st and 3rd brigades of the 1st Australian Infantry Division would mount the attack. Brigadier-General Nevill Smyth, a 58-year-old British officer, first cousin of the famous Robert Baden-Powell and winner of a Victoria Cross at Khartoum, commanded the 1st Brigade, comprising soldiers from New South Wales. Smyth had earned the nickname 'Sphinx' while in Egypt because of his quiet but determined demeanour. His brigade would attack the left-hand section of Pozières Trench. Brigadier-General Ewen Sinclair-MacLagan, a 57-year-old Scotsman with a booming voice, commanded the 3rd Brigade. His hard doers from the frontier states of Western Australia, South Australia, Tasmania, and Queensland had the tougher job — attacking the right-hand section of Pozières Trench, which intersected with the old German (OG) trench lines and would expose them to both frontal and flanking machine-gun fire.

Brigadier-General John Forsyth, a Brisbane-born son of a builder, commanded the Victorian 2nd Brigade. It would act as a reserve, carrying up ammunition, rations, and water to the other brigades. Forsyth, 49 years old, the least experienced of the three brigade commanders and the only native Australian, was a quiet, sensitive man, known affectionately to his men as 'Dad'.[58]

Would these men be competent leaders in battle? Birdie expressed confidence in the leadership of the British commanders, Sinclair-MacLagan and Smyth, but had reservations about Forsyth, which he had outlined in a letter to the minister for defence in late 1915: '[He] strikes me as having not fully risen to the occasion and has always given me the impression that the command [brigade] is just a bit too big for him.'[59]

Was Birdie's judgement sound, or did he display a bias toward British professional officers commanding Australian units? The Australian government, which desired the appointment of Australian officers whenever possible, had previously queried Birdie's recommendation to appoint British officers to divisional commands when the Australian Imperial Force reorganised in Egypt, reasoning that the Gallipoli campaign must have unearthed quality Australian candidates.[60] Eric Andrews, in his book on Anglo–Australian relations, *The Anzac Illusion*, wrote that Birdie did seem reluctant to appoint Australians in that instance. Under government pressure, Birdie reviewed his appointments, but nevertheless remained somewhat uncomfortable with colonial Australians holding key commands.[61]

For instance, while he expressed 'complete confidence' in Hooky Walker as a divisional commander, he did not have 'anywhere near the same confidence' in the Australian, Major-General James Gordon Legge, who commanded the 2nd Australian Division. Nationalist and imperialist leanings had subsequently formed among Anzac officers, with each faction harbouring differing views on who was best suited to fill key commands.[62] What no faction seemed to question was the leadership skills of Hooky Walker, who continued his preparations to capture a village that no Anzac had heard of a week earlier.

What was known about Pozières, a village that correspondent John Masefield described as having 'no interest and no importance' to anyone before the war?[63]

Before the war, it would have taken just over half an hour to walk the arrow-straight, poplar-lined Bapaume road from the market town of Albert to Pozières. Along the way, dirt tracks ran off to the small villages of La Boisselle, Ovillers, and Contalmaison. A hastily dug trench cut across the Bapaume road and looped around Pozières, protecting it from frontal and flanking attacks. The British called it 'K Trench' north of the road, and 'Pozières Trench' south of it. It was protected by belts of barbed wire — 15 feet deep and firmly secured by iron corkscrew stakes — as well as lines of dirty sandbags and mounds of white chalk fill. The village, behind the trenches, was screened by a small clump of trees.

A German blockhouse, soon to be known as Gibraltar, sat just off the main road. Its shell-scarred upper chamber, built of steel grid and concrete, had observation slits that provided clear views across the shallow valleys back to Albert. Its two deep underground chambers were constructed of reinforced concrete 12 inches thick, and could house up to 40 men. Gibraltar's heavy machine guns posed a significant threat to any troops foolhardy enough to attack the village frontally.

Before the war, about 350 villagers had lived in and around Pozières. The last of them fled when the offensive started, delaying only to bury their possessions. Their pink-brick cottages and barns, made of coarse clay slapped over wooden frames, had since been reduced to rubble. The Germans had demolished many of them, retaining only the cellars, which they deepened and reinforced with sandbags and concrete to protect them from shelling. Passageways linked the cellars to the village's underground water wells.

The ruins of the village hugged the road for about 1000 yards. Five hundred yards beyond this were two other trenches spaced about 200 yards apart — Old German Trench One (OG1) and Old German Trench Two (OG2). They straddled the Pozières ridge, spanning the entire battlefield, from the Somme valley to the river Ancre. The Germans had clear fields of fire for hundreds of yards in all directions, from both the village and the OG lines.[64] The British had penetrated the OG lines up to within 600 yards of the village, but German barricades and bombers blocked any further advance. Most importantly, the Germans held the junction between the OG lines and Pozières Trench, which allowed them to move fluidly between both locations.

There had already been five costly attempts to capture Pozières. On 1 July, the British 8th Division advanced up the Bapaume road, but machine-gun fire from La Boisselle and the blockhouse Gibraltar cut them down and pushed them back into no-man's-land.[65] Another four attacks occurred between 14 and 17 July. On 14 July, the British 34th Division seized a section of Pozières Trench but, after heavy fighting, the Germans repelled them. The next day, the division attacked from the south at 9.00 a.m., but intense machine-gun fire again stopped it cold. Another attack at 6.00 p.m. captured some ground and got the division within 300 yards of Pozières. The heavy bombardment supporting their attack that day shrouded Pozières in clouds of pink dust and flattened every building, but the Germans still managed to hold on. According to Charles Bean, there was little to show for the efforts of the British to that point, beyond the crumbled bodies of their soldiers hanging from the German wire entanglements.[66]

On the evening of 17 August, the fifth attack was raked by fire from at least ten machine guns and floundered after a 70-yard advance. In response, Brigadier-General Sir Henry Page Croft of the 68th British Brigade, who was justifiably frustrated by the failures, requested that the village again be systematically pounded by the heavies.

That same day, Haig had relieved the Fourth Army of its duty of capturing Pozières and allocated the task to Gough's Reserve Army.[67] Haig believed that the Australians were 'valuable reinforcements' who could resume what had become a fruitless struggle against an enemy too far entrenched in Pozières to be removed without large casualties. Foxcroft and his fellow members of the I Anzac Corps had arrived on the Somme, but their story was only beginning: they had the hopes not only of Australia but also of Haig's headquarters riding on them as they marched toward the battlefield. One Anzac sensed these expectations when a British soldier remarked: 'If you Anzacs can take and hold Pozières we'll believe all we've heard about you.'[68]

CHAPTER TWO

Foreboding

'Words cannot describe the utterly smashed condition of the ground here. Unexploded shells, debris, equipment were everywhere among the shell craters and in the mouths of the dugouts were corpses.'
— Private Eric Moorhead's diary

By midday on 19 July — the day after Gough had ordered Hooky to attack Pozières — Birdie and White had finally established their I Anzac Corps headquarters in a magnificent old château in the village of Contay. The opulent white-stone, two-storey building was surrounded by a high ornate fence and was guarded by two Anzacs. The Australian flags that hung from the front gate and the château's highest window fluttered in the summer breeze, reminding everyone that the Anzacs had arrived on the Somme. A shanty of tents had quickly sprung up on the château's immaculately maintained lawns, serving as temporary offices for staff who couldn't be squeezed into its main rooms.[1]

From this day forward, White would have his office light burning into the small hours of the morning. Bent over his wooden desk while smoking a pipe, he would study battle plans, thumb through piles of memoranda, respond to correspondence, read intelligence reports, and draft orders.[2] As soon as these orders were typed, numbered copies would be handed to waiting despatch riders, who would slip them into their leather satchels and motor away to hand-deliver them to one of over 20 formations participating in the coming attack. These orders sent soldiers such as Foxcroft into battle. They also focused on ensuring that all preparations for the coming attack were thorough: that assembly trenches and their approaches were carefully dug, bombardments and barrages were adequate, and the German wire entanglements were cut. Although White had previously orchestrated the evacuation from Gallipoli, the reorganisation of the Australian Imperial Force in Egypt, and the transfer of the corps south, it was the drafting of these orders for the coming battle that appeared to weigh most heavily on his mind. 'I often wonder how long one can go on under the strain,' he wrote in a letter to his wife, Ethel, in early 1916.[3]

His letters to Ethel throughout the war were disarmingly honest. He wrote about a range of subjects: his feelings of depression and loneliness, the stressful nature of his duties, his immense homesickness ('I am longing so to be back with you and the little fellows'), and his hope that the war would end someday. 'In the meantime it is cutting out some of the most precious years of our joint life and these I grudge,' he wrote.

On other occasions, when watching the columns of fresh troops marching toward the front line, he would contemplate their small chances of coming out unharmed, compared with men in past wars. In one letter he lamented: 'There will be such a lot of people at the end of this war who are not normal on account of the life here — and this is even more hateful a prospect than being blotted out.'

Birdie, unlike White, appeared to express no such misgivings. Despite the impending battle, he continued his daily routine. A dapper little man with a wispy moustache, Birdie always rose before 6.00 a.m. so that he had plenty of time to inspect his men. He took his responsibilities seriously: a few sandwiches for a breakfast on the run and no time for lunch — that way he could inspect even more troops, present more medals, and shake more hands. Not even the occasional shell could stop him. He promised his men that they would soon have a chance of open fighting, which he thought they would prefer to trench warfare.[4]

When Birdie had finished inspecting troops, he would arrange for his charger to meet him ten miles from headquarters so that he could gallop home across the fields and through the woods. Birdie meticulously recorded these daily gallops, which he rarely missed throughout the Pozières battle, in his diary.[5] Back at Contay, he would pursue his love of letter writing, corresponding with governor-general Ronald Munro Ferguson; journalist Keith Murdoch; the minister for defence, Senator George Pearce; and the Australian high commissioner, Andrew Fisher. His letters, which could run from eight to 15 foolscap pages, constantly eulogised his value to the Anzacs. And therein lay one of Birdie's key strengths: what he lacked in operational and organisational ability, he made up for with his finely honed political instincts and ability to promote himself. Iven Mackay thought he only ingratiated himself with the Australians to keep fresh the 'Good old Birdie' image.[6]

Birdie had commanded the Anzacs since November 1914. Some Australians believed that Major-General William Bridges, commander of the Australian Imperial Force, should have filled the post, but Birdie was undisputedly the right man for the job. He had all-important British connections: secretary of state for war Lord Horatio Kitchener was the godfather of his daughter; senior officers Ian Hamilton and Launcelot Kiggell were dear friends; and he knew Haig from his Clifton College and Sandhurst days. He also understood how the British army worked and, as an 'English Christian gentleman', formed part of its inner sanctum in a way that Bridges never could.[7]

Birdie's most important leadership quality was that he was a man among men, a front-line commander of soldiers rather than an organiser who sweated over staff plans. Kitchener thought that this quality made him ideally suited to the individualistic Australians and New Zealanders. Australian brigade commander Brigadier-General John Monash agreed; in 1915, he recalled Birdie talking to privates, buglers, drivers, gunners, colonels, signallers, and generals, and felt that 'every time he has left the men with a better knowledge of his business than he had before'.[8] But Birdie wasn't perfect. General Sir Ian Hamilton, commander of the Mediterranean Expeditionary Force, alluded to some of his limitations in a private letter to Winston Churchill: '[Birdie] has never commanded anything in peace except, for less than two years a brigade. For your business [Gallipoli] he will not quarrel with anyone, not at any price.'[9]

White had worked as Birdie's chief-of-staff from October 1914. He had two qualities that were immensely valuable to Birdie. First, he had a prodigious appetite for administration and planning. Birdie could afford to delegate virtually everything to him and be confident that it would be well managed. Second, he didn't compete for the limelight. Bean thought White, although ambitious, was too modest to promote himself. Despite this, his reputation quickly grew. Bean admitted to falling under White's spell, 'but who did not ... everyone on this divisional staff knows his value.'[10]

While Birdie inspected, White worked. He seemed to wear the worries of the corps. In the coming weeks, the lives of thousands of men would rest on his decisions. He felt acutely that he would be responsible, even when tired and worn, for double-checking the intricacies of artillery plans that, properly executed, protected thousands of men; he would be responsible for drafting important orders in which one turn of phrase incorrectly interpreted by a field commander could have tragic consequences. With Gough hovering in the wings and goading the corps, his job would be even harder. In a letter to Ethel, he couldn't help comparing his 'tired' state of mind with that of his 'bright and happy' general: 'Without any fear of responsibility and with a sort of fatalism that what he does will go well, his mind never seems distressed with vague imaginings.'[11]

By contrast, White admitted to suffering from 'appalling anxiety'. He confided to Ethel that in the days before the Gallipoli evacuation he had felt 'nothing but the thump' of his heart against his ribs. Years earlier, he had implored Ethel never to mention to anyone the frequent anxiety attacks and migraines he suffered during heavy bouts of work, fearing that his colleagues would consider him unreliable.

Why was such a capable officer plagued by bouts of anxiety? His biographer, Rosemary Derham, wrote that, when White was 15, drought and his father's failed businesses left his once-prosperous family penniless. White, who at the time was attending the prestigious Eton Preparatory School in Brisbane, had dreamt of becoming a barrister, but was forced to leave school to take up a job as a clerk with the Australian Joint Stock Bank on a salary of one pound per week. The drudgery of the bank clerk's work was as 'bitter as gall to him', wrote Bean in *Two Men I Knew*, 'and the monotony and lack of intellectual interest, or of any promise of it in the future, lay heavily on his spirit'. The family's changed circumstances deeply affected White. 'Each day met me filled with fear and foreboding,' he wrote to Ethel, recounting his youth, 'each day instead of getting up to bless, one gets up with all sorts of anxieties.'

White's life changed when he joined a friend, a volunteer soldier, on an outpost exercise one weekend. It whet his appetite for soldiering, and by 1897 he was commissioned as a junior officer in the militia regiment. Soon after, he was appointed to the Queensland Permanent Artillery.

After the Boer War, White was invited to study at the prestigious British Staff College at Camberley. He would not have fitted in immediately: he was of Irish descent, penniless, and uneducated, and there was no tradition of soldiering in his family. White felt compelled to spend much of his meagre allowance on keeping a horse and a part-time groom so he could participate in the college's ritual fox hunts. He did so at the expense of much-needed home help for Ethel and the children.¹² Slowly, White ingratiated himself to the college's junior officers. They admired his strong work ethic and spirited, if unrefined, riding skills. Their acceptance must have been very important to him.

Although White bore more of the administrative load than Birdie, his hard work was well recognised. By 1916, he was considered the rising star of I Anzac Corps. He appeared to have shaken off the lingering insecurities that had plagued his early career, and his lack of education and humble beginnings no longer seemed to trouble him. He felt confident in the company of army commanders such as Gough and enjoyed their respect. Small things such as Gough asking after Ethel's health meant a lot to him; it showed he was part of the fold. White was partly anxious for British approval because he firmly believed in the British Empire; he thought the maintenance of British ideals to be for the benefit of mankind.¹³ His imperialist views set him apart from other Australian officers, such as 2nd Division commander Major-General Gordon Legge, who were decidedly Australian nationalist in outlook. Despite White's growing stature, he was uncomfortably conscious that the vast and crucial operations on the Western Front were new territory to him. His guiding principle of 'never do anything by halves' would be challenged by Gough, who seemingly favoured timeliness over exhaustive planning.

Arthur Foxcroft's C Company, 4th Battalion, was part of Hooky Walker's 1st Division, which would storm Pozières around midnight on 23 July. After making battle preparations in the staging town of Warloy on 19 July, Foxcroft's platoon packed up and marched off for the firing line at 5.30 p.m. They arrived at Albert, which sat on the cusp of the front line, just on dusk. Many of its buildings were ruined; shards of glass littered the cobbled streets, and most windows were shuttered. Most of its 7000 pre-war inhabitants had fled. Those remaining hawked souvenirs or eggs to the passing troops at wildly inflated prices.

The platoons marched by the magnificent basilica Notre Dame de Brebières, which completely dominated the skyline. The sheer bulk of its brick foundations suggested it had been built to last a thousand years. But now, hundreds of shells pitted its arched neo-Byzantine-inspired ceiling and brick walls. Only a few shards of stained glass remained fixed in the windows. Its giant bell tower remained intact but, bizarrely, the golden statue of the Virgin Mary and baby Jesus perched above it leant at a precarious angle. Some passing troops thought the leaning statue resembled Australian swimmer Fanny Durack diving into the Coogee Baths; others irreverently christened it 'Annette Kellerman', after the first woman to attempt to swim the English Channel. For Paul Maze, the statue conjured up a more haunting image: that of the Virgin Mary casting baby Jesus from her outstretched arms into the battle's fires.[14]

The marching columns snaked their way from the cobbled streets onto the open, grassy fields, east of Albert, where battalions often bivouacked before marching the last leg to the front line. The sun receded behind the hills. The heavy bombardment of Pozières threw out flickering light that sporadically illuminated the darkness.

Foxcroft's platoon halted about three miles past Albert and slept the night in old, broken trenches. Corporal Apcar de Vine, who 'dossed' down close by, complained that he got absolutely no sleep that night because of the deafening noise of shells and cannons.[15]

From his broken trench, Foxcroft could probably whiff the fetid air of Pozières. The next day, he would be sent to the front line and be close enough to see its ruins; the day after that, he and the other Anzacs would storm it and, he hoped, etch the division's name into the history books.

By the time Foxcroft awoke from what must have been a fitful sleep at around dawn on Thursday 20 July, Hooky's 1st Division had completed its relief of the British 2nd and 68th brigades, which had been holding the sector opposite Pozières. The next few days, courtesy of Gough's decision to delay operations, provided Hooky's division with much-needed time to prepare more thoroughly for the attack.[16] His troops, such as Foxcroft, would have the chance to familiarise themselves with the battlefield; his staff officers, such as Thomas Blamey, would have the necessary time to develop and disseminate their battle plans; and his brigade commanders, such as Ewen Sinclair-MacLagan, would have a window of opportunity to improve their tactical position prior to the commencement of the main attack.

Hooky's 12 infantry battalions were staggered between the new front-line trenches, which were approximately 300 to 400 yards from Pozières, and Albert. At dawn, those reserve battalions near Albert began their final, slow ascent toward Pozières, marching in formations of half-platoons spaced 50 yards apart. Foxcroft's platoon passed by masses of British guns covered with camouflage netting, lined up wheel to wheel into the distance. These field batteries had bombarded the Germans for eight consecutive days prior to the 1 July attack, and were now pounding Pozières. 'All sorts and sizes of British artillery around us. Over 1500 guns just here, covering a 400 yard front,' noted Foxcroft.[17] As platoons passed by, the belching guns sent waves of warm, compressed air over them.

The platoons passed through the British old reserve and support lines and what had been no-man's-land three weeks earlier. Upon reaching La Boisselle, a small village that straddled the Bapaume road, the tired troops threw down their haversacks and rested. The fortified village — now just a patch of rubble and pulverised brick strewn with corpses — had formed part of the Germans' original front line.

Perhaps the Australians, after seeing La Boisselle's mangled corpses, realised the terrible destruction that a battle could deliver. French liaison officer Paul Maze, who was working with the Australians at Gough's request, recorded in his autobiography the macabre scene that La Boisselle presented: the hot sun had blackened and grilled the bodies of dead German and British soldiers, and human refuse was intermingled with rusty barbed wire. In the village's cemetery, headstones had been uprooted, coffins shattered, and cypress trees splintered. A headless statue of Christ completed the scene.[18] Foxcroft's notes reflected this state of destruction: 'Place in an awful state, gear, rifle, pieces of dead, rubbish all over the place,' he wrote.[19]

Iven Mackay was similarly affected, recording in his diary that there was barely a square foot of soil that had not been torn about by high explosives.[20] The destruction the soldiers witnessed at La Boisselle would become only too familiar in the coming weeks.

Later, rested and fed, some of the platoons marched from La Boisselle to the Chalk Pit. Just under a mile from Pozières, the Chalk Pit was a gateway between purgatory and hell; beyond it was the beginning of the front line. Its deep, chalky banks afforded some protection from shelling, but past them one's life was perpetually in danger. Many men later recorded their relief upon returning to the Chalk Pit, or their anxiety upon leaving it again for the front line. It acted as a dump for ammunition, a medical-aid post, and the most forward point for the field kitchens.

On the night of 20 July, carrying parties ferried ammunition and supplies up to the front line. The constant shelling lit up the sky, making it possible to read newspapers and write letters. John Harris tried to settle his men, who sheltered in narrow 'possies' — little more than cavities gouged out of the trench walls. 'The frequent explosions and the impossibility of lying down properly, made sleep at night almost out of the question,' he recorded in his war memoirs.[21] For many soldiers, it would be the second night without sleep, but certainly not the last.

Since 13 July, Hooky's chief-of-staff, Thomas Blamey, had been circulating general staff memoranda and divisional orders, as well as conducting divisional conferences concerning the looming battle.[22] (These memoranda and orders, which are archived at the Australian War Memorial, demonstrate that he was a careful and methodical planner who left little to chance.) Gough's delay provided Blamey the critical time he needed to distribute these documents and organise the necessary conferences to discuss them prior to the attack.

On Friday 21 July, divisional, brigade, and battalion officers conferred to discuss the fine detail of Blamey's battle plan. Second-Lieutenant Walter Claridge, a wool classer, attended one of these conferences. He furiously scribbled down page after page of instructions about lighting red flares as each objective was captured; the importance of those reinforcing rolling up their sleeves for easy identification; the need for all men to carry an extra 100 rounds of small-arms ammunition, two bombs, and two sandbags; and the necessity for at least four men to be posted at the entrance to every communication trench leading toward the enemy.[23] Iven Mackay attended a divisional conference the same day and wrote 12 pages of notes, covering every possible contingency. 'Battalion commanders were issued with so many maps that their bulging pockets had no room for anything else,' recorded John Harris.[24]

By midnight on 23 July, the commanding officers would have the first wave of troops in the jumping-off trenches, dug roughly 150 yards from the Germans; the second wave in the front trench; and the remaining waves staggered evenly further back.

Gough's postponement also provided Sinclair-MacLagan with the opportunity to capture the important German-held junction on the crest of the ridge, where Pozières Trench intersected with the OG lines. The British, who held the southern portion of the OG lines, had previously reached within 50 yards of the stronghold, but heavy machine-gun fire had pushed them back. Sinclair-MacLagan's 9th Battalion would attack the junction in the early hours of Saturday 22 July. The plan was for trench mortars to bombard the strongpoint thoroughly until 2.30 a.m. on Saturday morning, followed by a light barrage of 18-pounder shells to prevent the Germans from manning their machine guns. Two groups of about 50 men, under lieutenants Charles Monteath and Frederick Biggs, would then attack it.[25]

Sergeant Philip Browne, a blond, beanstalk-thin geology student from Queensland, was among those who would participate in the night attack. Days earlier, the 20-year-old had written a letter home, predicting that his 'lot' would soon see some of the fighting. He finished by writing: 'Please god we will come through safe.'[26]

By Friday evening, Monteath and Biggs' troops had positioned themselves in forward posts in OG1 and OG2. Darkness gradually replaced sunshine, and then zero hour approached. Platoons readied themselves. In the minutes before they were to advance, Monteath and Biggs listened for the mortar shells, but they heard nothing. Unbeknown to them, the mortars had expended their pitiful 14 rounds by 2.10 a.m. — for the last 20 minutes before the 9th was to advance, there was no bombardment.

Just after 2.30 a.m., the troops advanced toward the stronghold. The dim light thrown out by the rising moon only helped the Germans to see them. They hurled egg bombs — about the size of cricket balls and much lighter than their British equivalent, Mills bombs — at the Australian attackers. Machine guns joined in; the rattled troops bunched together and fell in heaps.

Browne, in support, watched the debacle unfold. He handed over his platoon to his corporal and rushed forward, from shell hole to shell hole, delivering a load of bombs to the stranded men. He also volunteered to carry some of the wounded back. Then, as he climbed from a low trench, he crumpled in a heap. No one knew exactly what had happened, whether small-arms fire, a whiz-bang, or shell fragments had hit him. They did agree — as each witness recorded in their statement to the Red Cross, who investigated soldiers reported as missing and wounded — that he died instantly.

The raid was aborted. The critical strongpoint remained in German hands, meaning that deadly crossfire from the German positions on the crest of the ridge, where the OG lines intersected with Pozières Trench, could compromise the attack planned for the following night.

The next morning, some soldiers crawled out into no-man's-land and dragged Browne's stiffened body into a shallow shell hole.

According to their Red Cross statements, they covered it with a few shovelfuls of dirt and placed a rough wooden cross at the head of the makeshift grave. In the confusion of the weeks that followed, its location would be forgotten. Browne's body was never recovered; he was one of the first Australians among the Somme's many missing.[27]

Some time later, 21-year-old Sergeant Freddie Barbour would sit down in a quiet place and write a letter to Browne's parents, James and Jessie. The boys had studied together at Toowoomba Grammar School, the school of choice for the well-to-do graziers and farmers of the Darling Downs district. Both were outstanding students, winning university scholarships, but the Great War had lured them away. By the time they were at Pozières, these smart, energetic young men had been promoted to sergeants.

Barbour would try to explain the circumstances of his mate's death as best he could and to offer some condolence. 'Deeply as we all regretted his death,' he would write, 'there is not one of us but envies him so glorious a death in his country's service, and I cannot say how proud I am to have been his friend. May we all do our duty as well and honourably.'[28] The idealistic tone of Barbour's letter varies remarkably little from the thousands of other letters sent by soldiers and officers to grieved parents.

Six months later, Barbour would die from wounds. Army protocol at the time dictated that his commanding officer send a letter of condolence to his parents. While there is no record of it, undoubtedly it would have been written in a similar style.

The only lingering reminder of Freddie and Philip is the inscription of their names on the bronzed honour boards at Toowoomba Grammar School. What the boards will never tell us is the snuffed-out potential of these young men. They don't reveal the long and painful odyssey that Browne's parents undertook to locate their son's remains, writing heartfelt letters to the Base Records Office well into the 1920s, or the sense of complicity that they must have felt for having signed his consent forms.[29] What James and Jessie would have found difficult to comprehend, along with thousands of other parents who would lose children in the coming months, was how their beloved could simply vanish from the Somme.

CHAPTER THREE

Fromelles

'O dauntless heart of youth!
Against grim bastions hurled
Your name shall keep the house we build
Secure against the world.'
— Vance Palmer, 'The Signal'

While the Australians completed their preparations for the 23 July attack, Haig most likely contemplated their chances. He must have realised that the inexperienced Australians, teamed with the talented but impetuous Gough — who had been promoted to army commander only three weeks earlier — was a volatile combination.

Haig rarely interfered with his generals' plans. He set the broad strategy and left the finer detail for them to work through. However, on 20 July he had departed from his *modus operandi* — he had visited Gough's headquarters in the small farming hamlet of Toutencourt to discuss the coming attack. He warned Gough that he had to go over all detail carefully, as the 1st Australian Division had not been engaged in France before and had possibly overlooked some of the preparations needed for this type of combat.

On 22 July, Haig visited Gough again to make sure that the Australians were given a simple task, reminding him that this was the first time they would take part in a serious, large-scale offensive against the German forces. The trouble was that there were no simple tasks on the Somme to give to the Australians.

Why was Haig so persistent in voicing his concerns about the Australians to Gough? On 20 July, he had received news that the 5th Australian Division — attached to the First British Army — had attacked near the village of Fromelles the previous evening, as Hooky's 1st Australian Division was marching through Albert toward the firing line. First Army reports indicated that the attack was 'only partially successful', a euphemism that would have worried Haig.[1] What did the puzzling term 'only partially successful' mean? What was the purpose of the 5th Division's attack and what impact would it have upon the I Anzac Corps' planned operations at Pozières?

In the early days of the Somme offensive, Haig had hoped that his armies would break through the German lines. His intention, upon breaching their line at one weak point, was to strike hard at other points where there were few reserves, and ultimately turn a local retreat into a withdrawal. Accordingly, on 5 July he had ordered the British armies along the Western Front to select points at which they would attempt to rupture the German line. XI Corps commander Lieutenant-General Sir Richard Haking suggested that, in his sector, a prominent German salient near Fromelles, the 'Sugarloaf', offered a favourable chance of capture.

Already, only two weeks into the Somme offensive, any thought of an easy breakthrough had vanished, but the attack that Haking had proposed weeks earlier was still being considered. It was planned as a feint to make the Germans think that they were being threatened so they might stop transferring troops to the Somme.

Haig was lukewarm about the idea, believing it should only continue if its architect, Haking, was absolutely assured that the artillery and ammunition in the north were sufficient to cover the attack.

Haking's superior, First British Army commander General Sir Charles Munro, also had concerns. He sought assurances from Haking that he could fulfil Haig's requirements. Haking believed that he could.

Haking decided that the 5th Australian Division — which had recently relieved the 4th Division when it transferred to the Somme — would lead the attack, along with the British 61st Division. According to Ross McMullin's account of the Fromelles battle in the biography *Pompey Elliott*, the proposition of the pending attack excited the 5th Division commander, Major-General James 'Big Jim' McCay. Although his division had been the last to land in France, he hoped it would be the first to make a name for itself in battle. His subordinate, Brigadier-General Harold 'Pompey' Elliott — who commanded the all-Victorian 15th Brigade, one of three Australian brigades participating in the feint — apparently didn't share his commander's enthusiasm, later claiming that he would have protested about having to attack such a position. 'Not that it would have done much good,' he wrote in a letter afterward. 'McCay was terribly anxious that it shouldn't be stopped and made no mention of the difficulties facing us.'[2]

Those 'difficulties' included the need to rush the registration of the heavy guns, insufficient artillery to subdue machine-gun emplacements and blockhouses, lack of communication trenches for troops to get to the front line, the requirement for troops to cover up to 400 yards of exposed and cratered ground, and the overambitious objective of capturing three lines of trenches.[3] In addition, the 5th Division had been in the front-line trenches only a week and had little combat experience.

In the days before the planned feint, dark rainclouds replaced the sunshine. Then the weather broke; sheets of rain lashed Fromelles, filling the trenches with mud and bogging down the troops. Haking postponed the attack, and his superior, General Munro, had the option of cancelling altogether. But Haig, now sold on the idea, wished for the operation to be carried out as soon as possible, weather permitting, and provided that Munro was satisfied that the available artillery and ammunition were 'adequate both for the preparation and the execution of the enterprise'.[4]

On 19 July, at about 6.00 p.m., the 5th Division troops — laden with haversacks, picks, shovels, bags of bombs, and other equipment, each soldier's kit weighing about 70 pounds — began their deadly journey across no-man's-land. Many were fatalistic. The Germans had already hoisted a noticeboard that taunted them, 'Advance Australia — if you can!'[5]

As the troops began to advance over the flat sweep of meadow, Germans shells fell heavily among them — unbeknown to the Australians, the German artillery observers stationed a mile back in the trees and roofs along Aubers Ridge and atop the Fromelles church tower could easily make out the commencement of the attack. 'The enemy bombardment was hellish, and it seemed as if they knew accurately the time set [for the attack],' recorded Lieutenant-Colonel Frederick Toll, 31st Battalion.[6]

The whole front erupted in noise. Whining shells, shouting men, stuttering machine guns, and the deafening crash of bombs all combined to create a terrific din. 'You could see machine guns knocking bits off the trees in front of the reserve line and sparking off the wire,' remembered one soldier.[7]

Elliott noticed at about 6.15 p.m. that the sound of the Germans' heavy artillery and musketry had died away. He assessed this as a positive sign. At 6.30 p.m. he reported that the attack had succeeded.[8]

His mood must have plummeted when the first detailed situation report, handwritten and with 'urgent' scrawled upon it, arrived just after midnight at his headquarters, a few hundred yards behind the front line. It stated that the attack had failed completely, with those reaching the enemy's trench killed or captured: 'Very many officers are casualties ... it seems impossible to reorganise ... Reports seem to be unanimous.'[9] Apparently, the German fire at 6.15 p.m. 'had only ceased because the attack had been shot to earth'.[10]

The inexperienced and demoralised Australians, according to one observer, retired in what appeared to be a panic, 'like a crowd running across a field at the end of a football match'; the retreat resembled a shambles.[11]

On the morning of 20 July, Charles Bean overheard that 'the 5th had their little show last night'. He commandeered White's car and sped north to see what had happened, arriving at 5th Division headquarters just after 1.00 p.m. to be told: 'It's all over, you know. We're back in our own trenches.'[12]

Bean then visited, at their respective headquarters, the three Australian brigade commanders who had been involved in the attack. He wrote that the 8th Brigade commander, Brigadier-General Edwin Tivey, 'looked quite overdone, his eyes like boiled gooseberries', after two nights without sleep. Tivey was anxious to reassure himself that his brigade had tried hard and done as well as those brigades on Gallipoli: '1700 — that's about as heavy as some of the brigades lost on the [Gallipoli] Landing, isn't it?' he queried Bean. When Bean visited Elliott, he described feeling almost as if he was in the presence of a man who had just lost his wife: '[Elliott] looked down and could hardly speak — he was clearly terribly depressed and overwrought.' Brigadier-General Harold Pope, 14th Brigade, 'rather disgusted' Bean by 'the boastful way he talked': 'Well — we were the only brigade that didn't come back till we were told to,' Pope crowed. Bean suspected that Pope had been 'refreshing' himself after the strain of the attack. Indeed, later that afternoon Major-General McCay found Pope in a drunken stupor, unable to comprehend an order or perform any part of his duties. He immediately called for his discharge and return to Australia.[13] Pope had unravelled after one day of battle.

It is clear that Fromelles had a debilitating effect on its commanders, who faced the combined challenges of sleep deprivation and immense emotional strain in the lead-up to and during the savage battle. Their experience would be a prelude to the strains that Walker, Sinclair-MacLagan, Smyth, and Forsyth would be exposed to over the coming days at Pozières.

While Bean talked with the brigade commanders, the survivors cleaned up the mess in the trenches: they collected the dead, tended to the wounded, and rescued those stranded in no-man's-land. The scene was appalling, recorded Lieutenant Hugh Knyvett in his biography, *'Over There' with the Australians*: 'If you had gathered the stock of a thousand butcher shops, cut it into small pieces and strewn it about, it would give you a faint conception of the shambles that those trenches were.'[14]

Captain Thomas Barbour recounted just one example of the carnage — the horrific sight of a soldier with both legs blown off crawling on his stumps across no-man's-land. 'He was last seen moving slowly into a sap where he no doubt perished,' he said.[15]

The feint shattered the Australian 5th Division: about half of its attacking troops were killed, wounded, or captured. It suffered 5533 casualties in 27 hours. The date 19 July 1916 remains the bloodiest day in Australia's history.

The carnage at Fromelles particularly shocked Bean, White, and Elliott. Naturally, they thought someone must be to blame. They asked uncomfortable questions immediately after the battle, and well into the 1920s and 1930s. Bean wanted to know why 'second rate territorials' (the 61st British Division) had been used in the attack, and why a 'fine division' (the 5th Australian Division), which had only been in the trenches for a week, had been sacrificed.[16] White, who hated what he called 'these little unprepared shows', could not understand why a feint had been required at all.[17] Elliott, who claimed in a letter to Bean in 1926 that he was always of the opinion that 'success was impossible' because of the distance his troops had had to cover to reach the German trenches, was the most scathing. He asked why Haking hadn't supported the attack with more artillery and why

Haig hadn't checked Haking's plans more thoroughly, or cancelled the attack.[18] In 1930, an embittered Elliott delivered a lecture that largely blamed the British commanders for the debacle. Elliott committed suicide a year after delivering his caustic talk; he was quite possibly another victim of Fromelles.

Newspaper articles and books written by survivors after the war continued to raise uncomfortable questions and apportion blame for the disaster. In 1920, *The Argus* featured an article on Fromelles under the headline 'What Really Happened' and concluded, somewhat confusingly, that the botched attack was 'a glorious failure'.[19] Ninety-five years after the battle, the discovery of the unidentified remains of Australian and British soldiers in an unmarked mass grave just outside the village resurrected these uncomfortable questions.[20] Emotions still remain high, with one historian recently likening Haking's planning to a 'dog's breakfast'.[21]

The prospects for the Australians attacking at Fromelles — as they were for the British attacking along the Somme and the Germans attacking at Verdun — were always bleak. Even if preparations had been perfect (and they never were) and all the trenches captured and held (which they never seemed to be), artillery would not have been able to support them indefinitely, and the Germans would have undoubtedly counterattacked. But the costly gamble had to be taken as part of a broader strategy aimed at achieving a breakthrough on the Somme: if the Germans had hesitated for one moment in sending troops south, it might have provided the critical window of opportunity that Haig so desperately sought to break through their defences. It might just have made the Australians' job at Pozières a touch easier.

The lesson of Fromelles was a brutal one, and it would have dire implications for the I Anzac Corps marching toward Pozières: war on the Western Front was completely different from anything the Australians had ever experienced. A feint like Fromelles only constituted a minor part of the overall Somme battle plan; it could take up to 40 or 50 attacks like Fromelles, all ending in carnage, to pierce the German line — if it could be pierced at all.

Battles like those on the Somme no longer had defined start or end points. They were rarely decisive and were more about attrition than breakthrough. Battle plans were always clouded by uncertainty and indecision; there were no sure paths to victory. And it seemed, irrespective of whether it was a major offensive, feint, or minor raid, and whether it was a success, draw, or failure, that the outcome was always the same: mass carnage.

The Australians had hoped that the Great War would be an opportunity to prove the nation a valuable member of the British Empire. They had anticipated short, set-piece battles and quick victories. Fromelles demonstrated that this was an illusion. In reality, the Somme was a human-mincing machine on a scale 20 times larger than Fromelles. British divisions were marching into it with metronomic regularity, to be ravaged and spat out days later with casualty rates similar to those of Australia's 5th Division.

Later that day, Bean returned to the Somme and met with an anxious White, who was grappling with some significant operational problems. 'Tomorrow is a more important attack,' he reminded Bean. White explained that critical issues still remained unresolved: there appeared to be 'no definite written arrangement' for the complex artillery plan supporting the 1st Division's advance, even though he had 'begged' the Reserve Army for it, and the objectives for the night attack still remained uncertain, although he had implored Hooky to take more than just the 'first miserable trench' in his midnight attack.[22] Would the Australians succeed and add fresh laurels to their name, or would they fail, their bodies becoming intermingled with those of British soldiers that hung from the German wire entanglements in front of Pozières? Perhaps White — late that night, while sitting at his desk, smoking his pipe — reflected on the Fromelles carnage, and pondered, in light of the problems he now confronted, whether it would be repeated at Pozières, with him there to witness it.

CHAPTER FOUR

Lurid Clouds of War

'If the motherland was in danger, so was the Commonwealth. If Great Britain went to her Armageddon we, as Britishers, would go with her.'
— Sir John Forrest, minister in Australia's first federal parliament

The morning of Saturday 22 July saw bright sunshine burn off the dawn mist. By mid-afternoon, when Charles Bean ventured up to an advanced post near Pozières Trench to sketch the lay of the battlefield in his diary, it had ripened into 'bright hot day'. As Bean worked forward, he observed that the Anzacs who sheltered nearby in shallow red-earth trenches were in good spirits.[1] Looking back, it is hard to fathom how these men, who would soon be called upon to kill others without hesitation — to shoot them at close range, drive a bayonet through their bellies, or bludgeon them to death — could feel this way. Although, according to Bean, outwardly the Anzacs displayed good spirits, what emotions did they experience privately? As each minute passed and they edged closer to their reckoning, did they feel a heightened sense of anxiety, apprehension, or fear?

Private Walter Wright, 4th Battalion, revealed his state of mind in a letter he wrote some time before the battle: 'Can't help wondering what fate holds in store for me. Will my luck go west? Whatever it is I guess I'll take what is coming to me.'[2]

Captain William Donovan Joynt, 5th Battalion, remembered one soldier expressing the unease felt by many: 'Well, I suppose others before us have gone through the same ordeal and come out of it all right. But I wonder if they felt fear and did they overcome it?'[3] Joynt summed up the prevailing emotion among his men as fear of 'being afraid'.

Lance-Corporal Douglas Horton, a 26-year-old schoolteacher from Mittagong assigned to the 2nd Battalion, describe how his platoon attempted to pass the time by singing songs and swapping jokes. Behind the lightheartedness, Horton sensed a quiet confidence within his platoon, noting: 'Every man was sure of himself and being sure of himself was sure of the man next to him.'[4]

To occupy themselves and possibly block out unsettling thoughts, the soldiers packed and repacked their haversacks, shaved, wrote letters home, watched the bombardment, or tried to snatch some sleep. Some huddled together and played hands of Housey-Housey and Crown and Anchor. Others lay in the grass, watching the aeroplanes circling overhead or the odd lark fluttering about the scarred fields.[5] 'The Battalion was restless all day,' summed up one battalion history. 'No one could settle down.'[6]

Each soldier prepared for battle in his own way. Some kept crumpled copies of Henry Lawson's stirring verse 'The Star of Australasia' inside their pocket-sized diaries.[7] Reading the verse must have helped to fortify their resolve. Lawson, the 'grey dreamer', didn't write soft and soapy poetry; his verse cut like a farmhouse axe. He prophesied: 'I tell you the Star of the South shall rise — in the lurid clouds of war.'[8] He promised them all — clerks, jackeroos, labourers, or drovers — that one great battle was their destiny, and after it their exploits would be remembered for the next 1000 years.

'The day is near when Australia's boys will once again be given an opportunity to show the World what we are made of,' wrote

Lieutenant Harold Malpas in a letter before the battle. 'Tomorrow we hope to be on the road to Berlin ...'[9]

Arthur Foxcroft would have been sitting quietly among his platoon cobbers, scribbling notes in his diary, which records: 'We are getting ready for our first big battle ... We are to take Pozières and must not retire unless beaten back in hand to hand fighting and must not fire a shot unless forced to.'[10] Other soldiers, like Arthur Thomas, immersed themselves in writing what they knew could be their final letters to loved ones. 'This is my last letter before going into a stunt,' he explained to his wife and children. 'God bless you, all my loved ones; pray hard for me.'[11]

Some 'cleanskins' observed the grim Gallipoli veterans — many of whom were distinguishable by the Australian flag tattooed on their arms, as well as brown, leathery skin cured by the Asian sun — for clues on how to prepare for battle. 'The boys at Gallipoli made a name. Now we'll make one too,' vowed Bendigo boy Private George Londey.[12] The veterans sat quietly; a nod here, perhaps a quiet word there, would have guided the 'cleanskins'. Underneath their seemingly calm exterior, they were probably equally anxious. Nothing on Gallipoli would have prepared them for what they were about to confront. 'You can't tell me that all the troops do not feel fear,' remarked one Gallipoli veteran as he watched the heavy barrage falling upon Pozières. 'They must!'[13]

Late in the afternoon, officers inspected their platoons to make sure that each man had everything he required — ammunition, gas masks, wire cutters, and signalling flares. After a late tea, rations were issued and water bottles filled. Under a glaring sun, the laden troops marched in single file toward the firing line, taking only the occasional breather to wipe the sweat from their flushed faces.[14]

Although the staff officers and commanders responsible for orchestrating the looming battle were many miles behind the front line, their diaries, letters, and memoirs reveal that they experienced emotions similar to those felt by their troops. At I Anzac Corps headquarters, White paused from his work to write to Ethel. His letter indicates that his immense responsibilities, combined with feelings of homesickness, had drained him. 'Ethel, you must pray that I may endure to the end,' he wrote.[15]

Meanwhile, outside the corps headquarters, 21-year-old Lieutenant John Treloar sat in one of the tents pitched on the château's lawns. As supervising clerk, he would play a critical role in the battle by overseeing the Central Registry, responsible for distributing all orders, intelligence, and memoranda flowing in and out of the corps. It was a 24-hour-a-day job — the Central Registry's messages fired the war machine. Treloar's diary, mostly recorded in shorthand script, shows a thoughtful man — it describes how, as he sat sorting through piles of correspondence, he could see 'flashes of the guns preparing for the attack'. Treloar had served on Gallipoli and had a 'goodly number' of friends in the fighting units; he felt anxious about how they would fare.[16]

At about the same time, Gough gave one last briefing to Paul Maze at Reserve Army headquarters. Gough, as an army commander, could not witness the attack firsthand, so Maze would be his eyes and ears. 'I could feel his keenness as he was explaining things on the map,' wrote Maze.[17] Gough wanted him to remain in close contact with the attacking troops and to make sketches illustrating the lay of the land. This meant that Maze would be going over the top with the Anzacs.

Meanwhile, at divisional headquarters at Rue Pont-Noyelles in Albert, Hooky Walker and his staff feverishly completed their final preparations. His staff were not only responsible for coordinating the movements of their own troops, but also for liaising with a huge supporting ensemble of formations, each critical to the attack's success. Many things had to go right for Hooky's plan to succeed; only a few things needed to go wrong for it to fail. Hooky told Bean that he feared his beloved 1st Division would be 'knocked out' in the attack.[18] Amid the frenetic preparations, Thomas Blamey sought higher guidance: 'God grant me a clear brain to plan and think for it.'[19]

Birdie's diary shows that late in the afternoon he visited Hooky to check the preparations. That evening, he dined with a friend from Gallipoli days, Lieutenant-General Aylmer Hunter Weston, whose VIII British Corps had almost been completely wiped out on 1 July — a feat that Birdie, no doubt, would not care to emulate.

As Birdie dined with Hunter-Weston, Bean worked his way along a series of 'lonely' roads and shallow trenches toward Sinclair-MacLagan's 3rd Brigade headquarters, located in a dugout somewhere near the village of Contalmaison. On the horizon he could see bursting shrapnel that resembled the bright flashes of a match striking flint. Bean, who was travelling alone, heard a voice from the shadows: 'Anyone going from here along the road is to prepare for gas.' As Bean fumbled with his gas mask, he wondered whether he would ever find the dugout from which he hoped to monitor his first big European battle.[20]

Long, grey shadows cast themselves across the battlefield; the last patches of lingering sunlight disappeared. The attack would commence in a few hours.

The burning question, looking back on the eve of this important battle, was why did so many Australian men find themselves about to be thrown into battle against Germany, the undisputed world military superpower, to capture a tiny village — why did Australia, a minor outpost in the Southern Hemisphere, feel compelled to fight someone else's war? To answer this, we must return to 1914.

The assassination of Archduke Franz Ferdinand, heir to the throne of the Austro-Hungarian Empire, by a Serb nationalist in Sarajevo, Bosnia, was first reported in Australian newspapers on 29 June 1914. The importance that Australians placed on this event was reflected in the Monday edition of *The Sydney Morning Herald*, which devoted the same column space to the murder as it did to England's thrashing of Australia in a rugby league Test in Sydney. The historian Ernest Scott, in *Australia During the War*, indicated that Australians, possibly preoccupied with the pending federal election and Norman Brookes's quest to win the men's singles title at Wimbledon, didn't appreciate the country's gradual drift toward war.[21]

On 29 July, the British government sent a cablegram to Australia, warning: 'See preface defence scheme. Adopt precautionary stage. Names of powers will be communicated later if necessary.'[22] The cablegram was a prearranged signal that war was likely, and an instruction to implement certain steps in a defence procedure laid down in 1907 by the Committee of Imperial Defence. Australian prime minister Joseph Cook met with his cabinet on 3 August and agreed to despatch 20,000 Australian troops to support the British government in the event of war. A cablegram informed London of Australia's proposal; on the next day, Britain accepted the offer.

By early August, the mood among Australians had transformed from cursory interest in European affairs to enthusiastic anticipation of war. This shift was nowhere more evident than outside the *Argus* newspaper outlet in Collins Street, Melbourne, on the morning of 4 August. A crowd of hundreds gathered, eagerly awaiting the newspaper's special midday edition. *The Argus* reported that police on duty were unable to stop the crowd from gaining access to the delivery counter, where copies of the special edition would be handed out. 'What's the news, tell us the news,' the seething crowd yelled.[23]

A day later, on 5 August, London sent a cablegram to all state governors in the Commonwealth, announcing that war had broken out between Great Britain and Germany. With Britain at war, so too was Australia. Ernest Scott wrote that when the call to arms came in August 1914, the response in Australia was 'immediate, it was jubilant, and it was unanimous'.[24] Yet what did Australians believe they were fighting for? The Australian government had no war aims beyond those of Britain, and theirs only made vague references to upholding the London Treaty that guaranteed Belgium's neutrality, which Germany had violated by advancing westward through its territories. Harry S. Gullett, in his October 1914 article 'United Empire', claimed all that mattered was kinship: 'There is no reasoning about it; it is not a matter of head but of heart. We have merely answered the call of race. We are fighting side by side with Britain because of our British blood.'[25]

Although Gullett's sentiment may appear naive, it accurately reflected the nature of the relationship between the two countries. Australia and Britain were inextricably bound by constitutional, social, and economic links. Gavin Souter, in *Lion and Kangaroo*, explained that Australia was still constitutionally tethered to Britain in 1914. Australia's constitution prevented it from making any formal treaties with foreign states; in fact, Australia had no diplomatic status abroad. The Parliament of Westminster could pass or void legislation applicable to Australia. In many matters, the prime minister and his parliament were subservient to the governor-general. If the prime minister wished to communicate formally with his opposite number in a foreign country or even in Britain, he had to do it through the governor-general and the Colonial Office. There was, therefore, no need for cabinet to discuss the merits of entering the war: London would decide this. If war was declared, the cabinet simply had to decide to what degree it would support the empire.

Constitutional bonds were underpinned by strong social links — 98 per cent of Australia's population was of English, Irish, Scottish, or Welsh descent.[26] Its national identity was closely linked to Britain's; many people still referred to themselves as 'independent Australian–Britons'. Schools reinforced these close ties: in 1900, every school was provided with a Union Jack flag and a recommended ceremony for saluting it; world maps were pinned to every classroom wall, with Britain's vast empire shaded in red; and Australians solemnly observed Empire Day each year. 'We were encouraged to believe that we were English in all respects but born and living in Australia.

The word Australian was seldom if ever used,' recalled Donovan Joynt in his autobiography.[27]

Australia's economy was also tied to Britain's. Australia's development largely depended upon the flow of British capital. In *The Anzac Illusion*, Eric Andrews explained that in the 1870s, Britain was Australia's main trading partner, accounting for two-thirds of its exports and imports.[28] The governor-general summed up the net effect of these strong links in August 1914: 'There is indescribable enthusiasm and entire unanimity throughout Australia in support of all that tends to provide for the security of the Empire in war.'[29]

On 15 August 1914, Scottish-born Brigadier-General William Bridges was chosen to lead the expeditionary force of 20,000 soldiers that Cook had promised Britain. *The Sydney Morning Herald* reported that volunteers rushed forward to offer their services.[30] By mid-September, Bridges had a full complement of soldiers, who would form the 1st Australian Infantry Division of the Australian Imperial Force.

Why did tens of thousands of men leave their jobs, families, and homes to enlist in Bridges' expeditionary force? Were they all selflessly motivated to offer their services to the empire? Although Bridges' men were, undoubtedly, infected by a spirit of imperial enthusiasm, Jane Ross in *The Myth of the Digger* suggested there were also other reasons why they enlisted: some joined because they were unemployed, and a number were excited by the opportunities for adventure. The diaries and letters of those soldiers poised to storm Pozières in July 1916 suggest that Ross's research was accurate. For Foxcroft, soldiering offered the prospect of steadier employment than farming during the severe drought of 1914. He also expressed a patriotic desire to offer his 'services to the empire' to 'fight against the Germans and her allies'. Iven Mackay and Donovan Joynt were citizen–soldiers, and so joining the expeditionary force upon the outbreak of war seemed the natural thing to do, although Joynt also recognised it as the start of a 'stirring adventure'. Similarly, the 11th Battalion history recorded that many Outback workers from the frontier state of Western Australia downed their tools and rushed to Perth to join up, filled with a spirit of adventure.[31]

Gallipoli led to a surge of enlistments. Lloyd Robson said that the first enlistment period (August 1914 to June 1915) was marked by minimal official efforts to stimulate recruiting, and there was an average of 9940 enlistments per month. The second enlistment period (July 1915 to August 1916) was fuelled by recruiting drives but, more importantly, by the Gallipoli campaign, which many Australians believed was the most important event in the nation's short history. The campaign, wistfully reported in the newspapers, appealed to the imagination of Australian men. A few months after the landing, in July 1915, monthly enlistments peaked at an all-time high of 36,575 — a significant increase on the previous peak of about 20,000, achieved in August 1914. The overall enlistments for this second period averaged 14,640 per month — a 47 per cent increase on the first. According to Ernest Scott, no Australian enlisting in 1914 and early 1915 could have predicted that nearly 60,000 of their fellow soldiers in the 'prime of life and physical capacity were marked for death, and that 140,000 more would suffer maiming, as a consequence of what had happened at Sarajevo'.[32]

Why did Australians place such high importance on Gallipoli and why did it motivate thousands of men to enlist? Prior to the Great War, Australians struggled to define themselves and their place in the world. Although federation had legally linked all the colonies into one commonwealth, nothing seemed to link its disparate people. There was little in the Australians' early history, wrote Robert Hughes in *The Fatal Shore*, that citizens could point to with pride.[33] Henry Lawson, whose rousing poetry captured the nationalist mood of Australians at the turn of the century, believed that war would be the glue to bind the colony into nationhood. He predicted in 'The Star of Australasia' that one day the boys in the 'city slum' and in the 'home of wealth and pride' would unite and 'fight for it [one home] side by side'.[34] Therefore, on 25 April 1915, when 48 wooden rowboats beached on what was to become known as Anzac Cove, they were not only laden with Australian troops but also with the high expectations of all Australians who sought to forge a national identity.

The nine-month Gallipoli campaign gave Australians what they sought: a 'baptism of fire' to crown the nation's bloodless federation. Australia's flag was stained with the blood of 8700 boys, and their sacrifice proved that Australia was a country worth dying for. Robert Hughes believed that Gallipoli was Australia's equivalent of Thermopylae, while Charles Bean suggested that it contributed to Australia becoming fully conscious of itself as a nation.[35] Australians gleefully drank from the Anzac chalice; the nation had finally made its spectacular debut on the world stage.

The British viewed Gallipoli differently from the Australians. For them, the evacuation and Allied casualties — 205,000 — represented an unmitigated disaster. There was no grandeur in defeat. Their international prestige took a battering because Turkey, a corrupt empire thought to be on the brink of collapse, had defeated them. Politicians lost a measure of faith in their military leaders, and tightened their rein on them. The architect of the campaign, Winston Churchill, lost his position as Lord of the Admiralty, and Ian Hamilton, commander of the Mediterranean Expeditionary Force, never held a command of any substance again. The failure contributed to the downfall of the British prime minister, Herbert Asquith, in late 1916. The British did the obligatory post-mortems, assigned blame, and then consigned the whole regretful episode to history.

Gallipoli inspired the boy who was to become my great-uncle, 14-year-old Ernie Lee, to join up. Lee's family came from the bush town of Mossiface in Gippsland, Victoria, where his father, Herman, ran a selection called Greville Farm. For 15 years, Herman had struggled to clear the gnarly land, but it would not give. It gradually wore him down, crippling his back and breaking his spirit.

The Great War, not farming, was what interested Lee. A few weeks after the last troops evacuated Gallipoli, he bought his first pair of long pants, caught a cable tram up Swanston Street, and presented himself to the recruiting officer at Melbourne Town Hall. On 8 January 1915, Lee completed his attestation papers: he falsely recorded his name as 'Ernest John Jeffries' and stated that he was 18 years old, a trained mechanic, and that his parents were deceased. Lee's papers, which are in the National Archives of Australia, reveal that he weighed only 115 pounds and was a shade over five-foot tall when he enlisted. Within months, this 'boy–soldier' would find himself on the Western Front alongside Gallipoli veterans.[36] Like many of the soldiers who enlisted in 1915, he had little idea of what lay in store, and how dramatically the experience would change him.

CHAPTER FIVE
Storming Pozières

'If I fight, I win.'
— attributed to Confucius

By Saturday 22 July 1916, Hooky Walker's 1st Division troops were prepared for what was to become the first crucial stage in the campaign for Pozières. They almost certainly knew the importance that British high command placed on gaining the village. What they could not possibly have known was how many of them would die or be maimed in the coming days in order to capture a few miles of cratered landscape, or what emotional and physical scars they would bear for the rest of their lives.

The battle plan was relatively straightforward. The Anzacs would aim to seize three objectives: Pozières Trench; the light railway that sat in front of the hedges on the outskirts of the village; and the portion of the village south of the Bapaume road. The Anzacs would attack from the south-west in three staggered lines. Each line would consist of three waves of troops spaced 20 to 50 yards apart, with scouts and wire cutters in the first wave, the main attacking force in the second, and parties carrying bombs, shovels, and supplies in the third. The first line was to leave their freshly dug jumping-off trenches at 12.30 a.m.; the other two lines, positioned further back,

STORMING POZIÈRES 55

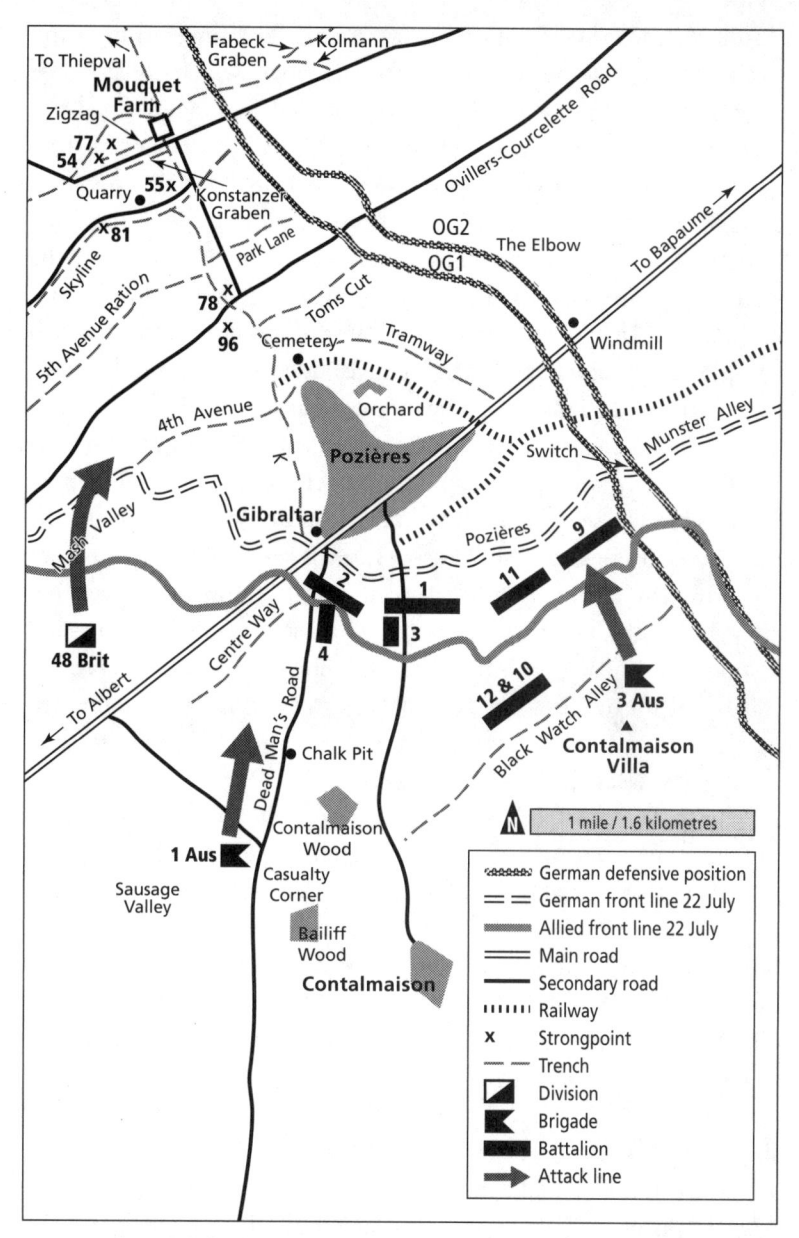

Map 3. The Battlefield Between 22 July and 5 September

would then leapfrog the first line at preordained times to move on to their respective objectives. A lifting barrage, which consisted of a wall of continuous shellfire that extended in range at planned intervals, would be employed to neutralise the Germans further back from Pozières Trench and to protect the advancing troops. The 48th British Division would attack from the north side of the road, hoping to capture a series of communication trenches that led to the village and intersected with K Trench. The theory was impressive, yet attacking at night and relying on numerous armies to execute a complex preparatory and lifting barrage added a significant degree of complexity to a relatively simple infantry battle plan.

By late afternoon, the final movements of Smyth's 1st and Sinclair-MacLagan's 3rd brigade troops were almost complete. Those responsible for seizing the first and second objectives were in the front-line area before dusk. Those responsible for capturing the third objective would begin their final ascent toward the assembly trenches after dark at 10.00 p.m.[1] Paul Maze, who accompanied the first and second lines through the trenches, described the scene: 'Everything was burnt up by the sun; the light was still very glary ... The men carrying heavy loads leaned and rested against the hot parapet, wiping the sweat off their flushed faces.'[2]

As the troops trudged forward, the shells of the preliminary bombardment screamed overhead and hammered Pozières, prompting Maze to speculate as to whether there would be anything left of the village to take. According to the *Official History*, the intense bombardment that he witnessed reflected British command's determination 'to make a certainty of Pozières this time'.[3] Maze admitted to feeling apprehensive as he trudged past the 'scarlet-faced Australians', who had their shirt sleeves rolled up and appeared to be preparing for battle by either having tea or cleaning their rifles by sliding the breech up or down.

Maze recalled that, gradually, moist evening air replaced the relentless heat of the day, and faint dew dusted the broken ground.

As the sun receded behind the hills and 'nature sunk into a peculiar stillness', he began to feel strangely detached from the shells rushing past and their resounding crashes upon impact. His apprehension gradually ebbed, replaced by a momentary sense of peace. He arrived at a reserve position packed with Australians awaiting the cover of darkness to proceed to their assembly positions, and remembered a soldier asking, 'Well Captain, are you coming over with us tonight?' He felt strangely glad to say that he was.

He continued moving through the trench. 'Men were merely moving shadows, barging into me with their kit,' he recalled. At one location, he observed a group attending to an officer who, upon looking too long over the parapet, had been shot through the head. It prompted Maze to assess his chances of surviving the attack. 'I could not easily give up life,' he concluded. It seemed too alluring and precious: 'Its grip on me was tightening, and more than ever I wanted to live.'[4]

Unbeknown to the Australians shuffling through the trenches, the Germans were aware of and prepared for the midnight attack. Their intelligence had gleaned a critical advantage when a captured British soldier disclosed that Pozières was about to be stormed. Defences were bolstered; fresh troops from the 117th Division were moved in to replace the weakened Burkhardt Division and cover the vital area between Thiepval and the Bapaume road. German commanders sent notes to the front lines to stiffen the resolve of their troops. 'Not an inch of trench must be abandoned to the enemy ... and if the enemy penetrates ... drive him out at once,' read one note.[5] First German Army commander Fritz von Below, who held the sector that included Pozières, sent an apocalyptic standing order stating that the enemy should have to carve its way over heaps of corpses to advance.[6]

As magnificent as its armies were, Germany was feeling the immense strain of fighting multiple enemies on multiple fronts.

United against the Germans were the British, Russians, French, Italians, Canadians, Australians, New Zealanders, South Africans, Indians, Portuguese, Serbs, and Belgians. By Germany's own admission, its armies had suffered a staggering 3.1 million casualties since the war started.[7] The elite divisions had wilted under the constant strain, and the reserves were not of the same fighting calibre. The Germans undoubtedly knew that if they didn't hold their fortified positions on the Somme at locations such as Pozières, they could possibly be swept out of France and back into their homeland. Commanders, referring to the ruined villages on the Somme, forewarned their troops: 'My boys, there you see what will happen if you let the English and French drive you back into Germany. Those villages will be your villages and towns. The misery of those old men and women and those children will be the misery of your father, mother, your wife and children.'[8]

The tremendous bombardment of Pozières, which reduced the village to a heap of powdered foundations, took its toll on the Germans. One soldier, who probably expressed the dread of many, wrote in a letter to his wife: 'The Gods only know if I am writing for the last time ... I have given up hope of life ... to my last moment I shall think of you. There is really no possibility that we shall see each other again. Should I fall — then farewell.'[9]

Just after 10.00 p.m., the Germans, who had been awaiting daily the attack on Pozières, launched a precautionary barrage of high-explosive shells, shrapnel shells, and phosgene gas, aimed at disrupting the Allies' attack preparations. It disorientated some of the battalions attempting to reach their assembly trenches. Other battalions were still short of their intended positions at 10.00 p.m., having lost their way or become entangled with neighbouring units. The disorientated 10th Battalion stumbled about aimlessly in the shadows while their guides argued among themselves; eventually, it had no other choice but to retrace its footsteps back to the starting point, and set out again. Elsewhere, 4th Battalion soldiers lost their bearings when gas shells (which, upon explosion, sounded like a paper bag bursting and had the pungent smell of crushed nettles) began falling among them. The 3rd Battalion, after wandering in the 'outer darkness' like 'tourists', managed to reach its assigned location about four hours early, at 9.00 p.m. With time to spare, the officers attempted to reorganise their attacking lines; however, constant German machine-gun fire and shelling confused the men, resulting in the lines becoming muddled. Fortunately, the shrapnel shells 'burst high and though the pellets rattled down like hail no one was hit', John Harris noted.[10]

Despite the initial confusion, the Australians gradually reached the assembly trenches, which resembled ditches freshly prepared for drainpipes, just before midnight. 'The atmosphere became tenser,' recalled Maze, and except for a few runners 'threading their way through with messages, movement had completely ceased'.[11] Nineteen-year-old dental apprentice Lance-Corporal Ben Champion, of the 1st Battalion, couldn't stop urinating as he waited anxiously for the Allied barrage to begin. 'When it did, it seemed the earth opened up with a crash,' he recorded in his diary. 'The ground shook and trembled … it was impossible to hear ourselves speak.' He recounted how men crept together for protection, and no motioning from officers could make them move apart.[12]

Ten minutes after midnight, and 20 minutes before the Allied barrage lifted, the first line of Australians left their jumping-off trenches and crawled over the thistle tufts to within 40 yards of Pozières Trench. As the new moon peeked over the horizon, flares lit up the sky. At 12.23 a.m., according to Douglas Horton, word passed along: 'Five minutes to go.' At 12.24 a.m., six minutes before the attack, a German rocket flare burst into stars, and machine guns opened fire. The increase in retaliatory fire from the Germans worried some Australian officers: had they spotted their troops crawling toward Pozières Trench? Would they now respond with a crushing bombardment? Yet, to the officers' relief, the German fire gradually subsided to levels expected on an ordinary night — possibly because the Germans had expected the attack on Pozières to fall between

1.00 a.m. and 2.00 a.m. At 12.26 a.m., word was passed along: 'Two minutes to go.'[13]

'Exactly at the tick of 12.28 a.m.,' recalled Sergeant Raymond Brownell, who was manning an artillery battery a few miles back in Sausage Valley, 'we got "Action, Gun, Fire", and all hell let loose.'[14] According to the *Official History*, the full fire of the 1st Australian Division's field artillery burst upon Pozières Trench. For two minutes, gunners such as Brownell fired as fast as they could load, while the troops crouching in the front line watched as Pozières Trench was illuminated by 'a continuous band of bursting shrapnel'.[15] As the Australian barrage obliterated Pozières Trench, the British 25th and 48th division batteries simultaneously fired on the north side of Pozières, and the British 34th Division and some French artillery fired on the OG lines.

Hundreds of troops on the slopes to the rear of Albert watched the spectacular bombardment, which was visible for nearly twenty miles around. The *Official History* described the skyline as alive with light: 'Flashes like summer lightning were quite continuous, making one flickering band of light.' Bean recorded in *Letters from France* that it was 'the most fearful bombardment' he had ever seen.[16] Paul Maze remembered hundreds of shells shrieking overhead and bursting; he described 'tongues of flame ... rising, glaring on lines of waiting men memorised by this unprecedented burst of sound'.[17]

The Germans retaliated with artillery and machine-gun fire. 'As we lay out among the poppies in No-Man's Land we could see the bullets cutting off the poppies almost against our heads,' recounted Sergeant Harry Preston, 9th Battalion, in the returned soldiers' magazine *Reveille*. 'A man beside me was crying like a baby, and although I tried to reassure him he kept on saying that we would never get out of it.'[18]

At exactly 12.30 a.m., the Australian artillery falling on Pozières Trench lifted to the second line. Foxcroft barely heard the order: '12.30 a.m. Fix bayonets and over you go lads.' He could not hear the guns for excitement. 'Sky one blaze from fire from guns. I had [my] helmet dented by shrapnel just as I jumped into No Man's Land,' he wrote in his diary.[19] Maze heard the clash of steel as men around him fixed their bayonets, and Harry Preston saw men scrambling to their feet. 'Taking this to be the signal for the charge I jumped up and dashed across,' he recalled.[20]

Troops stumbled forward over the rough ground, illuminated by rockets and star shells. Maze remembered bullets hissing past them. A man in front of him tottered and fell. 'I could hardly control my legs as I leapt to avoid his body. The ground seemed to quake under me. Everything appeared to be moving along with me, figures were propping up and down on either side over the convulsing ground,' he wrote.[21]

As Foxcroft advanced, a shell exploded close to his platoon commander, William Clemenger, partially burying him. The rest of the platoon continued on. 'Lieutenant Clemenger funked it and pretended to be gassed,' noted Foxcroft, somewhat harshly.[22] In fact, Clemenger was evacuated in a state of shock. As evidence of the bombardment's intensity, a week later, when he was examined at the 4th London General Hospital, Clemenger was still suffering from poor memory, insomnia, bad dreams, and slight tremors.[23] Many Australians would experience similarly debilitating symptoms over the next few days.

Almost 2000 troops advanced in dense formation — about one man to every yard — across a one-mile front, toward the German trenches.[24] They didn't march or slope arms as they had practised in parade-yard drills; it was simply a case of getting there as best they could. The sporadic machine-gun fire did not slow them.

'Our artillery prevented the Huns from coming out of their burrows,' wrote Foxcroft in his diary. 'Met a few Huns in shell holes on the way over demoralised by the intensity of our bombardment, and settled them.'[25]

Through the glare of German star shells and flares, Private Peter Smith of the 4th Battalion could see ghostly figures moving amid the smoke of battle. 'Every now and then a shell landed, and created more casualties,' he remembered.[26]

Elsewhere, Horton glimpsed his first German: he had his rifle to his shoulder, a finger crooked on the trigger, standing in a trench but without making the slightest movement. Horton realised that a bursting shell had killed him, leaving him standing as he had been.[27]

Iven Mackay described how surviving Germans emerged from their dugouts like drunken men, mumbling in a half-dazed way, 'Mercy, *Kamerad*.'[28] They were captured, bayoneted, or shot dead. Private Herbert Mobbs, from Murray Bridge, South Australia, had expected hand-to-hand fighting with the Germans, but said, 'All we could see was their arms and legs sticking out of the ground where they had been buried by our shells.' He recalled finding some dugouts and how he and the others he was with shouted to the soldiers within to come out: 'They started yelling "Mercy *Kamerade*" and stayed there so we threw bombs down to them.'[29]

Maze continued to advance with the Australians. At one point, he paused to scan the chaotic battlefield. He remembered seeing wounded men scattered everywhere, some crying in pain, others tearing open and applying their field dressings, and more screaming for stretcher-bearers.[30]

As the battle raged, Charles Bean sat quietly in Sinclair-MacLagan's crowded dugout, where he observed proceedings and occasionally took longhand notes of important conversations and orders. Hours earlier, he had set out alone from Fricourt in search of Sinclair-MacLagan's headquarters. After leaving the village at about 9.00 p.m., Bean had become disorientated by the onset of darkness and the heavy and prolonged bombardment. He described in his diary how he was forced to fit his gas helmet quickly when some gas shells 'plopped' close by, and how he couldn't breathe properly inside the helmet, which made him feel sick. However, with the help of some British signallers who kindly acted as guides for the last part of his journey, Bean located the thick beams of Sinclair-MacLagan's dugout entrance at about 12.15 a.m. He recorded how he ripped off his helmet and then half-fell down the dark stairway and over some tired runners into the lower-chamber headquarters, his 'awful series of adventures with gas shells and shrapnel' finally over. From his quiet corner in the dugout, Bean recorded that gas, with its aromatic smell, wafted through the headquarters. Sinclair-MacLagan's officers, seated around a candlelit table, worked with their gas helmets on. Outside, explosions — about three-and-a-half to the second — erupted continuously.

'They ought to be in by now,' speculated Sinclair-MacLagan, whose wire communication to the assaulting battalions had already been severed by shelling. As a result, he had only a vague grasp of how the battle was unfolding, and was almost solely reliant on the snippets of information his runners delivered to him. Gas, shelling, and severed communication wires weren't the only difficulties Sinclair-MacLagan faced: his officers and orderlies were exhausted but they had to be kept awake at all costs to monitor the battle's progress, draft orders, and scrutinise incoming messages from battalions and divisional headquarters. 'Don't let him sleep,' Bean overheard some whispering. 'Kick him, don't let him sleep.'[31]

Unbeknown to Sinclair-MacLagan, the first line of troops had captured Pozières Trench. 'We immediately set to work to improve our position,' said Preston. 'The dead bodies which had to be thrown out were used in building up the parapet.'[32] The first attacking line had to stay put at Pozières Trench while the second line leapfrogged through them onto the second objective, the shallow trench near the orchard. According to the *Official History*, an officer commanding the second line kept shouting 'keep on moving'; some men of the first line abandoned their position and followed him. On reaching the orchard, the troops threw their bombs into the dugouts and chalked the battalion's name on an abandoned 5.9-inch howitzer before moving on.[33] No one could accurately distinguish the British barrage from the German counter-bombardment; it was simply one illumination of bursting shells and flares all round. Some soldiers advanced into their own barrage, which blew them to bits. About 140 men of the 11th and 12th battalions made it through the barrage and chased the fleeing Germans as far as the windmill on the crest of the Pozières ridge. Sergeant Wally Graham of the 11th Battalion remembered thinking: 'Christ! The road's open to Berlin!'[34] However, officers persuaded the isolated men to return to their own lines. Only about 90 made it back through the barrage.

Resistance from the critical OG lines intensified. Officers despatched additional troops to help out. Preston's party bombed their way into the trench and barricaded their gains. The Germans, in an attempt to trick the Australians, put helmets and caps on their rifles and walked along the trench with them held above the parapet. 'When our men put their heads up and attempted to shoot them, they were shot by other Germans further along the trench,' recalled Preston.[35]

The Bapaume road was the third and most distant objective. About 2000 troops of the third attacking line were supposed to start their advance from the Chalk Pit at 1.00 a.m., but the three waves within the attacking line became entangled in the darkness. In some places, those carrying shovels led the attack; in others, the scouts lagged behind. The troops passed through Pozières Trench, which 'was dotted with little groups of men, some cheering wildly, some singing, some groaning', recorded the *Official History*.[36]

The Germans' intense shelling killed many officers of the third attacking line. Leaderless groups became confused. Some soldiers forgot the instruction to advance in the correct formation; others advanced obliquely across the battlefield. Harris tried to coerce the men to straighten up, but quickly found himself deserted by all except his batman. Harris continued forward, eventually stumbling across what he described as a 'confused mass of men' belonging to different battalions.[37]

Despite the chaos, Maze struggled on. Near the outskirts of the village, he came across the remains of a blown-up railway track. 'It flashed through my mind that General Gough had asked me to look out for a light railway. This was it,' he recorded.[38] Most soldiers of the third line regrouped at the railway track, which was a designated rallying point, and started out again, feeling their way through the shell holes, splintered trees, building rubble, and tumbled framework of cottages. 'Lashed by sprays of dust and broken brick, we stumbled over stones and shell holes,' noted Maze, who was almost certainly advancing with the third line of troops. They reached the Bapaume road. 'We ran into a hail of bullets as we struck some cobble stone, which must have been the main road,' he remembered. 'The men staggered across it, all lit up by the sudden glare of Verey lights.'

With their three objectives captured, the Anzacs dug a new trench line with the few shovels they had, hoping to consolidate their position before daylight. By 2.30 a.m. the troops had successfully dug a trench running the length of the village, parallel to the Bapaume road, only bending back as it approached the uncaptured portion of the OG lines 600 yards in the distance.

'From rifle flashes coming from the rising ground it seemed that the right [flank of the attack] hadn't progressed far into the village,' Maze speculated. He was right: the 9th and 10th battalions, responsible for capturing the OG lines, ended up about 600 yards short of their objective, leaving a dangerous gap in the defences.

Hooky Walker responded quickly upon hearing the news: 'The position on its [3rd Brigade] right flank became somewhat critical and I moved up the 7th Battalion from the reserve brigade to Black Watch Alley at 4.30 a.m.,' he noted in the divisional diary.[39]

The three German battalion commanders defending Pozières were in their dugouts when the fighting started and knew nothing of the battle's progress. Finally, one runner got through at 3.40 a.m., reporting the critical situation of troops closing in on its forward headquarters. The German commanders called for reserves.

Heavy British machine-gun fire and shelling repulsed the troops despatched from Courcelette to counterattack.[40]

The advancing Anzacs left in their wake a battlefield littered with dead and wounded. Nothing could be done for the dead, but 'the wounded were collected and carried back to the dressing stations,' recalled Captain Geoffrey Drake-Brockman. 'It was horrible to watch the shells bursting among them where they lay in long lines awaiting removal to clearing stations and hospitals.'[41]

However, being evacuated from Pozières did not guarantee safety. Private Frank Shoobridge, a stretcher-bearer who hailed from Tasmania, described in his diary how the wounded started coming in faster than the medical orderlies could get them safely into dugouts. 'Being full we had to put them out in the open where many of them got wounded again after we had dressed them,' he recorded.[42] The regimental stretcher-bearers couldn't cope with the immense workload. Hooky later admitted in his report on operations that the number of stretcher-bearers in the division was quite inadequate for the large number of casualties sustained. Subsequently, a great many were borrowed from other ambulances.[43]

Due to the shortage, many of those with light wounds tried to make their own way back to the aid posts. 'It is awful to see crippled men staggering back with the help of a shovel, stick or anything,' wrote Lance-Corporal Roger Morgan of the 1st Field Ambulance, 'just crawling along until at last they either reach help or fall exhausted on the road.'[44] Private Peter Snodgrass, a 31-year-old shearer from Western Australia, recollected one particular man with a bandaged ankle, two bandaged knees, a gunshot wound to the shoulder, and his shattered and badly bleeding arm in a sling, refusing to be stretchered out because there were many more urgent cases than him.[45]

'The scene is terrible,' wrote Morgan of dead and dying men lying on top of the other. 'Many of them were blown to pieces where they lay on the ground.'[46] Morgan recorded that one of the dying soldiers kept repeating to the orderlies: 'Stop the bleeding boys and I'll get back to the Mrs. and Kids'.[47]

Drake-Brockman remembered the excruciating wait for bearers while he sheltered in a shell hole with Major Leslie Mather, who had been shot through the neck. Mather became more and more yellow as time passed. 'He vomited all over my tunic. I wiped off the vomit with a stick. I watched, waited and wondered: would they ever return with a stretcher?' Drake-Brockman wrote.[48] He didn't realise the shocking conditions the bearers were working under — they had to traverse shell craters and work their way through clogged communication trenches to reach the aid stations, sometimes arriving exhausted or wounded. Many simply failed to return.

A tired Frank Shoobridge was within 100 yards of an aid post on his fifth trip when shrapnel burst overhead. 'Stredwick, who was carrying in front, was hit through the thigh and head and I got a bit in the knee and splinters in the face,' he explained in his diary. Another man tried to find fresh stretcher-bearers, but the patient died before he reached the dressing station. Shoobridge carried Stredwick, who was bleeding profusely and almost unconscious, back to an aid post. 'He went down on a stretcher and that was the last I ever saw of him.'[49] Sydney Stredwick, a chemist from Kyneton, died from his wounds two days later.[50]

Many of the wounded had to be attended to outside aid posts, under the German counter-barrage. Some aid posts in captured dugouts had their entrances facing the incoming German shells. On returning to the 11th Battalion's aid post early in the morning, Albert Coates discovered that a shell had killed all the wounded. 'What a sight. Mangled remains on the stretchers,' he remembered.[51]

Despite the casualties — which, by the Somme's standards, were relatively light — the 1st Division's attack was a resounding success. The British bombardment had completely destroyed the village, and the troops had captured their three objectives.

Yet not everything had gone to plan. Sinclair-MacLagan's 9th and 10th battalions hadn't captured the 600-yard stretch of the OG lines, leaving a dangerous gap that a German battalion could advance through undetected. The shelling had destroyed thousands of yards of carefully laid telephone wire, forcing Smyth and Sinclair-MacLagan to rely on runners to get their messages through. Also, on the other side of the Bapaume road, the 48th British Division, which had been swept with intense machine-gun fire, had only captured a small section of their intended objective — the communication trenches leading to the village. This meant that the Australian and British troops were separated by pockets of Germans, who continued to fight stubbornly.[52] Follow-up attacks would be required to dislodge them.

Hooky had to secure his gains quickly; the Germans would soon retaliate with their own bombardment and counterattack. He also had to plan for the capture of northern Pozières and the OG lines. Correspondent John Masefield best described the pending challenge: 'The tactical aim of the Australians was to drive the enemy off the high land. The tactical aim of the enemy was to shell the Australians off it.'[53] Capturing southern Pozières was only the first phase in what would be a long and exhausting battle for the Australians. In the coming days, Hubert Gough would harangue I Anzac Corps to capture northern Pozières and the Pozières ridge, and then swing around to the west and strike toward the formidable Mouquet Farm.

CHAPTER SIX
Consolidation

'*The most dangerous moment comes with victory.*'
— Napoleon Bonaparte

Despite the intense fighting of the previous few hours and the absolute exhaustion of many soldiers, the Australians had to set about consolidating their trenches before the German counterattack they feared was coming. As the first light of dawn came over the ridge at about 4.00 a.m., Paul Maze observed that the Australians were much further into the village than he had first thought. 'In front of us earth was being rapidly shovelled out of a trench, and we could see the heads of a few men busily consolidating the position,' he recorded.[1]

Elsewhere, Vickers and Lewis gun crews rushed forward, engineers and pioneers dug support and communication trenches, guards escorted prisoners out of the village to holding cages, officers sorted stragglers and lost men back into their correct platoons, and reinforcements came forward from the brickworks, located near Albert, to replace those killed or wounded.[2]

Just after daybreak, a British spotter aeroplane swooped low over the village. The pilot sounded his klaxon horn in sharp bursts, signalling to those below to light their green flares to show him where the new front line was. But the pilot couldn't see any flares because the mist and smoke were too heavy; the location of the front line was unclear.[3] As a result, wrote Arthur Foxcroft, 'our artillery didn't know how to "range" their guns so we got some of our own shells as well as Fritz's'.[4]

As the sun rose, the exhausted men congratulated each other on their success. 'We were surprised by how few casualties had been sustained,' wrote Douglas Horton. 'Satisfied with ourselves, we lay on the parados of the trench basking in the sun.'[5]

Another satisfied soldier pencilled a letter home. 'Mum, I don't think I will ever forget the fighting last night,' he wrote. 'Don't ask me how we took Pozières. But, Mum, we did it. That's all I know … and that's all that matters.'[6]

Maze, after the heavy fighting of the previous night, welcomed the morning solitude. 'Strangely enough, precarious as our position was, we felt protected,' he recorded.[7] The *Official History* attributed the morning lull — the artillery of both sides was almost silent — to the gunners being tired and the respective staff 'as yet uncertain where their own or the opposing infantry were situated'.[8] Australian soldiers felt safe enough to venture out into the open to gather up ammunition that lay scattered all over the ground; it was now desperately needed for the inevitable German counterattacks. The 3rd Battalion history compared the strange lull to the windless centre of a cyclone, with the front line taking on 'almost the semblance of the peaceful Fleurbaix-Armentières "nursery"… '.[9]

The quiet period provided some men the opportunity to snatch sleep for the first time in two or three days. The 3rd Battalion history observed that the silence allowed many Australians, fatigued by the strenuous digging and brutal fighting, to drop in their tracks and fall asleep.[10] 'Huddled up in strange and contorted attitudes in the trenches, or stretched out in shell holes in the rear,' wrote John Harris, 'they slept as soundly in all the discomfort and danger as if they had been in feather beds.'[11]

Suddenly, around daybreak, the peace was shattered by rifle shots from across the road. 'As we were standing-to a sniper got busy and "pipped" a few of our men off,' Peter Smith recalled.[12] Some soldiers darted across the road and hunted for the snipers, while others, according to Bean, 'ratted' for Germans in dugouts and cellars, chasing, shooting, and bayoneting those who got away. After Foxcroft finished improving his new trench he joined the soldiers in 'chasing huns and smoking them out of their cellars'.[13]

'We lost a number of men to snipers that day,' Lieutenant Elmer Laing wrote in a letter to his parents. 'I wanted to take a party out and clear them but was not allowed to.'[14]

The outbreak of German sniping permanently ended the fleeting peacefulness experienced that morning at Pozières.

At about the same time Foxcroft was 'ferreting' Germans from their dugouts, Douglas Haig awoke at Val Vion Château to reports that the Australians had captured most of Pozières. It was the only success of the British 'double-fisted' attack that had been delivered by Haig's Fourth and Reserve armies; as the *Official History* observed, 'no inch of ground was gained' on the whole front east of Pozières. Despite Haig having carefully planned the manner and timing of the attacks with his army commanders the previous days, it appeared that the Germans, strengthened by fresh reserves, had successfully repelled most of the assaults.[15]

The weight of expectation upon Haig during the Somme offensive must have been suffocating. The Allies, both on the field and off, looked to Haig to break the deadlock on the Western Front.[16] Haig appeared to cope with the immense pressures imposed on him by the Allies, British politicians, and his enemies by maintaining the same routine, irrespective of the highs and lows of battle. Charteris closely observed Haig's daily schedule. He documented in *Field Marshal Earl Haig* that his bedroom door opened punctually at 8.25 a.m. and he would go for a short walk. At precisely 8.30 a.m., he would come into the mess for breakfast. At 9.00 a.m., he would go into his study and work. Any matter brought to him was dealt with immediately. He seldom used the telephone, as he believed conversations on it were inaccurate and liable to distortion, no doubt favouring the candour of face-to-face meetings. He preferred that a staff member use the telephone on his behalf, reasoning that his staff were better placed to verify information provided by subordinates.

At 11.30 a.m., he would see his army commanders or department heads for their scheduled daily meetings. Haig's personal staff noted these officers' symptoms of anxiety as they waited to be ushered into his study for their rigidly timetabled interviews. Undoubtedly, Haig — with his direct questions, insistence that officers refrain from using notebooks, and reputation for ruthlessly removing incompetent officers — had the capacity to intimidate his army commanders and department heads. Although he occasionally berated an officer, most walked from his study with their nervousness replaced by marked signs of restored confidence. Haig never took notes and rarely had a paper on his desk.

At 1.00 p.m., he would have lunch. He would then motor out to the headquarters of an army, corps, or division. On the return trip, he would arrange for his horse to meet the car and ride with his escort to within three miles of his headquarters. From there, he would walk. He would then have a bath and do some physical exercise. Haig would work in his office until exactly 8.00 p.m., when he would have dinner, usually with a visiting guest, such as French commander General Joseph Joffre, King George V, British prime minister Herbert Asquith, secretary of state for war David Lloyd George (Kitchener's death in 1916 had resulted in Lloyd George taking on the war ministry), newspaper proprietor Lord Alfred Northcliffe, or war correspondent John Masefield. After dinner, he would work until 10.45 p.m., and then retire to bed at 11.00 p.m. He rarely varied from this routine, except during major battles. Distinguished guests conformed to it. So many hours for work, exercise, and sleep; he focused his whole mind and life on the Somme offensive.

Haig's immersion in the war meant that he dealt with people in a clinical and dispassionate manner. He was a composed rationalist who preferred to make decisions based on facts; opinions weighed little with him. Once he made a decision, the meeting ended. 'Though completely courteous,' remembered Charteris, he 'was cold and formal. He appeared to treat those with him rather as a doctor would a patient.'[17]

Why was Haig, as Tim Travers observed in *The Killing Ground*, so obsessive about order and the need to rigidly adhere to the same schedule? Why did he deal with people so clinically? Perhaps he derived some comfort from maintaining the routine and keeping an emotional distance from the officers who reported to him. Perhaps it gave him a sense of control, a feeling that he was on top of things.[18] After all, the four walls within his château were possibly the only things he controlled completely. The war had its own trajectory; no man could command it any more than a man could hope to direct an earthquake.

Despite the setbacks of 23 July, Haig seemed to draw some satisfaction from the Anzacs' efforts. They had broken one of the two buttresses, Pozières and Thiepval, on the enemy's northern flank of the battlefield. He wrote in his diary: 'The capture of Pozières by the Australians will live in history.'[19]

While Haig pondered how the 23 July setback would reshape his Somme strategy, Australian prime minister William Morris 'Billy' Hughes was returning to Australia, sailing on the *Euripides*, after four exhilarating months in Britain.[20] Welsh-born Hughes, judged by today's standards, was a man of extreme opinions: he advocated the White Australia policy, compulsory military training, and racial purity, and he viewed war as a natural Darwinist phenomenon to re-establish the world order at the expense of weak and corrupt races. The Labor leader held contradictory views: he was a fervent Australian nationalist but, unlike many in his party, also had a passionate belief in the British Empire. John Charteris aptly summed Hughes up as a queer combination of socialist and imperialist.[21]

Hughes had visited Britain on the basis of an informal invitation, issued to all colonial prime ministers by the British government, to discuss the war effort. Once there, he immediately struck a chord with the public. Although 53-year-old Hughes was small, nearly deaf, and had a squeaky voice, his frail body housed a magnetic personality and a sharp mind that could comprehend the most complex information and convert it into simple, emotive messages that the average person could understand.[22] In a series of bellicose speeches, he questioned the British government's lack of vigour in executing the war, and its lack of any discernible plan for winning it. 'You cannot have a great nation when the basis is rotten,' he lectured one audience in Cardiff, Wales. 'You must face these facts. You cannot shut your eyes and say, like the pacifist, that we should have no war …'[23] For all his preaching Hughes was right: Britain hadn't yet established a war economy that could adequately supply the front line, as the munitions shortage of 1915 had demonstrated. Furthermore, no central body was responsible for coordinating the Allies' war strategy, and Britain had no unified council devoted to managing its efforts.[24] Hughes, unencumbered by party loyalties and with no fear of upsetting the current British prime minister, Herbert Asquith, let rip, saying whatever he liked. The more his message seemed to resonate with the British people, the more extreme his speeches became. The rewards of his 'fiery crusade' included several honorary doctorates, the regard of King George V, and the applause of the British press, who, according to his biographer, W. Farmer Whyte, declared: 'An ounce of Hughes is worth a pound of Asquith.' Bean described the visit 'as a personal triumph for Mr Hughes'.[25]

Australia's war contribution gave Hughes's voice credibility — Australia had about 300,000 men in uniform by June 1916. As evidence of Hughes's growing stature, he was invited to attend a British cabinet meeting on 9 March, and in June, due to popular insistence of the public and the press, the inter-Allied conference on economic issues, in Paris.[26] Before the war, it would have been inconceivable that a dominion prime minister would be afforded such prominence.

The British admired Australia's efforts on Gallipoli, and appreciated its growing role on the Western Front. Haig desperately needed its four divisions in France to wage the later part of his Somme offensive, and Hughes had promised even more troops.[27] A shrewd political tactician like Hughes would likely have recognised that he had to convert his increasing popularity into political clout. Despite his visit to Britain being hailed as a triumph, Hughes must have realised that he only attended the British cabinet meeting as an observer rather than as a representative of Australia. At the inter-Allied conference he represented Britain, not Australia. Australia did not have the status of allies such as Japan, China, Belgium, and Portugal. No doubt, Hughes was still irked by Britain's decision to deploy its Anzac troops on Gallipoli without prior consultation with the Australian government.

On 1 June 1916, Hughes had tried to exercise his clout when dining at Haig's General Headquarters in France. He insisted that the Australian divisions should fight as an army rather than being scattered across different corps, and that this army should be placed under one commander, preferably Birdie, who would be responsible to the Australian government.[28] Haig politely refused the request, writing to Hughes some time later: 'I cannot form an Australian Army now, nor can I place all the Australian Forces in France under General Birdwood's command.'[29] Haig needed his forces to remain fluid; he didn't want the whims of a colonial government to restrict him. An emboldened Hughes wasn't deterred; he would persist with his agenda.

Battalion commanders, including 26-year-old Lieutenant-Colonel Owen Howell-Price of the 3rd Battalion and 34-year-old Lieutenant-Colonel Iven Mackay of the 4th Battalion, continued to meet with their officers throughout the morning to discuss their position, sort their soldiers into the correct units, inspect the freshly dug trenches, and thin the line of surplus troops — who were now overcrowding the trenches. Within hours, the two commanders would receive operational orders from divisional headquarters outlining their next objective.

Howell-Price and Mackay each commanded a battalion of about 1000 men. In the pre–Great War army, which traditionally made appointments based on seniority rather than performance, there had been only a handful of men who led such large numbers of troops, and they'd been groomed for it all their soldiering careers. (Just over a year earlier, the 3rd and 4th battalions had been commanded by Lieutenant-Colonel Astley Thompson and Lieutenant-Colonel Alfred Bennett, who were both 50 years old.) Howell-Price and Mackay's early promotions were due, in part, to the transformation that the Australian Imperial Force had undergone in Egypt in early 1916 in response to a flood of new recruits. Birdie, who oversaw the transformation, was adamant that this was a young man's war, and Howell-Price and Mackay's promotions reflected his thinking.[30]

Were these two men too young and inexperienced to hold such important commands? Bean seemed to think that opting for an energetic commander such as Howell-Price, who had a Military Cross and strong organisational skills, was a much better proposition than handing out commands to soldiers based on seniority. He believed the latter approach had already saddled units with commanders who were entirely lacking in the right spirit to discipline troops, select quality subordinates, and foster morale.[31]

Howell-Price and Mackay had much in common: mixed with their youthfulness was a streak of cold determination of which Haig would have approved. Each had strict self-discipline and determination — perhaps inherited from their fathers, who were both in the clergy. Each seemed also to have absorbed and assimilated the lessons of the new, industrialised form of warfare, which was fought with artillery and machine guns rather than muskets or swords; coordinated at army and corps level rather than regiment and battalion level; and contested across trench networks spanning multiple countries, rather than over open plains. They placed emphasis on careful planning and the crisp execution of battle plans, not on the military routines often valued by older officers, such as marching smartly, rolling up a greatcoat correctly, or conducting parade-ground drills. And they shared a love for their men: the commanders' thoughtful acts — Mackay, for example, organised half a pound of fruit cake for each man in his battalion on the anniversary of the Gallipoli landing — demonstrated this affection (and no doubt contributed to one soldier declaring that Mackay was the fairest man he had ever known).[32] But it was a tough love: both men had already demonstrated on Gallipoli and now at Pozières that they were capable of throwing their soldiers into battle, possibly toward certain death, without a moment's hesitation.

Mackay, the son of a Scottish preacher and raised in the Calvinist tradition, was strict with his troops, earning him the nickname 'Iven the Terrible'. One officer remembered Mackay, armed with a rifle and a pistol, and Mills bombs bulging from his pockets, continually inspecting the battalion's defences. 'I don't know how the Old Man kept going. Nothing showy about him. You knew that everything was under control once he arrived,' observed one soldier.[33]

Howell-Price left the safety of his headquarters to personally direct affairs in the village that morning, as did Mackay. Howell-Price, the son of a Welsh clergyman, was one of five brothers to enlist in the Australian Imperial Force. On Gallipoli, he revealed himself as a talented trainer and organiser of men. Howell-Price's troops considered him strict and resented his four-hour drills aimed at improving discipline — perhaps because of his youth, the commander took his responsibilities too seriously to be popular with his officers and men. Despite this, the 3rd Battalion history conceded that underlying his sternness and austerity was a deep and single-minded loyalty to his men.[34]

Both men's company and platoon commanders, who, on this morning, were busy organising their units, were often young men, only 21 or 22 years old. Military experience, some higher education, a modicum of common sense, and a little time in the trenches on Gallipoli seemed the main qualifications needed to command a company or platoon. They would be the ones to execute Howell-Price and Mackay's orders in the coming days, to cajole one more effort out of their exhausted troops — like Foxcroft, who hadn't slept since Friday — even if they didn't have one to give.

At about 5.30 a.m., as Howell-Price and Mackay organised their troops, several hundred Germans were seen massing at the OG lines. The Lewis gun crews — about 16 of these guns had reached the village with the first attacking troops the previous evening — would be vital in defending the Anzacs' newly captured position. The crews braced themselves for the attack. The Lewis gunner, who fired the weapon, had to be careful because an ammunition pannier could be fired off in six seconds flat. He had to be sure of his targets and fire in short bursts, otherwise his valuable supply of ammunition would be expended quickly.

The Germans pinpointed the gap between the OG lines and the village. They advanced in tight formation, offering themselves as easy targets. Harry Preston recalled: 'They came towards us like swarms of ants rushing from shell hole to shell hole.' The Lewis guns hammered away. In Preston's trench, the men, full of confidence, lined the parapet and emptied magazine after magazine into the attackers.[35]

'It was almost a shame to shoot,' recounted one soldier. 'Our machine guns mowed them away.'[36]

Some Germans tried to surrender. 'Although their hands were upraised, they met a volley from our trench,' Maze recalled. 'Those who got through squatted at our feet, happy to be prisoners and out of the war.'[37] Others caught in the open and exposed to Lewis gunfire hid in shell holes; a few minutes later, still under heavy fire, they scurried back across the Bapaume road and sought cover in the hedges near the village.[38]

The purpose of the German attack was most likely to probe the line and try to establish the size of the gap. The German doctrine of recapturing all forfeited ground meant that more counterattacks would follow. One thing became clear from this attack: the Lewis gun — the Germans called it the 'Belgian rattlesnake' — would be a critical weapon in blunting those counterattacks to come. It was relatively light, weighing only 27 pounds, and had great firepower; however, the slightest amount of dirt in its breech jammed it.[39] The *Official History* reasoned that, with Lewis guns positioned along the front, the well-entrenched Australians were more than capable of shattering any future counterattacks; their main risk would be being crushed by German artillery fire.[40]

Douglas Haig was responsible for setting the broad strategy of the Somme offensive, which ultimately determined the nature and shape of the Anzacs' fighting around Pozières. In response to changing circumstances on the battlefield — such as the setbacks of 23 July — Haig would, naturally enough, recast key elements of his approach. His reshaped stratagem would then be communicated to Gough's Reserve Army staff, who would be responsible for converting it into high-level operational plans. Eventually, Haig's strategy would cascade its way down through multiple operational layers — corps, divisions, brigades — to battalion commanders like Howell-Price and Mackay, who would be responsible for executing discrete sets of orders that would collectively deliver the outcome Haig desired.

There were also factors beyond empirical measures of yards gained and lives lost that would influence Haig's strategic decisions, including external pressure from the Allies and British politicians, and Haig's inherent character traits (his bulldog-like tenacity meant that his natural inclination would always be to cling to his enemy's throat).[41]

Haig's response to these factors would determine the Anzacs' role in the offensive over the next six weeks.

Some time after the Australians captured Pozières, Haig penned a letter to Lady Haig, protesting that the War Office insisted he provide interviews to war correspondents for propaganda purposes.[42] Yet although Haig did not approve of the practice, the outcome was, to his surprise, that British newspapers wrote favourable stories about him; they portrayed him as in possession of the infinite wisdom of Solomon and able to impose his will upon events — a chess master effortlessly moving his pieces about the board. These stories further strengthened the public's belief in Haig, whom they seemed to trust as they trusted God.[43] No one considered for a moment that he, too, might be overwhelmed by events.

In reality, Haig did have complete responsibility and accountability for the British Expeditionary Force, but this did not equate to complete control. His fate, and that of the Somme offensive, depended upon many things beyond his grasp. He relied on the home front to raise the requisite recruits and supply adequate munitions; he depended on his French ally to contribute divisions to the offensive; and he counted on his political leaders for backing, and to stop vacillating between an eastern and western strategy. On top of this, his enemy, the most technically advanced nation in Europe, refused to yield a single inch of French soil.

Each day that his armies failed to break through, Haig's political masters and Allies became increasingly concerned that his Somme strategy was flawed and his leadership unimaginative. The War Council sought reassurance from Haig that his heavy losses would be rewarded with significant gains. How could he promise this? His French ally goaded him to strike the enemy harder, in order to relieve the pressure upon Verdun.[44] Would he have to destroy his own army to save theirs? The British public, who monitored the official *communiqués* in the newspapers that reported constant successes, expected Haig to deliver a swift and decisive victory.[45] Haig dared not shatter their rising spirits.

Haig's biographers — both supporters and detractors — seemed to agree unanimously that he was single-minded and tenacious in his pursuit of a 'victorious end' to the Great War.[46] Therefore, it is unsurprising that he decided to continue the Somme offensive, albeit on a lesser scale until adequate men and munitions were accumulated for a full-scale resumption in September.[47] Despite the lack of British success on 23 July, he would drive at the enemy with all the endurance his armies could muster in order to wrest the advantage from his German adversary, chief of the great general staff General Erich von Falkenhayn. 'The war must be continued until Germany is vanquished,' Haig declared in his diary in late July.[48] He wouldn't shrink away from this goal in the face of horrific casualties.

Haig had confronted von Falkenhayn in battle the previous year, when the German threw his armies at the Belgian city of Ypres in an effort to break through to the vital channel ports. Haig's divisions initially inflicted massive casualties but, outnumbered, gradually buckled under the unrelenting pressure of the Germans. The important city seemed lost, but then, inexplicably, von Falkenhayn halted the offensive, believing that victory lay beyond his grasp. Alistair Horne speculated in *The Price of Glory* that von Falkenhayn, although ruthless, was at critical moments plagued by 'indecision and excessive prudence'.[49] Perhaps at Ypres, it was von Falkenhayn's inherent cautiousness, rather than his misinterpretation of battlefield data, that turned a potential victory into a half-success. Had von Falkenhayn possessed more tenacity and persevered, he might have turned the tide of the war. Two of Haig's biographers — Gerard De Groot and Andrew Wiest — believed that Haig learnt from the incident and would have been determined not to repeat von Falkenhayn's mistake.[50] John Charteris, Haig's confidant, summed up the prevailing creed within Haig's headquarters on the eve of the Somme battle: 'If we face losses bravely we shall win quicker and it will be a final win.'[51]

At 6.15 a.m. that morning, Haig instructed his army commanders to cease coordinated general attacks and, instead, commence local actions at selected points to improve their tactical position prior to launching another general attack in September. Although Haig wanted to maintain the pressure on the Germans, he couldn't afford to expend troops and munitions at the rate he had in the first three weeks of July. Haig's amended policy aimed to keep the Germans off balance while he accumulated men and munitions in the reserve areas. In response to this policy, I Anzac Corps and III British Corps would develop plans to capture the remainder of Pozières and the OG lines.[52] With the cessation of general attacks, the Australians' local attacks toward Pozières would undoubtedly attract greater attention and prominence, not only from Haig, but also from their German adversary.

As it turned out, however, just as Haig was meeting with his army commanders, the Germans launched their retaliatory action against the Australians.

Like the British, the Germans had formidable artillery on the Somme. Their standard tactic after losing a trench or village was to lay down a curtain of fire upon its approaches, to prevent their adversary from bringing forward fresh troops, food, water, and ammunition. This increased their chances of recapturing lost ground when they inevitably counterattacked.

At 6.25 a.m., about an hour after their initial attack, German shelling began. Shells shrieked over the heads of those Anzacs sheltering in the village, exploding about a quarter of a mile back, on the village's approaches. The ground shook and convulsed. Billowing clouds of acrid red dust hung in the air. The Germans had boxed Pozières off from the rest of the world — a tactic they had perfected after using it against the French at Verdun. Pozières's approaches were soon littered with the bodies of Australian runners, pioneers, stretcher-bearers, ration parties, and engineers who couldn't make it through the barrage.[53]

Despite the danger, Bean noted that it became a matter of pride for men to carry food or ammunition to their mates waiting for them in the firing line; they understood that their 'burden must be delivered, barrages notwithstanding'.[54]

While German shells fell on the approaches to Pozières, Australian troops doggedly continued 'ratting' in northern Pozières. They worked their way through a series of German dugouts and cellars, throwing phosphorous bombs into them rather than inviting the occupants to surrender. Bean described this 'grim sport': Australians could be seen chasing terrified and shrieking Germans and bayoneting them, or shooting from the shoulder at those who got away. One German with a Red Cross insignia on each arm surrendered to Second-Lieutenant Fred Callaway of the 2nd Battalion. 'He clung to me crying for mercy,' Callaway explained in a letter to his sister and aunt. As a precaution, he felt beneath the prisoner's coat and found a dagger and a revolver. 'I pointed to his red cross and then the revolver. He only cried.' Callaway raised the revolver to shoot him, but the German fell down and grabbed his knees, begging for mercy. 'I hadn't the heart to shoot him in cold blood, but he deserved it,' he wrote.

Although the enemy soldier had gained a reprieve, Callaway still had to find a guard to escort him to the rear, through the bombardment, before he reached the relative safety of a large open-aired prisoners' cage.

Not all Australians were as forgiving as Callaway; many shot German soldiers as they left their dugouts to surrender. 'I saw some awful cold blooded acts but you can't blame the men, they must protect themselves,' reasoned Callaway.[55]

Lieutenant Elmer Laing, a farmer from Western Australia, whose platoon was clearing dugouts in northern Pozières, was involved in one such incident. A German in a wireless station tried to give himself up as soon as he saw Laing's men upon him.

'Come out, you ——,' yelled one of Laing's men.

Laing heard him and rushed back, shouting at the soldier to shoot the 'swine' or else he would. The soldier shot dead the defenceless German.[56]

This didn't seem to be an isolated incident. Laing's letter to his parents suggests that his platoon had a premeditated plan to kill surrendering Germans: 'The Huns saw our chaps coming with bayonets fixed and cleared or tried to surrender, but it was too late.'[57]

Killing prisoners was illegal under international law.[58] The Allies understood the importance of appearing to fight fairly and not committing acts considered heinous, such as killing unarmed prisoners.[59] But, on the Somme battlefield, the Australians faced a practical dilemma. By abiding with international laws that prohibited the killing or wounding of unarmed men, they risked their own lives. It seemed much more expedient to throw a bomb into a dugout than try to entice its occupants out when they might meet with resistance. Earlier that day, a German sniper had shot one of Laing's fellow soldiers as he stood alongside him. Another German had fired at Laing three times.[60] Perhaps Laing decided not to take further chances.

Many Australians also became suspicious of surrendering Germans after hearing that 19-year-old Gallipoli veteran Lieutenant Walter 'Tiny' Host, a popular officer of the 2nd Battalion, had been killed by a prisoner.[61] Accounts differed as to how he died. One eyewitness told the Australian Red Cross enquiry that Host had arrested nine Germans in a dugout. 'His men wanted to finish them off, but the Lieut. stopped this,' claimed this eyewitness. 'Thereupon a severely wounded German picked up a bayonet and ran him through the body.'[62] Another witness disputed this version of events, claiming that shrapnel struck Host as he escorted the prisoners out of Pozières. Whatever the case, the rumour conveyed a subtle message: when it comes to the enemy, don't take any unnecessary chances.

In a way, it is unsurprising that the Australians killed surrendering Germans. English instructional officers in training camps, such as the notorious 'Bull Ring' at Étaples on the French coast, conditioned them, through repeated bayonet practice drills, to kill without hesitation.[63] It was difficult to switch off this instinct simply because an enemy soldier who was a threat a moment earlier had suddenly raised their hands in surrender. 'They will fire at us right up to the time we hop into their trenches, and then they fling up their hands and cry, "Mercy, comrade,"' explained one soldier. 'How can we give them any mercy after seeing them shoot down our cobbers?'[64] Even Bean, with his Victorian values and sense of fair play, reasoned that it was idle for men so caught to expect mercy.[65] Fred Callaway feared that, in the confusion of battle, a prisoner might manoeuvre behind troops and shoot them in the back. 'Our lads know this and take no chances,' he explained in a letter home.[66]

Sometimes, the sheer practicalities of the battlefield offered no alternative to killing prisoners, as Iven Mackay explained in his biography, *Iven G. Mackay*. 'Many [German soldiers] remained in their dugouts, terrified, and had to be bombed and bayoneted out,' he wrote, recounting an incident during the Pozières attack. 'Some never came out. A number of the Germans taken prisoner would not, through pure fright cross No Man's Land. They had to be killed.'[67]

The killing of prisoners during that first morning of the Pozières battle sits uncomfortably with the Anzac legend that flourished after the war. It also posed a problem for correspondents like Bean, who asserted that the Anzacs were fierce fighters — brutal in the heat of battle — but also had a chivalrous side that meant they were fair to their vanquished enemies afterward. According to Alistair Thomson, who analysed Bean's representation of Australian manhood during the Great War, Bean sometimes explained away these unsavoury incidents, claiming that soldiers of all nationalities committed them and that the war-mongers were ultimately to blame.[68] On one occasion, when German prisoners told Bean that Australians had machine-gunned German stretcher-bearers and killed inmates in a hospital, he quickly discounted these events, claiming that the machine-gun fire must have been indirect and the Australians couldn't have known that the Germans were wounded.[69] Frenchman Marc Ferro, in *The Great War: 1914–1918*, claimed that there was also an element of self-censorship at play that suppressed the reporting of these incidents, as no one wanted to be seen as 'doing down the side'. Rather, 'responsible authorities' focused on stimulating the nation's will to fight, which meant that people had to be shown they were 'fighting for the Right'.[70]

Throughout the morning, many Germans, shaken by the previous night's bombardment, gave themselves up and staggered in, 'like drunken men', according to Foxcroft.[71] Australians began taking souvenirs from their prisoners — grabbing at their helmets, cutting buttons off their tunics, taking their watches, and unlooping their belt buckles. The Germans were given cigarettes and chocolates as compensation. Officers frowned on 'prospecting' and warned looters that the enemy shot prisoners on whom any German buttons or papers were found.[72]

This prospecting was the first contact that many Australians had with German soldiers. At best, they may have observed prisoners working at the port at Marseilles when they had docked there in March; or perhaps they had glimpsed the fleeting, grey uniforms in the opposing trenches near Armentières. Yet many now saw their adversary up close, usually in compromised positions: Mackay observed them with their hands up, surrendering, and mumbling in a half-dazed way; Coates surveyed them scattered across the battlefield bearing horrific wounds, crying out for help; Foxcroft watched them shuffling like drunken men back through the lines; and 3rd Battalion troops caught sight of their pale and haggard faces, etched with signs of intense mental and physical strain.[73] Did they see hulking beasts, half-ape and half–Neanderthal man, raping and pillaging their way across Europe, or dishevelled men in dirt-smattered grey uniforms? Perhaps these Australians caught the Germans' downcast eyes and glimpsed something of themselves in them.

Foxcroft's diary provides an insight into his attitude toward the Germans after the Pozières attack. Foxcroft described how he entered a cellar, decorated with furniture and hanging pictures, knelt by the corpse of a German, and picked through his belongings for souvenirs.

He came across some worn black-and-white photographs in the tunic pocket. One was a portrait of the dead man. He had a long, boyish face and a pencil-thin moustache, with black hair poking from underneath his cap. In another photograph, the soldier's parents, young wife, and infant son posed in a sunlit garden. It was probably taken in the hot summer of 1914, just before he marched off to war.

The third photograph, an intimate portrait of the soldier's wife, showed dark eyes, a soft complexion, and thick black hair neatly gathered in a bun. The young woman would be unaware of her husband's fate — unaware that he was a corpse on the dirty floor of a dugout in a foreign land, with an enemy soldier picking through his most intimate possessions. Foxcroft did not record his thoughts about the photographs, but it is hard to imagine that he was not affected by the personal nature of them. We do know that he mailed them home to his parents, writing: 'I am sending some photos I got from a dead Hun and any card or anything I send home please keep for future reference.' Did Foxcroft intend to return the photos to the soldier's wife? Were they simply souvenirs? His diary does not reveal his motivation, but the photographs must have held some significance for him, as he kept them in his possession for the rest of his life.[74]

Private John Bourke was more open with his thoughts. He recorded in his diary that, while sheltering in the lower chamber of a blockhouse, he found a heap of cake boxes made of cardboard and sewn in with calico. He had received similar parcels from Australia. The addresses were in a child's handwriting, as were one or two of the letters. In another corner, he found a rolled-up coat. 'I opened it out, and found it stained with blood, and there right between the shoulders was a burnt shrapnel hole,' Bourke wrote in his diary. 'The owner of the coat was a German, and, some might say, not entitled to much sympathy. Perhaps he was not, but I couldn't help but feeling sadly of the little girl or boy who sent the cakes.'[75]

Back at I Anzac Corps headquarters, John Treloar, who was responsible for processing documents taken from German prisoners, expressed similarly conflicting emotions: 'Most [documents] seem to contain photos of people most wonderfully like ourselves. Often there are picture postcards of little children.' But he couldn't reconcile this image of Germans with that promoted by the press, as his diary entry indicated: 'One's thoughts go to the *Lusitania* outrage, and one wonders how it is that a nation who must have some love for children can be guilty of the atrocities they have committed.'[76]

Foxcroft's, Bourke's, and Treloar's diary entries suggest they understood that the Germans were not the ruthless barbarians they were often portrayed as in newspapers and recruitment posters. The Australians at Pozières did not, by and large, view the Germans with sympathy, but many of them perhaps saw that they had more in common with the enemy than they had first thought.

Charles Bean had stayed up until dawn on 23 July, monitoring the battle from Sinclair-MacLagan's dugout. After snatching some sleep at divisional headquarters, he visited the outskirts of the battlefield in the early afternoon. He chatted with some men with light wounds coming back down a dusty track from Pozières. 'I wish the people of Australia could see what we saw,' he wrote in his first Pozières despatch, published in the Melbourne newspaper *The Herald* on 27 July 1916. Bean described how the men he spoke to, who had just passed through the shelling and were still buoyed by adrenaline, talked quickly and paced around, fidgeting, smoking, unable to sit still, and sometimes shaking or ducking involuntarily as a shell landed close by. Bean spoke to one youngster, his hand heavily bandaged, who said: 'I hope I am not going to lose my fingers. I reckon I ought to be good for a number of the beggars yet.' Another man passed him, stripped to the waist, covered with bandages, a German helmet on his head. 'It might be worse,' he told Bean.

Bean's despatch, under the headline 'Fight For Pozières Vividly Described', had an exuberant tone. In one section he referred to the 'glamour of affairs' on the battlefield, while in another he described the 'great, cheery, strong-faced fellows' he saw going up the track to Pozières — how they were 'trotting beside a great gun team, whose easy-limbed drivers looked as if the men were part of the horses'. He also described the ordinary parties of bronzed, keen-eyed men, occasionally with a cheek bleeding from a cut, walking through shellfire as if going home to tea.[77]

Perhaps Bean's exuberant mood was justified: the Anzacs had done what the British troops had failed to do — they had captured Pozières. Furthermore, casualties were relatively light, and although the German bombardment was heavy, the British guns would soon counter it. Or perhaps Bean's upbeat tone masked darker feelings about the battle. Was it possible that he crafted a positive despatch because he didn't want to be seen 'doing down the side'? Bean's diary, in which he recorded his unguarded thoughts, provides some clue — his brief entry on 23 July suggests that he was, indeed, cheered by the Australians' performance at Pozières.[78]

Bean's high-spirited despatch was a noted departure from his usual writing style. Back in 1915, he had made it clear in his diary that he didn't want to be like other correspondents who told 'nonsense' stories, like those of Germans enlisting in the Australian army and then shooting Australian troops in the back, or of Australian soldiers leaving their sickbeds in droves to return to the front. Bean knew these stories were rubbish. 'I have asked the nurses. I have asked the men,' wrote Bean of his investigation into the second 'nonsense' story. Bean, who had spent almost two years with the Anzacs, covering their every major battle, was perhaps more qualified than any other correspondent to refute these stories. Yet choosing to be a stickler for the truth came at a cost: *The Argus* and *The Age* often wouldn't publish his bland despatches, instead preferring the highly colourful inventions of other correspondents, which the public seemed to lap up. British war correspondent Ellis Ashmead-Bartlett — who wrote the stirring and subsequently famed despatch that described the Anzacs as 'a race of athletes' whose landing on Gallipoli was the finest event of the war — was almost certainty a purveyor of what Bean labelled 'wretched cant'. Bean admitted that Ashmead-Bartlett's exaggerations made it a little difficult for him, presumably because it made his own despatches sound dull.[79]

Bean maintained these same cautious reporting standards in France. He deliberately avoided heralding the Anzacs every time they left their trenches when they were in the nursery sector at Armentières. He had explained to *The Times* readers back in June 1916 that the Anzacs did not want the public attention that was directed at them after their recent trench raids: 'They well know that their mettle has not been tried in France.'[80] But Pozières had changed things — the Anzacs' mettle had been tested and they had succeeded in achieving 'a victory of importance on the Western Front'.[81] The Anzac story was taking shape. It would be another seven days before Bean visited the village to experience the truth of Pozières: the putrid smell of rotting corpses, the unsettling sight of rows of cottages reduced to rubble, the sad spectacle of men driven mad by the German shelling, and the ghastly scene of endless shell craters littered with human body parts.

While Bean gathered material for his despatch, Maze contemplated leaving the village so he could report back to Gough: 'I had to think about getting back to Army Headquarters. It was important to let them know the conditions.' Maze worked his way through the shelling that fell violently upon the approaches to Pozières. His autobiography provides an insight into what the Australian ration parties, runners, stretcher-bearers, and reinforcements must have experienced:

> Everywhere men were held up on their way to the village, waiting all the time for the shelling to ease off; whole parties had been blown to pieces … From one place I had a glimpse of the previous night's No Man's Land pitted with fresh shell-holes, most of them rimmed with motionless human forms.

The Albert basilica, in the distance, acted like a guiding beacon for Maze. 'Every step towards it was a relief,' he wrote. In order to avoid the clogged trenches, he climbed out onto the open ground, which was pitted with shell holes. He became aware of an iridescent sky, and: 'I suddenly realised that I was alive. I turned to look back at Pozières in the distant crest where it remained in continuous volcanic convulsions.'

Within an hour, Maze had reached Albert and commandeered an army car, and was hurtling toward Gough's army headquarters. From the car's window, he could see columns of singing Anzacs and an endless procession of lorries making their way toward the front line.[82]

Throughout Sunday, conflicting reports arrived at Hooky's headquarters about the number of Germans troops defending northern Pozières. Some reports said the Germans had been reinforced, while others claimed they'd abandoned their positions. In spite of the confusion, Hooky and Blamey drafted operational orders to capture the rest of the village. They would first barrage the northern side of the road, then bring in fresh troops from General John Forsyth's 2nd Brigade, which had been held in reserve, and Nevill Smyth's 1st Brigade, to advance in extended formation (which required the troops to move forward spaced well apart) at about 4.00 p.m.

Then Gough intervened. 'Instructions were received from Reserve Army by telephone to cease firing on the village, as it was reported to be unoccupied,' recorded Hooky. Gough claimed that the Germans had already fled Pozières, and requested that immediate patrols, with no supporting barrage, be sent out to verify this. Hooky complied. 'These arrangements conflicted with the plans I had made and I cancelled the previous orders accordingly,' he recorded in his operational report.[83] The *Official History* observed that some Australian soldiers, who had been subject to sniping throughout the day, were angry when they were told that northern Pozières was supposedly empty.[84] At about 5.00 p.m., the first patrols probed the remainder of the village. Some of these patrols contained tired men who hadn't slept for days because they had participated in the night attack and had dug trenches the following day. The men also felt edgy because of the constant sniping and sporadic shelling throughout the day. One soldier who almost certainly felt the strain was Lieutenant George Walters, a 25-year-old clerk from Western Australia, who was unusually quiet before setting off on patrol. Being 'rallied' about it by his platoon, he replied: 'I'm going to get mine tonight. I know I won't come out of this stunt.' According to the 11th Battalion history, those around him laughed, while George 'just shook his head and gave a wintry-sort of smile'.[85]

Then, all of a sudden, flares arced into the sky. Third Battalion soldiers saw 'shadowy forms' quietly steal across the front about 50 yards away from them. Some soldiers prepared to open fire, unaware that the shadows were the patrolling Australians. Thankfully, before anyone could fire, Private Claude Dowling of the 3rd Battalion walked forward, confirmed their identity, and prevented a near tragedy.[86]

Forsyth's fresh 8th Battalion, which until now had been held in reserve, moved up into the village and swept northward through the ruins just before midnight. They encountered sporadic sniping and stray shells, but most Germans, when challenged, ran to K Trench or the OG lines. One even jumped on a bicycle lying against a wireless station and pedalled for his life.[87]

While supervising operations, an officer of the 11th Battalion saw a shell burst in the distance; at the same time he noticed a man topple over. In the fitful light, the slightly wounded officer limped across to the body. He turned it over and discovered that it was George Walters. 'His premonitions had been realised,' recorded the 11th Battalion history.[88] George's mother, Mrs Mary Alice Stewart of Kalgoorlie, Western Australia, would duly receive notification of his death and receipt of his personal belongings, which included George's rosary beads.[89]

The Australians had chalked up their first 24 hours in Pozières. Foxcroft's last diary entry for 23 July summed up what had been an exceptionally trying day: 'No sleep since Friday night, lost nearly all our mates something awful.'[90]

CHAPTER SEVEN

The Pozières Ridge

*'Pozières was like wandering through the regions
of the damned, inhabited only by the dead.'*
— Walter Belford, *Legs-eleven*

Early on 24 July, Hooky Walker and Thomas Blamey would have experienced a feeling of momentary jubilation upon realising that Pozières was in Australian hands. Blamey wrote that its capture was most brilliant exploit of the battle and gushed that the Anzacs were the finest fighting unit in the world.[1] However, as the *Official History* pointed out, the whole purpose of the operation was not to consolidate but attack. It is almost certain that the mood at divisional headquarters was doused when Hooky received a telegram from Gough, prodding him to act with vigour and immediately capture the Pozières ridge, and then swing around to the west and strike toward Mouquet Farm.[2]

Hooky carefully constructed a plan to capture the OG lines that straddled the Pozières ridge. The 1st Division, supported by a lifting bombardment, would launch two attacks on the OG lines at 2.00 a.m. and 3.30 a.m. on 25 July.[3] The advance would be more complex and dangerous than that of 23 July. The first difficulty facing Hooky was that the Germans could easily see the Australians advancing from

Pozières into the open fields to dig their staging posts and jumping-off trenches. The second was that Allied artillery observers couldn't see the reverse side of the Pozières ridge; therefore, the Germans could bring up their reserves unnoticed. The third was that there was only one route to the village, which meant that the fresh troops leading the attack would have to travel over the same ground; the attack times were staggered to account for this. Then, once the troops reached Pozières, they would have to manoeuvre in the dark until they were square-on to the OG lines, rather than perpendicular to them. The midnight attack on 23 July had demonstrated that troops became easily confused and disorientated in the darkness, sometimes advancing in the wrong direction or becoming entangled with other units.

The battle terrain also posed a risk to Hooky's plan. The attack front — 1000 yards north and 600 yards south of the Bapaume road — was similar to that of 23 July, when his division had been fresh and at full strength. Would Hooky have the number of troops needed to carry out the attack? In addition, the men had to advance up a gentle slope for about 600 yards. For local farmers, the gentle rise would have been barely noticeable, but for a soldier weighed down with his haversack, ammunition, a rifle, bombs, and an entrenching tool it could mean the difference between life and death. German sentries positioned at the peak had good fields of vision and were likely to spot the advance, and the slope had no protective folds or gullies for the Australian soldiers to shelter in to avoid German shelling and machine-gun fire.

It was the German machine-gun crews positioned on the peak that posed the most significant risk to Hooky's plan. They would have clear and unimpeded fields of fire between the OG lines and Pozières, which would turn this strip of land into a killing field. These crews had attained a formidable reputation since 1 July, when they cut through the British like a sharpened scythe through hay.[4] The seven- to eight-men teams were the best trained and the most disciplined soldiers of the German army, and rarely surrendered their guns — which meant they suffered high casualties when their positions were overrun. Those captured discreetly removed the badges from their tunics to conceal their identities, realising they risked rough handling from their vengeful captors.[5]

The Germans' standard gun, the Maschinengewehr 08, was solid and reliable, fed by fabric belts that each contained 250 bullets. Although the gun was capable of firing around 400 to 600 rounds a minute — the equivalent firepower of 60 to 100 rifles — the crews fired in much shorter bursts to economise on ammunition and avoid overheating the gun's barrel. Along with its firepower, the Maschinengewehr's distinctive noise terrified many soldiers: when fired, it sounded like a huge hammer striking an anvil. On a quiet evening, its report carried across the battlefield, causing men to cower in their trenches even though they were in no immediate danger from the bullets.[6]

The gunners had positioned themselves on the ridge in strongpoints — usually elevated positions with clear fields of fire at junctures where a trench intersected another trench, or road, or railway track — protected by mounds of soil and rows of sandbags. The crews trained to bring an unloaded machine-gun up from a dugout and be ready to fire within 30 seconds.[7] They would hold the OG lines at any cost.

On the fine morning of Monday 24 July, Arthur Foxcroft and other soldiers of the 1st Australian Division experienced their second dawn at Pozières. The *Official History* recorded that the soldiers were 'very tired but in high spirits', and still practically untouched by the German barrage.

At about 7.00 a.m., Foxcroft's platoon was getting its issue of cigarettes and rations when they heard a deafening whine overhead. Seconds later, it was followed by a terrific explosion that shook the earth, throwing broken bricks, masonry, and black smoke into the air.

When the dust settled, they could see a gaping crater gouged out of the earth. Then, another thundering whine and ear-splitting explosion: the German barrage of the previous day, which had fallen a quarter of a mile back on the village's approaches, had now been redirected onto Pozières and the troops that sheltered in the trenches there. Foxcroft realised what was happening, later writing in his diary that 'the huns [have] concentrated all their big guns on us'.[8] The shellfire was from 5.9- and eight-inch German howitzers. Those caught directly under the barrage, like John Harris, could see the descending shells in their last 40 feet of flight. Harry Preston, who was sheltering at the northern end of the Bapaume road, could see them 'like black streaks coming down from the sky just before they hit the ground'.[9]

The German gunners, positioned on the reverse slope of Pozières, behind the village of Courcelette, repeatedly loaded their shells into the breech of their heavy howitzers before seeking shelter behind a protective barrier of sandbags. The guns then let out an almighty belch, hurtling their shells through the sky, like comets, for the next 15 seconds. Their 5.9-inch shells — known as 'coal boxes', or 'crumps', because of the sound they made when they landed — looked like 'swift dots of black' as they rushed earthward and threw plumes of black smoke and dust into the air upon detonation.[10] The Anzacs particularly feared the 9.2-inch shell, which made a whining sound when travelling through the air; its high trajectory and size meant it caused considerable damage upon impact. The pink dust clouds from the explosions could be seen from Albert. Soon, a thick film of dust covered everything, including rifles and machine-guns, which had to be cleaned continually, otherwise they jammed. The unrevetted trenches were unable to withstand the blasts and collapsed like books closing shut, burying those inside. The men used whatever they had — spades, tin hats, their hands — to dig out the buried. Though these men were often exhumed alive, the *Official History* observed that 'their nerves had naturally been subjected to the most violent shock'.[11]

'Smashed our trenches in, made big gaps in our lines, heavy losses,' recorded Foxcroft.[12]

Elmer Laing, whose platoon was sheltering in northern Pozières, wrote that the shells came over in shoals, 'blowing in our trenches, burying men'.[13] Charles Bean, who listened to the guns at a safe distance, agreed with Laing's description, estimating that about 140 artillery blasts could be heard every minute.[14] Despite the heavy barrage and the fact that the Germans seemed to have pinpointed his platoon's location, Laing's men stuck it out. 'They deserve all the thanks,' he wrote to his parents.

The German artillery also seemed to have registered on Howell-Price's 3rd Battalion troops, who were sheltering in trenches adjacent to the Bapaume road. The shells, which appeared to come from the front, right, and rear, caved in the trenches and buried the occupants. 'The obvious folly of siting a trench along a main road and packing it with men became apparent,' reflected the 3rd Battalion history. 'There was nothing to do but try and keep the trenches clear and dig out the men who were buried.'[15] Despite the obvious dangers, Howell-Price — who described in his operational report that the bombardment was the most intense he had ever experienced — remained in the village all day, doing his best to keep up the spirits of the men. No doubt Howell-Price's selfless approach reassured his men, who, according to the battalion history, were terribly frightened by the 'storm of shell that rained upon them without intermission for nearly 12 hours'.

The bombardment, which had begun at 7.00 a.m., continued until 7.00 p.m. Iven Mackay initially thought the barrage signalled that the Germans were 'on the verge of making a massive riposte'.[16] False alarms were continually raised: Peter Smith described in his diary how he rushed for his rifle upon hearing that a counterattack had commenced, but it turned out to be a party of prisoners hurrying along an old trench, their guards battling to keep pace.[17]

The bombardment prevented anyone from entering or leaving the village. The exhausted Australians only received half of their daily rations. The wounded could not be transported out — 'the stretcher-bearers are having a terrible time some blown to pieces together with their living freight,' recorded Albert Coates in his diary.[18] Telephone wires remained severed; commanders relied on runners, as well as pigeons, which shellfire sometimes shredded, to get their messages through. The dirt road leading to the village, heavily pounded and littered with dead, would later become known as Dead Man's Road.[19] 'Many men buried or torn to pieces by the high explosives,' noted Coates. 'For a mile behind the trenches it is a perfect hell of shellfire.'

The troops worked hard to reconstruct their battered trenches; however, as fast as one portion of the trench was cleared, another was blown in. 'There were no dugouts in which men on post could take shelter, and the only thing to do was grin and bear it,' recorded John Harris.[20] Owen Howell-Price, Harris's commanding officer, paced up and down the trench line, continually cajoling his men whenever the shelling eased to dig deeper trenches. Perhaps the weary troops wondered whether they were digging their own graves.

All British artillery attempts to counter the German barrage failed. An aeroplane sent up mid-morning tried to direct British counter-barrage fire, but the German guns didn't let up. At 7.00 p.m., II British Corps fired a paltry handful of shells into Courcelette. 'Our artillery is not replying,' observed one British gunner in despair, as he watched the plumes of smoke and spurts of fire leaping into the air from the ruins of Pozières.[21]

Eventually, the shelling on Pozières slackened. The 3rd Battalion history recorded that half its troops in the front and support lines had been killed or wounded, while the survivors were parched and exhausted.[22] Foxcroft's platoon had been hit hard: 'What was left of us hung on until 5 p.m. when B Company relieved us ... We went back to support lines and mustered 13 men out of a platoon of 60.'[23] According to Bean's tally of casualties, almost 2000 Australians had been killed, wounded, or captured in the fighting of the previous two days. The 2nd and 11th battalions suffered most, losing almost

1000 men.²⁴ The 11th Battalion history, *Legs-eleven*, summed up the collective experience of its troops, and possibly all Australians — it asserted that Pozières on 24 July 'was certainly the world's most frightful spot that day'.²⁵ What the Australians didn't realise was that the next day would be much worse.

When Hooky's troops awoke to their second dawn in Pozières — the sun slowly rising above the horizon to replace the dull first light — they had no premonition of what they would confront over the next 24 hours. They didn't realise they would be expected to attack the OG lines on the Pozières ridge in the early hours of Tuesday 25 July and that the Germans were planning their own counterattack to recapture the village at 4.30 p.m. the following day.

On 24 July, preparations for the Australian attack continued throughout the day and into the evening. Just before dusk, the British and Australian heavy batteries had methodically shelled the OG lines.²⁶ As the German bombardment had prevented them from digging jumping-off trenches, they would have to rely on a solitary line of white tape to mark the jumping-off points. The engineers responsible for laying the tapes, unnerved by the heavy shelling, had positioned the last portion of the tape obliquely to the OG lines, rather than square on.²⁷ This meant that those troops starting out from the mislaid tape risked advancing across the battlefield rather than directly toward the OG lines.

The first attack, south of the Bapaume road, would start at 2.00 a.m. Two companies of Lieutenant-Colonel Carl Jess's Victorian 7th Battalion would advance in the arc between the Bapaume road and the old light railway; Lieutenant-Colonel Frank Le Maistre's Victorian 5th Battalion would advance in the arc between the railway and Pozières Trench, while the 10th Battalion would protect and bomb up Le Maistre's right flank.

By 10.00 p.m., darkness shrouded the battlefield. At 12.00 a.m., Jess's 7th Battalion was supposed to move up to the assembly area;

however, one company got caught behind the 5th Battalion troops, who were sharing the same approach. Subsequently, only one of Jess's platoons — fewer than 60 men — made it to their attacking position between the road and railway line.

When the British hurricane bombardment lengthened from OG1 to OG2 at about 2.00 a.m., the first waves of Le Maistre's 5th and Jess's depleted 7th battalions advanced. 'Rallying round their officers,' recorded the 5th Battalion history, 'the men sought the enemy in all directions, much to the danger of their comrades.'[28]

Within minutes, it became obvious that Jess's plan was in disarray. The Germans responded to the Australian advance with a counter-bombardment. Machine guns opened up with fierce crossfire, which meant that the Australians were targeted by guns positioned on their flanks. These well-placed guns laid down interlocking fields of fire and inflicted many casualties on the advancing troops.[29]

Twenty-year-old Private Vincent Keane of the 7th Battalion sensed that things were going badly when he came across a sergeant standing still in no-man's-land, seemingly oblivious to the bombardment.

'What are you doing?' yelled Keane.

'Keep quiet,' the sergeant shouted back. 'I'm thinking things out.'[30]

While the sergeant thought, troops struggled across the cratered ground. George Londey of the 5th Battalion remembered dozens of flares going up from the German lines, and intense machine-gun fire. 'Our artillery kept a screen of fire in front of us but owing to having a very hazy idea of the direction we were to take and the distance to go I think some of us ran under our own shellfire for a while,' he recorded in his diary.[31] Some soldiers got lost in the darkness, while others advanced across the battlefield rather than directly toward the OG lines. 'There was a moment of wild confusion in which the line split into groups, each searching for [OG1], some making south-east, others north-east,' Londey noted. Those who eventually stumbled on OG1 discovered that shelling had demolished the trench; all that remained was a series of linked shell holes littered with abandoned equipment.

One company of the 7th Battalion got lost in the darkness. Shaken by the deafening noise of exploding shells, they inadvertently advanced toward Pozières rather than the OG lines. Eventually, Private William Peach's company came across a trench and captured it. 'We were greatly surprised when B Company charged us a few minutes later with bayonets fixed,' Peach noted. It was their own communication trench. 'Lucky we got them to understand things and both companies set out in search of the enemy.'[32]

The German shelling and machine-gun fire pinned Jess's lone platoon down well short of the OG lines, leaving Le Maistre's northern flank exposed. Meanwhile, some of Le Maistre's troops had stumbled through to OG2, while the Germans were still holding sections of OG1. Twenty-six-year-old Private Eric Moorhead of Malvern, Victoria, was one of Le Maistre's soldiers groping about in the darkness. He wrote in his diary that there was confusion, disorder, and a lack of discipline; officers argued about what to do: 'Orders were given to two companies to hold and consolidate the trench — two officers to get on and take the next.' Moorhead claimed that a drunken officer gave the order to continue onto OG2, which was nothing more than debris-filled furrows along a line of splintered trees.[33]

Meanwhile, the Germans had infiltrated OG1, where only a handful of Australians remained. Captain Cyril Lillie made the decision to evacuate OG2 and retake OG1. Fortunately, those soldiers who risked being cut off discovered a communication trench linking the OG trenches, and worked their way back to OG1, unsighted by the Germans. 'We were ordered to cease digging in,' recorded Moorhead. 'We then retired to our first line of captured trench, all our work being wasted.'

The wounded had to be left behind — 'All I could do was to leave water bottles in their reach,' remembered Londey.[34] A party later returned and tried to rescue the men. 'The horrifying part is that not all the men were brought in and are out there still unless the Huns found them,' recorded Londey the next morning. 'Poor old Ruggles must be out there still. It is worrying me every moment.' Unbeknown to Londey, his mate, Private Charles Ruggles, was dead.

The 5th Battalion tried to hold OG1, rather than withdraw, while both sides furiously pitched bombs at each other in a desperate battle for control. The Germans were able to work their way up on the Australians' flanks. The Australians responded by cobbling together barricades with anything they could get their hands on, in the hope of slowing them down. Despite 'the dead and dying and wounded, the smell of blood and explosives', as George Londey described it, the 5th Battalion clung onto the position.

Sinclair-MacLagan reinforced Le Maistre's beleaguered 5th Battalion with 7th and 9th battalion units, who ferried boxes of bombs forward so the surrounded soldiers could continue fighting. In support, riflemen and Lewis gunners trained their guns on the OG lines and fired at the Germans whenever they raised themselves to throw their bombs — in some cases, severing their outstretched arms.[35]

By 8.00 a.m. on 25 July, the 5th Battalion troops had secured a section of OG1 between the road and the railway line. It represented about a quarter of their intended objective, and provided no tactical advantage. Holding the isolated section of trench would cost lives.

The second attack, north of the Bapaume road, was timed to start at 3.30 a.m. on 25 July. As planned, prior to the attack and sometime after midnight the 12th Battalion left the relative safety of the village to dig posts in no-man's-land, but were caught in a torrent of crossfire directed at the attacking battalions on the south side of the road. Trapped in the open, they had no choice but to withdraw.[36] The Western Australian 11th Battalion, one of the units responsible for attacking to the north of the Bapaume road, suffered a shattering blow as it approached Pozières from the relative safety of the British lines. *Legs-eleven* explained that as the troops moved through the village, some men fell from unexpected rifle fire coming from their rear. They fired back wildly into the darkness. As the light gradually improved,

Lewis gun officer Lieutenant Louis Le Nay began to peer through his field glasses toward the enemy. Something seemed wrong: in the grey of daybreak the uniforms looked remarkably like their own, even down to the red-and-white unit badges on their tunics. 'For Christ's sake, stop firing. They're our own chaps!' yelled Le Nay. The ceasefire whistle sounded, and the shooting stopped abruptly. The soldiers threw their rifles down in disgust, but bodies lay everywhere. Some 11th Battalion troops cursed, others stood quietly in disbelief, and others abused those they thought responsible for the death of 14 comrades.

Following the incident, the 11th Battalion troops struggled to describe their feelings. Captain Walter Belford commented: '[S]ome boys were so shocked by this mistake that war, which up to this time had been a kind of game, even if a deadly one, ceased to interest them.' Others blamed the tragedy on staff officers, who were responsible for the organisation of battle activity.[37] The *Official History* attributed it to the officers being unaware of neighbouring units' orders due to the damage to communication wires.[38] Understandably, the soldiers lost a measure of confidence in the 'brass hats'.

Brigadier-General Nevill 'Sphinx' Smyth commanded the five battalions responsible for taking the OG lines north of the Bapaume road. He'd received a rough outline of orders earlier in the day, telling him to attack the following day, Wednesday 26 July.[39] Divisional staff communicated the correct orders to him at about midnight. He recalled his officers, who had been dismissed some time earlier. Lieutenant-Colonel Iven Mackay remembered Smyth, in the dim light, calmly dictating new orders to a small crowd of battalion and company commanders. He remembered them listening intently, many with unlit cigarettes pursed on their lips. Smyth's cool composure amazed Mackay: he was 'not too upset by the emergency'.[40] When Smyth finished, the officers scrambled away and roused their sleeping men.

The main objective for Smyth's troops was K Trench, which ran along the forward edge of the village and on to Mouquet Farm.

Belatedly, at 3.55 a.m., the lead companies of Mackay's 4th Battalion worked their way down the winding trench, flushing the Germans out into the open country. Apcar de Vine recalled that the trench was captured as far as the cemetery. 'Many Germans hid in the shellholes, which provided excellent targets for our machine guns and snipers,' he wrote in his diary.[41] The *Official History* noted that many Germans, finding their way out of K Trench barred, tried to surrender. The Australians, realising that managing hundreds of prisoners while in the midst of battle would be dangerous, continued to fire. It was another example of the practicalities of the battlefield taking precedence over moral or legal obligations to show mercy to surrendering or unarmed enemy soldiers.

A group of Australians, led by Sergeant-Major Frank Goodwin, a farmer from Geelong, managed to push up the trench for about a mile. In the grey of dawn, they crossed a slight rise and found themselves standing upon the ruins of the soon-to-be-famous Mouquet Farm.[42]

At dawn, the full extent of the failure became clear. Yet who was to blame? Could Le Maistre have halted the attack south of the road if he had been made aware of the 7th Battalion's chaotic preparations? Would the result have been different if Smyth had received the correct orders earlier? Why were the 11th and 8th battalions unaware of each other's movements?

What lay at the heart of the failure was poor communication. Despite the technological advances of this war — aeroplanes, machine guns, and new forms of artillery — communication methods remained antiquated. Commanders often couldn't contact their artillery, troops, or fellow commanders during an attack because bombardments cut the telephone wires, even though they were buried up to six feet underground. Runners were unreliable and slow to cover the cratered ground; sometimes they got lost or were cut down by shells. Signalling aeroplanes depended on clear weather and an experienced signaller being on hand. If communication couldn't be guaranteed, it became impossible to coordinate multiple battalions and synchronise their movements with artillery units.[43]

Without the immediacy of telephone communication, commanders often received cryptic messages from runners that were hours old and out of date. They had to carefully assess the scant information they received. Was it still relevant? Had circumstances on the battlefield changed? Could the sender be trusted to interpret events accurately?

The Australians attacked at night to minimise casualties and catch the Germans off guard. Yet this tactic had drawbacks: troops were often exhausted during the attack, sometimes going without sleep for 48 hours beforehand; they were easily confused and disorientated in the darkness, which contributed to the 8th and 11th battalions firing on each other; and it was hard for them to distinguish objectives, as evidenced by Le Maistre's 5th Battalion unwittingly passing through the partly demolished OG1 trench.

The small Allied foothold in OG1 provided no tactical advantage and would needlessly chew up lives as long as the Australians clung to it. The 1st Division had expended most of its reserves; those unscathed were exhausted and incapable of mounting another attack. The weakened division was susceptible to counterattack. Luckily, the Germans' planned 4.30 p.m. attack would be, according to Bean, 'more or less shattered' by its own disasters.[44]

Hooky Walker, in his detailed report to corps headquarters, avoided referring to the attack as a failure:

> I would like to bring to notice the spirit of initiative shown by all subordinate commanders from brigadiers to platoon leaders and the gallantry and tenacity of the troops throughout the whole of the protracted and trying exercise.[45]

He appended to the report an itemised list of so-called trophies that the division had captured, including prisoners, right down to spare parts and toolboxes. These 'trophies' provided little consolation for the enormous losses of life.

Just after daybreak on Tuesday 25 July, the Germans opened up with a bombardment that was heavier than the previous day's. Sergeant Leonard Elvin of the 1st Battalion wrote in his diary that it was 'simply murder', with shells 'falling like hail during a storm'.[46] An exhausted Arthur Foxcroft tried to get rest for an hour or two, but was afraid to go to sleep for fear of being buried by shells. 'Wounded lying all along the trench waiting to be taken in. Could not tell whether they were alive or dead,' he recorded.[47]

At about 10.00 a.m., and again at 1.00 p.m., the shellfire eased for a short period. During the first interval, units of General John Forsyth's 2nd Brigade — which had been largely held in reserve, providing carrying parties in support of the other brigades — began to take over positions in and around Pozières from troops of the 1st and 3rd brigades.[48] Lieutenant-Colonel Gordon Bennett, the 29-year-old commander of the relieving 6th Battalion, reconnoitred his new position under the heavy bombardment before leading his men forward. 'I moved into Hell itself,' he recorded.

Bennett selected a line of defence. He knew he couldn't bring the battalion through the barrage without heavy losses. 'I prayed most earnestly to the Almighty for His Guidance,' he recalled. Then, suddenly, the shelling stopped, and most of his men got through to Pozières.[49] Yet the last platoon found themselves caught in the open when the bombardment recommenced; over 20 men were lost within a few minutes. The platoon's commander, Second-Lieutenant Henry Eggington, was left with a portion of his intestine hanging out. 'The Medical Officer quickly effected temporary repairs and sent him back to hospital with little or no chance of recovery,' the lieutenant-colonel noted.[50] Luck, or some form of divine intervention, seemed to favour Bennett, yet Eggington did not share in this. He survived, but became an invalid and lived out his days on a pension of four pounds a week.[51]

The state of Pozières shocked Bennett's men. 'The village is absolutely frayed to the ground, which in turn is a succession of deep shell holes,' wrote Lieutenant Matthew Abson in his diary. 'There are many dead bodies, German and Australian in varying stages of decay.'[52] Bennett's biography explains how he set up his battalion headquarters in a pine-covered shelter after his team dragged away the stiffened corpses of dead Germans that blocked the entrance. After setting to work — with their only light coming from a flickering candle stuck to a makeshift table by its own grease — exploding shells continually showered them with clods of earth, occasionally snuffing out the candle.[53] Hurricane bombardments, lasting half an hour or more and increasing in intensity, fell upon the Australians throughout the afternoon of 25 July.

John Harris, a schoolmaster at the prestigious Church of England Grammar School in Sydney, had participated in the midnight attack on 23 July and suffered under the German bombardment on 23 and 24 July. He was evacuated from Pozières and hospitalised on 25 July, shaking and suffering from tremors. What was this psychological sickness?

Since early morning on 23 July, Harris had busily walked the trench line, encouraging his troops and supervising the consolidation of the battalion's position. The schoolmaster's leadership must have comforted many of the Grammar School old boys scattered throughout the 3rd Battalion.[54] Howell-Price, in his report on operations, singled out Harris, commending his energy in organising the consolidation of the position, writing that 'he inspired and gave confidence to his men by cheerfulness and his disregard of danger'.[55] Harris must have been completely exhausted when he collapsed sometime on 24 July. The 3rd Battalion history gave some sense of the strain he had worked under for those three days. It explained how Harris summoned his platoon sergeants to a meeting to discuss the deteriorating situation, only to arrive late and find them blown to bits; and how, on the evening of the 23 July, his troops — braced for a German counterattack — almost opened fire on some shadowy figures across the road, who turned out to be other Australians.[56]

Harris spent most of 24 July digging his boys out of collapsed trenches. Late that afternoon, without warning, an exploding shell pushed a barrow-load of bricks over him. Something must have snapped; he seemed to suddenly break down. Although his commander needed every officer he could muster, he had no choice but to send Harris back to battalion headquarters for a rest.[57]

Harris's experience was common among the Australians sheltering at Pozières. Across the entire front, initially dozens and then hundreds of men descended into a catatonic state marked by symptoms of confusion, paralysis, tremors, anxiety, and shaking. 'I have had much luck and kept my nerve so far,' explained one soldier. 'The awful difficulty is to keep it. The bravest of all often lose it — one becomes a gibbering maniac.'[58]

At about the same time Harris collapsed, other troops began wilting under the strain. Major Verner Rowlands of the 2nd Battalion reported to the 1st Brigade headquarters that he had eight men praying to be seen by the doctor. 'The remainder are in a shocking state ... they seem to be nearly in a state of exhaustion.'[59] Some observers compared the phenomenon to that of a boat's mast creaking and then suddenly snapping under the strain of a torrid gale. Soldiers referred to 'broken' or 'shattered' nerves, and the medical fraternity called it neurasthenia, but its most common and evocative label was 'shell shock'.

By Tuesday 25 July, shell-shock cases had reached epidemic proportions, enough to threaten the Australians' hold on the village. On Saturday, there had been a handful of cases reported; on Sunday, 31 cases. On Monday, when the barrage shortened its range and pounded the village, 70 cases. By the end of Tuesday, there were over 200 cases, representing 20 per cent of all casualties that day. Shell shock also affected British troops: they had had 1387 reported cases in France for the whole of 1915, yet from July to December 1916 it escalated to over 16,000 cases.[60] The rise was almost certainly linked to the increased frequency, length, and severity of the bombardments throughout the second half of 1916.

Some officers, such as Captain Hubert Harris of the 2nd Field Artillery Brigade, didn't try to diagnose soldiers, but removed them from the line immediately. 'I do not consider it mattered much if the case was of stark fear or genuine "shell shock",' wrote Harris in his war memoirs, 'the former had to be evacuated to the ambulance because of the disastrous morale effect of a badly frightened man on his comrades.'[61] Australian medical officers quickly had to work out how to treat such victims. They recommended shorter periods in the line to combat exhaustion — which they considered the largest contributing factor to breakdown under shellfire — but this wasn't always practical under the German barrage. It became clear that there needed to be a way to treat these men within the confines of the village. One medical officer improvised his own homespun remedy, short-circuiting the need for evacuation: 'When men reported to me saying they were shocked, I made a comfortable rest for them; endeavoured to reassure them.' He then administered a mix that included morphine. 'I repeated this in half an hour. At the end of three quarters of an hour I was able to rouse them and the men would volunteer they felt better and would return to the line.'[62]

After collapsing, Harris was sent to battalion headquarters, where he rested as best he could; he could hear the muffled explosions of shells outside the dugout. When his rest period was up, he stepped groggily out of the dugout, just as a German shell exploded close by. 'It killed a man that had just stepped out of the dugout in front of me and knocked me down to the bottom of the steps with the dead man on top of me,' he recorded in his war memoirs. It 'terminated my further interest in proceedings'.[63] Harris had severe shell shock; he never returned to the line.

Mild shell-shock cases were evacuated to the corps rest station at Vadencourt.[64] Severe cases, like Harris, were evacuated to casualty clearing stations, which were out of artillery range. The two stations initially allocated to I Anzac Corps — nos. 3 and 44 British casualty clearing stations at Puchevillers — had six operating tables filled continually day and night for the first three days of the Pozières battle. After an extended rest, many soldiers returned to the line, but those with severe symptoms of 'nervous breakdown' were hospitalised, and recovery could be slow.

Shell shock did not discriminate. It could take hold of the brave, the shirker, the young, the old, the officer, or the private. Iven Mackay had been surprised when one of his battalion officers, decorated for bravery on Gallipoli, was found cringing in the corner of a dugout throughout the German bombardment. Mackay treated the man with the utmost respect, easing him out of the trenches and putting him in charge of a training battalion far from the fighting, where he might slowly recover. But he never did — even the explosion of training shells would set him trembling. When he eventually returned to the line, he broke down in a matter of days.[65]

Even if men did not display the classic symptoms of shell shock, it didn't mean they escaped its effects altogether. For several days after a battle, the noise of shuffling feet, an opening door, a passing cart — in fact, any movement at all — sounded to many like an approaching shell. 'We found ourselves flinching involuntarily on and off all day,' said one soldier.[66]

Even though Harris escaped Pozières, the war seemed to have destroyed him. He explained in a letter to his school magazine that after Pozières he lived a disconnected kind of existence as a sort of hanger-on to the division: 'I have never been quite right since P[ozières] and the H.Q. people have made that the reason for putting me on odd jobs.'[67] In the summer of 1917, Harris returned to his battalion. His personnel dossier indicates that his 'nerves' gave way again when his company passed through a barrage on the way to Polygon Wood in Belgium in September 1917. When shells exploded close by, Harris fell to the ground, shaking uncontrollably. He was evacuated to the field ambulance. The examining medical officer remembered him as suffering from tremor of the hands. He 'only answered questions slowly and after some delay'. His commanding officer found him to be imbecilic; all he could say was that he was 'feeling stupid'. Harris was diagnosed with shell shock for a second time.

Harris's file tells us that his commanding officer, Lieutenant-Colonel Donald Moore, believed the man could no longer stand the strain of action. 'Harris broke down in a similar manner the day after he led his company in the attack upon Pozières,' he explained in his report to Hooky Walker. On reviewing the situation, Hooky agreed.[68] Harris forfeited his command and, after a short stint in Egypt working at a reinforcement camp, applied for discharge. He returned to Australia a few months before the war's end. There was probably no marching band or heaving crowd to greet this war-damaged soldier; he would likely have quietly slipped back into civilian life. The war spawned thousands of John Harrises, who silently bore their terrible burden through the 1920s, 1930s, and 1940s. For them, perhaps the war never ended.

By Tuesday evening, the Australians had moved the front line forward about 600 yards by linking most of their forward posts, which they had dug the previous day; however, they lost many men in completing the task. Those soldiers still alive were too exhausted to repel a counterattack, should it come. Forsyth's relieving 2nd Brigade had only been in the line for 24 hours and had already suffered 1336 casualties.[69]

As a result of the German bombardment, an enormous plume of dust, smoke, and gunpowder shrouded Pozières. 'Terrible day for our boys,' said Lieutenant Ernest Holmes, 1st Division Artillery. 'They got shelled to pieces in Pozières ... Never witnessed such heavy shelling in my life as I saw today.'[70] Bean said Pozières was pounded more furiously than before: 'It seemed to onlookers scarcely possible that humanity could have endured such as ordeal.' The plume of red and black dust hanging over the village reminded him of a wild Broken Hill dust storm.[71]

Why couldn't the British guns knock the German guns out of action? Urgent pleas for counter-barrages were sent to divisional, Reserve Army, and then Fourth Army headquarters throughout the day, but nothing happened. The artillery observers claimed they couldn't direct counter-fire because of the dust plume over the village — and because the German guns were well hidden in Courcelette, on the reverse side of the Pozières ridge.[72]

What the Australians garrisoned at Pozières didn't realise was that its own artillery was stretched to breaking point and starting to buckle under mismanagement. David Horner's book *The Gunners* described how, after nearly a week of incessant firing, the buffer springs of the 18-pounder guns were nearly worn out. As a result, guns recoiled metal on metal, and had to be pushed back into their original firing position after each round. Their spring coils failed, and could only be returned to their original length by using up to 50 gunners and a thick rope to stretch out their compressed coils. These problems with the 18-pounders placed an extra load on the howitzer batteries. 'I had to cover the whole front of the brigade,' explained Captain Jeremiah Selmes of the 101st Howitzer Battery, 'and from 9 a.m. to 8 p.m. when I ceased to fire, I had expended 1672 rounds, completely using up all available ammunition.'[73]

The divisional ammunition columns also struggled to keep up supply to the field guns. They were already making up to three trips per day and working through the night. Three teams of two horses pulled the ammunition limbers. The limber drivers maintained a frantic pace, galloping all the way — particularly through the crossroads registered by the German guns. The potted roads sometimes snapped the horses' legs, and shellfire killed drivers and horses. The worst part for the drivers was seeing their limbers run over the bodies of the dead, although they realised this was the price to be paid for getting the ammunition through. Between 20 and 29 July, these columns would supply a staggering 80,000 rounds of 18-pounder, almost 9000 rounds of 4.5-inch, and over two million rounds of small-arms ammunition.[74]

Haig, aware of the haze, visited Birdie at his Contay headquarters and demanded that he immediately replace his long-time artillery adviser, Brigadier-General Charles Cunliffe-Owen, with the more experienced Brigadier-General William Napier, as Cunliffe-Owen had 'no experience of our present artillery or methods'.[75] Birdie complied. For Haig, it was another frustrating example of the old Gallipoli gang not appreciating the vital importance of artillery on the Western Front. 'I would be failing in my duty to the country if I ran the risk of the Australians meeting with a check through faulty artillery arrangements,' he later wrote in his diary. Disturbingly, months earlier Bean had predicted that the artillery would let the Australians down frightfully some day, writing in his diary: 'It's a puzzle to me why Birdwood keeps these people.'[76]

The early hours of Wednesday 26 July were spent trying to capture the remainder of OG1 and OG2, as Gough had ordered. The attacks were feeble, half-hearted, and unsuccessful. At daybreak on 26 July, the Australians braced themselves, wondering whether the Germans would bombard them for a third day straight. At 7.00 a.m. the bombardment came: gas shells musty with chloroform, sweet-scented tear shells that made eyes water, high-bursting shrapnel, and huge black clouds from exploding 5.9-inch shells.[77] The Australians crawled out of their trenches and into shell craters to escape the bombardment.[78]

Casualties mounted among the 2nd Division troops, who had just entered the line to relieve the 1st Division, while remnants of the 1st Division wondered whether they would make it out of Pozières alive. Carl Jess recorded the toll upon his officers with sobering regularity: '... Lieutenant Wright, brought in — shell-shock; 1.50, Lieutenant Hamilton, wounded; 2.45, Lieutenant Sutherland, wounded; 3.30, Lieutenant Hoban, wounded (lost leg since).'[79]

Hooky, sensing the imminent destruction of his once fine division, ordered that one battery of the 1st Anzac Heavy Artillery be solely devoted to counter-barrage work. Its commander protested, claiming that it would cost him his precious daily quota of shells. Hooky argued that his troops must be protected, and appealed to the commander of the Reserve Army's artillery for help, but he claimed he was already doing everything possible to suppress the German bombardment. It must have frustrated Hooky that most batteries sat silent, their forward observing officers claiming they were unable to direct fire owing to the haze.[80]

Back in the village, heavy shelling rocked Gordon Bennett's headquarters, which was made from pine logs. 'My men are being unmercifully shelled. They cannot hold if an attack is launched,' Bennett reported to his commander, General Forsyth. 'The firing line and my headquarters are being plastered with heavy guns and the town is being swept with shrapnel.'[81]

'Losses now heavy, many men are buried and suffering from shell-shock,' reported Iven Mackay that evening. 'Stretcher-bearers and runners very tired.'[82]

Late in the afternoon, a flurry of German rockets and flares curved into the sky. Soldiers panicked; officers doubted they could hold against a German counterattack. Sheltering in Gibraltar and with only one telephone working, Carl Jess phoned brigade headquarters, pleading: 'Consider relief imperative as we could not resist attack if this is the preparation of it. 6th and 8th battalions endorse this.'

Brigadier-General Forsyth considered Jess's desperate message. Pozières would be his last battle. Something inside of him must have snapped; he replied firmly, 'Men must and will fight if necessary.'[83]

Like Forsyth, Brigadier-General Sinclair-MacLagan and his staff at 3rd Brigade headquarters were utterly exhausted, having worked continuously, sometimes in suffocating gas masks under the poor light of acetylene lamps. One officer observing their work said they appeared to be walking in a trance. Tired runners, who snatched whatever fitful sleep they could before being called upon to deliver another message, clogged the dugout's passageways. One runner, unable to cope with the strain, blew his brains out.[84]

The three days between 24 and 26 July were possibly the most trying ever experienced by Australian soldiers. The troops suffered three days of intensive bombardment that was arguably the heaviest yet seen on the Somme. Lieutenant Colonel Elliott, who fought with the 12th Battalion throughout the war, described the shellfire as the worst he had ever suffered.[85] In the coming days, the burden of fighting under these trying conditions and seizing the important OG lines would transfer from Hooky Walker's spent 1st Division to the relatively fresh troops of the 2nd Australian Infantry Division.

CHAPTER EIGHT

The Price of Glory

'A soldier will fight long and hard for a bit of coloured ribbon.'
— Napoleon Bonaparte

Just before dusk on Wednesday 26 July, Major-General Gordon Legge, commander of the 2nd Australian Infantry Division, departed his temporary headquarters at Rubempré and motored toward Hooky Walker's divisional headquarters at Albert. In a few hours, Legge would assume command of the Pozières sector, relieving Walker and his chief-of-staff, Thomas Blamey, who was 'tired to death for want of sleep'.[1] As Legge hurtled toward Albert, his 5th and 6th brigades progressively relieved the 1st Division troops, while his third brigade, the 7th, remained in reserve at Tara Valley.

The shattered 1st Division troops waited impatiently throughout the night for Legge's troops to relieve them. Donovan Joynt was thankful when the 24th Battalion relieved his 8th Battalion at about midnight, recounting in his autobiography that his handover was quick and brief. 'I only waited to point out, "there's your front. I can't tell you where my flanking posts are — I haven't got any and haven't seen them."'[2] The relieving troops noted that Joynt's men were 'nerve shattered and very shaky from the effects of the heavy bombardment'.[3]

By the time Brigadier-General Sinclair-MacLagan was finally relieved, he had been without sleep for five nights and six days. He climbed over the sleeping and tired runners that choked the dugout's passageway, and then trudged through broken trenches, toward Sausage Valley, while a bombardment fell around him. He eventually climbed from the confusing network of trenches and worked his way back across the open ground. An even heavier bombardment blocked his way forward. Exhausted and frustrated, Sinclair-MacLagan collapsed into a shell hole. 'I'm damned if I'm going through that,' he said to himself. Meanwhile, runners and stretcher-bearers, focused on their tasks, hurried by the shell hole, oblivious to the brigadier-general sheltering there. An hour later, Sinclair-MacLagan picked himself up and continued on.[4]

In the early hours of 27 July, Iven Mackay's 4th Battalion troops prepared for their relief. 'Wake those men up and tell them to get ready,' ordered one of his lieutenants, George Pugh. But it soon became clear that the men he referred to would never leave Pozières — a thick film of dust obscured their faces, suggesting that they had died days earlier, and churned-up dirt from the bombardment had subsequently settled upon them.[5]

An exhausted Mackay led the last remnants of his battalion out of Pozières just before daybreak. At about the same time, the relieving 5th Brigade reported to Legge that all was 'quiet in Pozières'.[6] At sunrise, Charles Bean watched as Mackay's troops, in twos and threes, straggled in and gathered around the cookers. He walked among the 'overstrained' men — dirty, unshaven, with their clothes torn and mud-stained — as they got some food and coffee from the stoves; he compared their animated conversations to the wild chatter of schoolboys. Bean wrote in his diary that their stories seemed unbelievable; he doubted whether they could be taken literally on account of the men's high-strung condition.[7] Some soldiers, like Peter Smith of the 2nd Battalion, avoided the chatter and sat quietly, savouring the pleasure of a cup of hot cocoa — the first drop of anything warm for three days — from one of the cherished coffee stalls. Chaplain Walter Dexter, with the support of the Australian Comforts Fund, had established the stalls near the front line to provide soldiers with hot drinks and biscuits.[8] For many of Mackay's troops, the desire for rest outweighed their need for food: 'We all feel completely knocked and glad of the opportunity to take our boots off and get some sleep,' wrote Apcar de Vine, 'neither of which I have had since the 22nd'.[9]

A tired Douglas Horton remembered throwing his overcoat down and then himself upon it and within a few minutes being dead to everything: 'The dew was thick but that did not matter. We have drawn on our stock of endurance to the last ounce.'[10]

The 1st Division rollcalls after breakfast were a sobering reminder of the terrible price that had been paid to capture and hold Pozières. Smith recorded that only 203 men answered the 2nd Battalion rollcall; three days earlier, it had been 1000-strong. Out of 181 men in Frederick Callaway's company, only 39 answered. Arthur Foxcroft's platoon had been cut to pieces: '14 answered the roll in our platoon out of 60 men. One officer, one corporal, 12 privates,' he recorded in his diary.[11]

With rollcalls complete, the adjutants tallied the casualty lists. The 1st Division had suffered a staggering 5285 casualties — almost 50 per cent of its strength — in capturing the impregnable fortress of Pozières and unsuccessfully attacking the Pozières ridge.[12] It seemed that Hooky's premonition of his division being 'knocked out' in the attack had been realised. Although the 1st Division's casualties were heavy in the two night attacks, it was the four days of the continuous bombardment that had obliterated its ranks.[13]

How did the soldiers, junior officers, and commanders feel about their experience at Pozières? The boyish enthusiasm of the soldiers, a week earlier so strong for war, ribbons, and glory, had disappeared. 'I can tell you I should never have got out alive,' recalled one soldier.

'I had a terrible shaking up ... Some of the men went mad ... I hope the war is over very soon.'[14] Another soldier, caught under the German bombardment, declared: 'This war is a disgrace to Christianity.'[15]

An embittered Eric Moorhead claimed that the Australian officer leading the botched attack on the ridge-top trenches was 'filled to the neck with rum'.[16] The battalion history, written in 1921, supported his views, admitting that 'a liberal issue of rum had infused some of the officers and men with more than their habitual recklessness'.[17] The *Official History* mentioned it, but only as a footnote. Although it conceded that even the Germans' official historian had stated that the Australians were 'inflamed with alcohol', it rebutted the accusation, claiming that after careful investigation the allegation proved false.[18] In 1934, White criticised the draft *British Official History* for documenting the incident, claiming he doubted it had happened, and that even if it did, mentioning it served 'no good purpose'.[19] The issue of consuming alcohol during battle was a sensitive one at the time, particularly as *The Sydney Morning Herald* had recently published an article accusing the Germans of abhorrent battle tactics, such as attacking with Apache weapons (long sticks studded with nails), while stimulated with ether (a British officer had said they reeked of alcohol).[20]

The 1st Division soldiers leaving Pozières were different men from those who had stormed it five days earlier. Sergeant Ted Rule of the 4th Division, who watched the beleaguered troops march through Warloy, said he would never forget the sight. 'Almost without exception each man looked drawn and haggard, and so dazed that they appeared to be walking in a trance, and their eyes looked glassy and starry,' he wrote in his memoirs. 'In all my experience I had never seen men quite so shaken up as these.'[21]

Bean was also shocked by the state of the troops, noting that when they reached bivouac in Vadencourt Wood and had washed, shaved, and rested, 'they were strangely quiet ... far different from the Australian soldiers of tradition'. Bean wrote in the *Official History* that they were like 'boys emerging from a long illness'.[22]

Despite the catatonic state of the troops, their commanders drew some satisfaction from the expensive victory. 'Pozières is ours, captured alone by our division,' wrote Thomas Blamey in a letter home. 'We are all very proud of the feat. Our plan, which was chiefly mine, led to a brilliant success ...'[23] Birdie sent a note to Hooky saying he was chuffed with the division's magnificent efforts, and thanked them for taking Pozières:

> I well know how grateful the Chief and everyone else are at the work done by the division. I only wish that I could thank everyone individually and wish, too, that there were a sufficient number of V.C.s [Victoria Crosses] to go round for the very large number of officers and men, who I am sure have deserved them.[24]

Birdie's jaunty note suggests he was more concerned with medals won than men lost. Bean noted in his diary that even Birdie's fellow British officers suspected he was climbing on the shoulders of the Australians simply to further his career.[25]

Junior officers were less than enamoured with their costly victory. There seemed, according to one officer, an utter lack of any skill behind the attacks, which had wasted thousands of men. Battalion histories written after the war often voiced the junior officers' malcontent. The 11th Battalion history, *Legs-eleven*, summed up what seemed to be the prevailing opinion, writing of the horrific casualties that 'it was a terrible penalty to pay for the small advance made, much as it was lauded at the time'.[26]

What no one questioned — whether soldier, junior officer, or commander — was that two Australian divisions had been mauled in less than a week. Casualties topped 10,000: the 5th Division had suffered 5533 casualties at Fromelles; the 1st Division, 5285 at Pozières.[27] The 1st Division endured arguably one of the heaviest barrages experienced by the Australians throughout the war — according to the *Official History*, 'better or worse than Pozières' became the standard by which shellfire was measured by the Australian Imperial Force.[28]

While the battle seemed to have weakened the bond between soldier and staff officer, it appeared that the relationship between soldiers was strengthened. A man's 'only real support is the comfort of his mates', reasoned Geoffrey Drake-Brockman.[29] Frederic Manning, an Australian enlisted in the British army who fought on the Somme, described the bond in his semi-autobiographical book, *The Middle Parts of Fortune*. He wrote that at one moment a particular man may be nothing at all to someone, and the next minute that person will go through hell for him. 'It's not friendship. The man doesn't matter so much; it's a kind of impersonal emotion, a kind of enthusiasm, in the old sense of the word.'[30] The shared experience of battle apparently strengthened this bond: 'We help each other. What is one man's fate today may be another's tomorrow. We are all in it up to the neck together, and we know it.'

The 2nd Division troops almost certainly sensed they were in it up to their necks as they marched toward Pozières. 'Oh don't worry you will all be skittled,' one soldier warned 19-year-old Melbourne clerk Private Fred Hocking of the 23rd Battalion. 'In an attack up there the first wave gets cut down to the last man.'[31] Private Vic Graham, a 19-year-old mechanic from Moonee Ponds, Victoria, noticed the stink in the air near Pozières. He now understood what the French peasants meant when they whispered '*Bo coo Australie, fini Pozières*' (as Graham wrote it in his diary). It translated roughly to 'a lot of Australians finished at Pozières'.[32]

The troops were appalled by the state in which they found the village. 'It was just a heap of rubble and dust, shredded tree trunks, deep shell holes, and upturned earth,' explained the 17th Battalion history. All that remained of the orchard were 'tree stumps that appeared grotesque in the half light, bearing a weird resemblance to human shapes'.[33] Private William Clayton of the 6th Machine-gun

Company wrote in a letter home that the only indication that Pozières was ever inhabited was the thousands of bricks scattered and broken over the ground. 'The main track through Pozières was recognisable only by the large number of dead men and horses that were there,' he commented.[34]

The relieving troops busied themselves with fixing their battered trenches before the bombardment recommenced. The 24th Battalion deepened its trench, which, in several places, was only 18 inches deep. 'We worked like niggers, and by daylight had it down to about 3-feet, 6-inches,' Private Arthur Clifford recorded in his diary.[35]

Brothers Alec and Goldy Raws were among the relieving troops of the 2nd Division. Margaret Young and Bill Gammage documented their war years in *Hail and Farewell*. They recorded that Robert Goldthorpe — 'Goldy' for short — was the younger of the two, half a head taller than his brother and much fitter, after months of working in sugarcane plantations up north. He enlisted in Melbourne in January 1915 and completed his training locally, in Broadmeadows. Before sailing to Egypt, he visited his family in Adelaide. His father, John, a Baptist preacher, remembered the all-too-brief stay and the painful parting: 'We said goodbye to him near the Buckingham Arms, where he took a tram into the city and caught the Melbourne express.'

Alec was nicknamed 'Little Raws' as a child because of his slight build and poor health. Although he suffered from bouts of 'the shivers' and fainting, it appeared that no doctor accurately diagnosed his condition. No doubt the mild winters spent at his grandparents' house improved his frail health. After finishing school at Prince Alfred College in Kent Town, South Australia, Alec became a journalist and later secured a job with *The Argus* in Melbourne. Upon fronting up at a recruiting station in July 1915, he was surprised, on account of his occasional fainting spells, to be passed fit for service — he thought the reduction in recruiting standards must have helped to get him through.

Why did Alec feel compelled to enlist, even though a doctor had warned him to avoid excessive strain? Although Alec had a close relationship with his brother, this didn't appear to be the influencing factor. Alec was imbued with strong principles, which seemingly guided his decision to enlist: 'I am prepared to abandon all my comforts, all my life, all of everything, to fight for principles which, I hold, mean everything to the modern world,' he wrote.[36]

John seemed downcast upon hearing that Alec had enlisted. 'We felt it a good deal,' he wrote in his autobiography. Alec, aware of his father's concerns, tried to justify his decision in a letter, explaining his belief that the salvation of the world depended upon a speedy victory for the Allies: 'Holding such views, how can a man, judged to be physically fit for the purpose, reasonably hold back? I think that, looking at the facts in this light, you will agree with me.'

By March 1916, the brothers were in France and had both achieved the rank of lieutenant. Alec was the more outspoken of the two; being a political journalist, he was unusually articulate. He had strong political convictions, leaning toward the left side of politics; he had been active in the formation of the Australian Journalists' Association. With this unique background, it is unsurprising that Alec's expansive letters to his family and friends throughout July and August — to become possibly the most quoted in popular histories of the Somme and Pozières — were vivid and controversial. He cast a light on many uncomfortable themes that official histories largely avoided: incompetent leadership, cowardice, officers threatening to shoot their soldiers, and accusations of murder.

On 27 July, Alec and Goldy's 23rd Battalion shifted closer to the reserve trenches.[37] Although in the same battalion, the brothers hadn't yet seen each other. 'Though I believe he passed through the base where I camped the other night,' explained Alec in a letter to his mother, 'he [Goldy] has moved, whence and to where I am not permitted to tell.' Although neither brother realised it, their battalion would soon shift up to the front line to lead the attack upon the OG lines; it was quite possible they would never meet again.[38]

Major-General Gordon Legge's 2nd Division consisted of Brigadier-General William Holmes's New South Wales 5th Brigade, Brigadier-General John 'Jack' Gellibrand's Victorian 6th Brigade, and Brigadier-General John Paton's 7th Brigade. Legge was the only Australian divisional commander on the Somme.[39] Although Legge had served as Australia's representative on the Imperial General Staff in Great Britain before the war, he hadn't formed strong relationships with British officers, as White had during his tenure there. Therefore, Legge seemed to be excluded from the tight circle of British-trained officers into which White and Birdie fitted in comfortably.

Legge's inexperienced 2nd Division had served on Gallipoli, but had never fought a major battle before. His divisional staff had no experience in managing large-scale attacks, and his troops lacked training in trench warfare. The objective that Gough had set for Legge's division was daunting: to capture the trenches rimming the Pozières ridge and then strike out north toward the ruins of Mouquet Farm, the last obstacle that stood between the British and the impregnable fortress of Thiepval.

Legge received Order Number 16 from Birdie on Thursday 27 July, which instructed his division to attack the OG trenches. The attack had to be at night, but Legge could decide its timing.[40] In theory, he could take time to prepare thoroughly, but in reality time pressures demanded that he attack immediately. Gough had previously goaded Birdie, demanding action, but now he pressured Legge — who, understandably, 'tried to fall in' with his directives.[41] Gough most likely exerted pressure on Legge via Birdie, whom he met with almost daily, but also directly, when the two met every few days.[42]

For Legge, selecting the attack date was a balancing act: wait too long, and the German bombardment would leave him no soldiers with whom to attack; rush, and he risked compromising critical preparations. He eventually decided to attack on Friday 28 July — a bold decision considering that his headquarters had only arrived at

Albert on 26 July and assumed command from the 1st Division at 9.00 a.m. on 27 July.

Holmes's 5th and Gellibrand's 6th brigades entered the line on 25 and 26 July, while Legge held Paton's 7th in reserve. Holmes's brigade immediately became involved in contesting a portion of the OG1 Trench. Over 24 hours of vicious fighting, conducted almost exclusively with bombs, the Australians failed to gain a single yard of ground, but suffered heavy casualties that Legge could ill afford — of 54 bombers of the 18th Battalion, only seven came out unwounded, and the *Official History* recorded that all of the 5th Brigade's bombers had been killed, maimed, or exhausted in the fighting.[43]

In 1914, Legge was considered someone to watch. His résumé read well: he had completed a Bachelor of Arts, a masters degree, and a Bachelor of Laws; he was admitted to the Bar in New South Wales in 1891; and he had gained valuable war experience in 1899, commanding an infantry company in the Boer War. He was an architect of many reforms in the Australian army, such as compulsory military service, which Lord Kitchener, on his visit to Australia in 1910, had recommended. But with reform came conflict; Legge seemed to revel in it. His 'style and ideas' undoubtedly alienated his 'orthodox and plodding' British superior, Brigadier-General Launcelot Kiggell, when he served as Australia's representative on the Imperial General Staff between 1912 and 1914. His role in London was reduced to being little more than an observer.[44] For Legge, whose big frame, thick moustache, and closely cropped hair accentuated his imposing nature, getting the job done seemed more important than making friends.

Legge discovered on Gallipoli that his forceful approach had consequences beyond sacrificing the odd friendship. Although he missed the early months of the campaign, Legge was later appointed 1st Australian Division commander after the original commander, Major-General William Bridges, died. Legge's subordinates, such as brigade commanders John Monash and James McCay, argued against the appointment, feeling he was now junior in rank to them and without experience in the campaign; it seemed that McCay could 'hardly stand the idea' of reporting to him. Legge then clashed with Birdie over proposed tactics for the 1st Division's planned assault on Lone Pine.[45] What also irked Birdie was Legge's tendency to communicate directly with the Australian government — it is likely that Birdie, the consummate politician, and sensitive to criticism, believed that this should be his sole domain.[46] Legge, however, perhaps reasoned that the Australian government should hear about the welfare of its troops from an Australian officer. His fate at Gallipoli was soon sealed: Birdie, apparently realising that the peninsula wasn't big enough for both men, pushed him sideways into the role of forming the 2nd Division in Egypt.[47] Legge must have felt slighted by the arrangement and would likely have wanted to repair the damage done to his reputation.

Legge was universally recognised as a good administrator and a prodigious worker. He possessed the constitution of an ox and, with the occasional cup of tea and biscuit, could work for 18 hours a day and still feel fit at the end of it.[48] But was he a 'fighting solider'? His appointment to a field command was viewed as something of an experiment. His only recent command experience was limited to organising the Australian Naval and Military Expeditionary Force for service in New Guinea.

Many British officers and imperialist-leaning Australian officers, including White, also resented Legge's 'holier than thou' Australian-nationalist bent.[49] He'd previously clashed with White in Egypt over the appointment of British officers to posts he thought should have been taken by Australians. Chris Coulthard-Clark, in *No Australian Need Apply*, wrote that Legge disputed Birdie's decision to appoint Hooky Walker, rather than himself, temporarily in charge of I Anzac Corps in April 1916. 'He [Legge] does not have the full confidence of those serving under him, while Walker most distinctly does,' Birdie curtly explained in a letter to governor-general Sir Ronald

Munro Ferguson.[50] The tactful Bean thought Birdie passed over Legge because of his inclination to 'cry out Australia for the Australians', meaning Legge lobbied for Australian officers rather than British officers to be appointed to senior roles in the Australian Imperial Force.[51] Pozières would provide Legge the opportunity to prove his detractors wrong.

Like clockwork, Pozières came alive with the crash of shells at 9.00 a.m. on 27 July — the Germans were bombarding the village for a fourth consecutive day. Arthur Clifford had just finished digging a deeper trench when it started. 'The Germans did not spare us once daylight revealed our whereabouts,' he noted.[52]

The troops in and around the village had no duty that day other than to remain there hour after hour. One officer remembered a group of men caught under the bombardment trying to occupy their minds by playing cards. As one player was killed, another close by would take his hand. When the officer passed their way again, all four players had been killed.[53]

The Australians were still overcrowding their forward trenches. As the hours continued, the casualties became sickening in their number. Shelling targeted Holmes's troops. 'We sat in Kay Trench, hour after hour, waiting to be killed or buried by the collapsing banks,' remembered Clifford. 'By evening, half of my company was gone.'[54]

Legge's preparations appeared to be running into trouble. He had already lost valuable reserves, and the 1st Division's artillery commander told him he couldn't guarantee that belts of barbed wire in front of the first and second trench would be cut, due to the haze hanging over Pozières. If it remained uncut, advancing troops risked becoming entangled on it. Patrols sent out throughout the hot and cloudless day brought back mixed reports, saying that the wire protecting the German trenches had been cut in some places but remained intact in others. Spotter aeroplanes sent up to assess the state of the wire reported back that dust and smoke had obscured their view. Pioneers attempted to dig jumping-off trenches along the length of the old railway line but, as soon as they were close to completion, German shelling destroyed them. Even if they had remained intact, the soldiers still would have had 600 to 700 yards of open ground to cover — three times the distance recommended by General Headquarters. With no other actions planned that night, the Germans could concentrate the full weight of their artillery on the Australians. German artillery observers had seen the Australians digging their trenches, and expected an attack.[55]

Legge's preparations may have seemed flawed but, with Gough's continued goading and the relentless shelling of his troops, there seemed no alternative but to adhere to his tight schedule. Bean had once warned Birdie that Legge had a tendency to jump to big conclusions without working out all the finicky detail between.[56] Yet in this case, it was impossible to check such detail. By necessity, Legge's headquarters was in Albert, close to decision-makers like Gough and Birdie; this prevented him from going forward to observe preparations. He relied on his officers to be his eyes and ears but, unlike Hooky, he did not have an officer of Blamey's calibre upon whom to depend. Although Legge had elements of true genius, he possibly didn't yet have the experience to pick up those subtle clues that things were awry.[57] With the chaos thrown up by war, Legge likely reasoned that no one could expect arrangements to be perfect.

Legge perhaps sensed that the fighting in the OG trenches had weakened Holmes's 5th Brigade; and the heavy German bombardment, Gellibrand's 6th Brigade. In a bold move, he brought forward Paton's fresh 7th Brigade to lead the attack. The other two brigades would now protect its flanks. Gellibrand thought Legge was courting disaster, as the 7th did not have time to get its bearings or complete reconnaissance — aside from which, it was the weakest of the three brigades. In Bean's opinion, it was plagued with bad discipline and officers of poor quality, who were often appointed based on seniority rather than performance.[58]

Jack Gellibrand, by this point, 'seriously doubted' that the attack could succeed.[59] Gellibrand — a tall man with a thick moustache — usually wore a private's tunic and a battered felt hat, and lived simply among his men. A deep thinker prone to theorising, his unconventional opinions and behaviour polarised others: William Bridges criticised his performance on Gallipoli, and Birdie disliked his choice of dress and blunt manner, while White thought he had the tendency to wilt in situations of pressure.[60] Although Gellibrand had a strained relationship with some peers, after he had transferred to his 2nd Division he had formed a close relationship with Legge, who had enough faith to appoint him commander of the 12th Battalion, and, in March 1916, the 6th Brigade.[61]

Gellibrand moulded his staff into a tight and cohesive team. Lieutenant Richard Casey said the commander had a rare gift of being able to conceal his rank and age. 'This gave the younger man a degree of confidence in expression and discussion that was very marked and most useful, so long as it wasn't abused,' he observed.[62] Doubtless, some officers of the hierarchical British army considered this egalitarian management approach heresy.

Could Gellibrand be a decisive leader in battle? There had already been murmurings that his brigade headquarters, set up two miles behind the front line, deep inside a captured German dugout, was too far back to control the battle. And it was 16 years since his last field command, leading a company in South Africa.[63] Pozières would be the biggest challenge yet faced by Legge or Gellibrand in their professional careers. Gellibrand already feared that the attack to seize the OG lines would fail; no doubt the planned operation under these trying conditions would not only cost more lives in the coming days, but would also end promising careers.

CHAPTER NINE

Legge's Reckoning

> 'Never interfere with an enemy that is in the process of committing suicide.'
> — attributed to Napoleon Bonaparte

On Friday 28 July, Gordon Legge — imbued with a sense of optimism and possibly unaware of the difficulties facing his troops — continued his hurried preparations for the attack upon the OG lines.[1] His pioneer battalions dug strongpoints between Pozières and the OG trenches; heavy batteries carried out their preparatory bombardment; 7th Brigade officers — who hadn't yet occupied any part of the front — completed a rushed reconnaissance of the attack area; and brigade commanders reviewed divisional orders. Many troops in the front line for the first time were unnerved by the heavy shelling and the stink in the air. 'Some of the old hands in our platoon were just as nervous and scared-looking as ourselves,' recorded Private Walter Elkington, of Bingara, New South Wales, in his war memoirs.[2] Private Ernest Norgard spent long hours thinking of home to distract himself from the barrage and the awful smells.[3]

At sunset, Paton's untried troops marched toward the front line while officers, who had probably just received the coded message indicating the attack time ('pays will be issued at 12.15'), synchronised their watches.

Heavy German shelling had continued to hamper Legge's preparations throughout the day, inflicting 1521 casualties on his division by the day's end. Legge's 6th Brigade commander, Jack Gellibrand, estimated that two of his battalions — the 22nd and 24th — had lost 25 per cent of their strength from the shelling.[4] Gellibrand, sensing the depressed mood of his troops, issued the following message: 'It has been said that when you go out 25% of you will be killed. You will be killed if you go forward, you will be killed if you go back — It is better to be killed going forward.' There is no record of how Gellibrand's troops responded to his sober message, although it is difficult to imagine it motivating them.[5]

Legge's three brigades would each play a role in the attack. Gellibrand's 6th Brigade would attack with one battalion — Goldy and Alec Raws's fresh 23rd — in the northern sector of the battlefield, toward the Ovillers–Courcelette track. Paton's 7th Brigade would spearhead the attack with three battalions — the 25th, 26th, and 28th — in the arc between the Ovillers–Courcelette track and the Bapaume road. Holmes's 5th Brigade would launch a subsidiary attack south of the Bapaume road, using the 20th Battalion. Bean doubted the wisdom of allowing Paton's brigade to lead the attack, noting in his diary that Legge had placed the troops 'into trenches they don't know and opposite a front they haven't any experience of'.[6]

Legge, like many commanders new to the Western Front, had little appreciation of the best artillery plan to support an attack and dutifully accepted the one presented to him by the divisional 'artillery commanders', making only one alteration.[7] By the period of the Somme battles, artillery management had evolved into a complex science that was beyond the grasp of many infantry commanders. Artillery was divided between the division, corps, and army. Planned bombardments, like the one preceding the 2nd Division's attack, could have a number of objectives — destroying trenches, subduing counter-barrages, protecting advancing troops, cutting wire, or deceiving the enemy. A bombardment could be a mixture of shrapnel shells to cut wire, high-explosive shells to destroy trench positions, smoke to cover the advance of troops, or gas to disorientate the enemy. Add to this the different calibres of guns, fuse types, and explosive mixtures, and it was little wonder that there seemed to be 'a squad of mathematicians around every gun, doing sums, reading graphs, setting sights, calculating fuse lengths and getting in each others way'.[8]

The plan the artillery commanders presented to Legge was for the 2nd Division's attack to be preceded by 12 minutes of silence from midnight, followed by an intense three-minute barrage at 12.12 a.m. Legge's alteration was to request normal fire from midnight until 12.14 a.m., followed by one minute of intense barrage. At 12.15 a.m., the barrage delivered by six Australian brigades and two British divisions would lengthen as troops moved forward.[9] The final plan contrasted with the bombardment preceding the 1st Division's attack on Pozières, which had lasted days and destroyed virtually everything; this time, planners deemed surprise to be critically important. Yet, unbeknown to the Australians, the Germans had watched them dig their jumping-off trenches and lay out their white tapes to mark the assembly areas well before the attack commenced.[10]

Brigadier-General James Birch, Haig's artillery advisor at General Headquarters, was concerned with Legge's artillery plans. That evening, he told Haig that the 2nd Division would attack virtually without artillery because they believed that machine-gun fire could not do them much harm. Birch was referring to the original artillery plan that called for 12 minutes' silence, possibly unaware that it had changed. Haig, somewhat uneasy about Legge's seemingly slapdash plan, wrote in his diary: 'The Australians are splendid fellows but very ignorant.'[11]

Legge's troops had mixed emotions about the looming attack. Some, like Charles Turner, were fatalistic. 'Our battalion the 23rd is going into the front line of trenches tonight and making a charge upon the German trenches tomorrow,' he recorded. 'There is a chance that there will be a lot of us never come out of it.'[12]

Fred Hocking, also of the 23rd Battalion, mocked his major, who told him: 'There will be very few men if any in the trenches.'

'Not arf,' responded a disbelieving Hocking.[13]

Twenty-one-year-old Bunbury farmer Corporal Percy Blythe wrote that every 28th Battalion man was 'game and anxious' and not one man doubted 'himself or his comrade'.[14]

By dusk, the artillery batteries had completed their preparatory work, and troops, including Turner, Hocking, and Blythe, had worked up to their assigned locations. They passed Holmes's brigade, which had been in the line for the last few days. 'Most of them were broken men: big strong fellows shook like leaves,' noted Western Australian farmer Corporal Francis Mauger.

Toward midnight, the battlefield, dusted with dew, remained 'uncannily quiet', as a German soldier reinforcing Mouquet Farm noted.[15] At Gellibrand's brigade headquarters, officers anxiously scanned the night sky, watching for flashes: a flurry of flares would mean the Germans had spotted the Australians, whereas none would suggest all was well. While his officers peered into the darkness, Gellibrand — who, Bean noted in his diary, was as 'cool as ice' that evening — stole short naps in his wallpapered and wood-panelled underground bunkroom.[16] At 11.40 p.m. the southern part of the battlefield suddenly lit up like day — masses of red and white flares fizzed into the night sky, flowering to light before falling slowly to earth.[17] Without any shelling to keep the German forward sentries in their dugouts, they observed Holmes's 20th Battalion working toward them.

A minute later, a bouquet of fizzing red flares shot into the sky from two places, signalling for intense German artillery support in those southern sectors. It came almost immediately: shrapnel pellets ripped through what was left of the foliage, tearing at leaves and smacking against broken trunks; machine-gun fire raked no-man's-land, striking the Australians just a few yards from the trenches they had crawled from. 'Pieces of shell were whizzing and humming

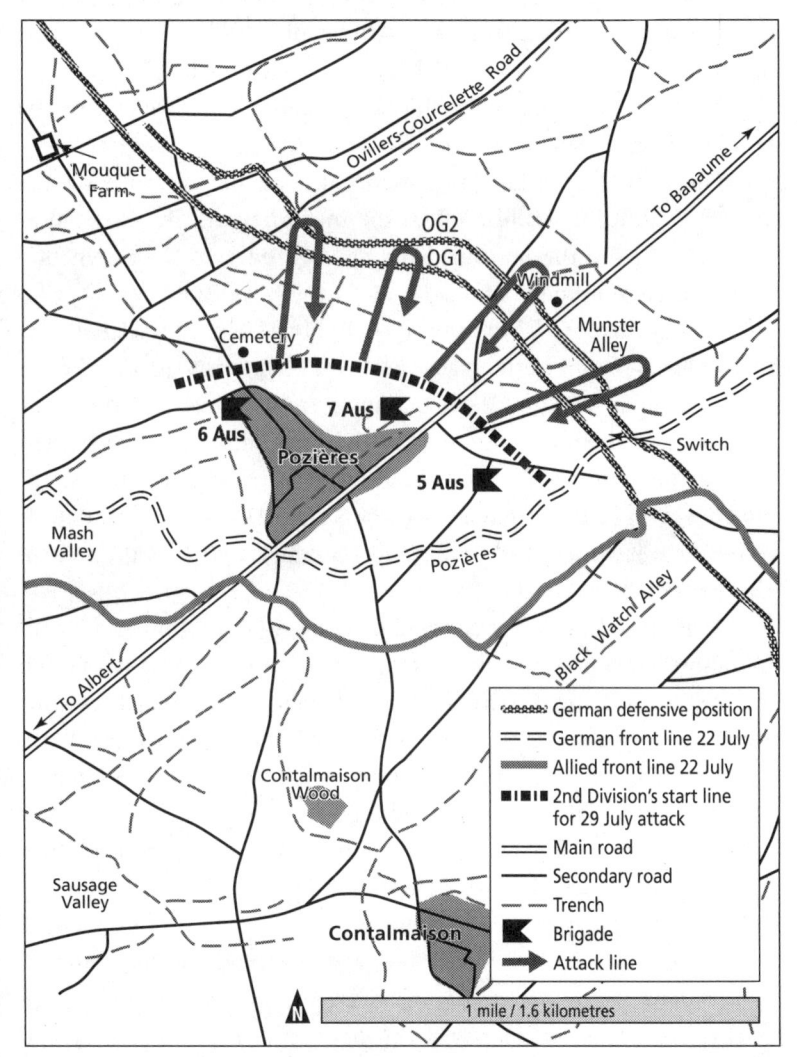

Map 4. 2nd Division's Advance on OG lines

and the ground seemed to heave as if an earthquake was on,' remembered one soldier.[18] Trench mortar crews worked frantically to silence the German machine guns, but failed.[19] The 20th Battalion diary summed up the debacle: troops were disorganised and out of position, and did not get forward at all. The battalion suffered 60 casualties.[20] Holmes's subsidiary attack south of the Bapauame road had failed before the main attack at 12.15 a.m., north of the road, had even been launched.

The light from the flares made any further advance by the 20th Battalion impossible. When the machine-gun fire subsided at about 3.00 a.m., the few survivors crawled back to their trenches, leaving their wounded stranded.

Paton's three fresh but untested battalions were to attack between the Ovillers–Courcelette track and the Bapaume road.[21] When midnight came, Paton's 28th Battalion troops crawled from their trenches and shell holes toward the OG lines, aiming to be closer to the German lines when the one-minute hurricane bombardment ended. Having left its trenches, Ernest Norgard's platoon found itself under heavy artillery fire; some soldiers crawled back to the trench, about 60 yards away, to seek shelter.

At 12.08 a.m., an alert German machine-gunner spotted the 28th Battalion's advance, and fired at the men. Other Germans saw the Australians moving up the hill toward them, and opened up with machine guns and rifles.[22] At 12.14 a.m., the firing dropped off, suppressed by the one-minute hurricane bombardment. Stretcher-bearer Private Tom Young remembered the troops continuing their uphill advance as if they were marching on a parade ground with their own shells screaming overhead and the German shells blowing them to bits. 'The men dropped like flies, the German wire remained intact and they could go neither forward nor back,' recalled Young.[23]

Soldiers in the first waves discovered the German barbed wire uncut. Some hacked their way through using rifle butts and wire cutters, while others wrenched out the corkscrew stakes with their bare hands. Wire snagged uniforms and flesh while the Germans sprayed them with fire. Percy Blythe sought shelter in a shell hole under the German entanglements, realising he couldn't advance any further. He threw his bombs at the Germans, then checked on the wounded caught on the wire and tried to drag them to a safer position.

German flares and exploding shells illuminated those hopelessly 'hung up' on the wire. The remaining waves of soldiers surged forward, oblivious to the problems of the first waves, leading to a bunching in no-man's-land.[24]

Nineteen-year-old Private John Stuart, whose father had only permitted him to enlist on the condition that he served with the Red Cross, watched this hopeless spectacle unfold.[25] 'Men were dropping killed and wounded everywhere. It was sickening to hear the moans and groans of our chaps,' recalled Stuart.[26]

'In about 15 minutes the 28th had ceased to exist as a Battalion,' recorded Francis Mauger, who was also caught in no-man's-land. 'The Germans had a perfect barrier of bursting bombs all along their wire, and in a few minutes it was all over. We never had a chance.'

The Germans' ability to target Australians was made easier by the seemingly insane requirement for troops to wear metallic discs between their shoulder blades, in order for observers in spotter aeroplanes to assess how far they had advanced. Commanders had reassured their men that the Germans could not see the discs.[27] Private Percy Perry of the 25th Battalion was one of the many troops who begged to differ: he recorded that the German flares 'reflected on the tins tied to their backs', resulting in 'dozens of machine-guns blazing into them'.[28]

Paton's 25th and 26th battalions fared marginally better than the 28th. They came across tracts of cut wire and broke through, securing a section of OG1. Some continued on, storming OG2, but uncut wire and machine-gun fire thwarted their advance. At 12.50 a.m. the situation was considered hopeless and the troops withdrew.

The 23rd Battalion, on the northern edge of the attack, initially advanced unimpeded by the firing that slowed Paton's battalions; however, within minutes they encountered another problem: they got caught in their own bombardment and became hopelessly mixed with Paton's men. Fred Hocking, caught in the shelling, recalled an officer shouting, 'Come on 23rd', even though he and the others, who were 'loaded up [like] pack horses', were already going as fast as they could across the shell-churned ground.[29] Second-Lieutenant Goldy Raws tried to settle his men, urging them to keep their line. His advancing troops could not find the dirt track to Courcelette. Raws must have realised that in the darkness they had passed over their objective — he urged those within earshot to double back.[30] Eventually, the troops made their way back to the shell-damaged track and began digging a new trench to protect Paton's right flank. Fred Hocking wasn't among them; a shell had exploded a few yards in front of him, taking off his commanding officer's head and wounding him. Hocking lay in no-man's-land, blood spurting from his wounded leg. 'I'm done for,' he thought, as he later recounted in a letter.[31]

As Gellibrand's 23rd Battalion troops dug in, word came that Paton's 26th Battalion, to their right, had withdrawn, leaving their flank exposed.[32] To address this danger, Gellibrand's troops hastily dug a new section of trench that connected with the old Pozières Trench. It was complete by 9.00 a.m.

The attack across the entire front had stalled. Some officers considered the situation hopeless and withdrew their troops. A few tried to rally them for another attack, but no men seemed interested.[33] Survivors pulled comrades from the wire into shell holes. Even though he had a badly shattered jaw, Private Thomas Jackson dragged Sergeant Lewis Marshall, whose shoulder blade had been practically blown away, into a shell hole. 'He offered to bandage me up and did his best to try and persuade me to make for our lives. I would not go,' recorded Marshall, who perhaps preferred the temporary safety of a shell hole to the risk of running across open ground swept with explosions and gunfire.[34]

Australians sheltering further back in reserve at the Pozières Cemetery watched as a steady stream of wounded men returned from the front line. Later, unwounded men began to stream back as well. 'Where are you going?' asked one man.

'Back to Sausage Valley to reorganise,' they were said to have replied.³⁵

Private Walter Elkington was one of the 20th Battalion soldiers in reserve, responsible for carrying loads of bombs forward to the attacking troops. He was just about to race through the barrage to the front line when an officer staggered into the trench and announced that the attack had ended in failure.³⁶

The 6th and 7th Brigade headquarters were virtually cut off from their crippled battalions because shelling had severed nearly all telephone wires. Gellibrand slept on in his dugout bunkroom, only waking occasionally to receive messages from runners or signallers. An anxious Paton, also cut off from his troops, repeatedly phoned Gellibrand, alarmed about the uninterrupted machine-gun fire and the lack of news on the battle's progress. At around 2.00 a.m., the first uncertain reports filtered through to Gellibrand that the attack 'didn't come off'. By dawn, which came at 4.45 a.m., he had enough snippets of information to realise that the attack had failed.³⁷

In the half-light of dawn, a heavy mist shrouded the battlefield, hiding the horrors of the previous night. Under its veil, stretcher-bearers collected the injured. The wounded and the lost tried to work their way back to their own lines. As the light increased, the Germans could see the countless Australians lying on their wire entanglements 'in a carpet' — in some places two or three men deep. One German regimental history described it as 'an appalling sight'.³⁸

The Germans tended to the wounded Australians close by and refrained from firing on the stretcher-bearers. The seriously wounded, who couldn't be moved, were left to die. Sometimes the German soldiers gave them comforting a drink of spirits to help with the pain, but mostly they ignored them, instead rifling through their belongings for rations and souvenirs. Private Wisbey Sinclair lay near the wire all night while German soldiers diligently foraged through the pockets of the dead and helpless. He heard a German walking toward him so he 'played possum'; another German later attempted to take his watch. When the soldier discovered that Sinclair was alive, he called his comrades. 'They got my groundsheet from my pack, spread it on the ground, lifted me on it and carried me into their front line trench,' wrote Sinclair.[39]

Lewis Marshall was hiding in a shell hole when dawn broke. A few Germans 'came over and spoke', and two picked him up. They accidentally wrenched his shoulder; Marshall lost consciousness. 'When I came to, I found myself in a deep dugout,' he later wrote. He was treated there and then transported away on a makeshift stretcher. He spent the rest of the war as a prisoner.[40]

German intelligence officers interrogated their Australian prisoners, including Marshall and Sinclair. According to German records of interviews, some distraught prisoners divulged nearly every detail of the attack. Others said that they were sick of the war and happy to be taken prisoner.[41] A German officer observed that a few prisoners who had already fought on Gallipoli were of good military bearing, although the majority, who had arrived as reinforcements, left a rather lamentable impression: 'Apparently they only volunteered for military service because it offered a cheap way to see something of the world and a chance to play at soldiering on the side.'[42]

Some prisoners did not make it back for interrogation. Sergeant Bruce Drayton recounted an exchange between 20-year-old Private Noel Sainsbury and a German officer. 'Are you a machine-gunner?' the German officer asked the wounded Sainsbury.

'Yes sir,' replied Sainsbury.

The officer drew his pistol and shot him through the chest and head. 'That is the way I deal with English swine.'[43]

It seemed machine-gunners received rough handling in both German and Australian hands.

The heavy German shelling slackened about mid-morning, by which time a shimmering heat had burnt off the morning mist, revealing iridescent blue skies. The battlefield remained strangely quiet. Fred Hocking, who had been stranded in no-man's-land since just after midnight, was one of the few wounded to make it back. He explained in a letter to his father how he bound his wound with a mud-stained puttee and crawled toward his own lines: 'I'd gone what must have been 100 yards but what seemed a life time journey when I found one of my sergeants in a shell hole ... We hailed each other with delight and started afresh.'[44] By late afternoon, the cries from the wounded in no-man's-land became weaker and less frequent; fewer men returned to the lines. Over the next two days, the odd man made it back, but most of the remaining wounded were either captured or died from their wounds.

Survivors assembled in Sausage Valley. Officers and soldiers reflected quietly on the wretched attack. 'Our Colonel stood on the side of the road as we passed and he was not ashamed of the tears that were plainly visible on his face,' remembered 22-year-old Private Edgar Morrow, 28th Battalion.[45]

At the 23rd Battalion's rollcall, Lieutenant Goldy Raws, along with 325 other men, did not answer. Raws was posted as missing. 'I heard that he was seen badly wounded but cannot vouch for that,' speculated a soldier some time later. 'As a rule if anyone goes beyond the objective and heavy artillery fire is on, it is unlikely that they will come through alive.'[46]

Alec Raws heard of Goldy's disappearance, but he was unsure of what had happened. 'He could not have died in agony because our stretcher-bearers were out in no-man's-land that same night, and then next day, and he could not have been missed,' he wrote reassuringly in a letter to his older brother, Lennon. 'Possibly too, he may have been taken away wounded by a British brigade on our left.'[47]

Goldy was merely one of over 1000 soldiers killed, missing, or wounded in the failed assault. The attack had shattered Paton's brigade: his 28th Battalion suffered over 470 casualties; its four company commanders were dead or wounded. Paton's 25th Battalion suffered 343 casualties; the 26th Battalion, 297.[48] Edgar Morrow remembered the survivors of Paton's brigade gathering around the cookers for a warm meal. 'Normally it's three to a loaf and a scarcity of bacon,' he noted. 'But that morning we could have two loaves and as much bacon as we could eat.'[49]

The Australians' fight for Pozières had been raging for a week. In the battle's first days, Hooky Walker had captured Pozières with light casualties. In the following days, the front line had barely moved forward. Instead, soldiers such as Arthur Foxcroft and John Harris had suffered under an unrelenting German bombardment, which eventually broke Harris's spirit and destroyed Foxcroft's platoon. When Legge's troops took over the line mid-week, the same bombardment killed Goldy Raws. It seemed that the second week of fighting would be more of the same: the remorseless Gough would continue to thrust Legge's division at the ridge-top trenches in a piecemeal fashion and, once the 2nd Division was totally spent, the 4th Division would be shunted forward to take its place. It appeared that Gough's and Haig's objectives were at odds: Haig wanted to conserve troops prior to his September offensive while Gough could only seize the ridge by employing more troops. In the meantime, the Australian troops, who had previously harboured dreams of victory and glory, were being ground to ash. What would August bring?

CHAPTER TEN

Promised Land

'You can no more win a war than you can win an earthquake.'
— attributed to Jeannette Rankin, the first woman elected to the United States Congress

That morning at divisional headquarters, Legge attempted to piece together what had happened. In his report on the operation, he tried unconvincingly to present the capture and holding of a small stretch of trench that Gellibrand's 23rd Battalion had dug as some kind of minor victory. He also vigorously defended the 7th Brigade's performance, stating that the troops had conducted themselves excellently: 'And the advance of the three battalions ... in the centre particularly well carried out as on an ordinary parade.'[1] Legge's praise couldn't hide the facts: his division had failed miserably in its attack, casualties were severe, and his shattered battalions were now vulnerable to counterattack. His division had suffered 1500 casualties in the two-day bombardment and, according to his report, another 1372 in the attack. Charles Bean concluded that the attack had been a 'wholesale failure', partly due to the short, 'ineffective' bombardment.[2]

While many commanders basked in the glory of the 1st Division's success — Walker, Birdie, White, Haig, and Gough — Legge's failure would be shunned. Over the next days Birdie, Gough, and White would carefully distance themselves from Legge. Gough's staff would subtly plant the seed with Haig that Legge was to blame for the failure.[3] Birdie would have no doubt reminded everyone that Legge had decided the attack's timing. Someone had to be blamed for the wanton waste of men, and Legge seemed a convenient scapegoat.

Had Birdie and White contributed to the disaster? The straight-shooting Gellibrand blamed them, saying that Birdie and his staff should have provided Legge with a really good team; he said that everyone knew the 2nd Division's staff was of poor quality.[4] It was a fair criticism: White should have worked more closely with Legge in checking the plan, making sure that it had every chance of success, and Birdie should have shielded Legge from Gough's pressuring.[5] (Admittedly, no one ever wanted to take on the prickly Gough, who had a reputation for dealing ruthlessly with over-cautious commanders — and Birdie would have known that corps commanders were not a protected species, as Gough had recently sacked Lieutenant-General Sir Thomas Morland, X British Corps commander.)[6]

Although White should probably have shared some of the blame for the failure, Birdie already seemed to have his scapegoat, and White was too valuable to lose. In his *Official History*, Bean largely absolved White of blame, claiming that he was 'full of misgiving' prior to the attack, but had for once allowed the confidence of others to bear down on his judgement.[7] White later admitted in a candid conversation with Bean: 'I was sure it was wrong, I was sure things were not ready but everyone was so eager. I gave my consent — through weakness I suppose.'[8]

News of Legge's failure soon reached Haig. 'I think the cause was due to want of thorough preparation,' he concluded in his diary. He cited four shortcomings: the attacking troops were not formed square to the objective, the advance was made over 700 yards, one brigade arrived late and didn't have a chance to reconnoitre, and the hurricane artillery bombardment lasted for only one minute before the attack. After lunch on Saturday 29 July, Haig motored out to Gough's Reserve Army Headquarters in the hamlet of Toutencourt. He impressed upon Gough and his general staff officer, General Neill Malcolm, that they must supervise the plans of the I Anzac Corps more closely. 'Some of their Divisional Generals are so ignorant and (like many Colonials) so conceited, they cannot be trusted to work out unaided the plan of attack.'[9]

Haig then travelled to I Anzac Corps headquarters at Contay and summoned Birdie and White for an impromptu meeting. Haig didn't like Birdie — he considered him a shameless self-promoter who put popularity ahead of discipline, an amateur who thought he knew all about war on the Western Front because he'd been on Gallipoli. Birdie may have been the Australian Imperial Force's 'kingmaker',[10] but in Haig's world he was an outsider — an Anglo-Indian officer, a relic of the Kitchener era who didn't have the brains to attend Staff College.

Haig rarely showed emotion, but when he did, according to Charteris, there was a telltale broadening of his accent toward Doric.[11] That afternoon, it must have been broad. The private conversation — reconstructed from Haig's diary entries, Bean's notes, and White's correspondence with Bean in 1928 — was brutally frank. Haig launched into Birdie:

> You can't come here, as you do, after your victories at Gallipoli and imagine you can tackle this enemy as you were fighting the filthy Bashi-bazouks! You're not fighting the Bashi-bazouks now! This is serious scientific war and you are up against the most scientific and military nation in Europe.

Pointing to a map, Haig recounted the attack's shortcomings. Pozières, he said, had been captured thanks to 'very thorough artillery preparation' and the French had often spent up to a fortnight in taking such villages. An artillery bombardment of only a minute was simply inadequate. As for Legge, he was overconfident and had rough-and-ready methods. Haig disparagingly referred to Legge as a 'buck-stick' (an Anglo-Indian colloquialism meaning a chatterer or braggart), who was 'quite confident upon no foundation of knowledge or experience'. White tried to interject on two occasions, but an angry Haig wouldn't let him speak, lecturing him: 'Listen to what I say young man, I am giving you the benefit of my experience.' The usually dutiful White bristled at what he perceived to be a severe dressing-down.

When the lecture ended, Haig walked to the door. White cleared his throat and, ignoring a warning headshake from one of Haig's staff, said, 'I can't let you go sir.'[12] He then went to a map and defended the 2nd Division point by point. He told Haig how Gough had pushed Legge into action without any regard for adequate preparations; he intimated that what the British staff officer had told him about the attack was untrue. He defended Legge, saying that, despite his casual demeanour, he 'had not undertaken the task in a light hearted spirit'.

Haig was known for bringing meetings to an abrupt end — Charteris recorded in his biography of Haig that the general had once ordered an officer who had vigorously defended his own point of view to leave the room. However, Haig heard White through. He then placed a kindly hand on White's shoulder and uttered approvingly: 'I dare say you are right young man.'[13]

White had taken a grave risk in challenging Haig. Why did he do it? Perhaps he did not want to see an injustice done to the Australians. Perhaps he sensed Haig's contempt for Birdie and feared that his own career could be affected; after all, he was the one who should have been supervising Legge's plans. Or perhaps White thought it was a good time to come out from behind Birdie's shadow — his private letters reveal that his relationship with Birdie may not have been completely harmonious. In September 1916 he would write to Ethel that Birdie had 'very little idea of the machinery which gets done all the things he wants'. Months later, he would criticise Birdie for not rewarding him with the honours he felt he deserved. His disapproval would peak in mid-1917, when he referred to Birdie as 'a man of no quality' in a letter to Jack Gellibrand.[14] No doubt White was loyal to Birdie, but perhaps even his loyalty knew some bounds.

The politically astute Birdie, who had said nothing during the meeting — Bean speculated that he was probably a little out of his depth — would have sensed Haig's contempt and realised that he could not afford to fail again. He believed there would one day be an official Australian army fighting in this war, with all the Australian corps in Europe consolidated into it, and he wanted to command it. Yet White seemed to be firming as a rival, even though he lacked divisional command experience.

Birdie and White, prior to the meeting with Haig, had conferred with Legge to discuss their next move. Could the 2nd Division mount another attack? The 4th Division was not ready to take over the line and, according to the *Official History*, Legge wanted to give his division another chance to leave Pozières as heroes, like the 1st Division. White and Birdie carefully considered his offer. They decided to give him one more chance, but this time White would closely supervise the plan. Perhaps Birdie and White's decision was influenced by the reports from Charteris's intelligence team that explained that exhausted German divisions were withdrawing from the Somme at an alarming rate. Their morale was reportedly irreparably damaged.[15] Perhaps the next defeat, like capturing the Pozières ridge, could bring this seemingly invincible foe to its knees.

Astonishingly, the follow-up attack on the OG lines was planned for the next day, Sunday 30 July. This date was chosen because the two neighbouring British corps would be attacking, which would hopefully tax the Germans' defences more severely. The main commitment from the conference was that the jumping-off trenches would be dug within 200 yards of the German trenches.[16]

After the conference, White, keen to avoid the previous day's mistakes, wrote out a detailed memorandum for Legge, describing what preparations had to be completed before launching the attack. White insisted that the whole operation had to be undertaken deliberately; the progress of the preparations would determine the actual attack date, he told Legge.[17] This was fine in theory, but would the impetuous Gough be as accommodating of White's advice as Haig had been? And with the Australians under a constant barrage, would they soon have too few men to mount a successful attack?

According to the *Official History*, on Saturday evening, 29 July, the planned attack for the next day was delayed because it became obvious that White's prescribed preparations would not be completed before Sunday evening. It appeared that the 2nd Division's initial attack date had been hastily selected in the vain hope of assaulting with the Fourth Army, rather than based on a realistic preparation time.

The Australians' preparations for the rescheduled attack were marked by sober caution. Legge's brigade commanders, perhaps sensing their troops' plummeting morale, baulked at the proposition of another night attack because the darkness, coupled with exploding shells and flares, confused their men. In response, Legge proposed a twilight attack, at 9.15 p.m.; however, this required the digging of separate approach trenches for each brigade so the Germans couldn't observe the attackers moving up to their jumping-off trenches. Legge believed these additional works would not be finished before 2 August.

The late arrival of orders for the digging of the jumping-off trenches, on Monday evening, threatened to delay the attack again. About 1200 yards of trenches had to be dug, which required 575 men to dig just over two yards each. An additional 450 men were allocated to digging the communication trenches that soldiers would use to reach the front line. Despite extensive efforts, several commanders were shocked the next morning when reports reached them that little progress had occurred the previous evening. Some officers reported that German shelling had prevented their men from digging. Legge's chief-of-staff, Colonel Arthur Holroyd Bridges, believed the troops were ignorant of the urgency. He wrote to Brigadier-General Paton, whose 7th Brigade troops were responsible for the task, telling him 'straight' that if casualties resulted from the digging, so be it.[18]

Legge and Bridges did not fully appreciate the appalling conditions their men were working under. Alec Raws, unfortunate enough to be leading one of the digging parties, recorded the horrors that he and other men experienced that night. Raws was bombarded all the way up the communication trenches. Once in no-man's-land, which was littered with stinking corpses, he could not find the appointed site and did not have the slightest idea where his or the German lines were. 'I would have gladly shot myself,' he wrote candidly in a letter to his sister. 'It was awful, but we had to drive the men by every possible means. And dig ourselves. The wounded and killed had to be thrown to one side. I refused to let any sound man help a wounded man. The sound men had to dig. Many men went mad.' Raws admitted that he threatened to shoot the broken men to shake them into activity.[19] Private Alfred Stewart, who sheltered in a trench close to Raws, was driven to despair by the shelling that night, writing in his diary: 'Thank God! our dear home folk, do not know what we have to go through here ... I wonder why this fearful war is allowed to go on, in what we call civilized times are we really civilized?'[20]

On Monday 31 July, Bean had trudged up to Pozières to view things firsthand. It was the first time he had visited the village since the battle erupted. The state it was in shocked him: the powdered debris of houses, he wrote in his diary, was spread like ashes six feet deep; the ground was as featureless as the Sahara, and 'level except for the shell craters which lay edge to edge'. In his 1917 book, *Letters from France*, he wrote that it reminded him of some 'broken down creek bed' in Outback Australia, 'abandoned for generations to the goats'.[21]

Bean then followed a small exposed track, ducking for safety every time a shell burst overhead, searching for the 19th and 21st battalions. He finally discovered the remnants of a deserted trench.

'There were only blackened dead and occasionally bits of men — torn bits of limbs unrecognisable — along it,' he recorded. He eventually stumbled upon a few tired men of Gellibrand's 6th Brigade, who would be expected to attack the OG lines in a few days' time.

Bean had soon seen enough. 'I know of nothing approaching that desolation ... there is no sign of life at all.'[22] With the help of a guide, he left the godforsaken village. That night, he camped near Bécourt Château, located between Pozières and Albert. The Germans' sporadic shelling of the nearby wood and the tormented cries of wounded men coming from the darkness affected him. 'I find this constant sort of shelling very trying when it's on,' he wrote in his diary.[23] Bean's biographer, Dudley McCarthy, believed his journey through the trenches that day left him deeply shaken.[24] It's quite plausible that he was experiencing the first signs of shell shock. 'I don't want to go through Pozières again,' he admitted. 'I have seen it now once — it was a quiet day. It was far worse than Fricourt and Boiselle.'[25]

As a steady stream of wounded passed by the château, Bean worked on his next despatch. He reflected on the tired troops he had observed that day: 'Of the men whom you find there what can one say?'[26] Surely Bean now realised that his romanticised image of the Anzacs at war was an illusion: they weren't sleeping comfortably under the open stars, but cowering in trenches under terrible bombardments; weren't using their bushman skills to cook meat or bake damper, but scavenging rations from their dead comrades; weren't trekking across the country on wild brumbies, but crawling on their hands and knees along broken trenches.[27] They were dying in droves due to this murderous industrialised war. There was nothing romantic about it.

Did Bean, having witnessed the horrors of Pozières, rethink the tenor of his most recent despatches, which had glorified the Anzacs' exploits?[28] It wasn't a straightforward question — Bean knew that the censors forbade criticism.[29] Furthermore, although committed to reporting truthfully, he refused to write anything that needlessly distressed soldiers' families, questioned authority, or second-guessed strategy.[30] We can only speculate why he chose to omit the hellish conditions at Pozières in his despatches: perhaps he reasoned that when fighting for civilization one had to expect a frightful toll; or that, if he described what he saw, the people at home might recoil at the war's terrible cost. It is possible that he viewed his despatches as a means to fortify their resolve to support the conflict — after all, he did believe that the Teutonic Hun had to be crushed.

Bean now appeared to be recording two versions of the battle. His despatches remained positive, telling of heroic acts, victories, and advances; his personal diary became more melancholy, giving vent to his own doubts. The 'truth' that Bean had vowed to record was becoming more difficult to grasp by the day.

While the Australians planned their next attack on the OG lines, concerns were intensifying in London about the Somme offensive. The War Council — a forum established by the British prime minister, Herbert Asquith, in January 1915 to decide wartime 'high policy' — wanted to understand the return that such large losses justified. General Headquarters despatches outlining advances were not enough. The offensive needed to shorten the war.

On Saturday 29 July, a nervous Field Marshal Sir William Robertson, chief of the Imperial General Staff, had written to Haig explaining that 'the powers that be' were beginning to get a little uneasy in regard to the situation — it seemed the field marshal had been unsettled by a damning critique penned and circulated to cabinet by Winston Churchill, in which he labelled the Somme offensive as 'disastrous'. Robertson's letter asked if the loss of 300,000 men would really lead to great results. If not, should they revise and limit their plans? Why did it seem that the British were bearing the brunt of the fighting, while the French seemed to be doing little? Had not the primary objective of relieving the pressure on Verdun been achieved, at least to some extent?[31]

On 1 August, after studying Robertson's letter, Haig drafted a response.³² Typical of Haig, it was unrelenting and unequivocal: 'Maintain the offensive!' He also warned that there would be more Sommes to come. 'It would not be justifiable to calculate on the Enemy's resistance being completely broken without another campaign next year,' he wrote.

Haig's alleged bloody-mindedness and obsession with wearing battles that cost hundreds of thousands of lives resulted in him becoming one of the most controversial and possibly vilified figures of the Great War. The boom in war books in the late 1920s and early 1930s fuelled the enduring image of Haig as a woodenheaded, red-faced, moustachioed general who sat in his château headquarters, well behind the lines, as he ordered waves of infantry through barbed-wire trenches. These books typically consisted of two types: political memoirs, such as those by Winston Churchill and Lloyd George, that shifted blame for the bloodshed from themselves to the generals; and anti-war stories by soldiers — such as Siegfried Sassoon's *Memoirs of George Sherston*, Robert Graves's *Goodbye to All That*, and Reich Maria Remarque's *All Quiet on the Western Front* — that portrayed the war as utterly futile.³³

On 1 August, as Haig drafted his response to the War Council, he would have sensed that his window for achieving measurable results on the Somme was closing. It was becoming more important that key strongholds such as the Pozières ridge, Mouquet Farm, and Thiepval be taken without delay so that he could launch his planned September offensive, which he hoped would bring the success he so desperately sought. All this depended on the Australians capturing the seemingly impregnable OG lines within the next few days.

On the evening of 1 August, the Anzacs cancelled their nightly artillery arrangements because troops complained that on previous evenings shells had dropped short and killed or injured those digging in no-man's-land. Consequently, the 7th Brigade reported the next morning that its forward line was almost finished, and the 6th Brigade reported its digging practically complete. Nevertheless, according to the *Official History*, the 2nd Division staff delayed the attack again to 3 August; they were confident that all works would be completed by then.[34]

However, at corps headquarters on 2 August, White, somewhat apprehensive after his dressing-down from Haig, carefully studied aerial photographs of no-man's-land to assess whether the freshly dug jumping-off trenches were satisfactory. He became alarmed by their poor state and rang Gough to express his concerns. Gough still wanted an early attack and said that he had been assured by Legge that preparations were adequate. 'Well you can order them to do it if you like and of course they will do it,' replied White; he then carefully explained to Gough why the attack should be delayed. Gough reluctantly left it to White to decide the issue. White, who suspected that Legge's officers were too optimistic about the state of preparations, postponed the assault for another 24 hours. Colonel Bridges, possibly sensing White's heavy hand in the division's change of plans, wrote to the brigade commanders: 'This gives us a bit more time for preparation, and more time to the Boche as well.'[35]

The following day, on 3 August — five days after the initial attack had been scheduled — Gough met with Haig and blamed the Australian corps for putting off the attack again. He told Haig he was so concerned with the delay that he had called for a written explanation. Haig wrote in his diary afterward that the delay was due 'to the ignorance of the Australian 2nd Division staff and that the GOC [General Officer Commanding] Legge was not much good'.[36]

The constant delays frayed the soldiers' nerves. 'Each night we expected to go up and take the ridge, but they kept on postponing it,' read Private Arthur Clifford's diary.[37] With each delay, rumours had circulated among the shaken soldiers: some believed the attack had been fixed for the following day, others claimed it had been further postponed, while most hoped it would be cancelled altogether.[38]

On 5 August, Field Marshal Willliam Robertson tabled Haig's reply to his letter dated 29 July. In responding to the War Council's concerns about the excessive loss of men, Haig reasoned: 'Our losses in July's fighting totalled about 120,000 more than they would have been, had we not attacked.'[39] Undoubtedly crude reckoning such as this led Haig's most fervent critic, future British prime minister Lloyd George, to conclude that he lacked those qualities which were essential in a great commander in the greatest war that was ever seen — 'it was far beyond his mental equipment,' he wrote.[40] In *War Memoirs*, Lloyd George defined the necessary qualities: the commander saw the ground upon which he fought, adapted to the changing conditions of war, and fostered innovation in his subordinates.[41]

Lloyd George's criticism of Haig might be seen as unfair — wasn't such a war beyond anyone's mental equipment? After all, by 1916, the greatest generals of the era had fallen on their swords. Russian general Alexander Samsonov had blown his brains out in a quiet wood after the annihilation of his army three weeks into the war. The nerve of German general Helmuth von Moltke gave way a few weeks later, after his armies were checked on the Marne. Haig's predecessor, General Sir John French, whose moods swung dangerously between unrealistic optimism and utter pessimism, was summarily dismissed only one year into the war.[42] All these men had struggled with the scope, scale, and complexity of the Great War.[43] Haig was one of few prominent commanders to outlast the war.

Before condemning Haig as a butcher and bungler, it pays to understand the immense complexities he faced on the Somme. It fell to Haig to oversee the logistics of the offensive and, as Charteris pointed out, it is inconceivable to imagine what it took to feed, administer, move, and tend to the medical and spiritual requirements of one million men, even if they were not engaged in fighting in a foreign country. The aftermath of each battle resembled the devastation caused by an earthquake or tornado, with buildings smashed, communications severed, supply lines wrecked, and thousands killed.

And the unrelenting office hours were far longer than those of a civilian officer in peacetime. 'There are few if any officers who would not do a fourteen-hour day,' Charteris noted.[44]

Over the course of the war, Haig's armies had expanded at a staggering rate. At the start of the war, the British Expeditionary Force consisted of about 70,000 soldiers in six divisions. By the time that fighting began on the Somme in July 1916, he controlled ten times that.[45] Even Lloyd George conceded that Haig had the overwhelming task of commanding a force 'five times as great as the largest army ever commanded by Napoleon'.[46] Haig's task was further exacerbated by the dearth of experienced officers available to command the divisions in his expanding armies.[47] Rapid promotions resulted; Gough went from commanding a brigade of 4000 to an army of 'half a million men' in a couple of years.[48] This pattern was repeated down through the ranks.

The gargantuan expansion of Haig's forces, according to Ian Brown's study *British Logistics on the Western Front*, placed enormous stress on the army's archaic systems. The daily needs of a single division filled one half of a train. For the Somme, 63 packed trains were needed per week.[49] Haig had to revolutionise the army's transport systems to cope, calling in civilian experts to transform each mode of transport — roads, canals, and rail — into an integrated network.[50]

Haig's rapidly expanding force also quickly outgrew its rudimentary communication systems. On the Somme, his armies communicated via a network of telephones linked by 7000 miles of buried cable and 48,000 miles of above-ground cable.[51] Yet once a battle erupted, shellfire inevitably severed some of these cables, leaving commanders, from brigadiers up to Haig, cut off from their front-line troops.

Haig's challenges were immense, and beyond the grasp of any mortal man. John Terraine, in *Douglas Haig*, noted that even the commander-in-chief himself conceeded this: 'I feel that one's best can go but a short way without help from above.'[52]

There was an air of nervous expectancy at I Anzac Corps headquarters on the muggy morning of Friday 4 August. After seven days of digging trenches, re-equipping soldiers, reinforcing platoons, and reorganising battalions, the day of the 2nd Division's follow-up attack on the OG lines had finally arrived. Birdie, as on most other mornings, was up by sunrise.

After leaving the divisional headquarters at Albert, Birdie recognised a group of soldiers gathered by a wood. They were Australians just out of the line, busy boiling tea, making damper, cooking beef, and cleaning up. He walked among them, animated and full of nervous energy, drawing from one and then another stories of the fighting they had just experienced. He knew some of the boys, having most likely met them on Gallipoli and in Egypt, and addressed them by their Christian names. He listened to their yarns; he seemed genuinely interested in what they had to say. In turn, the men felt familiar enough to invite him to have a cup of tea with the 'mob'.[53] Afterward, Birdie, as always, had one piece of parting advice: 'Write home and let your mothers know where you are, what you are doing and how you are,' he advised. 'If you don't they will write to me.'[54]

For Birdie, being a general seemed all about getting in among the men, feeling their presence, cheering them up, and maintaining their morale. Unwittingly, anticipating the nickname that would come to spread in 1916, he told newspaper proprietor Lord Northcliffe: 'My boys are good diggers. They dig deep and quickly and the trenches are so clean you could eat off them at dinner.' In turn, the men liked Birdie. Some battalion diaries recorded how he showed interest in them individually, in their home lives and the different parts of Australia they had come from. He was one of the few 'red-tabbed Johnnies' that could move among them unpretentiously.[55]

The trouble was that Birdie's leadership style appeared to belong to another era. Fostering an offensive spirit among the troops was not as crucial as closely overseeing the infinitely complex logistics of supplying them. Too often, Birdie seemed to neglect critical planning matters, leaving them for White to work through. Birdie, as a corps commander, should have been checking, questioning, overseeing, and improving these plans.[56] Two years earlier, when armies were smaller, no one predicted that corps commanders would be controlling such large masses of troops; now that this was a reality, no one was quite sure what they were supposed to do — least of all Birdie.[57] In 1914, a corps had been a grouping of divisions, their only permanent units a headquarters and a signal company. By 1916, the so-called corps troops had expanded to include artillery, engineers, intelligence, and administration staff. The corps commander thus became a vital liaison between the army (the headquarters responsible for drawing up directions) and the division (the formation responsible for carrying out the plan of attack).[58]

Yet Birdie's most troubling weakness was his lack of perspective. On Gallipoli he visited his men and then returned to headquarters without having received any reliable tactical information. 'I found that you could never rely on it being at all like the fact,' complained White.[59] Immediately before the Gallipoli evacuation, Birdie's thoughts were preoccupied with 'how surprised the Turks would be to find them [Anzac trenches] so clean and in such perfect order'. Pozières was no different — Birdie rambled on to Lord Northcliffe about how clean his boys' trenches were.[60] He told Lord Derby that the taking of Pozières wasn't 'such a difficult job'.[61] He recounted stories of troops bayoneting 300 Germans in the 23 July attack, which he thought vitally important because 'it does a lot of good in keeping up the right spirit of the men'.[62] Birdie appeared dangerously detached from the corps' important problems.

The troubling question was, even if Birdie were to choose to devote more time to organising the efforts of his divisions, did he have the brains to do it? On Gallipoli, Birdie's antics were a touch eccentric. At Pozières, they were becoming downright dangerous. What effect would his shortcomings have on the attack that evening?

While Birdie greeted his 'boys', the final preparations for the follow-up assault on the OG lines were completed. This time, the German trenches had been subjected to many days of heavy bombardment. Brigade diaries document the fact that additional stretcher-bearers had been organised to collect the inevitable casualties; mortar crews were ready to fire off the smoke shells to screen the troops' advance, and soldiers had been instructed — to their great relief — that the despised tin discs which had been attached to their backs could be hidden until they were required for signalling. Importantly, troops knew exactly what was expected of them: 'Our orders are, even if we are to go through Hell, we must take that position,' Arthur Clifford recalled.[63]

The Germans sensed that another attack was imminent. Throughout the day, Allied spotter aeroplanes had directed the British artillery's fire upon any dugout they saw, and the Germans were too scared to show themselves. 'Hostile airmen — always 6 to ten above us and only 100 metres up — none of our airmen and no anti-aircraft guns — nothing. It was enough to make one despair,' wrote a German soldier.[64] General Max von Gallwitz, commander of the First and Second German armies, tried to rally his troops for the inevitable, advising them in his order of the day that the enemy was expected to attack in strength during the coming days and that the decisive battle of the war would be fought out on the battlefield of the Somme. He finished by stating that the enemy's assault 'must be smashed before the wall of German men'.[65]

One German soldier who would form part of von Gallwitz's 'wall' watched the telling signs of the impending attack. 'In front of Pozières we can see the English working,' he wrote. 'Between 5 and 7 strongest English artillery fire and trench mortars. Thick clouds of dust make it impossible for our artillery to see the red lights fired by us.'[66] Another demoralised German soldier thought there was only one way to escape the looming battle: 'The best thing that can happen is to get a slight wound.'

The first waves of troops would leave their jumping-off trenches at 9.15 p.m., with subsequent waves advancing 15 minutes later. Gellibrand, frustrated by the communication problems that had plagued him in the first attack, had shifted his headquarters from Sausage Valley up to the Pozières cemetery, which sat on the cusp of the front line. Extra telephone wires were also laid and laddered to aid uninterrupted communication.[67]

At the allotted time, the Australians, having navigated their way to the jumping-off trenches without major incident, waited quietly in the warm dusk in the minutes before the attack. 'The men hardly dared look at one other,' remembered one soldier, 'the old hands were fighting grimly against the fear, the new hands were struggling against the oppression of an ordeal of which they knew nothing except by hearsay but which they felt was momentous.'[68] All knew that the first objective, the German front trench, was about 300 to 400 yards away, and that despite the numerous shell holes they ought to reach it in about six minutes.

At 9.14 p.m., just before the hurricane bombardment opened, three red German flares arced into the sky, bursting into stars. Seconds later, exploding shells illuminated the night: the final three-minute hurricane bombardment had begun. Across a front of about 1300 yards, over 1000 men had started their jog-walk across the dry, pitted battlefield. This time, at twilight, they managed to keep their footing. In spite of their natural instincts to maintain a safe distance from the exploding shells, they hugged the bombardment that edged forward in front of them (this method ensured that the attackers were on their enemy immediately after the barrage passed over their trenches). 'Onwards we floundered through the soft shell-torn ground,' remembered Walter Elkington, 'narrowly escaping a shell-burst alongside, over numerous dead men.'[69] The third, fourth, and fifth waves readied themselves for their advance 15 minutes later.

After five long minutes, the first wave of Australians reached OG1. The bombardment seemed to have done its job — very few

Germans had time to leave their dugouts and mount their guns, and there was only sporadic machine-gun fire. The 20th Battalion succeeded in capturing its objective. Its third and fourth waves leapfrogged through, capturing the second trench over the ridge, which was nothing more than a wilderness of craters and shredded wire entanglements. 'We did not find a solitary live German,' recorded Walter Elkington, 'although dozens of dead ones were lying about in what was left of the trenches.' The demoralised Germans withdrew over the ridge, leaving behind many valuable machine guns with the breech blocks removed.

North of the main road, Paton's three battalions crossed no-man's-land with little opposition. Gellibrand's 22nd Battalion, further north, adjacent to the Courcelette track, secured their objective. By 12.15 a.m., the 2nd Division had captured both trenches.

John Treloar, back at I Anzac Corps headquarters, had watched the wild flashes of light coming from the ridge, and wondered whether the division could hold on. 'The shellfire is terrific and the ground seems to be moving the whole time,' he recorded in his diary.[70]

Sheltering in Gellibrand's dugout, Charles Bean had been anxious about the attack all day. At about midnight, he heard five tremendous explosions from the other side of the ridge; objects were thrown hundreds of feet into the air. Bean interpreted this as a good sign, writing: 'looks as if [the] enemy were blowing up their ammunition'.[71]

The captured trenches had to be consolidated quickly — the ridge was a significant loss to the Germans, and they would doubtless retaliate. 'We feverishly set to work deepening our trenches and building up the parapets,' wrote Elkington.[72] The Germans shifted their bombardment to land just behind the trenches to prevent the Australians from reinforcing. Many digging parties, carrying much-needed picks and shovels, failed to make it through. Those who did were 'bombarded something awful and casualties began to occur in every shell hole'.[73] The 22nd Battalion had only brought a few picks and shovels forward, so that troops such as 20-year-old

Lance-Corporal William Hatcher, a farmer from the backwater town of Goyura, in western Victoria, had to dig with their entrenching tools. The Lewis-gun and Stokes-mortar crews, desperately needed to shore up the defensive line, were blocked from coming forward. Forward posts along the new front remained unlinked, meaning that pockets of soldiers were only vaguely aware of their neighbours' position. The Australians' hold on the OG lines remained tenuous.[74]

The expected German counterattack came quickly from the southern side of the Courcelette track, at 3.45 a.m. on Tuesday 5 August. It targeted Paton's weakened 25th Battalion, made up of troops from Queensland. Some Germans forced their way into OG1, and soldiers clubbed and jabbed at each other with rifle butts and shovels. The remaining attackers panicked, bunched together, and were met with machine-gun fire. Two companies were sent forward to support the exhausted Queenslanders, who feared that their newly won positions would be overrun. Some Germans, overwhelmed by machine-gun fire and trench mortars, sunk in to shell holes, while those near OG1 realised they were outnumbered, and surrendered.

A second counterattack came just on daybreak at the northern end of the OG lines, where William Hatcher and the other men of the 22nd and 26th battalions sheltered. About 150 Germans advanced from the valley in front of Courcelette. Snipers positioned 40 yards from OG2 initially prevented the Australians from returning fire, yet gradually Australian riflemen suppressed the fire, and the assault suddenly came to a standstill 200 yards short of OG2. 'As soon as those dirty Huns found they were in for a bad time they threw down their rifles and put their hands up and we were forced to take the lot prisoner,' wrote Percy Blythe. 'And you just ought to see them go back to our lines, they were anxious that the guard could not stay with them.'[75]

Captain Frank Corney of the 26th Battalion, who was sheltering in the trenches, remembered vividly, as daylight came, Germans popping up from the shell holes just in front of him, holding their hands up and coming in to be taken prisoner. 'In the distance you could see the German artillery and some infantry scampering for their lives over the hills and out of sight,' he wrote in a letter home.[76]

The Australians, in the morning light, surveyed their newly won position. Most had a clear view toward the German-held villages of Le Sars, Courcelette, and Bapaume. It was like seeing the Promised Land: green, open fields and unimpeded views as far as the eye could see; ripe wheat upon the far slopes; and a church spire rising through a clump of trees on a near crest.[77]

Walter Elkington, who was sheltering in a German communication trench when morning broke, liked what he saw. 'We had captured the Windmill [100 yards past the OG lines and adjacent to the Bapaume road] and its big dugouts and had the satisfaction of seeing about 300 Germans surrender to men on our immediate left,' he recounted in his memoirs.[78]

One surrendering German officer asked his captors, 'Are you in Courcelette?' The officer had incorrectly assumed that the Australians had advanced over the ridge and on to the German-held village of Courcelette, about two miles away.[79]

The German defenders had fallen into utter disarray. Their command structures had been savaged, they had few or no reserves left, the trench line protecting Courcelette was incomplete, and its batteries were dangerously short of ammunition. 'If the enemy's attack had continued,' recorded one German colonel, 'Courcelette would have been lost.'[80] Another thought it incomprehensible that the Australians failed to drive home their advantage: 'They would have been able to thrust deep into our hinterland without coming up against any considerable resistance, for the troops that had received the alarm were not in position.' German batteries, in panic, blew up their ammunition.[81]

The Australians, however, were grappling with their own problems. Their push forward had created an even greater bulge in the line. Shelling and sniper fire came from three directions. The second captured trench, on the reverse side of the ridge, could be seen easily by German artillery-observers stationed around Courcelette, and the first trench by those stationed at Thiepval. White concluded that it was unwise to advance any further because the bombardment made it impossible to supply the men, and 'it would be an impossible salient to hold'.[82]

'If only the three other Australian and some British divisions had been there,' lamented Jack Gellibrand after reconnoitring the position, 'they could have undoubtedly got through.'[83]

Unlike Gellibrand, Walter Elkington's thoughts were focused on survival rather than heroic advances. 'As soon as it became light, the German artillery commenced a desultory bombardment of our position,' he recorded in his memoirs.[84] Their heavies systematically worked along the lengths of the front-line trenches. The accuracy of the shelling improved considerably, aided by the morning light, as the troops pinpointed and systematically destroyed key Australian posts on the ridge that were vital for its defence. Artillery observers targeted anything on the ridge that was moving, even a solitary man running to the rear. Blythe recalled the Germans throwing everything at the Australians — whiz-bangs, high explosives, shrapnel, coal boxes, and gas shells — in an effort to blow them clean off the ridge.[85]

The communication trenches were also targeted. 'Being high up on the ridge of Pozières Heights, we could look down and see our chaps coming along the communication trench, and see the enemy shells bursting along it, sending up great clouds of dust, smoke and stones,' noted Arthur Clifford.[86]

In turn, the artillery supporting the Australians failed to inflict any damage upon the Germans withdrawing toward Courcelette. 'Barely a shot was fired,' complained Lieutenant Arnold Brown, a sheep farmer from West Perth. 'We had to sit and suffer the sight of the enemy gun teams limbering up and drawing their field guns to safety, later to again rain shells on us.'[87]

The 2nd Division had paid a terrible price to redeem its reputation. Of those lucky enough to survive the first attack, few came out unscathed in the second. Ernest Norgard, Frank Corney, and Edgar

Morrow, all seriously wounded, were evacuated to Britain. Lewis Marshall lay unconscious in a German field hospital.[88]

Percy Blythe, also seriously injured, had almost been blown off the ridge by an exploding shell. His personnel dossier indicates that he was evacuated with gaping wounds to his face and leg. As he lay in the 13th Stationary Hospital, his thoughts would likely have turned to his young wife, Mary. He must have felt comforted that she would be well provided for if he died — he had filled out his last will and testament before sailing for France, bequeathing everything to her.

As it turned out, Percy recovered, was awarded a Distinguished Conduct Medal, and later survived another serious wound. Yet, like many men, his luck eventually ran out. He died a few months before the war's end.

William Hatcher, also injured, was evacuated to the 3rd Casualty Clearing Station in Puchevillers. He had a gaping wound to his stomach, and Sister Aitken maintained a vigil by his bedside. In the small hours of the morning, William asked her to write a short letter to his parents, Thomas and Eliza, back in Victoria. Sister Aitken finished the letter the next afternoon. It explained that William had been admitted into the hospital on 6 August, severely wounded in the abdomen, and although everything possible was done to save him, his condition gradually worsened until he passed away. 'My heart ached for you so far away from your loved one,' she wrote. 'Rest assured we did what we could for him. He had a nice comfortable bed and every attention from us all. We did our best but the issue was in God's hands.'[89]

The Base Records Office mailed a bland letter to Hatcher's parents a few weeks later. The clerk handling it must have been overworked; the paper was positioned off-centre and he smudged William's name as he typed it into the allocated space. 'I regret to advise you that No. 739 Private W.L. Hatcher, 22nd Battalion, has been reported wounded,' read the letter, 'the nature of which is not yet known here. It is not stated as being serious and in the absence of further reports it is to be assumed that all wounded [sic] are progressing satisfactorily.'

Hatcher's parents received official word from the officer in charge of the Base Records Office on 17 January 1917 that William had died — almost six months after they had received Sister Aitken's letter.[90]

Although Alec Raws survived the battle and suffered no physical wound, his mind seemed damaged beyond repair. 'We are lousy, stinking, ragged, unshaven and sleepless,' he wrote in a letter to a friend, upon coming out of the line. 'My tunic is rotten with other men's blood, and partly splattered with a dead man's brains. It is horrible, but why should you people at home not know? Several of my friends are raving mad.'[91]

Gough and Haig saw things differently to Raws. Gough congratulated the division for inflicting a severe defeat on the enemy and securing the most valuable ground, while Haig considered their gain 'a fine piece of work'.[92] The unrelenting Gough immediately ordered another attack that evening toward Mouquet Farm.

Haig's and Gough's positive attitudes were possibly influenced by German papers unearthed by John Charteris's intelligence officers after the attack. The documents urged the German people to rise up in revolt and enforce peace on their rulers.[93] At I Anzac Corps headquarters, John Treloar reviewed similar letters taken from prisoners. Their families asked the soldiers to bring food home from the front. One writer predicted that there would be no third winter campaign.[94] It seemed plausible that the German armies could collapse imminently under the weight of the constant attacks.

Had the 2nd Division's expensive victory done enough to redeem Legge's career? Possibly not, given that he'd already fallen out with Birdie and did not have White's confidence. Bean, who seemed to reflect White's views on many issues, criticised Legge, writing in his diary on 5 August that he could not grasp a battle. Expanding on his criticism, Bean claimed that Legge had repeatedly failed to accurately assess his division's state of readiness for attacks. In reality, Legge's record at Pozières closely matched Hooky Walker's — he had had one outstanding success and one notable failure. Legge's effort was, perhaps, the more difficult of the two, as he carried out his first and second attacks on the OG lines under intense shelling and without the element of surprise. The main difference between the two commanders' records, reflected White in a conversation with Bean, was that Gough, who 'naturally wanted to push along as fast as possible', had pressed Legge into attacking in an under-prepared state on 28 July, while Hooky held his ground prior to the 23 July attack.[95]

Unfortunately, these facts regarding Legge's performance didn't seem to matter. Legge's abrasive personality had alienated his superiors, his fellow officers, and the British general staff. Birdie confided in a letter to Senator Pearce that he did not 'feel anything like the confidence in him [Legge] as a divisional commander I do in both Generals Cox and Walker when their divisions are engaged'.[96] Haig would be crucial in deciding Legge's fate, and he thought the major-general was not particularly capable. Sacking Legge outright, however, was almost certainly out of the question. As the only Australian divisional commander on the Somme, the Australian government would not have tolerated such a move and Birdie would be loath to sully his own career by attempting it. Rather, his preferred method was to push Legge sideways into a harmless staff role. The poised axe would fall in the winter.

Even though the Australians had captured the OG lines on 4 August and Field-Marshal William Robertson had presented Haig's reply to the War Council on 5 August, concerns about the Somme offensive still persisted. Robertson sent a private letter to Haig, warning him that Winston Churchill, General Sir John French, and others were trying to make mischief.[97] The whispers criticising Haig's leadership gradually increased. In late August, Bean condemned Haig's generals for suffering from 'a poverty of brains'; in November, Lloyd George claimed that Haig's judgement was 'clouded by the smoke of the battle'; and in 1917, war correspondent Colonel Charles

Repington criticised Haig's officers for failing to visit the front often enough.[98] These early disparate whispers, which eventually became a deafening roar after the war and blackened Haig's name, focused on three perceived failings: firstly, that Haig rarely left his château to visit the front line; secondly, that he had scant regard for the suffering of his troops; and thirdly, that he persisted with the costly Somme battle even when all hope of a breakthrough had disappeared.

The undercurrent to these devious rumours was that Haig was out of touch with his troops. Yet visiting the soldiers on the front line was not an easy task. Charteris said that one of the great difficulties for everyone at General Headquarters was to get away from their office often and long enough to keep in close touch with their subordinates and events at the front. Few could ever get further forward than the headquarters of the armies; the divisions were housed mostly in farmhouses, but these were within the fighting line. 'We all manage ... to see something of divisional headquarters, but it is only when there is some particular object, more than simply looking around, that one can give up time to go beyond them.'[99] Haig's diary makes no reference to him visiting a brigade headquarters in the first month of the Somme offensive.

What would Haig have gained by visiting the front line? He might have met a handful of soldiers and better appreciated the conditions they fought under, but he would likely have gained few strategic insights beyond that. Like his soldiers, he would have been lucky to see anything beyond the small section of trench he was in. It would have been an unnecessary risk to allow him further afield — in 1915, three of nine British divisional commanders had been killed or died of wounds at the Battle of Loos. Haig, who commanded the British First Army in the battle, would have likely realised that the British Expeditionary Force couldn't afford to suffer such losses, let alone that of its commander-in-chief.[100] Visiting the front line during a raging battle was thus nothing more than a symbolic act witnessed by a handful of soldiers. Birdie, no doubt, visited the fighting line more often than Haig but, at the same time, appeared completely out of touch with the pressing organisational issues of his corps.

Haig's critics also claimed that he was unmoved by his soldiers' suffering. Yet Haig was in some touch with his men and he did visit the wounded. In fact, according to historian Gordon Corrigan in *Mud, Blood and Poppycock*, their suffering made him physically ill — so much so that his staff, worried that it might affect his judgement, counselled him against it.[101] Haig was not alone on this count: his French counterpart, General Joseph Joffre, once said, after pinning a medal on a blinded soldier, 'I mustn't be shown any more such spectacles [otherwise] I would no longer have the courage to give the order to attack.'[102] In *The Great War*, Dan Todman noted that 'no general who cared too much about the lives of his soldiers could function in the attritional warfare of the Western Front'.[103]

The loudest whisper intimated that Haig was obsessed with battles of attrition on the Western Front. Lloyd George, for example, wrote that Haig had wastefully prolonged the Somme campaign after it had become clear that a breakthrough was unattainable.[104] However, Haig was in fact simply adhering to secretary of state for war Lord Kitchener's explicit directions. His instructions, dated 28 December 1915, stated that the defeat of the enemy by the combined Allied armies must always be regarded as the primary objective for which British troops were sent to France and, to achieve that end, 'the closest cooperation of French and British as a united army must be the governing policy'.[105] Haig had little choice but to continue to fight on the Somme — the Allies had agreed at the French headquarters at Chantilly in December 1915 to seek a decision there in 1916. The Somme was the juncture between the British and French armies, and the most logical place for the joint offensive.

In fact, many commanders adhered to the strategy of attrition, which by definition was prolonged offensives on the largest possible scale in order to wear down the enemy by slow destruction — or as Charteris crudely phrased it, to kill Germans. The Germans and

French practised it as well: it was von Falkenhayn's plan at Verdun, and Marshal Ferdinand Foch adopted a comparable *matériel*-intensive strategy in the later years of the war.[106] The events of 1914 had demonstrated that breakthroughs were a dangerous illusion, and Haig believed the other oft-mentioned alternative of pursuing 'easy victories in unimportant theatres' was a fool's option.[107] Charteris agreed: 'How on earth one can hope to beat Germany by killing Turks or Bulgars passes comprehension.'[108]

Several claimed that Haig abhorred the colonials. Even the Germans pedalled this view, claiming that the British did not send their own countrymen into the firing line on the Somme but employed colonial troops.[109] This simplistic myth still exists today. One popular Australian history, Noel Carthew's *Voices from the Trenches*, was adamant that 'Haig used Australians to sever barbed wire entanglements before the British went into action', and that 'Haig orchestrated the slaughter of Australians'.[110] What evidence supports this? Although Haig was stretched to the limit — 52 divisions were thrown into the summer offensive, three of which were Australian — he had shown extreme concern in how the Anzacs were deployed on the Somme. He demanded that Gough provide them a simple task; he heaped praise on them when they captured Pozières; he intervened on 29 July when he believed Legge's haphazard planning had contributed to the 2nd Division's failed attempt to capture the OG lines. In his diary, he devoted three pages to discussing the artillery arrangements for the 23 July attack, and he forced Birdie to dismiss artillery commander Charles Cunliffe-Owen, whom he deemed incompetent. He listened to alternative views from Australian officers such as White, and there is no evidence that he treated them any differently to the British troops. Admittedly, Haig didn't pander to their vanities like Birdie did, but he certainly didn't abhor them.

It is clear from the various biographical accounts of Haig that he lacked the spark of genius.[111] His limitations are well documented, but they are sometimes overplayed. While he may have lacked Winston

Churchill's brilliant intellect, he had an unshakable resolve — once he selected a course of action, he adhered to it strictly. He didn't have Birdie's magnetic personality, but proved more measured in his decisions. His skills suited him to the demands of the Western Front, which required an uncompromising commander who could adhere to a brutish strategy of attrition in the face of horrific casualties and the temptation to pursue perhaps less costly but most likely equally ineffective campaigns. His oft-quoted maxim, 'a mediocre plan consistently followed is better than a brilliant one frequently changed', summed up his steadfast approach.[112] Winston Churchill correctly said of Haig, 'He might be, he surely was, unequal to the prodigious scale of events; but no one else was discerned as his equal or better.'[113] Similarly, his most vehement critic, Lloyd George, admitted in the last paragraphs of his 2043-page memoirs that there was no known officer in the army who seemed 'better qualified for the Highest Command than Haig'.[114]

All morning on 5 August, the heavy German howitzers worked methodically up and down the OG trenches, churning up everything in their path. The bursting shells threw up clouds of white dust that created a haze along the length of the ridge. The worst thing for Private Robin Ferguson, a labourer from Linton, in country Victoria, was seeing all the dead and wounded lying about. 'You could do nothing for them,' he wrote.[115]

Walter Elkington recounted that the wounded had to remain in the trenches, and many died for want of attention: 'One man was badly shellshocked and the poor beggar had to endure the agony of shellfire all day long until he was taken out at nightfall, an absolute wreck.'[116] The coveted ridge that the Australians had fought so hard for was now one of the most dangerous places on Earth. Later, John Masefield would write that thousands of men were killed on that plateau, and buried and unburied, and buried and unburied again, until no bit of dust was without a man in it.[117]

By mid-afternoon, the situation on the ridge had become critical. 'There were too many men crowded into the front trenches,' remembered Arthur Clifford.[118] Finally, some battalions received orders to withdraw. In the confusion, other battalions withdrew without permission, leaving gaping holes in the line. By late afternoon, it became clear that the 2nd Division would be unable to hold it if attacked. Brigadier-General Holmes believed that his exhausted 5th Brigade could take no more, and requested immediate relief. Corps headquarters flatly rejected his request, replying: 'On no account will OG1 be evacuated. Men to go forward into shell holes rather than fall back.'[119]

At corps headquarters, the deteriorating situation weighed heavily on White's mind. In a letter to Ethel, he wrote: 'It is a horrid feeling that one is safe and in comparative comfort while those poor fellows are suffering under appalling shellfire.'[120] Despite his misgivings, the sober White would have realised that nothing could be achieved on the Somme without a colossal expenditure of ammunition and great losses of life. As for Birdie, he seemed somewhat concerned about breaking the news to Gough that there would be no attack northward that evening. Reluctant to disappoint his commander, he promised to launch 'minor' attacks on the German flanks instead.[121]

The capture of 2000 yards of the OG trench by the Australians marked the conclusion of the second week of fighting. They had successfully punched deeper into the Germans' lines; however, their position was now exposed to German shellfire from three directions. What would Gough expect of the Australians in the coming weeks — would he order them to continue to batter their way forward, at the cost of more lives, for minor tactical gains? Haig wanted to seize the Thiepval–Morval ridge prior to his September offensive, but how did he expect his divisions to secure and hold such a narrow frontage? White sensed this operational dilemma, which would potentially condemn more divisions to attacks along narrow fronts in the coming weeks if decisive action was not taken.

A German captured in the attack on the ridge summed up the apparent futility of the battle for both sides, taunting his captors: 'Nobody will win it.'[122] Many Australians at that point would probably have agreed with him.

CHAPTER ELEVEN

Folly

'You may call this war, I call it just sending men to be killed.'
— Correspondent John Masefield, *The Battle of the Somme*

The 2nd Division, in a staggering feat of endurance, had held the line for 12 days. But the division's gains had come at a high price: 6846 soldiers had been killed, wounded, or reported as missing. Of Legge's 12 battalions, five had suffered a casualty rate of more than 60 per cent.[1] Gellibrand, exaggerating, claimed he went into action 'with full numbers', but came out with not more than a 'baggage guard'.[2] Even survivors didn't escape untouched — many, for some time after their relief, shook like aspen leaves.[3]

From 5 to 7 August, the fresh 4th Division relieved the 2nd Division. Private Alfred Stewart of the 2nd Division described in his diary the strain of waiting to be called. On 30 July, he recorded how depressed the men were when they heard that they would not be relieved that day. Stewart received no further news the next day, prompting him to write: 'We are all frightfully unnerved and shaken and deserve relief and wonder that it does not come.'[4] On 2 August, he recorded: 'We are all as nervy as old women and have been under the strain for far too long and even our officers wonder why we are not relieved.' Stewart eventually made it out of the trenches on a stretcher. 'At 9 a.m. our wounds were examined and I was marked for England. Hurrah!!!' he wrote on 7 August.

Alec Raws's 23rd Battalion was also relieved. Away from the guns, he reflected on what he had just been through. 'I yet never conceived that the war could be this dreadful. The carnage in our little sector was as bad, or worse, than that of Verdun, and yet I never saw a body buried in ten days,' he wrote in a letter to a friend. 'The men who say they believe in this war should be hung.'[5] Away from the front line, Raws and his company commander, Captain Lionel Short, quietly discussed their experiences. It left Short feeling concerned: Raws, he thought, seemed obsessed with the horror of what they had just been through. 'It had not weakened his courage but it had affected his spirit,' he reflected some years after the war.[6]

It seemed that the spirit of the relieved troops of the 6th Brigade Machine-gun Company had been similarly damaged by the battle. Their history, *In Good Company*, described how, upon reaching the comparative quiet of a reserve position, some of the gunners broke down completely. None of them could sleep, although not one had slept a wink for over 50 hours. 'Some cried, others laughed and cried together, and one or two were merely moody and nerve-stricken,' the history recorded.[7]

News of the 2nd Division's withdrawal reached John Treloar at I Anzac Corps headquarters. 'A goodly number of my friends are in the 2nd Division and I am rather anxious to hear how they fared,' he wrote in his diary.[8] It is unclear whether Treloar knew the officers of Gellibrand's 24th Battalion — Major Charlie Manning, Captain William Tatnall, Captain Harold Plant, and Lieutenant James Carvick — who were killed by a single shell burst on the night of 7 August after they had come out safely from the front line. Upon hearing the news, Arthur Clifford wrote in his diary that 'this terrible loss was a hard knock' that 'had a depressing effect' upon the men.[9] Bean, shaken by the death of his good friend Charlie Manning, wrote despairingly in his diary, 'When will this awful war cease?'[10]

The 4th Division lacked battle experience — two of its brigades hadn't even conducted a trench raid, and the third had only a few days' experience in the front line on the Western Front. German intelligence noted that the division had few Gallipoli veterans. 'It consists almost entirely of inexperienced replacements,' one report noted.[11] However, Bean correctly estimated that about 25 to 30 per cent were veteran troops — mainly 4th Brigade soldiers — which was about the same ratio as the other divisions.[12]

The 4th Division troops, who came mainly from the outer states — Western Australia, South Australia, Tasmania, and Queensland — were considered willing fighters but lacking in *espirit de corps*. This was attributed, in part, to poor leadership, due to key positions being filled according to seniority rather than performance. The division's chequered reputation had spread throughout I Anzac Corps. 'Rotten lot; they reckon they can't be trusted in the lines,' remarked one soldier, while another believed that the divisional staff were mostly 'cold-footed birds, chucked out of the British Army'.[13]

The division's poor discipline while marching to the Somme in July had reinforced these opinions. According to the 4th Division diary, the troops' march discipline could have 'scarcely be[en] worse' — about 800 men fell out of the 12th Brigade's march.[14] The 4th Brigade's march discipline was just as bad, remembered Sergeant Ted Rule of the 14th Battalion: 'We had men lying out on the roads for miles, too exhausted to go further.'[15] The dreadful marching was attributed to a heavy drinking session the night and early morning before. The 4th Division commander, Major-General Sir Herbert Cox, drove out specifically to observe the march discipline of the 13th Brigade, which had set off at dawn for Herissart. Mid-morning, standing beside he road, he watched the troops struggle by.[16] Cox described the march discipline as deplorable, and saw many men — some still drunk — straggling behind their units in twos and threes, smoking and talking as they passed by. Some had hitched rides on wagons, while others had discarded their kit by the roadside or shoved it onto the wagons, which were covered in rifles and packs.[17]

Cox had been forewarned by Haig of the ignorance and conceit of the colonials and had drafted a damning circular to his officers on 14 July, claiming that for a soldier to fall out while still able to struggle forward was disgraceful. He demanded that, in future, officers march in the rear and record the name of every straggler. Slackers were to be dished out exemplary punishment. Over the following days, as punishment the division was route-marched with full packs by every road, hedgerow, and farmhouse in the district.[18] 'It's the hardest work I have ever done in my life,' Sergeant Henry Palmer of the 50th Battalion wrote in a letter home.[19] Some disgruntled soldiers questioned the practical worth of marching drills, wondering whether they had come to France to fight or 'to go touring the country like blanky Cook's tourists'.[20]

Cox, a sickly 56-year-old Englishman and an old friend of Birdie, wouldn't tolerate sloppy soldiering. He had learnt his soldiering on the subcontinent and was said to have a little of the hot Indian sun in his temper. According to the 48th Battalion history, whenever the sardonic Cox encountered his soldiers on the roads he subjected them to a strict examination; he aggressively fired questions and warned them that they were destined for 'some dirty work at the crossroads'. The troops bristled at the treatment and complained that these mocking examinations seemed to be for no other reason than Cox's enjoyment.[21]

Cox's abhorrence for sloppy discipline and the class-based attitudes he displayed toward the 'colonial' Australians alienated many of his troops. While many Australians, including Bean, celebrated the Anzacs' larrikin streak and egalitarian ethos — which manifested itself in what many believed were harmless behaviours such as failing to salute officers and demonstrating irreverence for social niceties and authority — some British officers, including Cox, thought this insolent behaviour was harmful to good soldiering.

British and Australians officers no doubt broadly agreed that discipline was a key ingredient to good soldiering. The trouble was, for many British officers good discipline extended to somewhat inconsequential matters, such as soldiers presenting neatly at all times. At Pozières, Australians tended to wear dilapidated uniforms, much to the annoyance of these British officers. Bean defended the Anzacs, as they could only replace their old uniforms, which were no longer issued, with British tunics, which they detested. An Anzac wearing a British tunic seemed 'to be the hallmark of a different being — a more subservient, less intelligent man,' claimed Bean. Australians, according to Bean, generally didn't fuss about their personal appearance, as it was viewed as 'unessential', whereas they were all in favour of whatever was deemed 'essential': they had a tendency to dress for practicality rather than neatness. By contrast, Bean continued, the British were 'apt to carry the regard for dress and unessentials to the most vicious extreme'.[22]

Unsurprisingly, many 4th Division soldiers with a somewhat more relaxed attitude toward discipline took umbrage at Cox's harsh response to their poor marching and the way he aggressively interrogated them. They no doubt reasoned that holding shallow trenches against repeated German counterattacks was the real mark of a soldier's discipline, rather than marching in perfect order or fussing over his personal appearance. One soldier wrote: 'Fritz couldn't fault our discipline, and he ought to know'.[23]

Along with apparently inflexible attitudes toward discipline, the British army also had a strict pecking order based on class distinctions: professional soldiers outranked volunteers, British-born subjects stood above colonials, and the public-school officer class were superior to their working-class soldiers. Australians — colonials and volunteer soldiers — resented the British class division that placed them on the lower rungs. These social distinctions sometimes resulted in conflict: one Australian officer, dressed in a private's tunic, recalled being spoken to like a 'lowborn dog' when he didn't return a salute to his British counterpart, who mistook him for a private soldier.[24] Unsurprisingly, Australians relished their capture of Pozières after the repeated failures by British troops because it contradicted their hierarchical view of the world.

Bean criticised the British class divisions, claiming that British soldiers were afraid of their officers and stood in awe of them as acknowledged superiors. 'But an Australian does not stand in that sort of awe of his officer because he is of the same class as his officer — there is no social difference,' he wrote in his diary. Bean said that the British army's class distinctions resulted in few of the lower ranks being promoted 'in the field' to officers, whereas Anzac commanders scoured their battalions for men of outstanding character for officer schools, with little consideration of their social background.[25] This meant that a talented private could progress through the Australian Imperial Force ranks, whereas this rarely occurred in the British army. One Anzac, whose story was recounted in the 3rd Battalion history *Randwick to Hargicourt,* realised the subtle differences in class attitudes between the two armies when he and some other officers entertained an Australian non-commissioned officer in their billeted house. He noted that the British officers in an adjoining billet were astounded by this behaviour. 'They did not understand the familiarity and friendship which always existed between officers and men in the AIF [Australian Imperial Force],' explained Eric Wren in the battalion history.[26]

Cox was reluctant to promote from the ranks. His inherent class bias was evident when he discussed with an officer the possibility of commissioning a sergeant. Cox vetoed it, arguing that none of those in the lower ranks should ever become officers as there could not be working-class men leading university graduates and businessmen.[27] Cox's stance was doubtless influenced by his experiences in the British army, as well as his postings in India.

The Anzacs, perhaps sensing Cox's class-based attitudes, constantly tried to ruffle his composure. On an occasion when Cox lectured a brigade during the Somme offensive, a drunken sergeant continually butted in, at one point objecting to the Germans using phosphorous. Cox took it in his stride, coolly replying: 'Don't you get burnt up. Anyway we can't spare you.'[28]

The Australians' supposedly distinctive views toward discipline and egalitarianism may have been exaggerated after the war, particularly by unit reunions, veteran organisations, and official institutions such as the Australian War Memorial. Perhaps it was one way of supporting Bean's view that the Anzacs were superior soldiers to their British counterparts, which was an important tenet of the Anzac legend. And this legend, which according to some scholars was constructed around the archetypical Digger, served a number of important purposes in broader society after the war: it provided Australians with a past they could live with, it personified an idealised national character, and it affirmed that a frontier or bush lifestyle produced an improved race of people.[29] Perhaps by elevating the Anzacs' exploits, Australia's national self-image proportionally strengthened.

Eric Andrews challenged the key tenets of the Anzac legend, pointing out in *The Anzac Illusion* that the discipline and class differences between the Australian and British soldier were not always as pronounced as many observers, including Bean, suggested — in fact, he believed they were generalisations that hid a more complex truth. For example, Australian officers weren't always promoted from the ranks, but came disproportionately from Protestant, non-manual backgrounds, such as commerce and clerical work. Furthermore, many Australian Imperial Force officers were British-born and schooled, having migrated to Australia some time before the war.[30]

What seemed to be the most important ingredient in leading soldiers on the Somme was the officers' — whether Australian or British — ability to adapt their command style to get the best out of their troops. Hooky Walker, a British regular officer who understood the Australians' nuances, succeeded in maintaining good disciplinary standards as well as earning the devotion of his men, but it seemed that the old-fashioned Anglo=Indian officer Cox couldn't adjust his style to the command situation he faced. As a result, no one was quite sure how this unlikely pairing — the undisciplined and individualistic Australians coupled with the crotchety Cox — would perform in the coming battle.

Cox's staff were predominantly professional British officers, while two of his brigade commanders, Brigadier-General Thomas 'Bill' Glasgow of the 13th Brigade and Brigadier-General Charles 'Digger' Brand of the 4th Brigade, were Australian soldiers. Brigadier-General Duncan Glasfurd, a career soldier of the British army seconded to Australia before the war to manage the cadet-training program, was Cox's third brigadier, and commanded the 12th Brigade. Glasfurd immediately clashed with his Australian-born 48th Battalion commander, Lieutenant-Colonel Ray 'Bull' Leane. On 5 August, Glasfurd ordered his 48th Battalion to relieve the 27th, which held the OG lines. Leane, a Gallipoli veteran, refused to comply, insisting that the German bombardment would needlessly slaughter them. Leane reasoned that it was better to risk a temporary penetration of the line than to suffer casualties passively in a congested front line. Glasfurd produced a written order. 'I was now faced with this problem,' Leane wrote in a letter in 1923, recalling the incident. 'If I obeyed orders I felt that the men would be shot to pieces ... If I disobeyed the order and lost the ridge my career as a Military Officer would be over.'[31] Leane refused to obey the order and defiantly left one of his companies in Pozières.

Leane was a strongly built man who had started a retail business in the Outback mining town of Kalgoorlie, and epitomised the mythical bushman of which Bean was so fond.[32] He did not disobey Glasfurd lightly; he had already reconnoitred the front line under bombardment and was aware of conflicting orders requiring commanders to thin out the garrison to prevent unnecessary casualties. Leane's behaviour was not a prelude to the Australian Imperial Force's command-and-control structure breaking down under pressure, but rather a case of an officer being confident enough to back his own judgement and question orders rather than treating them as gospel. Glasfurd, an old-fashioned soldier of the British army, was not ready to adopt a more consultative approach with his battalion commanders. The *Official History* noted that Leane and Glasfurd's relationship never recovered.

While marching toward the Somme in late July, the 4th Division troops came across remnants of the 1st Division. They watched the pitifully weak platoons stagger along the road, the strain of the previous week etched on their faces.[33] Despite the unnerving sight, the soldiers remained naively keen to enter the line. 'Every day our maps were studied and the rumours flew thick and heavy,' wrote Sergeant Ted Rule, a 30-year-old railway foreman from the dusty Outback mining town of Cobar, New South Wales, in his war memoirs. 'The know alls said that just as soon as we got the Windmill on the ridge on the other side of Pozières, we would put the cavalry in and then it was to be the finish of Mr Hun.'[34]

Days later, Rule found out that soldiering on the Somme was harder than the 'know-alls' made out. The citizen–soldier and Gallipoli veteran managed to get his platoon lost before they reached Sausage Valley. 'What, lost in daylight,' boomed his brigadier to the floundering men. 'Don't know what you will do in the dark.'

Like the 1st and 2nd divisions before it, the German bombardment cut through Cox's inexperienced troops on 5 August as they made their way to the OG trenches. When Leane's 48th Battalion eventually arrived there, they could not find the battalion they were to relieve — the 27th Battalion had already disappeared back to Sausage Valley without orders.[35] Leane's troops, unable to find their trenches, walked a mile past their allocated position and were lucky not to be mistaken for Germans upon their return. They eventually found remnants of the line, clearly marked with the dead and wounded that the previous battalions had left behind. Leane described the relief, which started on 5 August and ended in the early hours of the next day, under the heavy bombardment, as his worst experience of the whole war.[36]

The next morning, Sunday 6 August, Leane scouted his forward positions. His concerns about overcrowding the front line proved accurate — shelling had wiped out his two forward companies. 'There were masses dead and wounded everywhere,' he recalled.[37]

Preparations continued in anticipation of the Germans' assault. Soldiers sank trenches deeper into the loose, chalky soil and repaired the gaping holes in the trench walls. They scooped dirt out of the large shell holes in front of OG2 and converted them into strongpoints, which Lewis gun teams manned, and fighting patrols worked between, during the night.[38]

Ted Rule's platoon continued to work its way to the front line, passing through Pozières and into a blown-in trench. Dead men lay along it — some partially buried, with just an arm or a leg sticking out. 'It was the first time I had ever scrambled over dead ... I have never been so horrified in all my life,' recorded Rule.[39] The platoon reached battalion headquarters, located in a small German dugout. Rule asked an officer what the men of his unit had done with the blankets that each had carried in. 'His answer was that we would be damned lucky if we ever used a blanket again.'

The platoon made its way to the support lines. 'I've never seen men so closely packed in a trench,' remembered Rule. 'It was not a bit of wonder that men were being killed like rabbits.' Then he found the commanding officer of the 28th Battalion: 'I bailed him up and asked him what I ought to do.

'"Get up to the front line and help your mates," he replied. "You'll be attacked tonight."'

Late that afternoon, German aeroplanes flew low over Pozières, probably gathering intelligence for their field batteries. Cox's 'jumpy' troops raised false alarms after scattered groups of Germans were mistaken as the start of the counterattack. At dusk, some Germans reinforced the trenches protecting Mouquet Farm. The German bombardment eased in the evening but then suddenly started again, shelling Tara Valley, Bécourt Wood, and Sausage Valley, to the rear of Pozières. Leane thought this signalled the Germans' intention to launch an assault the following night.[40] The garrison had previously been thinned to prevent unnecessary casualties. Could more troops be rushed forward when the counterattack came?

While the Australians prepared to meet the German counter-attack, some Gallipoli veterans reflected on the first anniversary of Lone Pine. 'I was at the Pine,' crowed a digger to his mates. Lone Pine was a celebrated victory on Gallipoli, albeit one of little strategic importance. The Australians had rushed the Turkish position only to find that a roof of freshly cut pine logs protected them. Some clawed, scratched, and tore their way through; others entered through back entrances to capture the warren of trenches. As with the OG lines, capturing the trenches had been the easy part; holding it against desperate counterattacks chewed up countless lives. The Lone Pine veterans would never, in their worst nightmares, have imagined that they'd be caught in an even more ferocious battle exactly one year later. 'Everyone admits that this is worse than Lone Pine,' wrote Arthur Foxcroft.[41]

Brothers Joe and Bill McSparron had fought at Lone Pine. Their personnel dossiers indicated that before the war they had migrated from Ireland to Australia, seeking a better life. Two weeks after the war broke out, Bill left his chauffeuring job and enlisted. Joe, a Parramatta rail employee, joined six months later. 'Mother was advising me to wait a while before volunteering,' wrote Joe, 'but I have already done so and don't regret it in the very least, I believe it is every young fellow's duty.'[42] Bill's battalion led the charge upon the Lone Pine trench. He was never heard of again. Joe wrote a letter to their mother in October 1915 and offered some hope: 'I have spoken to WG's [Bill's] commanding officer. He knows there was a party of our men captured at the same time and believes there is every chance that Bill is among them.'

Exactly one year after Bill disappeared, 26-year-old Joe sat in a trench waiting for orders to attack when a shell exploded above him, wounding him and some other men. His friend, Private Jack Owens, tried to get near to check that he was alright, but the trench was too packed. 'Malone and the big cook, Wicky, were trying to push through; made things worse,' recalled Owens. They lost touch.

The next day, Owens wrote a letter to Joe: 'I am very sorry to hear that you were hit, but hope it is not as serious as we think.' He needn't have bothered; Joe had died. Like many mothers of Australian soldiers, Mrs Jane McSparron of Londonderry, Ireland, would pause on the anniversary of Lone Pine to mourn. It was a terrible tragedy of fate that her sons were killed on the same day, one year apart.

General Fritz von Below, commander of the First German Army, wanted the Pozières ridge back. On 5 August, he had drafted orders demanding its recapture, stating that Hill 60 (the Pozières plateau) had to be recovered at any price, for if it remained in the hands of the British it would give them an important advantage.[43] Attacks were to be made by consecutive waves, 80 yards apart. Troops who first reached the plateau had to hold on until reinforced, whatever their losses: 'Any man that fails to resist to the death on the ground won will be immediately court-martialled.'[44] It was a costly policy, but von Below was determined not to yield a single inch of hard-won French soil.

Fresh German troops rushed forward in preparation for the coming attack. A captured letter described the experience of a German officer caught up in the preparations. He recorded that, upon reaching Courcelette, an impenetrable cloud of dust enveloped the soldiers. Despite this, his company continued forward and relieved a full battalion. His men had to lie, crammed together, in shell holes in part of an old demolished trench:

The hundreds of dead bodies make the air terrible and there are flies in the thousands ... We have no dugouts, we dig a hole in the side of a shell hole and lie and get rheumatism. We get nothing to eat or drink ... The ceaseless roar of the guns is driving us mad.[45]

The Australians' conditions in the opposing trenches weren't much better. 'We all sat huddled in the bottom of the trench resting against each other's knees,' Ted Rule wrote in his memoirs, 'constantly showered with falling earth from the bursts.' He thought it strange that all the shells were bursting further back from the front line; he pulled his rifle a little closer.[46]

In the early hours of Monday 7 August, masses of German soldiers trudged toward the Australian lines; through the morning mist, Australian forward scouts could see them advancing up the ridge from Courcelette. General Fritz von Below had mustered all available troops for the attack, about 1500 in all: machine-gunners, pioneers, and *flammenwerfer* squads, all wearing their newly issued steel helmets, surged forward at about 5.50 a.m. in two extended waves. They reached the first trench almost without loss. 'We opened fire but we could not shoot them all,' remembered one Australian.[47]

The Australians fired SOS rockets, calling for artillery support. No support came because the rockets couldn't be seen through the heavy fog. In desperation, Ray Leane's battalion headquarters released a pigeon with a request for support.[48] Men in the advance posts, about to be overrun, panicked and ran back to OG1. The shadows of dawn partly obscured the Germans, who swept through the OG lines and made for Pozières. It seemed the tactic of thinning out the trench garrison would cost the Australians dearly.

Australians positioned in the support trenches further back at Centre Way and Tom's Cut braced themselves as the grey wave swept forward. 'Right in front of us we made out fleeing figures,' remembered one German soldier. 'Just then we came under a furious storm of concentrated fire from right and left.'[49]

Fortuitously, the pigeon had made it back to the corps cage in about 13 minutes, and the artillery was soon provided. The British barrage opened up and machine guns fired into the Germans. According to Leane, the barrage 'smashed' the German reserves advancing in close formation onto the OG lines, but those who had already advanced past it were now intermingled with the Australians.[50]

For Rule, the ensuing fighting presented a surreal scene: Germans and Australians scattered in ones and twos all along the side of the ridge were shooting point-blank at each other's faces: 'Others were fighting with the bayonet, this being one of the few occasions when bayonets were really crossed. Others were on their knees in front of standing figures, praying for their lives.'[51]

Gradually, the Australians wrestled the advantage back from the Germans, and after an hour the fighting subsided.

Rule left his support trench later that day to see the carnage. He claimed that the sights were enough to haunt a man for the rest of his days. The area contained more dead than he had ever hoped to see. Every shell hole had one or two men in it. 'Many of our boys who had been wounded in the German counter-attack were still lying about in the trenches ... Lots of the boys that were being found at this time had their wounds all fly-blown,' he recounted in his memoirs.[52]

The heavy German losses must have shocked General von Gallwitz. He castigated von Below for having inflicted another bloodbath, even though von Below had simply adhered to the German doctrine of recapturing lost territory at all costs. The counterattack represented the last concerted effort by the Germans to recapture the ridge and Pozières.[53]

The 4th Division's fighting strength had diminished before it had even started toward Mouquet Farm. In one day and two nights, Ray Leane's 48th Battalion had lost over half its strength: 20 officers and 578 men. The 45th Battalion had lost five officers and 340 men.[54] Despite the casualties, the 4th Division would push toward Mouquet Farm in the next few days. The Australians had secured the fortified village of Pozières and the OG lines on the ridge; they thought that capturing an isolated and ruined farmhouse would be a relatively straightforward and inexpensive task.

CHAPTER TWELVE

La Ferme du Mouquet

'The earth grew nothing, although watered with a rain more precious than any other it had known.'
— Captain E. Gorman, *With the Twenty-second*

On the misty morning of 5 August, I Anzac Corps staff turned their attention to Gough's order requiring them, at the earliest moment, to advance northward to Mouquet Farm and Thiepval. Cox's 4th Division would be responsible for pushing past the farm and on to Thiepval. John Masefield wrote that the Australians' push through the markless mud toward Thiepval marked the third sombre stage of their Somme battle.[1]

Mouquet Farm — known as 'Moo Cow Farm', 'Mucky Farm', or 'Muckety Farm' to those who struggled with the subtleties of the French language — was about 2000 yards from Pozières. In better times, if you had stood in the main street of Pozières and walked away from the village in a north-westerly direction, you would have passed some cottages, an orchard, a light-rail track, and a cemetery, and then dipped into a shallow valley. You would have crossed the Ovillers–Courcelette road that Gellibrand's 23rd fought so hard to secure, on to an 800-yard dirt track that would take you through a second valley and up a gentle rise to the doorstep of Mouquet Farm.

Gough believed that the farm had to be captured before Thiepval — 1500 yards away — could be threatened. Once the farm was captured, he would thrust his five divisions to the rear of Thiepval, and silence it once and for all.

After the momentous events at Pozières, capturing a ruined farm should have been a mere formality, but this was not the case. As the Australians advanced toward the farm, the Pozières ridge on the right and a dominating spur on the left hemmed them in. The German-held ridges either side gradually closed in on Mouquet Farm, funnelling the Australians into a narrow front. The restricted area meant the Australians could only attack with one or two battalions, while the Germans could respond with a concentrated bombardment from three directions.[2]

I Anzac Corps Intelligence didn't know much about *la ferme du Mouquet*, other than that it had once been a large brick farmstead owned by a wealthy farmer, with a dairy and stables attached. As a result of the previous six weeks of fighting, only smashed brickwork, twisted wrought-iron gates, caved-in cellars, and broken roof beams remained. When the Germans swept through the Somme Valley in 1914, Monsieur Vandendriessche, the farm's tenant, had probably shared the concerns of other French residents, but must have felt sure that his isolated farm would escape their interest. Yet the Germans started poking around the farm in early 1916 and immediately earmarked the farm as an important stronghold. For Major Hans von Fabeck, who was responsible for converting the neighbouring Thiepval into an impregnable fortress in April 1916, Mouquet Farm's deep cellars and elevated location meant that it was ideally suited, along with the nearby Goat and Stuff redoubts, to protect the village. He carefully engineered the Thiepval sector into an integrated defensive zone.[3]

The Australians, according to the *Official History*, had first to capture three lines of trenches before taking Mouquet Farm. The first, Park Lane, sat on the rise north of Pozières. The second, Skyline Trench, ran from a high spur, past a chalk quarry and into a shallow gully. The third and most important, Fabeck Graben, snaked along the second rise. The Australians assumed Park Lane and Skyline Trench, which appeared rough and disconnected from other trenches, to be only weakly held by German troops. The Australians expected a prompt advance and then greater resistance from Mouquet Farm, which lay beyond the second rise and would only be seen in the last 100 yards of their advance.[4] The Germans were determined to hold the farm no matter the cost, understanding that if it fell, so too would Thiepval.

Shell craters carpeted the path to Mouquet Farm. Some soldiers thought its approaches resembled a rough sea as seen from the beach.[5] The odd shattered tree stump and a lone upturned wagon broke up the brown expanse. It would have been impossible for those soldiers stumbling over the cratered ground to make out their objectives. Trenches were, in most cases, only a series of linked shell craters or shallow furrows. The loose dirt had been so churned up that a trench couldn't be dug without its walls caving in. Maps became useless because trenches were obliterated and then reconstructed elsewhere within hours.[6]

I Anzac Corps encountered significant logistical problems in its efforts to capture the farm. It was becoming increasingly difficult to keep the supply lines open so that the front-line soldiers could receive ammunition, water, food rations, and medical help.[7] As the Australians punched deeper into the German lines, they created a dangerous salient that allowed the Germans to observe their vulnerable supply routes from three vantage points.

As a result, rations parties stopped carrying food up from the field kitchens to the trenches in broad daylight, rather bringing breakfast, lunch, and dinner up together before daylight. Ration carriers, sometimes with hot boxes strapped to their backs, worked their way through crowded communication trenches in the early morning to ensure the soldiers received their rations. The soldiers typically

Private Arthur John Foxcroft of Gilgandra, New South Wales, enlisted on 30 August 1915. Almost a year later, when Foxcroft's platoon withdrew from Pozières, it could only muster 14 of 60 men. Foxcroft was wounded in August 1916 and evacuated to England.
(State Library of Victoria)

War correspondent and official historian Charles Edwin Bean meticulously recorded the Anzacs' exploits on the Western Front. As the campaign for Pozières progressed, Bean's diary entries became more scathing of British commanders, who he believed were mismanaging the offensive; however, his official despatches remained positive. *(Australian War Memorial)*

The village of Pozières, which had about 350 inhabitants, was positioned on a ridge and therefore had strategic value to the Allies and Germans. Concentrated artillery bombardments in July and August 1916 razed the village. After the battle, a noticeboard marked 'Pozières' was the only indication a village had ever been there. *(Australian War Memorial)*

General Sir Douglas Haig, commander-in-chief of the British Expeditionary Force from 1915 to 1919, was vilified for his role in the slaughter on the Somme. Haig was, in fact, concerned by how the Australians were deployed at Pozières, and intervened when he believed their preparations were inadequate.
(Australian War Memorial)

Commander of the British Reserve Army, General Sir Hubert Gough, ordered Major-General Harold 'Hooky' Walker's division to attack Pozières before it had conducted reconnaissance of the sector. Hooky claimed that Gough exhibited the worst generalship of the campaign.
(Imperial War Museum)

Major-General Harold 'Hooky' Walker, commander of the 1st Australian Infantry Division, was respected by his men for his methodical planning and concern for their welfare. British-born Hooky, who spoke with a refined accent and enjoyed the finer things in life, feared his division would be 'knocked out' in the attack on Pozières.
(Australian War Memorial)

A German soldier in April 1916 standing in a communication trench leading to Pozières. The Germans, anticipating an Allied offensive, carefully selected the highest ground along the Somme and constructed an elaborate defensive network of trenches, underground dugouts, fortified villages, and blockhouses. *(Australian War Memorial)*

Soldiers of the 4th Australian Division Ammunition Column posing with locals outside a French inn at Estaires, seven miles west of Armentières, in June 1916. 'But for realities there might not be a war on at all,' wrote Sergeant Philip Browne in the weeks before the battle for Pozières. *(Australian War Memorial)*

German prisoners making their way through the British lines on 1 July 1916, the first day of the Somme offensive. The practicalities of battle meant that it was sometimes more expedient to kill surrendering Germans than to risk lives escorting them from the battlefield. *(Australian War Memorial)*

A British soldier rescuing a comrade under shellfire on 1 July 1916. The wounded man is believed to have died 30 minutes after reaching the trenches. On the first day of the Allied offensive on the Somme, the British walked into a storm of steel and suffered 57,000 casualties. It is still the bloodiest day in British history. *(Imperial War Museum)*

Lieutenant-General Sir William 'Birdie' Birdwood posing with his favourite horse, a chestnut gelding. While Birdie meticulously documented his daily rides in his diary, he rarely recorded any insightful notes on the Pozières battle. *(Australian War Memorial)*

An unidentified Australian soldier shaving in a rear area, after being relieved from the front line on 27 July 1916. His spiked helmet (known as a *Pickelhaube*) and the leather satchels close by are spoils captured from the Germans. One battalion history noted that a little rest put new life into the soldiers after the heavy fighting at Pozières. *(Australian War Memorial)*

Brigadier-General Cyril Brudenell White, chief-of-staff of the I Anzac Corps, bore most of the administrative load at the corps headquarters. Australian-born White, although considered brilliant, was plagued by depression, loneliness, and self-doubt. He became increasingly disillusioned by the Allies' piecemeal attacks around Pozières. *(Australian War Memorial)*

Lieutenant John Treloar (right), of I Anzac Corps headquarters, was the supervising clerk of the Central Registry. The 21-year-old was responsible for overseeing the distribution of orders, intelligence, and memoranda flowing to and from the corps. On the Somme, Treloar worked in a tent pitched on the lawns of Contay Château. *(Australian War Memorial)*

Private Ernest Victor Lee of Mossiface, Victoria — the author's great-uncle — enlisted at 14 under the alias Ernest John Jefferies. After the war, newspaper articles glowingly referred to Lee as a splendid specimen of Australian manhood, but made no mention of his troubled past.
(Author's collection)

A column of 2nd Australian Infantry Division soldiers winding its way along the undulating roads of France, toward the trenches. After their time in dreary Armentières, the Anzacs welcomed the warm sun and blue skies of the French countryside. *(Australian War Memorial)*

Major-General James Gordon Legge, commander of the 2nd Australian Infantry Division, was the only Australian divisional commander on the Somme. Although Legge was universally recognised as a brilliant administrator, Bean thought his flawed judgement and limited experience prevented him from being a good leader in battle. *(Australian War Memorial)*

Major-General Sir Herbert Cox, commander of the 4th Australian Infantry Division, was an Anglo-Indian officer of the British army. Haig forewarned Cox of the Australians' ignorance and conceit, but the sardonic Cox remained determined to instil strong disciplinary standards among his men. *(Australian War Memorial)*

Brigadier-General John 'Jack' Gellibrand (third from left), commander of the 6th Victorian Brigade, having breakfast in Sausage Valley with seven Australian officers. Gellibrand claimed he went into action on 27 July 1916 with 'full numbers', but came out with little more than a regimental transport 'baggage guard'. *(Australian War Memorial)*

Four Australian gunners loading a shell into a 9.2-inch breech-loading howitzer. On average, British guns on the Somme fired, in a single day, as many shells as had been fired during the entire Boer War. *(Australian War Memorial)*

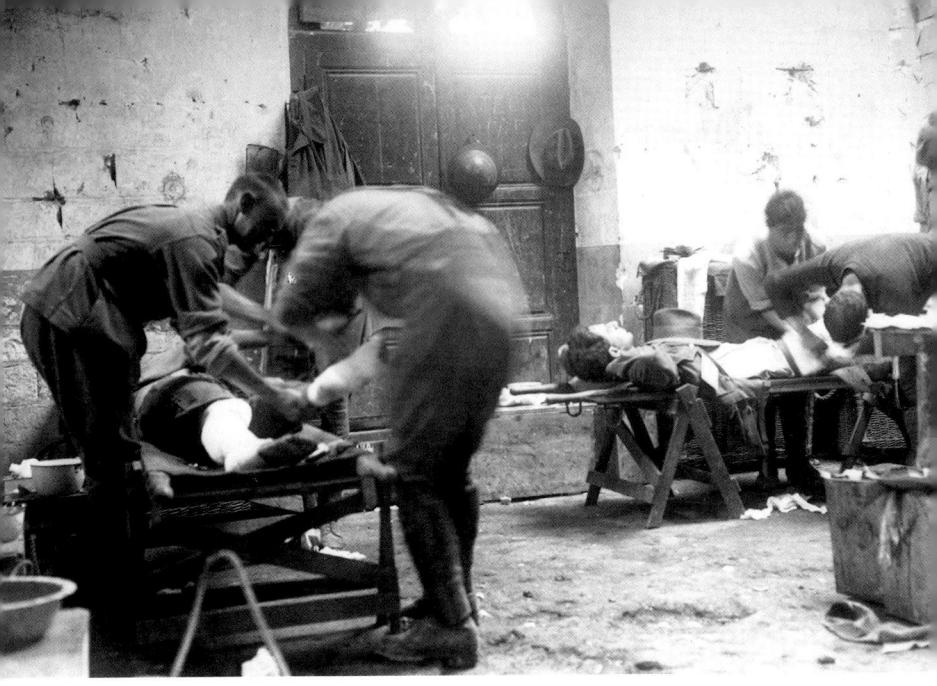

Members of the Australian Army Medical Corps dressing the wounds of Australian soldiers in Bécourt Château's converted chapel. The medical officers dressed up to 800 wounds a day and, as the campaign progressed, were forced to perform surgeries because the severely wounded would not survive the journey to the casualty clearing stations. *(Australian War Memorial)*

An Australian fatigue party from the 7th Infantry Brigade carrying empty sandbags past the shattered remains of Gibraltar. After its capture, Gibraltar became an important signal station. Whenever the wire between it and rear headquarters was cut, a new cable would be run; it was severed so often that a bundle of wires thick as a man's wrist protruded from the blockhouse. *(Australian War Memorial)*

An Australian machine-gun crew in action at Pozières. Allied and German machine-gunners inflicted horrendous casualties, and consequently were often treated roughly if captured. When German machine-gunners surrendered, they sometimes discreetly removed the badges from their tunics in order to conceal their identities. *(Australian War Memorial)*

After the capture of Pozières, one soldier said that the cratered village resembled a rough sea as seen from the beach. The lonely white cross marks the grave of Captain Ivor Stephen Margetts of Wynyard, Tasmania, who served in the 12th Battalion and was killed on 24 July 1916. In 1918, the Germans re-captured this area and Margetts' grave was lost. He is commemorated on the Villers-Bretonneux memorial. *(Australian War Memorial)*

Australian prime minister William Morris 'Billy' Hughes became convinced, upon his return from England in late July 1916, that conscription was the only option to replenish the Anzacs' strength following the battle for Pozières. He successfully lobbied to put the issue to a referendum, which was held in October 1916 and split the nation. *(Australian War Memorial)*

Birdie in Vadencourt Wood addressing soldiers of the 2nd Infantry Brigade on 28 July 1916, after their first tour at Pozières. Birdie preferred meeting his troops to office work. Cyril Brudenell White, his chief-of-staff, believed he had little idea of the administration involved in implementing his orders. *(Australian War Memorial)*

Stretcher-bearers of the 6th Infantry Brigade on 28 August 1916, passing the old cemetery of Pozières after coming from the line, near Mouquet Farm. The Australians and Germans had an informal agreement not to fire on stretcher-bearers, who were often forced to travel across open ground because trenches were clogged with troops. *(Australian War Memorial)*

OG1 Trench, north-west of the Pozières windmill. Private Eric Moorhead claimed that a drunken officer gave the order to capture OG2 Trench during the 25 July attack. After two failed attacks, the 2nd Australian Infantry Division finally captured the trenches on 4 August. *(Australian War Memorial)*

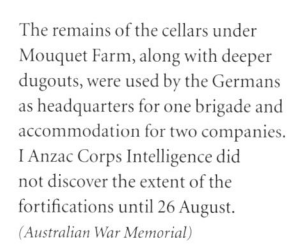

The remains of the cellars under Mouquet Farm, along with deeper dugouts, were used by the Germans as headquarters for one brigade and accommodation for two companies. I Anzac Corps Intelligence did not discover the extent of the fortifications until 26 August. *(Australian War Memorial)*

The skeleton of a German soldier near a dugout entrance on the Somme. The German army's standing order to maintain their position at all costs resulted in a sickening number of casualties. Total British, French, and German casualties were estimated at 1,043,000. *(Imperial War Museum)*

Leg amputees attending an Australian Red Cross Society telegraphy workshop at the 2nd Australian Auxiliary Hospital, Southall, England. An estimated 3000 men passed through the hospital over three years. *(Australian War Memorial)*

Shell-shock patients of the 3rd Australian Auxiliary Hospital in Kent awaiting their Christmas dinner in a ward decorated with streamers and garlands of holly. Recovery from this little-understood condition, which reached epidemic proportions at Pozières, could be very slow. *(Australian War Memorial)*

Soldiers and officers in July 1917 listening as the chaplain reads the service at the unveiling of the memorial to fallen members of the 1st Australian Division. Beside him, draped in the Australian flag, is the memorial.
(Australian War Memorial)

An Anzac scrutinises a grave near Pozières, along the line of OG1 Trench, in 1917. After the war, the remains of soldiers, which had been buried in graves scattered throughout the battlefield, were exhumed and interred in cemeteries. However, an estimated 4000 Anzacs who died at Pozières had no known grave.
(Australian War Memorial)

In the Somme valley today, fields still disgorge unexploded ordnance. The French Department of Mine Clearance recovers about 900 tonnes of unexploded munitions every year. Since 1945, approximately 630 French minesweepers have died handling such munitions. *(Author's collection)*

Many Australians marched past Plot 1 of Gordon Dump Cemetery, which has views down to Sausage Valley, on their way to the front line. Today, the cemetery contains 1676 buried, 91 of which are Australians. Gordon Dump Cemetery is one of 242 military cemeteries dotted around the Somme region. *(Author's collection)*

There are over 10,700 names etched onto the Portland limestone memorial panels at the Australian National Memorial outside Villers-Bretonneux. Four thousand Australian soldiers were posted as missing at Pozières. Their bodies were never recovered, or, if found, never identified. *(Author's collection)*

blasphemed the cooks for the meagre rations, probably unaware that the carriers had spilt most of it on the way up.[8] A reserve of 250 tins of water and a canteen selling tinned fruit, cakes, tobacco, and biscuits had also been set up close to the front line. Unfortunately, the tins, previously used for petrol, were often tainted with a faint residue of the fuel, prompting one soldier to comment that after taking a drink he 'was afraid if I put a cigarette in my mouth I should blow up'.[9]

The Germans typically shelled at meal times in order to interrupt the delivery of rations, and heavy casualties resulted. Captain Allan Leane's company of 55 men was responsible for feeding the 48th Battalion troops.[10] When Leane's company came out of the line, he only had 30 men left. 'We certainly got our share of it, maybe I put my cookers too close ... The casualties were very heavy but the regiment was looked after,' Leane explained in a letter.[11]

The front line lurched forward continuously, stretching medical arrangements to breaking point. The battalion stretcher-bearers struggled to cope with the flood of casualties, the 'lengthy and formidable' transports, and the constant shelling. In response, the number of regimental stretcher-bearers was increased, sometimes supplemented by bandsmen, who were adept at entertaining the troops out of the line; pioneers; and field-ambulance bearers. Field-ambulance bearers also remained behind to continue helping after their division was relieved, and relays were organised to ease the stretcher-bearers' workload.

With the front line fitfully moving forward, aid posts were soon too far back from the trenches, delaying the treatment of the wounded and exhausting the stretcher-bearers. In response, medical staff set up forward posts that shortened the carry distance. It sped up treatment, but exposed the wounded to shelling; in some cases, these aid posts were even set up in old German dugouts, with their entrances facing the German guns. Shells sometimes exploded in the dugout's mouth, killing or trapping those inside.[12] In an incident that Sergeant John Edey recorded in his diary, a doctor and his army medical sergeant were entombed in a dugout. Sensing that their chance of rescue was slim, they were considering taking an overdose of morphine when, at the last moment, they were dug out.[13]

From 8 August, the Australians would extend their advance northward from the Pozières summit into the shallow valley in front of the farm. This advance would result in the Australians losing visual communication with their brigade headquarters and artillery, which, in some cases, was over 2000 yards away in Mash Valley.[14] Signallers such as Private Harold Hinckfuss would have to adapt quickly to this new situation. Despite the difficulties, he understood that his duty was to 'get the message through at all costs'. According to Hinckfuss, most commanders had a magneto telephone. Shellfire constantly severed connections to these telephones, forcing signallers to spend hours listening in to conversations over a wire; that way, they knew when a connection was cut and could immediately repair it. Multiple trunk cables with numerous test points were also buried in trenches in an attempt to restore uninterrupted communication. Surface lines were laid when and where needed, then duplicated and laddered, which created a network of alternative electrical paths.[15] Despite these improvements, the wires rarely survived a heavy bombardment. In response, some signallers used large French electric lamps, which could send up to 30 messages a day, although they had the unfortunate side-effect of attracting German fire at night.[16] Others reverted to using carrier pigeons; signallers attached a small cylinder to the pigeon's leg, and filled it with messages written on custom lightweight paper. Pigeons were surprisingly reliable, but could only be released in daylight hours and calm weather. If mistakenly released into a westerly wind, they were sometimes blown over into the German lines. Soldiers often came across dead pigeons that shellfire had shredded.[17]

Despite these measures, commanders still relied on runners to relay messages. Unfortunately, runners' lives were sometimes risked to deliver trivial information. Iven Mackay recalled, when crouched over a map amid dozens of corpses and moaning wounded, a panting runner arriving with an envelope marked 'urgent and secret'. The note from Gough, presumably forwarded by brigade or divisional staff, said that a number of men had recently failed to salute his car, despite the general's flag being prominently displayed on the bonnet.[18]

This new phase of fighting along an exceedingly narrow salient was also characterised by German barrages that repeatedly destroyed freshly dug trenches. It would cause massive confusion: orders referred to trenches that ceased to exist or were not recorded on maps.[19] New maps were needed almost daily to cope with the ever-changing situation. The most reliable and important source of information for maps came from aerial photographs taken by the 7 Squadron, Royal Flying Corps, which were attached to the Anzac Corps.[20] Photographs taken in the early morning were developed and printed at the aerodrome, and then rushed by motorcycle to reach the corps, and later, the divisional headquarters, by late afternoon. The maps clearly showed new trenches, and helped officers set their objectives and accurately measure their troops' advances.

White and Cox would have hoped that these revised arrangements would keep the vital supply routes open and soldiers adequately supplied long enough for them to execute their next attack upon the farm. Time would tell whether the arrangements would hold.

On Tuesday 8 August, Birdie and White met with Cox to devise a strategy for the capture of the farm. In plans drawn up on 6 August, White had suggested the first two trenches as successive targets, but Cox now favoured only one, as he didn't want to end his first thrust at the bottom of the gully. The officers agreed that the attack's objective for that evening would be Park Lane Trench.

Although agreeing on the plan, White still harboured grave concerns that the isolated attacks across the entire line were uncoordinated and, in the case of the Australians, conducted on a much narrower front.²¹ The value of decisive and coordinated attacks seemed to have been forgotten: Rawlinson's Fourth Army, Gough's Reserve Army, and General Marie Émile Fayolle's French Sixth Army were each doing their own thing. 'They seem content to let each little lot plan its own attacks,' White remarked.²² White's opinion was accurate: the Reserve and Fourth armies seemed incapable of launching coordinated attacks and despite the best-laid plans, the French and British had to postpone joint attacks on 7 and 11 August.²³ On 11 August, Haig's ally, General Joffre, vented his displeasure with the situation, stating that he wanted to move away from small-scale battles to broad-front, multi-division affairs.²⁴

White also realised that he had to act quickly, as Gough wanted to launch his five-division attack on Thiepval by the end of the month. Railway timetables — of all things — dictated this timeline. The *Official History* noted that the generals speculated as to the exact date that a division would be worn out, and railway timetables were developed accordingly. The dates for transporting the Australian divisions from the Somme had already been decided. The Australian commanders had to speculate which vital points would be captured prior to their division's relief. Based on their forecasts, high command had expected the Australians to capture Mouquet Farm by mid-month.²⁵ Unfortunately, the chaos thrown up by battle rarely conforms to railway timetables.

White and Cox decided to capture Park Lane Trench using Digger Brand's 15th Battalion, supported by the 7th British Suffolk Battalion. They hoped that Park Lane would be lightly held. 'We go over the parapet and then our fate is sealed,' an officer wrote to his wife, upon learning that his battalion would lead the attack. 'I'll try for your sake to do well and come through ... God be with you Love for all Time.'²⁶

Just on dusk on 8 August, the 15th Battalion left its shallow trenches, traversed 200 yards of no-man's-land, and secured a section of Park Lane Trench. The 7th Suffolk Battalion on its left failed to capture a knot of trenches known as points 78 and 96.²⁷

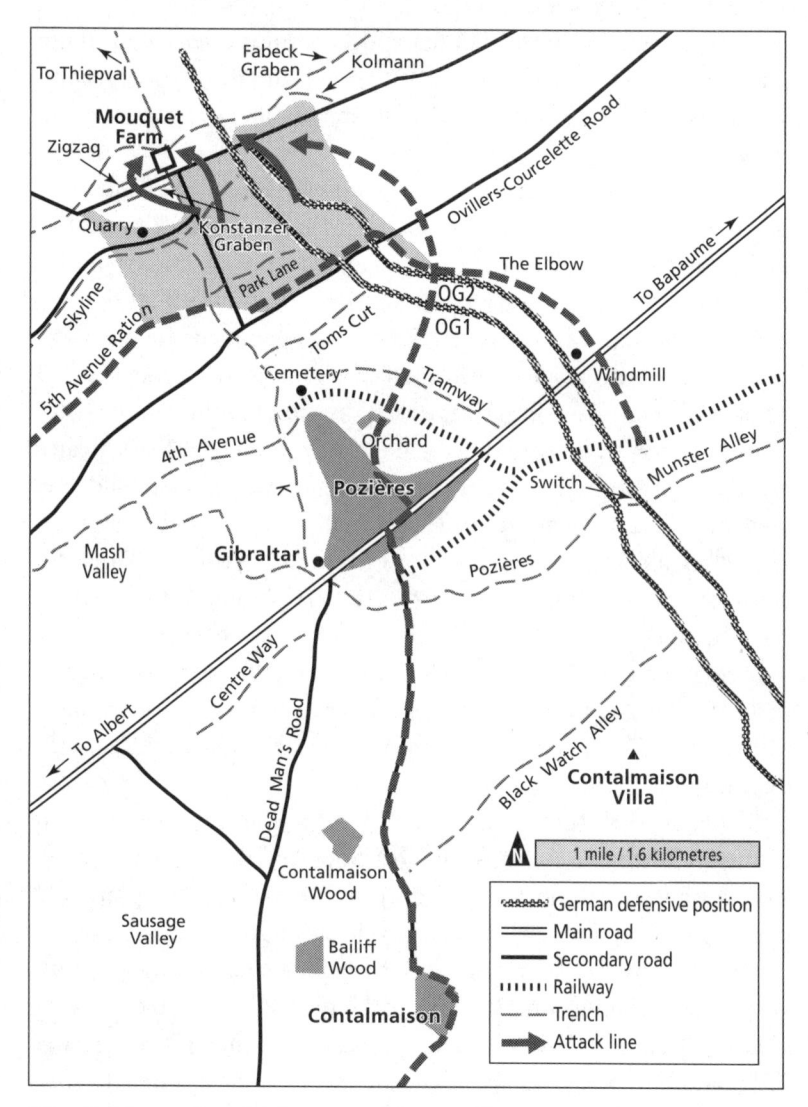

Map 5. I Anzac Corps' Advance on Mouquet Farm,
August to September 1916

Casualties were relatively light, thanks to inexperienced German soldiers initially mistaking the attackers for their own troops. Some Australians, unable to make out the shallow trench, settled 50 yards beyond it.

Charles Bean, who sheltered in Brand's 4th Brigade headquarters — a dugout in Sausage Valley — during the attack, was less enthusiastic about its supposed success. 'And so ends another expensive petty operation,' he wrote in his diary. 'With all the will in the world one cannot see a spark of the genius or imagination which one would like to see in the British plans. Have they a plan? At present it looks as [they] leave each division to think out its petty "stunt" and act on its own as it likes.'[28] At a tactical level, Bean's criticism of seemingly valueless advances was understandable. However, at a strategic level, Haig's plan was comprehensible: to secure favourable positions, such as Mouquet Farm and Thiepval, prior to the September general assault. Historian Peter Simkins recognised the differing perspectives of soldiers and generals on this matter, noting that 'the broader tactical benefits were not always instantly apparent to the officers and men who saw the strength of their battalions eroded by minor yet costly "line straightening" operations'.[29]

Cox ordered further minor raids over the next few days to capture additional sections and offshoots of the trench warren. The battalions, supported by accurate bombardments, gradually edged their way forward, inch by inch, through a combination of bombing raids and barricading. 'Everywhere successful; joined up with 15th Battalion on right; Suffocks on left,' wrote Lieutenant-Colonel Edmund Drake-Brockman, commanding officer of the 16th Battalion, in a message to divisional headquarters at 3.45 a.m. on 10 August.[30]

Birdie, Cox, and Gough 'heartily' congratulated Brand on his success. 'I was sure you would succeed fully,' wrote Birdie. It seemed a solid blow had been delivered upon the wedge that would drive the

Allies toward Thiepval. Gough's ambitious timetable of capturing the farm mid-month and Thiepval toward the end of the month might just be met, although no one was under any illusions: the next two trenches would be the most difficult and costly to capture.

As Bean and White feared, isolated attacks along a narrow front had become the Reserve Army's *modus operandi*. Resentment grew toward its supposed architect, the prickly and impatient Gough, who White considered dangerously impulsive.[31] White, like many Australians, couldn't understand why Anzacs were still being sacrificed to capture a seemingly insignificant farm.[32] No doubt White and Bean wondered whether it would be better and quicker for the British to launch one massive, full-blooded frontal attack upon Thiepval. As the *Official History* pointed out, attacking Thiepval's back door only resulted in difficult and expensive fighting.[33] Why had Gough chosen this course of action?

After capturing the OG lines, Gough's intent had been clear. From 5 August, he had ordered repeated attacks, with moderate numbers, toward Thiepval (although the first moderate thrust northward did not occur until 8 August, due to the exhaustion of the 2nd Division troops).[34] He wanted as few breaks as possible so that the Germans would be kept off balance. 'Once we allow him to get his breath back,' he told Birdie, 'we shall have to make another of these gigantic assaults by which time all the German defences will have been repaired and strengthened.' And his approach, although contrary to White's view, had some merit; the terrible losses of 1 July were still fresh in everyone's minds. 'I think our way keeps down casualties and brings the best results,' reasoned Gough.[35]

Gough believed that Thiepval stood in the way of achieving a breach. The futility of assaulting this stronghold frontally was there for everyone to see: the twisted and contorted bodies of the 36th (Ulster) Division troops, who had attacked the fortress on 1 July, still littered Thiepval's steep approaches. Gough was right: Thiepval was the most powerful German bastion on the Somme, and Mouquet

Farm was the best point for sapping toward it.[36] And according to Gough, it was working: 'We are breaking in bit by bit and must not stop until we have made the gap.'[37]

Just as important, Gough's 'penny packet' assaults complied in principle with Haig's directive that his generals attack with as little expenditure of fresh troops and munitions as possible (although the toll on those troops who were thrust forward repeatedly into the attacks was high).[38] Even if Gough wanted to chance another massive frontal attack, he didn't have the materials required to pull it off. Therefore, Gough's strategy was a logical response to the circumstances confronting him. Yet this provided little consolation for the Australians, who would have realised that they were simply one small cog in a gigantic enterprise and that, like those blackened corpses of the Ulster Division that lay on Thiepval's approaches, they too would be ground to dust. And all for some seemingly insignificant coordinates on a map — it seemed that minor successes on the Somme always came at a shocking price.

Even though Gough's strategy seemed well reasoned, albeit expensive, there were no guarantees that it was right or would be successful. Gut instinct, hunches, and time pressures had shaped it, along with the interpretation of uncertain battlefield data and questionable intelligence reports. Gough perhaps felt that his chosen path was vindicated by Charteris's intelligence reports, which suggested that the Germans' morale was irreparably damaged, and Haig's opinion that the Germans had used up 30 of their divisions in one month on the Somme, compared to 35 at Verdun in five months.[39] No doubt he also read captured German letters describing scenes, such as soldiers openly sobbing in their trenches, that suggested his enemy was under considerable distress.[40]

Gough favoured repeated attacks with moderate numbers, while White sought a coordinated effort across broader frontages — whose approach was right? Unfortunately, there was limited opportunity to mull over these options, as time remained the mortal enemy of strategy.

It was a case of a plan vigorously executed today being better than a perfect one enacted tomorrow. No one was certain there would be a tomorrow; the only certainty was that the prospects for the Australians were bleak.

As it turned out, White had good reason to be worried.

While the Anzacs slogged their way over a brown-cratered wilderness toward the ruins of Mouquet Farm in early August, 10,000 miles away in Australia the public closely followed their fortunes in the newspapers. The reporting of the exploits was anything but bleak. Ever since 3 July, when the Melbourne *Herald* had first announced that 'Britain's Greatest Battle' had begun, crowds had milled around newsstands, hankering for news. *The Herald* reported how the British public rejoiced upon hearing that the much-anticipated offensive had started, explaining that when the news was read aloud in theatres and music halls, audiences rose to their feet and cheered. The first sketchy reports, often received from *The Times* or Reuters, brimmed with confidence. One article declared that the 'opening moves of the terrific drama were played with strategic skill confusing the enemy'.[41]

Over the next three weeks of July, the newspapers reported a string of smashing British victories — on every front the news was good. *The Herald* reported that Lloyd George expected to snatch victory in the next few months and that German experts had admitted their victory was near impossible.[42] The war's end seemed imminent, with some experts predicting it would end in November 1916 or early 1917.[43] Only Australian correspondent Keith Murdoch expressed some concern, cautioning that the gains of the offensive weren't commensurate with the losses.[44]

On Monday 24 July, news had come that Australia's own Anzacs had captured the stronghold of Pozières. The Melbourne *Herald* reported that, even though the Germans had resisted fiercely, Australian casualties were light.[45] More detailed reports filtered through over the next few days. The paper told its readers on 26 July of heavy fighting, with soldiers describing Gallipoli as child's play compared to Pozières.[46] Hobart *Mercury* readers learnt on the same day that in hand-to-hand fighting the Germans were no match for the Australians, 'who simply love it'.[47] Melburnians would have lapped up Bean's despatch the following morning, under the giddy headline, 'Men Cross Zone of Death as if Going Home for Tea'.[48] The French, delighted with the capture of Pozières, applauded the Anzacs, who were described as 'hard as nails'.[49] In another article, a German prisoner of war was reported to have said that the Australians were brave men who seemed to have no fear of death.[50] *The Herald* told its readers on 7 August that the Anzacs, 'full of life and gaiety … were always anxious to get back to the firing line to show the Germans that if they were looking for more trouble they could have it'.[51]

The public drank willingly from the Anzac chalice. The praise was gratifying, particularly as it came at a time, as Joan Beaumont noted in *Australia's War, 1914–18*, when Australians were searching for a sense of what it was to be a nation, rather than a collection of colonies. Many Australians believed the struggle of war was the greatest test of a nation and found the newspaper reports of the Anzacs' exploits appealing. The correspondents, who embellished the soldiers' successes and omitted much of the devastation blighting the Somme, were laying the foundations of the Anzac legend.[52] According to historians Manning Clark and Ken Inglis, Australia was gradually acquiring its own secular religion (partly cultivated by overoptimistic reporting) that, after the war, would have all the symbolism of Christianity — a baptism of fire, selfless sacrifice, and sacred sites of worship.[53]

War correspondents faced many challenges in reporting the truth. The first was the Australian government's censorship laws. Australia's *War Precautions Act* was enacted in August 1914. Ernest Scott noted in *Australia During the War* that the far-reaching provisions of Section 4 of the act enabled the governor-general to make regulations to secure public safety and the defence of the Commonwealth, which empowered the censor to perform its function. Put simply, the act prevented any agency or person from eliciting any information that might be directly or indirectly useful to the enemy. It therefore prevented correspondents from mentioning the location of troops, the unit they belonged to, numbers of casualties, or anything else that could be seen as helpful to the Germans.[54] Under the strict interpretation of these vague laws, anything written about the rolls of honour or even the weather conditions risked censure. Rather than openly challenge the act, most willingly abided by it. Bean wrote in his book *Letters from France*: 'The war correspondent does not wish to give to the enemy for a penny what he would gladly give a regiment to get.'[55]

All correspondents' reports passed through the censors. Although the Act intimated that legitimate criticism would not be suppressed, publication of anything prejudicing recruitment efforts or discipline of the forces was censored. Emotive phrases, gruesome photographs, or exaggeration of successes or failures would not make it through.[56] The censors even dictated which British newspapers and what edition the reports were published in. On the Somme, a press officer located at Amiens carefully scrutinised Bean's articles. Bean noted in his diary that on 31 July 1916, the officer, Colonel Hutton Wilson, warned him that his recent articles contained 'too many exact particulars', such as attack times. Bean, although incredulous — he said to Hutton, 'surely the Germans know' — complied with the request.[57] Bean also relied heavily upon communiqués from General Headquarters, which, according to the *Official History*, were prepared more for the enemy's consumption than for the public, meaning that events were often represented through rose-coloured glasses.[58]

Since the beginning of the war, the military had controlled war correspondents tightly, including Bean. In 1914, the War Office banned them from the front line. By 1916, these restrictions were relaxed. Only a handful of correspondents were accredited to cover the Somme battle. ('We cannot conveniently control more than six correspondents,' was John Charteris's reason for accrediting so few journalists.)

Yet having accredited journalists on the front line didn't guarantee realistic reporting. As Martin Farrar explained in *News from the Front*, the army's accreditation system could vet correspondents and refuse access to anyone they felt might not share their view. Once accredited, the army assigned a liaison officer to parties of correspondents, who closely monitored their movements.[59] Bean, as Australia's official war correspondent, had more freedom than most to visit the front line, but at the same time he censored himself, electing not to publish anything that might upset his hosts and threaten his access to the front. And Bean had good reason to be compliant: in July 1916, the censors had stopped his early Somme despatches from reaching the British newspapers for a short period after a fellow correspondent allegedly objected to Bean's name appearing in them. Bean thought the complaining correspondent was jealous of his growing reputation. He later wrote in his diary that petty measures such as this, which seemed directed at controlling the amount of kudos the Australians received on the Somme, resulted in the public not having 'the least idea of the battle we are fighting'.[60]

As the battle ground on through August, the newspaper reports lost their euphoric tone. On 16 August, *The Herald* admitted that the Australians and British had suffered under 'appalling fire' for the previous nine days.[61] The reports now wrote of consolidating and straightening the line, rather than of breakthroughs. Readers sensed that the task confronting the Allies was much greater than first imagined. 'What one feels is that after all, our progress is insignificant, we have thrust back our foes a distance of one or two miles upon a front of 8 miles,' wrote one reader in his diary. 'What is this compared with the front line which is measured in hundreds of miles?'[62] In late August, *The Times* in London predicted that the war could last until 1918. John Treloar, at I Anzac Corps headquarters, got quite a shock upon reading it: 'The thought rather terrifies.'[63]

The newspapers repeatedly assured the Australian public that casualties at Pozières were light and many wounds slight, sometimes only scratches.[64] But the casualty lists published in the newspapers every second or third day grew at an alarming rate. Some families accused the government of reporting casualties inaccurately, claiming they had received word through unofficial sources, such as letters and cables, before they received official notification. On 12 August, the minister for defence, Senator George Pearce, publicly disputed the claims. Although he admitted that casualties had been 'fairly heavy', he advised relatives 'not to spend their money on cabling on the basis of the rumours'. Then, in an about-face, the government admitted on 29 August that there had been delays in reporting casualties, saying that the 'great loss of officers' had slowed the compilation of authentic information.[65]

Australians began to realise that the initial newspaper reports had been overly optimistic and misleading. Then, in late August, the massive casualty lists from the month before finally appeared in the papers, spilling over many pages. 'The casualty lists in the papers made it all clear to us. Every day we saw men and women wearing bits of black, and we knew others wearing no sign at all,' remembered one man. 'The pattern of the war was set.'[66] Between 2 August and 23 September, *The Herald* reported a staggering 21,000 casualties.

Yet it was often friends and comrades of those soldiers killed or wounded, and even medical staff, who provided next-of-kin with the first news of their loved ones' fate. The parents of Private Robert 'Roy' Smith received a letter from Sister Cunningham, who, sometime on 30 July, in Block A of Wharncliffe War Hospital in Sheffield, had sat by Roy's bedside and written on a Red Cross notepad, 'I am writing to let you know that your son Pte Smith arrived at our hospital two days ago, he is quite badly wounded in both legs and one arm and chest.' She then wrote, 'he is much better today than when he came in'.[67] These carefully crafted words suggest that Sister Cunningham wanted to offer some hope to Smith's parents, without creating false optimism.

Smith was one of Gellibrand's hapless 22nd Battalion soldiers who had sheltered in broken trenches between the orchard and the cemetery at Pozières for 'hour after hour' on 27 July under the German bombardment.[68] He was fortunate in one respect only: according to his diary, the shell that wounded him had killed the men either side of him. He was evacuated in a critical condition. He remembered lying on a hard stretcher and his badly smashed leg getting shaken about.

After a series of operations and some rest, Smith felt well enough to write a letter home to his mother, Mrs Annie Bennison of Prahran, Victoria: 'I have some bad news for you. I have been under four operations with my leg and at the last they had to cut it off above the knee. It was either lose my leg or go under myself.'[69]

Unlike Annie Bennison, Hester Allen, the mother of Robert and Stephen, did not receive any unofficial notification of her sons' fate when they disappeared on 14 August. Robert and Stephen Allen had decided to enlist together in July 1915. There wasn't much to keep them at home in the beachside suburb of Manly: neither had married, and they probably wouldn't miss their labouring jobs. It may have worried them to leave their widowed mother, who had struggled to care for them since they were boys, but their younger sisters, Florrie and Minnie, could be depended on to help out. Allocated to the 13th Battalion, the brothers sailed together on *HMAT Ballarat* in September 1915, arriving in France via Egypt.

Robert and Stephen had not answered the 13th Battalion's rollcall after the 14 August attack. It took another month before Hester received this tragic news through the official source, the Base Records Office. Hester and her daughters patiently waited for further information, but none came. Three months after their disappearance, Florrie sent a letter to Base Records, asking if they had any more news. A printed letter replied that 'no further report had come to hand'.[70] Florrie, no doubt desperate for more details, sent a letter to the brothers' company commander, Captain Theodore Wells. He didn't reply.

Hester Allen's search for news about her two missing sons mirrored that of thousands of Australian families in late 1916. Letters and cables from their loved ones' friends and comrades, no matter how painful they were to read, provided more texture to the circumstances of their disappearance than bland official sources.

Charles Bean believed strongly in the Allies' cause. Yet he was not merely an objective outsider looking in; he was part of the army machinery. Bean held the honorary rank of captain, wore an army uniform, and was recommended for gallantry awards. He prided himself on working obediently within the constraints of the army system, boasting that he'd never yet 'written one word that has given the staffs a seconds anxiety, although I have seen and known more of the war — and lived far more in the thick of it — than any other writer for the paper'.[71] John Charteris observed that the press censorship on the Somme worked very smoothly owing to the 'loyalty of the correspondents'.[72] The complicity between correspondents and the army became apparent after the war, when five British correspondents were knighted in recognition of their war efforts.[73]

Bean, along with most journalists, lacked the language to adequately convey the true horrors of the war. In *News from the Front*, Martin Farrar noted that 'high' diction terms such as 'to perish', 'the fallen', and 'the red wine of youth' appeared throughout despatches, making them read more like romance novels than news.[74] Jaunty headlines in Australian newspapers in July 1916 — 'Thrilling Episodes Described', 'Dazzling Courage of the Australians', and 'Cooee Frightens the Germans' — misrepresented to readers the nature of the fierce fighting at Pozières.[75] Even the Anzacs resented these simplistic reports. 'You can't imagine how fed up we all are with some of the English newspapers,' wrote one. 'Padded up with such rot as "the giant athletes leaping their trenches" makes one sick.'[76] Despite the soldiers' disgust, many, including Albert Coates, were reluctant to describe the horrors of the Somme in letters home 'for fear of

The Censors'.[77] Bean would later reflect in the *Official History* that readers yearned so much for success, were so expectant of victory, that they sometimes wrongly interpreted intermittent advances on the Somme for much more than their worth.[78] Perhaps their unquenchable thirst for victory clouded their interpretation of Bean's despatches.

Politicians naturally feared that unrestricted and graphic reporting of battles like that on the Somme could erode the public's resolve to wage war. 'If the people really knew,' reflected Lloyd George in 1917, 'the war would be stopped tomorrow. But of course they don't and can't know. The correspondents don't write and the censorship would not pass the truth.'[79]

In 1916, the Australian public and its soldiers were fiercely committed to the war. Often this commitment was expressed in opinions tinged with almost religious zeal. For example, the Melbourne *Herald* preached to its readers in early August that they fought the Germans 'so that the whole course of life may move upward, instead of downward'.[80] Private William Clayton's papers contained these fortifying words: 'Man has had to wade through a sea of blood to reach a higher plane in its slow ascent towards the goal of noblest aspirations.'[81]

Captain Stanley Cocking expressed his commitment to the war with similar fervour: 'I am here to kill a vile principle that, in the nature of things, necessitates the taking of human life.'[82] The reporting of the unadulterated truth risked draining away this incredible reservoir of support; politicians like Lloyd George no doubt wouldn't risk it. In addition, it would give the Germans an unfair advantage. Their propaganda machine would soon claim that the British high command had fed three inexperienced and untrained Australians divisions into Pozières, while the British divisions sat idle.[83] Perhaps fire had to be fought with fire.

The problem was that the gap between 'what was fought and what was talked' was so glaringly wide due to inaccurate reporting and censorship that it prevented Australians from fully understanding the war or having an informed debate about its merits.[84] Censorship, according to Eric Andrews in *The Anzac Illusion*, lessened the political awareness of Australians.[85] In 1917, Mr Justice Ferguson openly expressed his concerns about inadequate reporting: 'We do not know what brigade, what division or what battalion was at Pozières,' he told guests of the Institute of Journalists of New South Wales. 'The indifference to the war among so many people in Australia is largely due to the ignorance of what takes place.'[86]

In early August 1916, in the midst of the Somme battle, there was still the opportunity for Bean to rethink the tenor of his despatches. In the coming days, the battle would touch him in the most personal way. Would this trigger him to tell the truth about Pozières without fear or favour?

CHAPTER THIRTEEN

Kicking in the Back Door

> 'See that little stream. We could walk to it in two minutes. It took the British a whole month to walk to it — a whole empire walking very slowly, dying in front and pushing forward behind.'
> — Description of a preserved trench close to Thiepval,
> F. Scott Fitzgerald, *Tender is the Night*

By dawn on Thursday 10 August, Cox's troops had captured Park Lane Trench, the first of three German trenches protecting the farm. The divisions' next objective would be to advance down the gully, sweep up the opposite hill, and then capture the farm. The Germans' objective remained unchanged: thwart the advance at all costs. Predictably, they responded to the loss of the Park Lane Trench by shelling the Australians throughout 10 August. 'Fritz started a very heavy bombardment,' explained one soldier sheltering in a broken trench. 'All the time we were crouched in the bottom expecting every moment to be the last.'[1]

Between 10 and 15 August, Cox's troops steadily battered their way forward over the cratered landscape, while the Germans repeatedly counterattacked. The Australians' first minor attack was launched just after midnight on 11 August, when patrols pushed into the valley and established forward posts. The 13th Battalion history, *The Fighting Thirteenth*, recorded that the troops advanced about 200 yards without meeting the enemy: 'When our barrage became stationary, all dug in.' The Germans counterattacked twice, at 2.45 a.m. on 11 August and at dawn on 12 August, but failed to dislodge the Australians. Their counterattacks withered under heavy Lewis gunfire, with their losses, the battalion history notes, 'estimated at over 1000'.[2] According to British correspondent Philip Gibbs, Germans stood on their parapet calling their comrades back, 'trying to save something out of this senseless slaughter that had been ordered'.[3]

On 12 August, the 4th Division and the 12th British Division launched a second formal attack toward Skyline Trench at 10.30 p.m. 'With a sounding of whistles we charged like blue hell across those few yards,' recalled trainee schoolteacher Captain Harold Armitage, who, along with the other troops, 'shoved' forward and secured a position about 350 yards short of the farm.[4]

On 13 August, Gough, pleased with the previous night's success, ordered Cox's division to completely surround and capture Mouquet Farm. The *Official History* speculated that, at the present rate of progress, the Australians would be well past the rear of Thiepval before Gough launched his grand attack on it.[5]

The course of the battle for the farm changed just before midnight on 13 August, when the Germans recaptured Skyline Trench from II British Corps. The Germans had preceded their attack with overwhelming artillery fire that, at about 10.50 a.m., forced the British to retire from the trench. Germans massing near the trench throughout the day were repeatedly shelled by the British and Australian artillery, resulting in severe casualties. Finally, at 10.30 p.m., the Germans launched their attack and captured Skyline Trench, which was full of British dead killed by the earlier German artillery fire.

The Germans' subsequent heavy shelling compromised the Australians' preparations for their 14 August attack. Lieutenant-Colonel Arthur Ross believed that his 51st Battalion could not possibly attack due to severe casualties: 'Both 13th CO thinks, and it is my genuine (not depressed) opinion that it would be a mistake to press the offensive further locally in this salient,' read his note to brigade commander Bill Glasgow.[6]

Ross's soldiers also dreaded the prospect of another attack. 'By this time we had lost two-thirds of our men, we'd had no sleep since late on the 11th and the men were dead tired with three nights of hard, heavy digging,' recorded an exhausted Harold Armitage.[7] The 13th Battalion history explained that, after two advances and several defensive battles, all its troops were 'weary and nauseated in all their senses'.[8] Despite heavy casualties and the troops' exhaustion, Glasgow sent a note to his company commanders ordering them to attack. As planned, the 4th Division advanced on 14 August and successfully broke into a small section of Fabeck Graben — the last trench protecting the farm. However, after desperate fighting, the Australians forfeited the trench. The *Official History* observed that Gough's northward advance had met with its first check.[9]

Confusion about the location of the Australians' trenches, the onset of bad weather, and the further stretching of the Australians' supply lines marked the five days of desperate fighting between 10 and 15 August.

The *Official History* explained that, throughout the recent advances, British aeroplanes had swept low over the battlefield, trying to confirm the furthest point of the Australians' advance; however, those on the ground often refused to light flares, fearing it would reveal their position to the Germans.[10] This meant that Cox and White often had to plan their follow-up attacks unsure of the front line's position, and that some troops, such as those of Ross's 51st Battalion, were shelled by their own guns. 'Our artillery are bombarding our own front trenches (heavies!!!)' read Ross's note to brigade headquarters on 14 August.[11]

On 10 August, rain fell steadily across the Somme battlefield. Mist and heavy cloud replaced the clear skies of summer. The shapeless landscape, now shrouded with mist, swallowed men up. In the early hours of 11 August, Captain Francis 'Toby' Barton, a law student from

Sydney, left his trench with Sergeant John Riordan to meet up with another officer. Barton, with his characteristic 'pigeon-toed walk', courtesy of a bullet wound to the thigh on Gallipoli, disappeared into the fog.[12] Barton's men scoured no-man's-land, but found no trace of him or Riordan. 'Neither were seen again,' recounted one soldier. 'Had he met the enemy, "Toby" would have certainly sold his life dearly.'[13]

Back in Australia, Annie Riordan and Cecilia Barton pondered the fate of their lost sons. 'I only wish, Dear Mrs Barton, that I could send you some comfort in your trouble,' read Annie Riordan's letter. 'God, grant they are safe somewhere.'[14] Seven years elapsed before Cecilia received Toby's perished identity disc in the mail, after his remains were discovered in a shallow, unmarked grave.[15] Annie Riordan's son's remains were never recovered.

As the Australians pushed deeper into the German lines, they extended their supply routes further, making it even more difficult to carry up rations and remove the wounded. Glasgow's troops went without water for two days, and when it did arrive there were only a paltry seven tins to share around. As for the scant food, the men had no appetite. 'Men cannot eat,' explained Corporal John McPherson. 'Their stomachs get upset through seeing their pals get cut to bits.'[16] Men sat by helplessly as their wounded comrades died. Harold Armitage cared for his wounded batman, struck in the back by bits of shell, as best he could. He waited for stretcher-bearers, but none came. A relieving battalion promised to look after him. On the way out, the battalion was badly shelled and Armitage lost contact with his batman.[17]

Captain Pat Auld of the 50th Battalion explained to a wounded soldier that it was pointless waiting for stretcher-bearers, as most of them had been hit: 'Your only chance of getting out of here alive is to run down the trench and turn left at the end of it.' The badly wounded man staggered to his feet and stumbled down the trench. Auld saw him several years later in Adelaide, not much worse for the experience.[18]

The ramifications of the Australians' savage battle on the Somme were felt beyond the thin sliver of French farmland they fought and died upon. Charles Bean sensed the offensive's radiating consequences whenever he read letters from grieved parents: 'they show the way in which a scrap piece of iron flung at random on the hillside in front of Mouquet drives its course right through to the furthest end of the world.'[19] Bean was right; the consequences of the Somme offensive were spreading like the ripples across a pond. They were felt by the shattered troops of the 1st and 2nd Divisions and the headquarters staff who grappled with the battle's complexities. They radiated across the Channel, and were felt in the British military hospitals that were flooded with thousands of broken soldiers and by politicians unable to comprehend how the waste could continue unabated. The consequences crossed the oceans to Australia, exacting a toll on the families of the dead, missing, and wounded. Generations would not be spared: children would grow up without fathers, and wives would grow old without husbands. The tragic results of the battle would linger for decades.

The consequences of the battle were felt at divisional headquarters. After pressing forward between 8 and 13 August, the 4th Division's advance had ground to a halt. Cox would have realised that the Australians' first attempt upon Fabeck Graben Trench on 14 August had failed. Unbeknown to him, the Germans had captured vital documents beforehand, showing that the attackers were intent upon capturing Mouquet Farm that evening, no matter the cost. With their senses heightened, the Germans interpreted every movement, real or imagined, as an attack, and met it with shelling and machine-gun fire. The Germans believed they were attacked at 1.20 p.m., 5.45 p.m., 7.00 p.m., 7.45 p.m., and 9.40 p.m. Ironically, and as testimony to the confusion of the battle, they didn't mention the actual attack time of 10.00 p.m.[20]

At corps headquarters, two issues would likely have occupied White's mind. First, to meet Gough's timetable for capturing the farm, a follow-up attack would have to be organised immediately. But what tactics could he employ? The British shelling seemed unable to root the deeply burrowed Germans out of their shelters. The Australians, by contrast, had little cover; every time they dug a trench, it caved in. Second, the Australians' momentum was slowly winding down. The corps had been in the line for 24 days straight. They now attacked with 'penny packets' of two or three battalions, as compared to six or seven at Pozières. Weary soldiers now welcomed 'blighty' wounds, such as a shattered arm or leg, which would have them evacuated from the front to Britain.[21]

While White considered his options, Charteris considered intelligence reports, which in recent weeks had lost their optimistic tone. His latest report stated that the Germans were still fighting well, and the British would need all the months available to them before winter to grind them down. Charteris correctly sensed the changing mood in London: there seemed to be less enthusiasm for the offensive, and growing doubts about whether the Germans would break.[22] Historian Simon Robbins suggested that Charteris was torn between his perceived duty to support Haig and maintain his spirits, and the obligation to furnish him with objective intelligence reports.[23] Perhaps Charteris's competing priorities coloured his reports, resulting in reversals being downplayed and partial successes exaggerated.

At I Anzac Corps headquarters, John Treloar reviewed intelligence summaries, some likely collated by Charteris's team, which often featured captured letters showing the enemy's desire for peace. Treloar wondered whether the letters reflected the true state of affairs: 'I always have the feeling that they are picked out of a number of letters of a different tone and published because they will cheer us up.'[24] He and his team of clerks were exhausted after many weeks of manning the Central Registry around the clock. Treloar, who worked from 7.00 a.m. to midnight most days in an uncomfortable canvas tent, wondered how long his clerks could maintain their punishing routine. One day merged with the next; it seemed hard to distinguish weekdays from weekends. 'There is nothing but the name to distinguish them from Thursdays and Fridays,' he wrote in his diary.

The work particularly taxed his clerks. 'I didn't come away to be a blooming owl,' complained one after working a string of late evenings. His orderlies seemed to come and go. They felt strangely removed from the battle, stamping and filing papers while marching columns passed by. 'They become possessed to return and share the perils of warfare with their comrades, so off they go and often within a few days are reported "killed in action" ', wrote Treloar in his diary. While Mouquet Farm remained in German hands, there would be no respite for Treloar and his clerks.

At small staging villages behind the front line, relieved soldiers of the 1st Division were slowly recovering from their first stunt. The mid-summer days of late July and early August on the Somme were beautiful and warm. The country was at its best: the flowering flax created vast fields of deep and intense blues. The aroma of fresh grass, the sound of sweetly singing birds, and the tranquillity of the leafy lanes provided a wonderful tonic for the shattered men.[25] The soldiers slowly wound down and began to feel normal again. On warm summer nights, they often took off their puttees, rolled them up, and used them as pillows; they lay in the open fields among the long grass and fresh flowers, staring at the stars before finally falling into a deep sleep. 'It is beautiful among the trees,' recorded Albert Coates, 'after being like rats living in shell holes with dead and wounded men everywhere.'[26]

These soldiers tried to forget the war. Some immersed themselves in helping peasants to harvest their ripening crops. 'I remember seeing an Australian out in a field milking a cow,' observed John Treloar in his diary. 'Perhaps he enjoyed the work because of the home memories it brought.'[27] Others gathered in a shaded spot to toss the 'browns' in a game of two-up, or shed their clothes for a quick dip in a nearby stream — to the apparent shock of the local peasants labouring in the fields.[28]

As early as 27 July, rumours had begun to circulate that they would be returning to the line. Each man reacted differently. Some spent their money and enjoyed themselves one last time, getting drunk at an *estaminet* or purchasing a hearty meal. Vic Graham's mate urged him to clear out — perhaps go 'away without leave' to Paris — as he believed there was little hope of returning from such a place a second time.[29] Albert Coates had had enough of the senseless fighting; he didn't want to go back to Pozières. Only 50 men remained of his 1200-strong battalion that had landed on Gallipoli. He requested a transfer from the medical to the sanitation section, which was approved. On 3 August he began a job only cherished in wartime. 'Walking around the town inspecting latrines and water testing today,' he wrote of his new role with the Sanitary Hygiene Section, which supervised hygiene arrangements in the field to prevent disease.[30] Coates survived the war and became one of Australia's most eminent surgeons.

Others had no option but to return to the line. One man displayed a false bravado, claiming, 'Two or three good feeds and sleeps, and I will be ready to have another go at the bastards.'[31] Other soldiers would likely have laughed but no one would surely have believed him. The 1st Division troops had anticipated a long rest for reorganisation and re-equipping. However, in the coming days, their expectations would be shattered; as the rumours suggested, their spell from the trenches would be shortlived.[32]

From his billet in a small French village, Alec Raws was still grappling with the sad outcomes of Legge's failed 28 July attack upon the OG lines. His brother Goldy was still missing. On 12 August, the 23rd Battalion held a court of enquiry to ascertain Goldy's fate. Private John McGuire and Sergeant James Alliston were called as witnesses. According to the transcripts, McGuire heard Goldy's voice urging his men to remain in line during the attack; later, he saw him silhouetted in the light of a German flare. After digging in, McGuire asked after Goldy, but no one had seen him. This confirmed what Alec already knew, but what Sergeant Alliston had to say no doubt shocked him. In the aftermath of the attack, Alliston had suffered from shell shock. In hospital the day after Goldy disappeared, a medical officer asked Alliston about the officers of his battalion. Alliston said that Goldy was among the missing. The medical officer corrected him, saying that Goldy had passed through his hands with a wound to his head. Alliston couldn't recall the officer's name or where he had said Goldy was passed on to.[33]

Based on this scant evidence, the court recorded Goldy as 'missing'. For Alec, this offered some hope: 'Goldy is posted missing, but may be possibly wounded and temporarily lost in some strange hospital,' he wrote to his brother-in-law. 'I've told mother and father that he is wounded, but I don't know his whereabouts. I had to tell them something.'[34]

The practical consequence of the high Australian casualty rate on the Somme was the pressing necessity to recruit fresh men to replenish the gaps. In Australia, the wheels of the massive production line that recruited, equipped, transported, trained, housed, and finally sent men into battle continued to turn in August, albeit at a slower rate than in late 1915. The newspapers played their part in persuading men to volunteer. The Melbourne *Herald* regularly devoted its front page to pocket portraits of brothers — sometimes up to five — who had enlisted together. In August 1916, the newspaper applauded Mrs Campbell of Warrnambool for selflessly offering up her five sons in service of the country.[35]

In London, politicians such as Liberal member William Cowans contemplated whether the battered Australian divisions could replenish themselves. In the House of Commons on 10 August, he enquired if Australia would have any difficulty in keeping its forces at full strength, considering the lives they had lost on the Somme. 'I am confident that Australia will take all necessary steps to provide drafts to make good the wastage,' replied Lloyd George, then minister for war.[36]

Australia's war planners, plagued with falling voluntary enlistments, would not have shared Lloyd George's confidence. The enormous losses of Legge's division, coupled with those of Walker's 1st Division and McCay's 5th Division at Fromelles, had seriously depleted the Australian Imperial Force's reserves. More sapping battles were anticipated. In *Australia During the War,* Ernest Scott explained that, in response to these casualties, the Army Council (the supreme board administering the army, based in London) threatened to break up the 3rd Australian Division that John Monash was training in Britain so that the existing Australian divisions could be maintained in the field. It appeared to be a calculated move, as the Army Council rightly anticipated that the Australian government, and Birdie, in particular, would strenuously oppose it, given that both had been pushing hard for an Australian corps or army.[37]

Birdie and White thought it best to spell out to Australia their future manpower needs. Perhaps they could be supplied by voluntary enlistments. They requested 80,000 additional men over four months to replenish the five divisions.[38] This was above the 11,790 men they were anticipated to receive each month. The War Council accepted the estimate and cabled Australia with the colossal demand in early August. 'This is the only means of retaining the 3rd Division for service in the field,' read the cable. These numbers would be impossible to fulfil through voluntary enlistments, which had fallen to 6500 per month by mid-1916.[39] It appeared that the only way Australia could take the necessary steps to bolster its drafts was to introduce conscription. A crisis loomed on this issue; it would embroil the Australian Imperial Force and the Australian government and its people.

Australian prime minister Billy Hughes had the opportunity to achieve great things on the back of his growing reputation, but only at the cost of thousands more young lives in many more attacks like Pozières. The only way he could drive his political agenda was to answer the call to introduce nationwide conscription. Hughes didn't then realise it, but this would split the nation in two.

Amputee Roy Smith represented the Australian wastage that Lloyd George referred to. After a series of operations, his mangled leg had been amputated at the thigh, and his raw stump was mending slowly. 'It is a good cut and it takes a while to heal up,' he wrote in a letter home.[40] Shifted to the 2nd Australian Auxiliary Hospital in Southall, Middlesex, Smith noticed the deterioration in care, most likely due to the growing number of cases the hospital had to deal with in July and August. He wrote:

> My leg has not been dressed since Tuesday … one of the sisters must have woke up and came along to do my dressing; when she took it off it was green and smelt horrible. My dinner was stone cold and not very nice, I can tell you I never felt so homesick in all my life.

The specialist hospital where Smith convalesced fitted artificial limbs to amputees coming back from the Western Front. The flood of incoming cases overwhelmed and saddened the nurses. 'I have about 156 dressings to do for about 30 one-armed men,' wrote Australian nurse Sister Edith Avenell during a busy period for the hospital.[41]

'I was on duty with a ward of 15 patients who had three legs between them,' wrote another nurse. 'I felt a coward and shrank from meeting them at first, for they shamed me with the cheerfulness and independence.'[42]

Over 3000 shattered men passed through the hospital in three years. 'I am sorry for Australia but it will be nothing but broken-down men after the war,' despaired Avenell in a letter home.[43]

The newly designed high-explosive shells shattered the limbs of many soldiers apart from Smith. Geoffrey Noon explained in *British Fighting Methods in the Great War* that these shells broke up into jagged fragments, inflicting terrible damage by penetrating the skin and severing superficial veins and arteries before striking muscle, and possibly severing the nerves and large arteries and veins contained within it. If bone was struck, it would shatter into even smaller fragments.

These fragments would eventually exit the same way, making a larger hole on the way out.[44] These wounds were susceptible to gas gangrene because of the Somme's high manure content, causing the tissue of the affected limb to swell as the cells gradually died off. Doctors had few options to address these injuries — as in the case of Roy Smith's smashed femur — other than amputation.

Like Smith, infantryman Private Dan O'Brien from Charlton, Victoria, also had his leg amputated. O'Brien's 20th Battalion charged the Germans on 4 August, and just as he reached a German trench he was struck — 'I thought I was gone,' he wrote in a letter home.[45] He managed to crawl back to safety after sheltering in a shell hole all night. 'Next day two chaps carried me about two miles to the Dressing Station … I was on the point of death and they kept injecting me morphia to stop the pain.' O'Brien was eventually transferred to Southall. 'There were two operations and in the second one they took my leg off up near the thigh. So it will be "Old Uncle Dan and his Wooden Peg" when I come home.'

Smith wasn't sure what he would do when he returned home. He thought he could perhaps do his old job as a mechanic, but worried that the walk might be too far. The hospital offered technical training opportunities, and he started working in a factory with other amputees. 'All the other chaps have their wooden legs and when we are coming to work in the morning everyone knocks off work to watch us pass and they laugh at the others hobbling along on their legs,' he noted in a letter.[46]

Smith recovered slowly, returning to Australia in 1917. He must have wondered what his future would hold — would he be welcomed home, or would his pinned trouser leg be an uncomfortable reminder of a war that some Australians no doubt would prefer to forget?

The 4th Division's period of fighting concluded on 15 August, and its relieved units gradually withdrew from the front line. The *Official History* calculated that the 4th Division had conducted six successive night attacks over nine days, which had brought it within striking distance of Mouquet Farm. Correspondent Philip Gibbs described the fighting around the farm as 'hard and grim', as the enemy had 'done his utmost to check every yard of our men's advance by continual curtain-fire'.[47] The 4th Division's figure of 4649 casualties was marginally less than the 1st and 2nd Division's losses.[48]

Although the 4th Division had largely achieved its set objectives, its soldiers did not seem to be in a celebratory mood. Private Gilbert Jacob recalled looking back on the battlefield as he withdrew with a small group of walking wounded, one man out front carrying a white flag tied to a crooked stick. He saw an unbroken stretch of desolation, torn up a thousand times by the bursting of shells:

> It was worse than the desert, though, like in the desert, there was some tiny, yellow flowers. I stuck one in my coat and tried to whistle, but I felt so tearful that the third note stuck in my throat every time.[49]

While soldiers such as Jacob trudged back, their naive enthusiasm for war crushed and replaced with shattered nerves, bone-weariness, and tears, divisional headquarters hatched plans for yet another attack upon Mouquet Farm.

Birdie's diary and battalion histories show that he, in a feat of considerable stamina, distributed medals to nearly every battalion in I Anzac Corps — a major undertaking, considering there were 39 battalions in the corps and that each ceremony lasted many hours.

At a parade of 1st Division troops, Birdie announced, 'I have some wonderful news ... beautiful stirring news.'[50] He then dropped what was likely an unexpected bombshell: 'We will be in a serious action again within a few days.' The soldiers on parade couldn't believe it. 'You could hear going down the line, "You old bastard,"' remembered Ben Champion of the 1st Battalion. 'Birdwood must have heard it too, but he didn't bat an eyelid.' They had good reason to be angry: 50 per cent of the 1st Division troops had been killed or wounded in the first series of attacks, and subsequently they had only been reinforced to two-thirds of their original strength. Birdie tried to lift the troops' spirits with trite platitudes — he told them they had 'drubbed the Germans' once, and that this was their chance to 'kill some more'. The *Official History* said some men caught Birdie's spirit, while the majority thought his praise was idle flattery.[51]

Despite the loss of 5285 men from the division, the *Official History* explained that the brutal logistics of war, rather than Birdie's desire for further honours, dictated the 1st Division's return to the line. There simply wasn't the reservoir of fresh divisions to continually call upon as replacements; they had to be recycled whether at full strength or not. British divisions with similar, and sometimes heavier, losses had also been shunted back to the Somme for a second stunt.[52]

Birdie's bombshell deepened the Anzacs' growing bitterness toward the general staff. Some soldiers thought Birdie only used the Anzacs to make a name for himself. Bean noted in his diary that even Birdwood's fellow British officers thought 'he had come along too fast'.[53] When General Smyth asked for the customary three cheers for Birdie after one of his pep talks, Iven Mackay noted that 'the response was very ragged'.[54] The singing, joking, and high-spirited antics that marked the troops' mood in late July had faded, replaced by resignation to their pending fate in the mire and filth of the Somme battlefield.

CHAPTER FOURTEEN

Second Stunt

'Our nerves are bad but the heads are keeping us hard at it.'
— Corporal Arthur Thomas's diary

In mid-August, the 1st Division troops marched back toward Pozières. Birdie's news no doubt doused their relaxed mood. As they put their packs and blankets back into storage, some probably wondered if they'd ever return to reclaim them, or whether they'd ever get another chance to spend their French francs.

That night, the subdued troops slept in the remnants of a wheat field close to Albert. It rained and the fields turned into muddy clay, clinging to their boots and creating stagnant, foul-smelling puddles. Ground sheets prevented the men from sinking into it as they slept.[1] Many probably suffered a fitful sleep due to the mud and the odd shell landing in nearby fields.

The next day, they marched on to Bécourt Wood, just beyond Albert, and received water and iron rations — a tin of bully beef, two packets of plain biscuits, and a ration of tea and sugar — before continuing up the protective folds of Sausage Valley. They arrived at the Chalk Pit, the gateway between purgatory and hell. A quiet message was passed down the line instructing them to dump all supplies, equipment, and overcoats because they were going to attack Mouquet Farm.

During the three weeks of the 1st Division's rest, soldiers had rekitted, depleted ranks were replenished with reinforcements, platoons were drilled in modern warfare tactics, and soldiers were promoted to fill gaps in the officer ranks. The *Official History* recognised that within such a short time many of its troops were unlikely to have 'entirely recovered from strain' and may have, understandably, returned to the line determined to do their job but with 'deep bitterness in their hearts'.[2]

On a dreary Wednesday, 16 August, the troops tramped through the mud toward Pozières. Steady rain and thick mists had replaced summer sunshine. Major-General Hooky Walker assumed command of the front-line sector from Major-General Cox at 5.00 p.m. on 16 August. Hooky's division was expected to make two attacks in the coming days: northward to reach Fabeck Graben and enclose Mouquet Farm, and eastward to capture the new German front line opposite the windmill.[3] Gough told Hooky that his attack must coincide with the British and French offensive toward Guillemont on 18 August. Since the division's last stunt, the front line had shifted forward about 500 or 600 yards. Hooky would soon discover whether the spirit of his troops was adequately repaired to continue the push toward Mouquet Farm.

Hooky decided to tackle both objectives together on Friday 18 August by throwing the New South Wales 3rd Brigade at Fabeck Graben Trench and the Victorian 2nd Brigade at the strongpoints on the Pozières ridge, beyond the windmill. His immediate concern was, however, to ensure that his division — with its efficiency diminished from the last stunt — successfully navigated its way through the waterlogged approach trenches to the front line and then made the necessary preparation, such as digging jumping-off trenches and improving communications, prior to the attack two days later. Based at his Albert headquarters, Hooky wouldn't have realised how challenging these tasks would be.

The relieving troops trudged up the Bapaume road in drenching rain, occasionally slipping on the ground before entering First Avenue

Trench, which the pioneers were busily repairing. In a trench that was only three feet deep and shell-damaged, they threaded their way past soldiers' kit, mess tins, and discarded rifles.[4] Arthur Thomas of the 6th Battalion worked his way through the bog toward the windmill line, passing some of the wounded on the way there. He noted, 'so early in the morning, it has a bloody rotten effect on all of us'.[5] Lieutenant Matthew Abson, also of the 6th Battalion, wrote in his diary that the trenches smelt very badly of the dead, while Arthur Foxcroft, who trudged with other Victorian 4th Battalion soldiers toward the farm, recorded that the battlefield had barely changed since the last stunt.[6]

Eric Moorhead of the 5th Battalion moved into the reserve trenches, an area known as Death Valley. The name seemed deserved: 'Here a leg clad in Australian trousers protruded from the ground, there a German's hand, heads crawling with maggots and half eaten away protruding from the side of saps,' Moorhead recounted in his diary.[7] He wasn't exaggerating: Bean, who had followed a similar path, noticed a dead man's legs, a shoulder, and a half-buried body sticking out of the tumbled red soil. 'Bodies in a sort of decay, some eaten away to the skull,' he recorded.[8]

Upon reaching the trenches, 4th Battalion commander Lieutenant-Colonel Iven Mackay discovered that the relieved battalions of the 4th Division had abandoned two Lewis guns and some of their wounded comrades. Even worse, there were no British troops in trenches on his left for 500 yards. A disgruntled Mackay believed that 'a German battalion could walk through this vulnerable point and onto Pozières unmolested'.[9]

By Wednesday evening, the wet and tired 1st Division troops had largely taken over the 4th Division's trenches. The next day, 17 August, staff officers raised serious concerns about the location of the Australians' front line. The 4th Division's reported position before its relief seemed completely at odds with the position that the 1st Division now occupied. The 9th Battalion history, *From Anzac to the*

Hindenburg Line, attributed the confusion to poor communication, claiming that exhausted 4th Division troops 'could not give the relieving troops any information, but simply went out of the line as fast as they could'.[10] With no defined trench line, had the fresh troops settled in the wrong positions? Hooky's planned attack could not proceed until this problem was sorted out. Concerned, Brigadier-General Nevill Smyth personally reconnoitred the front line near a chalk pit called the quarry, which was about 250 yards from the farm. He believed the front line was not as far forward as the 4th Division had reported it to be, even though an aerial photograph showed a 'beautifully clean line dug' in the disputed location. Based on Smyth's reconnaissance, Lieutenant-Colonel Howell-Price's 3rd Battalion was ordered to withdraw from two advanced positions to allow the heavies to bombard in front of them.

'Why?' responded Howell-Price. 'It's 150 yards behind my front line.'[11]

Smyth was wrong. Aerial photographs taken later that morning confirmed that the objective set for the upcoming attack was actually the 1st Brigade's front line. Birdie visited Hooky's headquarters and confirmed the disturbing error. Hooky's staff redrafted and reissued orders. Hooky blamed intelligence officers for the confusion; he thought they too often stayed cooped up at headquarters rather than visiting the front. He demanded that they provide him with their daily reports in the future.[12]

The confusion about the location of the front-line trenches continued that evening when shells from the preliminary bombardment fell directly on Howell-Price's 3rd Battalion. Howell-Price sent a message back to headquarters:

> Can this matter have attention please? At present I am endeavouring by all means possible to stop our artillery from firing and now it is 45 minutes since I sent my first message and one gun is still firing with disastrous effect.[13]

Coupled with occasional desultory shelling from their own guns, the Australians were also shelled by the Germans. It seemed that the Germans had noted the activity opposite them in the early hours of 16 August, and rightly guessed that a major relief operation was underway.[14] Foxcroft, now a lance-corporal and one of the most experienced men in his platoon, had sheltered in the support trenches with his section since 4.00 a.m. the previous morning. Covered in mud, he kept a close eye on his anxious reinforcements. 'Standing to all night expecting huns to attack, some men in trenches for their first time, had [a] job to keep them awake,' he wrote in his diary. 'Had to dig half buried dead out of trench and build up parapet before daylight.' Foxcroft dug out his mate, Roy 'Bluey' Wilson, after an exploding shell buried him, only to discover that his head had been blown off. Foxcroft's sergeant, John May, was also blown to smithereens. When morning came, Foxcroft remembered that he and what was left of the platoon felt 'very tired'.[15]

Nearby, Sergeant John Edey, 5th Battalion, tried to manoeuvre his platoon up a narrow trench toward the front line. The shelling terrified his men, who became horribly bunched. A shell landed in the middle of them and practically buried them all. Edey tried to dig them out. 'All I could do was scrape down till I located a face, and then continue till I could locate another, and so on,' read his wartime diary. The soldiers were in terrible pain, with parts of their equipment sticking into their bodies. 'Faces, faces, was what I was after. Just to get them all breathing,' he recorded. As Edey exposed faces, he placed steel helmets over them to protect them from the shelling. 'In most cases the lower part of the legs were entangled, and so it was dig to the very end.' Disturbingly, as each man wriggled free, they disappeared toward the aid station, leaving Edey alone to complete the task.[16]

Edey's men scampering to the rear was an understandable reaction. George Londey's diary description of being buried under six feet of earth by a massive shell provides an appreciation of the sheer terror they must have felt: 'My toes were all I could move. There was one man two or three yards on my left buried up to the neck.'[17] Londey remembered verging on unconsciousness as the little air in the space near his eyes and nose became stale. He knew that life was being squeezed out of him and he feared that he'd be another of those killed, smothered to death.

After 20 minutes, Londey was dug out. 'I was sent out of the line and felt better when I got a stiff tot of rum,' he wrote in his diary. Understandably, men like Londey, after surviving such terrors, lost their will to fight.

Later in the day, a sergeant assigned a new platoon to John Edey, who assessed them as being 'a team of war babies, 16-year-olds; the first time in the line for them all'.[18] They arrived with a much-needed Dixie of stew: 'I had to stand over the newly arrivals and personally compel them to eat, they were that scared.' As Edey tucked into the stew, a shell burst overhead, breaking his leg and tearing his calf muscle. He made his way back to a dressing station, edging along the trenches on his elbows. I Anzac Corps could ill afford the loss of experienced Gallipoli veterans such as Edey.

It seemed that no one was concerned with being a hero anymore — most soldiers, among them Eric Moorhead, just wanted to survive. 'You would not have called us heroes if you had seen us,' he wrote in his diary on 17 August, 'quivering at the knees and smoking cigarettes to keep the nerves up.'[19] Even Moorhead's officers couldn't stomach the thought of another attack; he wrote that 'to get the battalion declared unfit many of us were practically ordered to parade sick'. The doctor at a dressing station in Fricourt didn't accept the exhausted men's claims, and they rejoined their battalion the next day.

Mackay sensed his men's utter exhaustion. Seven days of fighting in July and August had resulted in 741 casualties to his battalion: one hundred every day; four every hour; one every 15 minutes.[20] Mackay felt that his men could no longer withstand the rigours of war. Minor wounds, a scare, or a close shave had them scampering back to aid stations for treatment. He castigated them: 'A man is not wounded if his face is splashed with dust, or if a small clod hits his back. We must learn to keep cool and to steady the new men.' No one seemed to listen. One of Mackay's lance-corporals could not stand the strain any longer, and deserted. Mackay, who had always assiduously protected his men, would later promulgate the man's sentence, which was most likely to be death by firing squad — although these sentences were always commuted to penal servitude in the Australian Imperial Force.

News of the incident also troubled John Treloar. 'I realise that grave offenses must bring serious punishments,' he wrote in his diary, 'but I cannot help thinking of those who are interested in the man back home.'[21] It seemed odd that an Australian soldier could volunteer his services to the Empire and then risk being killed for later withdrawing the offer.[22]

Foul weather, confusion about the front line's location, and German shelling threw the 1st Division's attack preparation into the usual confusion. But what possibly concerned White, Birdie, and Walker the most was the fading resilience of their troops. Could these spent men muster another effort or two to take the farm before they completely unravelled?

Hooky Walker's eastward and northward attacks around dusk on 18 August followed a now well-established script; it was one that Charles Bean seemed familiar with, writing in his diary: 'without losing heart, anticipate getting in [to the trenches] but holding is another matter'.[23] As anticipated, the German bombardment compromised the digging of jumping-off trenches; battalion headquarters received written orders so late that they had to communicate them by phone to their companies; troops were shelled by their own guns; advancing troops captured some objectives, but were forced to retreat as their flanks were dangerously exposed; and many deaths and wounds resulted in trivial gains.[24] In one disturbing incident, troops in the supports refused to help others struggling to hold a position. The sights and sounds of a night battle — orange flashes, bursting flares, panicked screams, whistling bullets, yelled instructions, and muffled explosions — terrified the inexperienced reinforcements that had replenished the battalions. In a sign of growing discord between the Australians and Gough, Bean recorded in his diary a rumour that the general, displeased with the attack's failure, had the cheek to tell Hooky that he ought to go up Pozières and see things himself.[25]

No one seemed to recall whether it was the fifth or sixth attack toward the farm; each fatiguing effort seemed to merge with the next. Although the Anzacs' assault had failed to gain any ground, Rawlinson's Fourth Army attack upon Guillemont had some success, with the outskirts of the village being reached and held; however, the attack upon High Wood largely failed. The 18 August attacks aimed to straighten the line before Haig launched his mid-September offensive. Robin Prior and Trevor Wilson noted that Rawlinson, in his nibbling and poorly planned attacks, showed no sign of achieving this objective.[26] Rawlinson's operation suffered the same shortcomings as Gough's: piecemeal attacks delivered on narrow fronts with insufficient troops.

The continuing strain of repeated assaults and prolonged bombardments did, however, place further stress on the German defenders. All available reserves had been put into the line. The 28th Division's commander warned that he would no longer be held responsible for the defence of the second and third lines.[27] General Max von Gallwitz, concerned with the precarious nature of his defences, visited the front line. He realised that a further breakthrough would bring the enemy to the rear of Thiepval, making his own men's position untenable.[28]

Von Gallwitz needn't have worried. In the 1st Division sector, Hooky had already notified corps headquarters that, due to severe casualties, he doubted his men would be fit to engage in anything more than very minor offensives. Despite this, White requested that the division conduct one more limited action before its relief: could Hooky's division clear the Germans in front of Fabeck Graben and then secure the higher ground? This would straighten the line, making subsequent actions much easier to launch.

Hooky couldn't see the sense of such a 'half hearted' effort to clear an area about the size of a local park.[29] If he had to attack and incur casualties, shouldn't the objective justify the cost? Therefore, the revised objective included a large portion of Fabeck Graben.[30]

John Forsyth doubted that his brigade would be of much use in the coming attack. In a note to Hooky, he explained that in five days he had lost 850 men and he had two weakened battalions strung out over a frontage of 1500 yards, while a third verged on collapse after digging trenches and carrying out fatigues throughout the night.[31] With or without Forsyth, the formal attack in broad daylight would occur as planned on Monday 21 August. He hoped that the clumsy tactics previously employed by the Anzacs would be modified before the assault.

On Saturday 19 August, the clearing weather gave Foxcroft a chance to clean the mortar-like mud from his rifle. Absorbed in the task, he reacted slowly to the whine of a whiz-bang. Foxcroft explained in his diary that its explosion threw him to the muddied floor of the trench, showering him with dirt and knocking the air from his lungs. He lay still. After a minute, he tried to move his limbs. He could feel his legs, arms, and head, and as far as he could tell he didn't have a wound to his stomach or chest. It seemed that the fine, dusty soil, churned up by shell after shell, had muffled the blast and saved his life. Foxcroft thanked God for his luck.

His injuries were moderate: the top of his middle finger had been blown off, and shrapnel had lacerated his shoulder and face. A stretcher-bearer dressed his wounds. He worked his way back through the narrow trenches to a dressing station, where he felt safe enough to enjoy a smoke, a cup of tea, and a plate of hot soup.

An orderly snipped off the finger that hung by a sinew of flesh, and dressed the wound.

He arrived at the Canadian General Hospital at 4.00 a.m. the next morning and was taken to a makeshift tent with 40 beds. It took some time for his wounds to be treated, as others, including his mate Paddy South — a stretcher-bearer with his hand blown clean off — were priority patients.

The next day, Foxcroft received something that any man who had ever been under a German bombardment cherished. It wasn't a medal or citation, but a small tag with the handwritten words 'Evacuate to England' scribbled on it. Arthur's war was over for now; he had his 'blighty' wound that he would recover from in time.

On 24 August, he arrived at Dover and transferred to No. 1 Eastern General Hospital at Cambridge, which was packed with 62 beds in each ward. Foxcroft, for the first time in months, slept in a real bed with clean sheets and soft pillows. At the time, it likely would have seemed well worth the price of one finger.[32]

Second Division soldiers such as Alex Raws waited for the inevitable calling for their units to continue the fight around Mouquet Farm. Raws had recently been suffering from inexplicable fainting spells. 'It is difficult to know whether it is not just nerves,' he wrote in a letter to Lennon.[33] He expected their next fight to be short and sharp, on account of their diminished divisional strength; then, once they got through this, they could expect an extended period out of the lines reorganising and reinforcing. On Monday 24 August, he wrote to his father, hinting that the prospect of Goldy turning up alive was low, as he had not been found at any hospital:

> I write of him coldly and without emotion, because, Father, it is impossible that one give way to the expressions of grief just now. And I do trust that you and Mother, should good news not have reached you, will be able to sustain yourselves.

Alec then wrote a candid letter to his brother, disclosing that Goldy's death had shocked him more than he thought possible. He finished with a revelation:

> I honestly believe Goldy and many other officers were murdered on the night you know of, through the incompetence, callousness and personal vanity of those in high authority. I realise the seriousness of what I say, but I am so bitter, and the facts palpable, that it must be said. Please be very discreet with this letter — unless I should go under.

It was the last letter he ever wrote.

Like Raws, privates Denis Howard and Tod Nicholson heard the rumours that the 2nd Division would return to the front line. When confirmed, they decided to go absent without leave and visit Paris. The 6th Machine-gun Company history explained that with some cash, a little French, and a commanding officer willing to turn a blind eye, Howard and Nicholson set out for the French capital. The army, constantly on the lookout for deserters, had military police stationed at key points leading to Paris. Howard and Nicholson managed to board a train carriage occupied by two French soldiers, two elderly women, and a little fat boy consuming a pastry, who all initially suspected that the two men were spies. However, although they didn't understand the 'lingo', Howard and Nicholson shared a bottle of wine with their companions, and the sympathetic soldiers donated their overcoats to disguise them as French 'froggies'. Eventually they reached the city, where they noticed that a great commotion ensued whenever any of the locals discerned the word 'Australian' on the shoulder of their tunics. The men enjoyed hot coffee, biscuits, and cheese with some friendly Parisians, as well as the beautiful sights of Place de la Concorde, the Arc de Triomphe, and the Notre Dame cathedral. Howard marvelled at the Parisian streets, which were 'infested with small red taxi cabs which seemed to rush hither and thither without any regard for traffic rules'. Two a.m. found the weary men safe in a pensione. When they returned to the Somme, burdened with parcels of wine and food, their only punishment was a stern talking-to from their major.[34]

Soldiers such as Howard and Nicholson were more fatalistic after their first stunt at Pozières and were now prepared to break the army's rigid rules, knowing that they could be dead or maimed within the week. Often, jail seemed a more alluring prospect than another stunt.

Ernie Lee, the 14-year-old runaway who had landed at Marseilles in early June, seemed another Anzac contemptuous of the army's strict rules. At Étaples on 26 June, Lee had been charged with being asleep at, and then absent from, his post. Days later, he was found guilty of the charges. While his battalion fought on the Somme, Ernie served out a 28-day jail sentence; while he was serving, at home Herman and Mary Lee discovered that their son had enlisted, and at the request of the Australian Imperial Force completed a statutory declaration, revealing his true age.[35] Upon his release, Lee disappeared for 24 hours and was charged with being absent without leave and refusing to obey an order.

Strangely, Lee's jail sentence conflicted with the dates that the 1st Division returned to Pozières; it didn't make sense when the evening *Herald* claimed he'd fought at Pozières. Perhaps Lee had embellished his service record to acquaintances, or perhaps a journalist had incorrectly assumed that Lee, being part of the 17th draft of reinforcements for the 5th Battalion, had fought at Pozières.[36] In any case, he would soon find himself in much more serious trouble. Lee's behaviour, like that of Nicholson and Howard, was a prelude to the escalating disciplinary problems that the Australian Imperial Force would confront.[37] After the Somme, droves of disillusioned Anzacs would go absent without leave or commit serious offences, resulting in their imprisonment. This disturbing problem would tug at the fabric of the Anzac story.

As Raws, Nicholson, and Howard suspected, the 2nd Division relieved the 1st Division on 21 August. Holmes's 5th Brigade replaced Forsyth's weakened 2nd Brigade, which had suffered almost 1000 casualties since 15 August.[38] Those battalions not involved in the upcoming attack, such as Gordon Bennett's 6th — which had been under shellfire for six days — were relieved first. 'God how we welcomed our saviours who relieved us,' read a soldier's diary note. 'The men were so excited and nervy after their long trying vigil awaiting events, that they kissed each other.'[39]

In a last-gasp effort, Sinclair-MacLagan's 3rd Brigade, along with fresh 5th Brigade troops — about 1000 in all — would storm Fabeck Graben at 6.00 p.m. in the late afternoon light of 21 August and, it was hoped, capture about 1000 yards of the trench immediately in front of the farm. Bean, who observed the attack preparations at divisional headquarters, noted that 'there was a great deal of anxiety about this attack' although 'it has pleased the wonderful General Gough who controls this army'.[40]

Sergeant Dave Badger, a 20-year-old auburn-haired clerk from Peterborough, South Australia, didn't fancy his chances in the coming attack. Promoted to sergeant a few weeks earlier, he knew that for a few extra shillings he had to lead his men into attack. And he would have realised that those leading the attacks — sergeants and lieutenants — had a life expectancy measured in hours. He wrote a letter to his parents, preparing them for the inevitable. 'When you see this I'll be dead; but don't worry ... try to think that I did the only possible thing, as I tell you I would do it again if I had the chance.' Badger had reason to be melancholy: in the hour before the attack, the Germans' retaliatory bombardment cut down 120 men of his 10th Battalion, about 20 per cent of its attacking strength.[41]

Like Badger, 32-year-old Lieutenant Bert Crowle of the 10th Battalion had joined the Australian Imperial Force as a private in 1914 and worked his way up through the ranks, and would now lead troops into battle. Crowle stood only five-foot five, his slight stature akin to that of a jockey. It is hard to imagine him before the war, back in Adelaide, sawing timber, fixing joints, or laying foundations as a qualified builder.[42] It is also hard to imagine a recruiting officer accepting him as Australian Imperial Force material in late 1914, when recruiting standards were still high. Perhaps Bert's trade qualification got him across the line.

Lieutenant Alfred Hearps of the 12th Battalion had enlisted enthusiastically in August 1914, perhaps confident that his experience as a cadet lieutenant had prepared him for anything that the war might throw up. But the Tasmanian quickly discovered that he had no stomach for war. His casualty form records that he was evacuated from Gallipoli diagnosed with 'hysteria', a vague term that referred to the loss of control due to fear. Perhaps this term was used because 'shell shock' had not yet come into parlance.[43] The diagnosis was later changed to 'breakdown'.[44] When Hearps recovered, he was appointed company quartermaster sergeant, which kept him away from the front line. Unfortunately, the battalion's infantry sergeants and lieutenants had all virtually been cut down in the first attack on Pozières. According to the battalion history, *The Story of the Twelfth*, an unprecedented nine promotions were required to replenish their threadbare ranks.[45] There was no alternative but to promote Hearps to lieutenant and give him an infantry platoon to command.

When the whistles sounded in broad daylight on 21 August for the attack toward Fabeck Graben Trench to start, Badger, Crowle, and Hearps shepherded their 'shaken' men into no-man's-land.[46] Badger and Crowle's 10th Battalion troops advanced on the right flank. Shelling had obliterated their first objective, a newly dug German trench. Badger and two lieutenants led the troops through Fabeck Graben — which they mistook for their first objective — and into their own bombardment. Shellfire, machine-gun fire, and bombs killed or wounded half the battalion in about 30 minutes. According to the 3rd Brigade diary, only one 10th Battalion officer remained unwounded.[47] At about this time, two machine-gun bullets struck Crowle in the upper thigh, with a third ricocheting off the periscope in his pocket. The Germans quickly worked their way behind the stranded troops, and their fire came from all directions. Some, such as 26-year-old Private Alfred Beck, a labourer from South Australia, had no option but to surrender. He got a little past the German front line when a German grenade hit him in the back. 'I became unconscious and coming to found myself a prisoner,' he explained in an interview after the war.[48] Badger and about 30 survivors desperately tried to bayonet and bomb their way back through the German lines. By dusk, only a few had made it to their own lines.

Hearps's 12th Battalion advanced in the centre, directly toward the farm. Rather than stop at their assigned objective, which shellfire had obliterated, Hearps and Lieutenant Osmund Roper led their men 50 yards beyond the farm. Some Germans managed to manoeuvre behind them, cutting them off. About this time, a piece of shrapnel the size of a man's fist slammed into Hearps's neck; he collapsed. The shrapnel that struck him apparently came from a British gun.[49]

Hearps's Red Cross file tells us that his batman, Private Arthur Bean, remained by his side and tended to his gaping wound, while other survivors withdrew. Bean's Red Cross statement indicates that Hearps was in a bad way: barely conscious, blood gushing from his neck, and paralysed — the shrapnel had severed his spinal cord. Bean, a house decorator by trade, didn't know what to do. Hearps implored him, and then ordered him, to leave his side. Bean, understandably torn between his duty and the strong impulse to save his own skin, reluctantly complied. He promised Hearps that he would get help and return.

Sometime after dusk, Bean reached the Australian lines. 'How he had got back safely God only knew,' remarked Lieutenant Roper. Bean pleaded with Roper to send some men out to rescue Hearps. Roper said it was futile, as Mouquet Farm was in German hands, and forbade Bean from returning.

Hearps was recorded as missing at rollcall. His fate remained a mystery until a soldier found his body some time later, and returned his identity disc to a 10th Battalion officer.[50]

The next morning, 22 August, aeroplanes swooped low over the battlefield; spotters reported that many Australians were still forward of the newly dug trench line in shell craters.[51] Headquarters interpreted this as the advance still having some momentum, and they ordered fresh attacks. Yet there was no one to deliver them; by mid-afternoon, these isolated men had been rounded up and taken prisoner.

That same day, Australian fatigue parties — typically assigned to labouring jobs, such as repairing roads or scavenging abandoned equipment — cleared the trenches of dead Germans, mostly Bavarians and Saxons. One soldier asked his officer what the inscription on their belt buckles said. The officer roughly translated, 'God with us for King and Fatherland.'

'Well, God doesn't seem to have done much for these blokes,' the soldier replied.[52]

It seemed that God had no favourites — not even Dave Badger. According to the Red Cross's enquiry into his disappearance, a sergeant came across a handful of bodies on the German side of no-man's-land; it seemed a single burst shell had killed all of them. He collected up their identity discs and pay books. One belonged to Sergeant Dave Badger. Later, his body was recovered, along with a letter marked: 'To be opened in the event of my death.'[53]

Bert Crowle survived the machine-gun bullet wounds to his thigh. Stretcher-bearers walked four miles across open ground, one out in front with a white flag, to get him back through the lines to the 3rd Casualty Clearing Station. Yet, after three days of treatment, Bert realised things weren't good. The Somme soil, laced with manure, had possibly infected the wound. Surgeons removed pounds of flesh from his buttocks in an effort to excise the gangrenous tissue, but it had already gone too far. 'You must be prepared for the worst to happen any day,' he warned his wife, Beatrice, in a letter.[54] 'I am very sorry, dear, but still you will be provided for as I am easy on that score.'

Nurses placed salts in and around the wound in an effort to cleanse it, but Bert sensed it was all but futile. 'It smells rotten,' he wrote in the letter. He died the next day, on 23 August. His personal belongings were sent home; among them was a slightly damaged periscope.

Despite the attack's minor success — the *Official History* called it trifling — of capturing a small parcel of land to the right of the farm, it cost Sinclair-MacLagan's 3rd Brigade a staggering 840 men. Over 200 simply vanished — either killed, taken prisoner, or left to die in no-man's-land.[55] The 11th Battalion history criticised the stunt: 'Most of the boys felt … that good lives had been wantonly thrown away in an attack that had absolutely no hope from the first.'[56] The lasting consequence of this piecemeal action would be felt over the coming weeks in Australia. Soon, Mrs Hearps would open an impersonal letter from Base Records informing her that her 'beloved' son, Alfred, was dead; soon, Mrs Beatrice Crowle would receive a handwritten letter that her husband, Herbert, had written while he lay dying in a casualty clearing station; and soon, Mr and Mrs Badger would receive an envelope marked, 'To be opened in the event of my death', which had been removed from their dead son's tunic pocket and mailed to them by an unknown soldier.[57] The letter contained two important messages. The first: 'don't grieve, be proud'; the second: 'send someone in my place'.[58] Badger's personnel dossier indicates that his parents honoured his death wish, bundling his little brother Magnus, barely 18, off to war in early 1917 to take his place. The war, with its apparently insatiable appetite, had to be fed.

For almost a month, Bean had meticulously recorded the battle's progress. Although he had complete freedom to move about the battlefield, he realised it was impossible to record much more from his wanderings than the general condition of the fighting, the weather, the barrages, and the morale of the troops. The best way to capture the ebb and flow of the battle was to interview the officers and non-commissioned officers of a unit, but it had to be done within a week or two of their fighting. Otherwise, as Bean noted, memories dimmed and history was lost forever.[59]

Most evenings, Bean sat at his desk and transcribed the shorthand notes he had taken that day, finding that he was rarely disturbed in the late evening and early hours of the morning. 'Sometimes daylight would find me still at it,' Bean wrote of the habit he had formed on Gallipoli, 'occasionally by some strange process of mental effort, falling asleep at each full stop and then waking to write each successive sentence.'[60]

Bean made his second trip to Pozières on 17 August. Upon reaching the village, he noted that for a mile the desolate battlefield had been flayed, lying open to the sky. 'The whole flank of the ridge had been torn open,' wrote Bean in *Letters from France*. 'It lies there bleeding, gaping open to the callous skies with scarcely so much as a blade of grass or thistle to clothe its nakedness.'[61] Bean met with battalion commanders Iven Mackay, who gave him details of the previous night's counterattack, and Owen Howell-Price, who was crouched over a map and managing the sending up of flares to signal his position to a contact pilot; the pilot was circling his aeroplane above and hooting his horn. Bean noted that the officers worked away, seemingly oblivious to the shells that thumped close by.[62]

Bean's mood lifted on 22 August when he reunited with his cousin Leo Butler, who had thus far survived the fighting unharmed. 'I was immensely relieved to see him,' wrote Bean. 'I dreaded him being hit for Uncle Ted's sake.'[63] His delight would be shortlived. A few days later, on 24 August, Bean was visited by his brother, Jack. He brought the shocking news that cousin Leo had died. 'It was too sad and dreadful for words,' wrote Bean.[64]

Leo, a big, strapping man with blue eyes, a fresh complexion, and dark hair, was one of those men about whom Bean loved to write: a quintessential Australian. A handy sportsman and great cricketer, he had a sharp mind and was one of Hobart's most successful barristers. Bean said he was the finest specimen of manhood in all of Hobart.[65] To round it off, Leo had the egalitarian touch. Thirty-two and in a professional occupation, he didn't have to enlist, but, according to Bean, he couldn't bear the thought of shirking his responsibility to his country.

A fitting finale for Leo would have been a hero's death, mortally wounded while gloriously charging the German trenches or selflessly rescuing a fallen comrade. But the Great War had little respect for legend-making. According to Bean's diary and letters within it, while Leo was in the support trenches near Mouquet Farm on 22 August, a shell exploded around dusk, taking off a lower leg and smashing the other. Leo lingered on, drifting in and out of consciousness, trying to be cheerful. He was carried back to a casualty clearing station. Leo knew he'd lost a lot of blood; he remarked how much of it covered the stretcher he'd been carried in on. Leo whispered to the friend who accompanied him that all day he had felt that something was going to happen to him. A surgeon immediately amputated his bloody stump high at the hip, and took the toes off on the other foot. After the operation, Leo's voice was strong, but he had lost too much blood. He slipped into shock and died just before midnight on 23 August.[66]

After hearing the news, Bean searched for Leo's younger brother, Angus, in Amiens. He found him about midnight. 'The boy had been crying his eyes out,' wrote Bean, 'I could see that.' Angus said he was thinking of his father: 'I'm afraid of how it will affect him when he hears it.'[67]

Bean attended Leo's funeral, along with a few friends, a French labourer, and a peasant woman. The cemetery sat well back from the front line, among the wheat fields and rolling hills. As Bean watched Leo's rough, wooden coffin being lowered into a freshly dug grave, feelings of doubt plagued him. 'I couldn't help wondering whether it was worth it,' he later wrote in his diary, 'whether there is anything gained in this war that justifies such sacrifices. Leo would not have doubted it ... nor for one moment would he have questioned it. But I don't feel so sure of it.' Bean wanted to create a monument for the Australian people built on the exploits of the Anzacs, but the corrosive war leeched away at its foundation stones.

On 22 August, Legge's 2nd Division had relieved Hooky's 1st Division, which had suffered 2650 casualties in its second stunt. The *Official History* admitted that the task confronting the Australians had reached the stage where further progress was impossible.[68] Officers such as Iven Mackay doubted whether further gains could be achieved through 'tiddly-winking pushing and grabbing parts of trenches'.[69] Gough's ambitious plan of thrusting past the farm toward Thiepval now seemed doubtful.

The worn-out 1st Division troops, no doubt indifferent to Gough's grand plans, came out of the firing line in 'dribs and drabs', and after some rest marched to a railhead near Doullens.[70] On 27 August, they began their long journey to Ypres in dirty but familiar cattle trucks labelled '40 *hommes*, 8 *chevaux*'.[71] Donovan Joynt reflected on what his battalion had endured. Although proud that the Australian divisions were among the few to reach their objectives, he still felt that Haig and Gough had mishandled them and had repeated the mistakes of the Boer and Crimean wars. He then recalled the comments of British general Sir Ian Hamilton while inspecting Australian troops in 1912: 'It would take three Australians to equal one continental soldier.' Although undoubtedly filled with sadness, Joynt seemed proud that his comrades had forged an identity for the nation and, in doing so, had proved the general wrong.[72]

After travelling through landscape that showed little evidence of conflict, the troops detrained at Poperinghe, a village about eight miles west of Ypres. The quietness of this sector, coupled with the crisp autumn mornings, was a wonderful tonic for the troops. Shattered battalions would be gradually replenished, although Iven Mackay warned that, with the merest trickle of reinforcements coming in, it would be a slow process that would consume the remaining months of 1916.[73]

While the 1st Division troops rested, those of the 2nd Division would have justifiably wondered whether they would survive their second stunt — particularly as they had suffered a 50 per cent casualty rate in their first, and the task confronting them was deemed impossible.

CHAPTER FIFTEEN
Battering Ram

'For Christ's sake write a book on the life of an infantryman, and by doing so you will quickly prevent these shocking tragedies.'
— Private Arthur Thomas's diary

Bean, who became more scathing in his diary with each failure, was unsurprised by the 1st Division's lack of success on 18 and 21 August. How could a division in its second stunt be expected to perform as well as it did in its first, he argued, particularly as its depleted ranks had only been 30 per cent refilled, with the remaining 20 per cent still to be filled? A frustrated Bean believed that the Australian Imperial Force had 'broken itself' in repeated battering attacks on Pozières and now Mouquet Farm, but had received no credit for it from British officers and the censors because of petty jealousies. Bean confined his bleak assessment to his diary, while outwardly he fulfilled his official obligations unstintingly.[1]

The normally restrained *Official History* described the progress achieved in the 1st Division's two attacks as 'trifling'.[2] The division's lack of success was, perhaps, also due to the Germans reorganising their defences. 'We know exactly what we have to do,' wrote one of the farm's defenders, Lieutenant Tschoeltsch. 'We only have to hold our position and not be sent pillar to post.'³

Tschoeltsch had directed his men to rest on their haunches and focus entirely on blunting the repeated attacks. The next day, 23 August, First German Army commander Fritz von Below formalised this local arrangement by abandoning his standing order that every inch of ground lost must be immediately recaptured. Von Below's directive read:

> The battle that is now in progress consumes, in defence alone, so many troops that I am forced to issue orders that methodical counter-attacks, beyond minor ones of a purely local nature, are not to be carried except by my orders.⁴

The 2nd Division, which would undoubtedly suffer the consequences of the Germans' change in tactics, would now attempt to complete a task that the *Official History* admitted had reached the point of impossibility — the weakened battalions would grind through the mud into a narrowing salient while the German artillery inflicted maximum casualties. Gough would once again prod Legge for premature action on a battlefield that the War Committee in London conceded had come to a 'temporary standstill'.⁵

Second Division soldiers, returning to the line after a brief fortnights' rest, harboured the same bitter feelings as those expressed by the 1st Division soldiers. Their first stunt had been the most gruelling of any of the three divisions, which was reflected in their high number (6848) of casualties. Now they had little room to manoeuvre, with their front line butting up against what had once been the front gate of Mouquet Farm.

Which of the Legge's ragged brigades would renew the 'battering ram' attacks against the farm? Not Paton's 7th Brigade; it had been smashed up twice in its first stunt. Holmes's 5th Brigade hadn't fared much better. The *Official History* noted that Gellibrand's 6th Brigade was considered the strongest of the three, even though shelling had virtually wiped out his 23rd Battalion, and most of his other battalions, after reinforcing, could barely muster 600 men each.[6]

Gellibrand was informed that his 6th Brigade would resume the attacks and advance to the left and right of Mouquet Farm. The news infuriated him. At a corps conference on 22 August, he argued that such a large attack was beyond his men; they had suffered heavy casualties in their first stunt and had only been out of the line for 17 days. White, realising the futility of renewing a defeated attack without changing the method, agreed. He revised the battle plan, limiting the objective to capturing the trenches on the left-hand side of the farm and Zigzag Trench, which lay just beyond the farm. This would straighten the line for the 4th Division's follow-up attack in late August.[7]

Gellibrand also harboured deep concerns about the rushed preparations for the attack. 'So far as I can judge we have taken over an incompletely consolidated position without any communication worth speaking of,' he wrote to divisional headquarters. His soldiers noted that the front-line trenches were very shallow. 'Unless you crawled around on your hands and knees, you were in full view of the Germans,' recorded Arthur Clifford.[8] How would Gellibrand, whom Birdie once described as a 'rather delicate man ... prone to breakdown', respond to what appeared to be the unrealistic expectations placed upon his worn brigade?[9] The answer, as usual, was that he would focus on methodical planning and the careful management of his troops in the coming days to maximise the brigade's chances of success. He would continue his practice of communicating face-to-face with his subordinates in the fighting line, which he thought was the best way to relay his expectations and plans; he would also push his platoon commanders to monitor the condition and morale of their troops, firmly believing that until they knew how much 'beer or butter' their men could hold, they wouldn't get much value out of them in battle.[10]

Was Gellibrand prone to breakdown, as Birdie suggested? He was brittle under prolonged periods of strain, but so too were other officers, such as White — both men shared letters in 1917 confessing that their duties had exacted a toll upon their health. Gellibrand reasoned that few commanders could endure more than 48 hours of a raging battle. Bean's diary supported Gellibrand's assessment: he cited instances of commanders wilting under strain, including Major George Redburg of the 10th Battalion, who slept in his dugout on 21 August while the 'whole operation outside hung on his battalion', and his predecessor, 50-year-old Lieutenant-Colonel Stanley Price Weir, who asked for a return to Australia after suffering from exhaustion at Pozières. Gellibrand's brittleness under strain revealed itself in prickly and tactless behaviour toward other officers, which resulted in spiteful clashes with Charles Brand, whom he 'detested', and Arthur Bridges, whom he called a 'swine'.[11]

Gellibrand would have understood that the odds of his brigade succeeding in the attack were small. He could protest to his superiors about the senseless operation, but this would almost certainly end his career as a field commander. Haig and Gough had already dismissed a number of 'windy' officers who lacked the right offensive spirit.[12] Despite his misgivings, Gellibrand would rally his troops for the assault; although he cared for them deeply, he also possessed a quality essential to all commanders in battle — ruthlessness toward subordinates.

As expected, Gellibrand responded to White's revisions by throwing himself into the planning of the attack. Concerned about his poor lines of communication, he moved his headquarters forward to a dugout near the Pozières cemetery. He also shifted the brigade supply dump forward to alleviate some of the supply problems experienced by other divisions. Gellibrand then selected his 21st Battalion, which could muster about 700 men, to lead the attack. He decided to attack at 4.45 a.m. on Saturday 26 August, reasoning that the murky light of dawn might provide some cover for the advancing troops.[13]

Gellibrand sent patrols out to ascertain the location and strength of the German defences, but their reports proved inconclusive.[14] What the patrols failed to discover was that the Germans had evacuated their forward trenches to avoid heavy casualties from the British bombardment, but they aimed to reoccupy them at the exact moment the attack started. 'If anything went wrong, we should look stupid,' said the plan's architect, Lieutenant Tschoeltsch. 'If, on the other hand, we succeeded and we cleared this sector and reoccupied it at the right moment then the British would not get Mouquet Farm today.'[15]

As attack preparations intensified, Gellibrand sensed his men's depressed spirits. Arthur Clifford, who, along with many fellow soldiers, had unearthed stinking corpses while digging a trench, was no doubt justified in feeling bitter about the looming fight over a few yards of ground.[16] According to Gellibrand's biographer, Peter Sadler, whenever he was in the trenches Gellibrand moved up and down the line in his shabby private's uniform and tried to lift their sagging spirits by imploring them to 'box on boys, stick it out'. His soldiers sensed that his encouragement was genuine and conveyed in the same manner that a father would inspire a son.[17]

In the grey dawn of 26 August, Gellibrand's 21st Battalion, supported on its flanks by the 22nd and 23rd battalions, climbed from their trenches and advanced behind a barrage, which crept forward at 50 yards a minute. The troops' objective was to advance forward on about a 1000-yard frontage and straighten the line by capturing the dugouts within the farm, as well as numerous strongpoints that surrounded it. But, confused by the flares and noise coming from the farm's ruins, the troops inadvertently continued past their main objective, the 'barely traceable' Zigzag Trench. Captain Fred Sale realised the mistake and brought some men back, but the bombardment drowned out his shouts to the others. The main body of men advanced past the ruins of Mouquet Farm. They later tried to return, but inavertently bunched up, offering themselves as easy targets to the German machine-gunners.[18] At 7.00 a.m., a despatched pigeon reached battalion headquarters, informing them that the advance of the 21st had stalled and been driven back at various points. The news at 7.20 a.m. was just as grim: small parties of troops were still hanging on, but the carrying parties supporting them were dwindling due to shelling casualties.

German machine-gun crews, hidden in the ruins, spat bullets across the attack front continually, forcing the Australians to take cover in shell holes and ditches. Second-Lieutenant Alexander Beatty, a 27-year-old farmer from Yackandandah, Victoria, attempted to silence one of the machine guns so his platoon could advance. He told his batman, Private Stan Sedgman, to explain to his family if he was killed that he had died while trying to take a machine gun. As Beatty climbed from his shell hole, he was shot dead.[19] Bombing teams also tried to suppress the fire, but the Germans shot them down before they could get close enough to throw their bombs. The Australians could neither move forward or backward; they had no options other than to withdraw from their exposed position or surrender.

By 10.30 a.m., the fighting had petered out. Toward noon, the German shelling intensified again. That afternoon, the Germans attacked the remnants of the 21st Battalion sheltering in the shell holes and ditches around the farm. Some Australians forfeited their precarious positions while others, unable to safely work their way back to their own lines, remained in their shell holes and planned to return at dusk. For two days, Lieutenant Norman Cumming, a 23-year-old schoolteacher from Victoria who was wounded in the head and side, tried to reach the Australian lines with two companions, but he was eventually captured. About 60 other Australians were also taken prisoner.[20]

That night, the incoming 14th Battalion launched a follow-up attack. They captured a stretch of trench, but were later chased out by the Germans. A padre justified the assault to Bean the next day, saying: 'It was not successful as an attack but most successful as a raid.'

Bean was incredulous, noting in his diary: 'That is simply meaningless to me and I am not going to write up as a successful raid what was a failure as an attack.'[21] This incident illustrated that Bean's enthusiasm for the Somme enterprise, so obvious on 26 July, had dampened, most likely because of Leo Butler's death, not to mention viewing first-hand the desolation of Pozières and the results of five weeks of exhausting labour. Bean also seemed frustrated and somewhat constrained by his own strict standards of reporting, telling events truthfully and yet not writing anything that questioned military authority or strategy.

The objective of straightening the line had failed. Gellibrand's 21st Battalion was relieved that night. For the second time in two weeks, it had been shot to pieces, losing 13 officers and 444 men; the brigade, out of a fighting strength of 2500, had lost 896 men.[22] The front line remained unchanged. The Australians were unlikely to be beyond the farm before Gough launched his grand attack.

Some of those men had lost their lives before the attack had even commenced. Alec Raws had died during the changeover of the 1st and 2nd divisions. After the 23rd Battalion made its way through the bombardment and into its designated trenches, some men were reported missing. Later, three privates were found dead beside a junior officer, reported to be Alec Raws. His body had no wounds; concussion due to an exploding shell was probably what killed him. 'He should never have gone back into the fighting so soon,' reflected his friend and company commander Captain Lionel Short. 'I had the feeling that he had known he would not come out safely.'[23] He later wrote a letter of condolence to Raws' family. After recounting their close friendship, Short wrote philosophically: 'Well that is war. You go into a stunt and if you are lucky enough to keep your own life, [you] find that most of your friends are missing.'[24]

Between 27 and 29 August, the complexion of the battle changed. At a tactical level, Cox's 4th Division replaced Legge's 2nd Division. The 4th Division's re-entry into the battle marked the last opportunity for I Anzac Corps to seize the farm before it was rested at Ypres in Belgium for the winter months. The Germans also made a significant change to their command structure on the Western Front, replacing General Erich von Falkenhayn with Field-Marshal Paul von Hindenburg, who immediately revised their 'no retreat' doctrine. And the deteriorating weather transformed the battlefield into a quagmire.

On 28 August, Cox took full control of the front, and command of the last remnants of Legge's division. Despite two weeks' rest, many of Cox's troops, such as Sergeant Ted Rule of the 14th Battalion, were still rattled. 'The thoughts of another gruelling [sic] were not very welcome,' wrote Rule, and the thunder of the guns 'put the wind up us a little more'.[25] Dispiritingly, the line had hardly moved since their last stunt.[26]

As the 4th Division troops sheltered in their muddy trenches, White reflected on the Australians' past attacks. It seemed that every variant had been attempted: daylight, twilight, and early-morning attacks; creeping, lifting, and machine-gun barrages; two-, two-and-a-half-, and three-battalion attacks; advances to the left, centre, and right. White sensed that the forces previously employed against the farm were 'too light'.[27] The 2nd Division's last effort involved half a battalion. Also, unconfirmed reports from Australian soldiers and German prisoners suggested that the German positions within the farm were much stronger than first thought; apparently, their dugouts were capable of housing hundreds of soldiers. In response, White demanded that a whole brigade be thrown at the farm. Yet how would he shunt so many men forward without the Germans noticing them? And denser attacking formations would provide the German machine-gunners with splendidly uniform targets. Cox disagreed with White's edict, and was only prepared to spare two battalions for the attack. He ordered his 13th and 16th battalions to advance on Fabeck Graben and to capture Mouquet Farm on the way through on 29 August, exactly the same objective that the 13th Battalion had tried to secure just two weeks earlier.

Unfortunately, one critical piece of information about the farm's defences had eluded White, and it held the key to its capture. White and the divisional commanders thought Mouquet Farm was an uninhabitable pile of rubble. They assumed that the strength of the German position lay in its strong trench network and supporting dugouts located along the ridge line. Commanders remained baffled by the repeated reports of the Australians being fired on from behind after German positions had seemingly been cleared — how were the Germans infiltrating and outflanking them so easily? I Anzac Corps Intelligence headquarters' routine interrogation of German prisoners on 26 August revealed the answer: beneath the farm's rubble lay an extensive labyrinth of cellars, sometimes as deep as 30 feet and 28 steps down, reinforced with logs and linked by tunnels. The cellars held hundreds of men, and stores of munitions and food. Pulleys hauled machine guns up to firing platforms so that the farm's approaches could be sprayed methodically with bullets, 'even by a blind man'. Hidden entrances around the farm allowed the Germans to safely withdraw during bombardments and then suddenly reappear once the Australians attacked.[28]

In *Thiepval*, Michael Stedman attributed the farm's strength to the meticulous Major von Fabeck, who, upon arriving on the Somme in April 1916, had fortified Mouquet Farm, converting it into an underground fortress by late June. It contained regimental battle headquarters, shelter for 300 men, a telephone exchange, water supplies, and pumping equipment, as well as medical and rest facilities. He also set up a pumping station that carried water all the way from the station at Courcelette.[29]

It was a major failure of I Anzac Corps Intelligence headquarters that the full extent of the farm's fortifications remained unknown through most of August. The interrogation of German prisoners and French refugees on 5, 7, and 8 August disclosed information about the farm's deep shafts and underground rooms. Yet, even as late as 25 August, intelligence furnished reports to the divisions indicating that the farm appeared to be unfortified.[30] Hooky had previously criticised intelligence officers for staying cooped up at headquarters rather than visiting the front; perhaps this practice contributed to the oversight. The discovery demanded new tactics. White was right: a few companies of exhausted men couldn't take this position.

On 28 August, while Cox and White planned their next attack upon the farm, the Germans simplified their command structure on the Somme. Von Gallwitz's command responsibilities were trimmed; he forfeited control of von Below's First Army to concentrate on his own Second Army. On the following day, 29 August, General Erich von Falkenhayn was sacked. Field-Marshal Paul von Hindenburg assumed his duties as chief of the Great General Staff, with General Erich Ludendorff as his assistant. The news reached John Treloar at I Anzac Corps headquarters a few days later, who wrote in his diary: 'We also heard that von Falkenhayn had been dismissed and Hindenburg appointed in his place. The question then was, "who and what is Falkenhayn?"'[31] Treloar's diary entry suggests that the Anzacs, who were engrossed in their own affairs, paid little attention to the machinations of the German army supreme command. This was not surprising, considering that many Anzacs would not have even known the names of their British commander-in-chief or army commanders.

Von Falkenhayn's apocalyptic promise of bleeding the French white at Verdun had turned out to be an empty one. In fact, he had almost bled his own armies out on the Somme by adhering to the decision not to forfeit a yard of ground. Packed front-line trenches provided easy targets for British gunners, and doomed counterattacks resulted in sickening casualties. Upon coming to grips with the situation in the west, Hindenburg replaced the 'no retreat policy' with the concept of elastic defence: why not give up 1000 yards here or there of tactically unimportant ground if it meant conserving vital reserves? The attitude of German soldiers on this subject was summed up in a captured letter: 'We [the Germans] may lose a little more ground ... but we can afford to do that; it isn't our ground.'[32]

What did the command change signal to the Allies? *The Times* believed that it indicated the most dramatic change of the war, an admission of German failure.[33] Haig felt vindicated, citing it as clear evidence that his Somme campaign had worn the Germans down. 'There can be no question as to the right course to follow,' he wrote in his diary. 'Our offensive must be continued without intermission as long as possible.'[34] For the front-line soldier, this meant one thing: many more months in the Somme mud. One British officer caught in the mire surveyed his exhausted troops: 'All around me are faces which sleep might not have visited for a week. They have dark shadows under eyes,' he wrote in his diary. 'Voices too are tired and the very gait of men has lost its spring. The sap has gone out of them, they are dried up.'[35] These men, who had been reduced to husks, were incapable of continuing Haig's offensive.

Light rain had fallen across the battlefield between 10 and 18 August. A week of fine weather followed. Then, between 25 and 30 August, dark storm clouds brewed and heavy rain drenched the ground. By 28 August, many of the trenches were ankle-deep in water. Although the Somme's chalky soil drained well, the farming fields surrounding Pozières had an unusually high clay content. With little vegetation to bind the soil together, it became sticky 'yellow-red paste' that clung to the men's boots, tunics, and weapons. Trenches crumbled under the constant soaking. 'Talk about slush, it was up to your knees, and over in places, and just like glue,' wrote Lance-Corporal Ivan Harrison of the 14th Battalion in a letter to a friend. 'The chaps were continually getting bogged. Sometimes it took two or three of us to pull a man out of the mud.'[36]

Despite the rain, the Australians continued preparations for their 29 August attack. At 11.00 p.m. on 29 August, the 13th and 16th battalions would advance on a 1200-yard frontage in the hope of capturing the farm and the dugouts and strongpoints surrounding it. On the morning of the attack, the 13th Battalion history described the scene confronting the troops: 'Never has anyone seen a more miserable dawn ... From our trenches the outlook was even more foreboding; nothing but twisted, heaped and churned mud.'[37]

All day, German shells pounded the front line. Ration parties couldn't get forward, leaving the men with only their wet biscuits and rhubarb jam to eat. Soldiers crawled out of their waterlogged trenches and into muddy craters to avoid the shelling. By dusk, shelling had killed or wounded 90 13th Battalion soldiers. Those wounded had to be dragged through the sucking mud to aid stations.

Some men believed the rain would make the attack impossible. 'I thought our attack might be countermanded, but at 11.00 o'clock we heard the guns behind us open,' recorded an observer.[38] The attack would proceed, even though many rifles were clogged with mud and wouldn't fire.

At 11.00 p.m. on 29 August, the troops left their sodden trenches and shell holes with their tunics soaked, boots waterlogged, and weapons plastered with mud. The bombardment crept forward at its usual pace of 50 yards a minute, but the men, caught in the mud, couldn't keep pace. Guiding lights laid out earlier to direct them toward their objectives had been blown away or buried. Rattling machine-gun fire raked them. Some reached Fabeck Graben, but couldn't fire their rifles and Lewis guns because of the viscous mud coating them. Mud-encrusted bombs were impossible to throw accurately.[39]

Major Percy Black, a 38-year-old miner from the Southern Cross goldfields of Western Australia, was among those assigned the impossible task of capturing Mouquet Farm. Somehow, Black and his men managed to break into the farm. They quickly silenced the machine guns, throwing bombs down the entrances of the dugouts to clear them. The Germans responded by hurling the bombs back up the shaft, wounding the Australians who had thrown them down, or shooting at their attackers' legs. Meanwhile, Captain Ross Harwood of the 16th Battalion had seized Fabeck Graben, east of the farm. His

120-man company fought off repeated counterattacks.⁴⁰ A report despatched to headquarters prematurely declared that Mouquet Farm had fallen; despite the horrid conditions, the Australians seemed on the cusp of victory. They now had to link up their isolated positions.

Then, a German machine gun opened up from the northern end of the farm. The 50 prisoners that the Australians had captured in the farm had to be released. The battalion history, *The Old Sixteenth*, said that Germans suddenly swarmed from some dugouts missed in the advance, as well as from the farm's underground cellars. The besieged Australians fought their way through the Germans and back to their own trenches. One retiring soldier said he tried '14 bloody times to scramble out of a crater' but fell back on his end every time. Afterward, a muddied Ross Harwood fronted the 13th Brigade commander, Bill Glasgow. 'You went over pretty thin didn't you,' Glasgow asked, referring to the weight of troops employed in the attack. 'Thin as tissue paper,' replied Harwood.⁴¹ The two battalions had lost 459 soldiers in the fight.

The next morning, on 30 August, an aeroplane observer reported to headquarters that the bright-red fizzing flares laid out by the Australians to show the limit of their advance were barely forward of the jumping-off trenches. Another gruelling attack upon the farm had failed.

The 16th Battalion history, keen to protect its reputation, referred to the stunt as a 'non success'. They attributed this to the fact that the communication trenches were three feet deep in soupy water, and a large proportion of the rifles and Lewis guns were clogged with mud. The 13th Battalion history concluded that such a position should never have been attacked in 'nibbles' of a few exhausted men.⁴²

Brand's 4th Brigade operations report told a similar story, indicating that only 5 per cent of available rifles and light machine guns could be fired during the attack. Furthermore, the supporting artillery shelled up to 200 yards to the rear of the jumping-off trenches, rooting up all vital telephone wires, demolishing communication trenches, and inflicting untold casualties. By the time the heavies redirected their fire, they had expended their allocation of shells.

Ted Rule, two miles back from the front line, remembered one officer seconded to Brand's 16th Battalion returning the morning after the attack without his helmet and puttees, and covered in mud.[43] It seemed a fitting metaphor for the failed attack.

White mulled over the results of the attack. Irrespective of the rain, he thought too much had been asked of the battalions, which attacked on a frontage that a month earlier a whole division would have covered. Referring to his earlier conversation with Cox about the optimal deployment of forces, White confided to Bean: 'I wish I had been strong and asked for it to be done by a whole brigade.'[44] Bean concurred, writing that the army, which suffered from 'a poverty of brains', continually wasted opportunities to seize objectives like Mouquet Farm or Courcelette because of its insistence on attacking with too few troops. Bean maintained that to take a position that the Germans considered as important as the farm, one needed men to be 'swarming over it after the attack, like flies'. Bean's next diary entry revealed his disdain for Gough's tactics: 'It is all very well for army generals to sit with their maps and talk about attacking with patrols.' He believed Gough's theory was flawed and had never been proved against tough troops.

The battered battalions were relieved the next day. Mouquet Farm would not fall. 'A very wet, cold, muddy and weary lot were the 13th,' observed the battalion history, as its soldiers quietly trudged to the rear in the drizzle. The three miles to battalion headquarters took them over five hours to cover.

The consequences of the battle radiated out from Mouquet Farm to Australian homes. On 29 August — the day that Cox's 4th Division bogged itself in the mud trying to seize the farm — Reverend John Raws, the father of Goldy and Alec, celebrated his 39th wedding anniversary. In the evening, he received a telegram explaining that Goldy had been missing since 28 July. It seemed that Alec's letters explaining his brother's disappearance hadn't yet reached the Raws family. John telephoned Lennon with the news and then visited the Red Cross to see if they had any information on Goldy. John surely felt the sinking dread that every parent must feel upon hearing the news that their child's whereabouts are unknown. His treasured memories of Goldy, such as summer holidays at Port Elliot, his son's first days at Prince Alfred College, and their final parting near the Buckingham Arms, must have flooded back to him. Would he ever discover Goldy's fate?

Lennon Raws expected further bad news. 'When we received word about Goldy I felt that Alec had gone too, otherwise he would have been sure to have sent a cable to his parents,' read his diary notes.

Almost a month later, while John Raws prepared for a Baptist Union meeting, his phone rang: 'I had a telephone message from the military that Alec was killed in action, August 23rd.' The news shocked John. He cancelled his meeting and immediately notified family and friends. According to his diary, letters of sympathy poured in all of that day and the next.

Lennon was in his office when a visibly upset colleague came in: 'I have some bad news. Your brother's gone.' Stunned, Lennon remembered asking him to leave the room. 'The thought of what it meant to mother and father and a great love and pity for the two boys, swallowed up so suddenly in the black gulf of war, overwhelmed me and I burst into tears,' he confessed in his diary.

Lennon immediately travelled to Adelaide to comfort his parents. His father met him at the station. He noted: 'He was still under shock, but wonderfully brave although occasionally he would break down. Mother had to keep calm to help him, but we sorrowed even more for her because she could not find relief in tears.' Lennon stayed until Tuesday. 'It was one of those beautifully sacred times which come through sorrow,' he recorded. 'Helen [Goldy's, Alec's, and Lennon's sister] was over as well and we were united for the time being by a common bond which is too often broken by the friction of ordinary life.'⁴⁵

The family's despair over Alec's death would deepen after his grave, marked at the foot of a trench near the Pozières cemetery, was lost in the heavy fighting in 1918. His body, if later recovered, was never identified. If his remains were reburied in a grave, it would have had the simple inscription of 'A soldier known unto God'. His story was one of thousands similar, as many families had no site at which to mourn their loved ones, who had become lost amid the soil and mud of the Somme.

The 4th Division troops would attack the ruins of Mouquet Farm one last time on 3 September 1916. Over the last few weeks, I Anzac Corps had expended thousands of men to advance a few hundred yards toward the ruined farm. Whatever the outcome of the last battle, the farm had already seared itself indelibly upon the psyche of many soldiers. Equally, the ubiquitous sight and sickly stench of the dead would never leave them. They could not avoid fixing their eyes on the dead, as they seemed to rest in every shell hole, trench, crater, and sap; they were churned through every square yard of earth. Each shapeless body was someone's brother, son, husband, or father. It seemed an impossible task to recover and identify the remains scattered about the battlefield.

In the midst of battle, very little could be done about the dead. In early August, Foxcroft had written in a letter to his parents that those killed were left where they fell, and their pockets were not even checked nor discs even looked at. He wrote:

> You are known as dead by being missing at the assembly after coming out of the trenches ... If they are buried they are only to be rotted up by shells again and there is no time to do it until they got the Huns back and the cleaning up party buries the dead and picks up all the material off the field.⁴⁶

Bean also observed that little could be done when he visited 10th Battalion headquarters in mid-August. He shuddered when he observed the living sleeping just near the waxen dead. 'One is apt to think it is callous of the battalion to leave these men lying about,' he wrote in his diary, 'but the living are worn out [and] the dead are dead.'[47]

The corps' main priority in the battle area was clearing the dead away from the vital communication trenches so that the flow of troops was unimpeded.[48] 'Armed with shovels we used to follow up the communication trenches,' remembered Walter Elkington. 'Whenever we saw a body lying close to the parapets we would jump out of the trench and poke the body, crawling with maggots, into a shell hole and then pile the earth on top.'[49] The corps adopted the pragmatic approach that winning battles was the priority, whereas the dead could be properly attended to later.

As the Australians pushed the Germans back in late July and August, burial parties under the direction of a chaplain buried the dead quickly, usually in a disused trench or shell crater. It was a vile job: some corpses were bloated with blackened faces; some were skeletons picked clean by fattened rats; others were merely bits and pieces of burnt gristle scattered about the battlefield.[50] The smell of decaying flesh would have permeated the men's clothes and skin. Naturally, the soldiers' effort to identify corpses and mark their graves clearly was probably secondary to the need to complete their task expediently. Charles Bean observed one fatigue party burying 24 men along Chalk Pit Road. They simply tossed them into the nearest shell hole and covered them up. 'No time to get identity discs — they are generally rotted away. So the poor chaps go down as "missing",' he observed in his diary.[51]

Often, the burial parties bound the corpse's hands with signal wire, as if in prayer; wrapped them tightly in blankets; and then lowered them into the burial pits. After filling the pit, the fatigue party bowed their heads and pressed their hats against their chest while the padre said a quick prayer. Then it was on to the next batch.[52]

From August, the corps assigned 400 men to regular fatigues to bury the dead, but it made little impact upon the massive problem. When reports reached General Gough that the dead lay thickly about the approaches to Pozières, he implored that more resources be devoted to burying them so that the morale of the men would not be affected. Birdie despatched his chief medical officer, Colonel Courtenay Manifold, to investigate. Manifold, apparently shocked by what he saw, could see no easy solution. He reported that it was simply a question of military expediency as to whether the dead should be allowed to lie unburied or more lives should be risked by attempting to bury them.[53]

Away from the dangers of the front line, soldiers had more time to collect dead men's personal effects. 'Had a look over the field and got a few pay books from the dead,' explained Rollie Touzel, 'Handed them in so they could tell what happened to the owners.'[54] Sometimes, soldiers, such as Private Harold Hinckfuss of the 26th Battalion, went beyond this perfunctory duty. Hinckfuss came across a dead British soldier lying on his back; he knelt down to have a look at the prayer book protruding from the pocket. 'Inside was a name and address. I decided to take it and send it to the person,' Hinckfuss recorded in his autobiography. He posted it to England and later received a letter of thanks from a grateful relative.[55]

Ted Rule vividly recalled burying three men from his section in mid-August, including his good mate Jack Pearce, a labourer from Trawalla, Victoria. Before burying Pearce, Ted opened his tunic at the throat to get his identity disc, but it wasn't there. Instead of being on a piece of string about his neck, it was in his pocket. 'The thought of putting my hand into his pocket was repulsive,' wrote Rule in his memoirs. 'He was my pal, and somehow it was different; his half opened mouth and dulled eyes seemed to mock me.'[56]

Rule made sure his mate received a decent burial. 'One of the lads made a cross and put it over the grave ... Lieutenant Dean took a photograph of it and intended sending it to their mothers,' he recalled.

Tragically, Lieutenant Archibald Dean died days later, and the photographs and condolence letters were never sent. 'I know Jack Pearce's mother never knew what happened to him,' noted Rule, 'for I afterwards saw a letter that General Birdwood wrote to our C.O. inquiring to his fate.' It is not recorded how Mrs Helen Elliott, the widowed mother of Sergeant Jack Pearce, found out about his death. What is known is that Jack's grave was lost in the fighting over the next two years. Helen's ensuing years would have been a struggle without Jack, who was her sole support.[57]

While Anzacs such as Rule would endeavour to provide a decent burial to a mate, German corpses received little attention. Private Richard Walmsley of the 7th Battalion wrote in his diary that to avoid the smell of the dead Germans, they simply covered them over with a few shovel loads of soil.[58] After the war, some French farmers apparently preferred once again to shovel dirt over unearthed German bodies — easily identified by their grey uniforms — rather than complete the onerous paperwork that accompanied such discoveries.

While soldiers and their families grappled with the Somme's tragic outcomes, troops of the 4th Division prepared to play out the last act in the fight for Mouquet Farm. How many more men would be expended in the next few days to capture the ruined farm? Sergeant Leslie Parsons of the 51st Battalion captured the prevailing mood of those Australians soldiers preparing for the assault, writing in a letter home: 'I would sooner be on Gallipoli for another six months than spend a week more … in the Big Push.'[59]

CHAPTER SIXTEEN

Graveyard or Glory

'There is only one decisive victory: the last.'
— Carl von Clausewitz, military theorist

There was time for one last Australian offensive at Mouquet Farm before the Canadian Corps relieved the Australians and they were transferred north to Ypres. Canadian engineers were already busy erecting huts at Contay Château in anticipation of the changeover. John Treloar observed the 'happy' Canadians playing drums and blowing bugles as they marched toward the reserve areas, writing in his diary: 'I wonder what they will think after a few days around Pozières.'[1] Like the Australians before them, little did the Canadians, who were entering the Somme battle for the first time, know what horror lay in store for them.

It was planned that on 3 September Brigadier-General Bill Glasgow's 13th Brigade would attack the farm at dawn with three 'strong' battalions: the 51st (Western Australia), 52nd (Tasmania, South Australia, Western Australia), and 49th (Queensland). Although the attack was less than brigade-strength (four battalions), as White had previously sought, the facts that the frontage was limited to 1250 yards and the battalions' assembly trenches would be dug by other troops meant that the proposed force should prove adequate to break

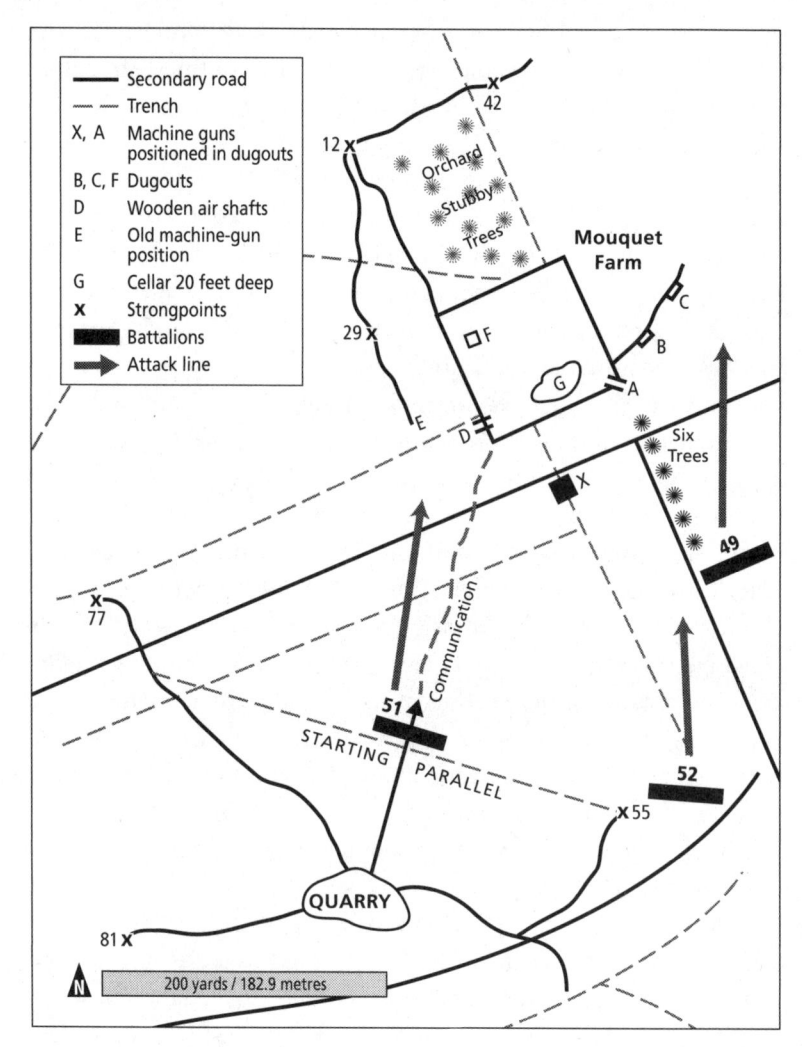

Map 6. 4th Division's Advance on Mouquet Farm

into and secure the farm.² The battalions' first objective was to storm and capture Fabeck Graben Trench — which, it was hoped, would block German reinforcements sweeping down into the farm — and then peel off to secure the farm.

On the same day the Australians attacked Mouquet Farm, Gough's Reserve Army would storm Thiepval from three directions. Further south, Rawlinson's Fourth Army and the French Sixth Army would attack Guillemont and Combles at noon.

Opinion was divided on the looming attack. Some soldiers felt that capturing the farm's ruins would be of poor consolation for the awful losses they had already suffered. Others believed that too much had been sacrificed to leave the battle for the farm undecided. General Cox, the last remaining Anzac divisional commander on the Somme, was desperate for the attack to be successful. He sent a message to his troops urging them to firmly hold any ground captured: 'The importance of holding on ... cannot be underestimated,' read Cox's circular.[3] One of his officers, Captain Charles Dawkins of the 51st Battalion, was as focused on surviving the attack, writing: 'God, I hope it's a success and I come through all right.'[4] Lieutenant Len Wadsley of the 52nd Battalion simply wrote of the fighting: 'We are all thoroughly sick of it.'[5] Wadsley possibly wondered why, after six failed attempts upon Mouquet Farm, the seventh attempt would be any different. Some time earlier, Wadsley had written a letter home explaining that he was preparing to fight in a fairly large offensive which 'may be the end of a good many of us and I may be one of the number ... I leave myself in the hands of the Almighty and trust him absolutely'. Wadsley had handed the letter to a mate. His instructions were, 'Post it for me if I do not come back.'

On 2 September, Glasgow's troops filed up the narrow communication trench from the Pozières cemetery to the quarry, which sat about 250 yards from the farm. They reached their position at 11.00 p.m., about six hours before zero hour. Just after midnight, Lieutenant Duncan 'Big' Maxwell of the 52nd Battalion synchronised watches with his platoon commanders, including Len Wadsley of 11 Platoon.

The Western Australian 51st Battalion sheltered in the trenches to the left of the farm. Captain Daniel McCallum, a bank clerk from

Kalgoorlie, and Lieutenant Bert Clifford, a farmer from Donnybrook, would have been bitterly cold that night because they and their troops had been ordered to leave their greatcoats and blankets behind. McCallum and Clifford were both in their mid-20s and had joined up as adventurous young men in 1914. McCallum and Clifford saw themselves as 'real hard doers', and were fiercely loyal to their battalion and outpost state. They would lead the first four waves of 51st Battalion troops into the attack.

Captain Howard Williams was another 'hard doer' of the 51st Battalion. The 23-year-old Williams grew up in Carlton, Victoria, and had studied at the University of Melbourne and attained a teacher's certificate from the Victorian Education Department before being lured away to the uncharted west. A year of soldiering must have aged him; his men said he looked about 30.[6] He would lead the last three waves of 'mopping-up parties', made up mostly of bombers, into no-man's-land. Their objective was to clear the farm's tunnels.

At 5.10 a.m. on 3 September, as the morning sun cast its orange glow across the clouded sky, four waves of Queenslanders from the 49th Battalion, who were positioned on the right flank, climbed from their shallow trenches and clambered toward Fabeck Graben. A barrage of high-explosive and smoke shells, mortar bombs, and machine-gun fire screened their advance. 'Rockets from both sides coursed through the half light in elegant curves,' remembered a German soldier defending the farm. 'The earth shuddered with the impact of heavy and super heavy shells.'[7]

The first wave of Queenslanders captured a subsidiary objective called Kollmann Trench. The second wave advanced and spread out in shell holes in front of Fabeck Graben to act as a security screen. Despite heavy machine-gun fire, the third wave went forward and broke into a small section of Fabeck Graben. They quickly cleared the trench of Germans and set up protective barricades. From their elevated position, they had clear views beyond the battlefield to the open country and the red-tiled roofs of the German-held villages Courcelette and Grandcourt. Some men diverted, as planned, to the farm and threw bombs down dugout entrances. The troops of the fourth wave, who were carrying picks and shovels, advanced and acted as a security screen for those soldiers who had seized Fabeck Graben. German machine-gun crews were slow to react, and were killed before they could mount their guns.

At the same time that the Queenslanders moved forward, seven waves of Western Australians from the 51st Battalion, on the left flank, climbed from their trenches and advanced toward Fabeck Graben. McCallum and Clifford led the first four waves into no-man's-land, followed by Williams and his three waves of 'mopping-up' bombers.

'We left our trenches somewhere before 5 o'clock in the morning. It was not quite daylight,' recalled Private John Cotter, a farmer and Boer War veteran of the 51st Battalion. 'We were instructed that we had to capture Mouquet Farm and a machine-gun strong post to the right rear of the farm ... We did not lose so many men crossing over.'[8]

Clifford and McCallum's companies advanced toward their objective, about 100 to 200 yards beyond the farm. 'We pushed on with the advance and got through a mess of barbed wire entanglements to the left of the farm,' remembered Cotter. Surrendering Germans spilt out of their dugouts with their hands raised.

After seven attacks, the Australians seemed close to securing the farm. Success, however, depended on the 52nd Battalion in the centre breaking into Fabeck Graben and linking up with the 49th and 51st battalions on either side of it.

As the protective barrage passed over the Germans' heads at about 6.30 a.m., their surviving machine-gun crews manned their weapons. Although it was unlikely they could see the 52nd Battalion through the smoke and dust, they fired in the direction they expected the attack to come from. As the fire intensified, some Australians panicked and sought cover in shell holes, while others ran back to their own trenches. Lieutenant Duncan Maxwell and Sergeant

Allan Black tried to settle them. Black then manned a Lewis gun and returned fire, eventually silencing one machine gun. The troops edged forward again and captured a small portion of Fabeck Graben. Germans hiding in the shell craters close by surrendered.

The 49th and 52nd battalions each held a portion of Fabeck Graben. The C Company of the 52nd Battalion had to fill the gap. Captain Ralph Ekin-Smyth, a portly 41-year-old customs officer from Woodville, South Australia, and a citizen–soldier for 25 years, led his company toward Fabeck Graben, but didn't recognise it because it had been destroyed by the bombardment. Ekin-Smyth's company kept advancing, and walked straight into their supporting barrage. It shattered the company in minutes, and an exploding shell blew Wadsley's head off. Sergeant Roy Pollard, who took over Wadsley's platoon, was unsurprised by his death. 'A few minutes before the charge, he told me that he felt as if he would not come out of it,' he explained in a letter to Wadsley's family.[9]

Ekin-Smyth gathered the survivors together; yet, as they retraced their steps, shrapnel struck the captain. Although seriously wounded, Ekin-Smyth yelled orders and directed his men with his cane. Confused and leaderless, some men panicked and again walked into their own barrage, while others streamed back toward their own trenches. The gap remained.

Maxwell, stuck in Fabeck Graben with his flanks exposed, sent a patrol out to contact Ekin-Smyth's company. The patrol leader, Lance-Corporal Ernest Green, found Ekin-Smyth lying in a crater and gave another man a hand to bind up his wounds. 'His left arm was broken in two places. While binding him up a bomb lobbed in the crater and struck Ekin-Smyth in the stomach killing him,' Green explained in his statement to the Red Cross.[10]

By 7.00 a.m., Maxwell had established all-important but very tenuous touch with the C Company of the 52nd Battalion. Meanwhile, Williams's 51st Battalion bombers had secured most of the farm's ruins. According to the *Official History*, they had worked their way from dugout to dugout, tentatively peering down their dark shafts. If shots rang out from below, Williams's bombers rolled grenades or phosphorous bombs down. Within minutes, smoke billowed from a dozen wrecked dugouts.[11]

At 7.30 a.m., Williams, in his temporary headquarters in a deep cellar, scribbled down a message and handed it to his runner. Some time later, the runner arrived at battalion headquarters at the cemetery. Williams's message read that Mouquet Farm had been captured except for a few isolated dugouts. The great news quickly spread among the nearby troops. '13 Brigade took Mouquet Farm and is still holding it,' recorded Harold Morris in his diary.[12]

Had Williams sent the message prematurely? Machine-gun fire soon intensified; large 9.2-inch shells exploded among the Australians, and those digging the communication trench linking the farm to the Australian trenches downed their tools and sought cover. By 8.00 a.m., the staff officers at headquarters had become concerned because no further messages had been received from the farm. Observers in spotter aeroplanes sent up to check the advance's progress returned with confusing information: the green flares that marked the advance's limit were seen scattered around the farm, but so too were red, yellow, and white ones.

The Australians held a large section of Fabeck Graben Trench. The Germans responded to this reversal by despatching reinforcements through the communications trenches toward Fabeck Graben. Pockets of Australians spotted the Germans advancing toward them, and desperately dug trenches to establish a continuous defensive line and prevent themselves from being outflanked.

Elsewhere, German reinforcements advanced from shell hole to shell hole toward the farm. They bombed and pushed back an Australian platoon positioned on the farm's eastern outskirts. The sight was a blow to the men clearing the farm's dugouts who, till then, had been 'confident they were winning hands down'.[13]

Meanwhile, Clifford and McCallum's battered companies managed to reach the north-east corner of the farm, as planned, and dug in. When the advancing Germans attacked them, Clifford and McCallum had little choice other than to hold their ground. Then there was a loud explosion and McCallum collapsed. 'He was hit in the head and also had several stomach wounds,' stretcher-bearer Private William Reith told the Red Cross enquiry some months later.[14] McCallum bled to death on the battlefield. Lieutenant Francis Bailey, 21, from Subiaco, took over his company.

Reaching the outskirts of the farm, the Germans flanked Clifford's isolated position. They entered the farm's hidden underground entrances and then manoeuvred behind Clifford's party.

Suddenly, a Lewis gun covering Clifford's party jammed. Moments later, Clifford received a message from 24-year-old Gallipoli veteran Lieutenant Ernie Smythe, who was protecting his exposed flank. Smythe wrote that he was being bombed out and couldn't hold on much longer. Clifford sent a short reply: 'Hang on at all costs.'[15] Only a handful of Clifford's men stood between the Germans and the farm. At 8.30 a.m., Clifford scribbled a note and handed it to a runner. It read:

> Being hard pressed. Enemy bombing up our trench from both ends. Strong point on our left rear has not been cleared, as they are sniping in our rear … Only have about 30 men with me. No sign of a communication trench to us from farm as yet. Lost trace of the 52nd. Believe we have gone too far.

Elsewhere, a German *Minenwerfer* crew fired its large two-gallon canisters, filled with scrap metal, into the sky. The canisters could be easily seen in flight, rising slowly and momentarily hanging in the air before tumbling over into the Australian positions. Deafening explosions shook the ground. Further back, German shells fell thickly in no-man's-land, the support trenches, and divisional headquarters at Tara Hill.

By 8.45 a.m., battalion headquarters had lost touch with Clifford and Bailey. Soon after, Bailey, who had only taken over his platoon's command an hour before, was sniped through the head and died instantly.[16]

At 9.30 a.m., with few men left, bombs running low, and Germans continuing to emerge from secret passages, Williams withdrew his troops from Mouquet Farm and returned with them to their own line. Somewhere along the way, according to a subsequent Red Cross enquiry, a bullet drilled Williams through the forehead, killing him instantly.[17] Clifford's men were now completely cut off.

The Germans, possibly sensing the shift in momentum, attacked Clifford's isolated position from all sides. Moments later, Clifford was shot dead; it was the second anniversary of his enlistment. Lieutenant William Halvorsen positioned himself between Clifford's limp body and the Germans. Halvorsen, also severely wounded, recalled later the hopeless situation confronting the stranded troops:

> All our Lewis guns had been put out of action ... runners were sent back for reinforcements and additional Lewis guns, but we received no response to these messages. The German barrage was on us and we were being persistently sniped.[18]

Halvorsen lapsed into unconsciousness.

The Germans infiltrated Ernie Smythe's isolated position, and he made for the farm. 'I saw him shot as he was running across No-Man's Land,' said an eyewitness. 'I don't know how badly he was hit.'[19] Another soldier later saw Smythe lying dead in a crater.

'We were surrounded,' remembered Private John Cotter. 'I went out to try and get assistance for the wounded men when I was rushed by about 30 Germans.'[20] Cotter and the remaining soldiers surrendered, concluding the Australians' last hopes of capturing the farm.[21]

Glasgow, in his dugout headquarters near the cemetery, forwarded reserves at 9.30 a.m. to help his besieged battalions. It was too late: they were unable to find anyone, and returned some time later.

Glasgow, although only 1000 yards away from the farm, responded to messages despatched by officers that were sometimes two hours old. He commanded companies that had ceased to exist.

Further back at Tara Hill, conflicting reports arrived at divisional headquarters throughout the day and into the evening about the attack's progress. At 12.50 p.m., the 13th Brigade reported that they had lost the farm; at 6.35 p.m., artillery observers stated that the Australians still held it. 'Latest reports show that we may still be in Mouquet Farm itself but this is unclear,' read a 4th Division situation report at 6.45 p.m. 'Two Coy's, 51st still out west of the farm. We are still trying to link up with them.'[22] The attempts would be futile, as Clifford's and McCallum's men were either dead, wounded, or captured.

The only thing left to decide was whether the Australians could hold the ridge to the right of the farm. Expensive attacks and counterattacks continued throughout the day as the Australians and Germans desperately tried to wrestle the prized ridge from each other, which by late evening was crowned with the twisted corpses of both sides. The next day, 'Big' Maxwell, whose 52nd stubbornly clung on to the ridge, wrote in response to the suggestion that his battalion was knocked out, 'Rot, we are going strong.'[23] The 450 casualties that the battalion suffered in the battle suggested that Maxwell was adopting a brave face.

Gough's offensive to capture Thiepval and Mouquet Farm had failed completely. At 6.00 p.m., he suspended all other offensive action, but confirmed an order for Glasgow to maintain his tenuous grip on the high ground near the farm. Although admitting that his Reserve Army had met with a large-scale repulse, Gough was adamant that it would be soon avenged. According to historian Martin Gilbert, Gough blamed his commanding officers' lack of 'discipline and motivation' for the failure to capture Thiepval. Gough was somewhat more generous toward the Anzacs, writing in his memoirs that the Australian officers and men had shown a fine spirit in attack, and steady courage under the constant shelling.[24]

Despite the frightening casualties and minuscule gains of the last attack upon Mouquet Farm, it still provided grist for the Anzac legend. Their ability to persevere with seven attacks, despite overwhelming odds and supposedly incompetent leadership, supported Bean's contention that the Anzacs' unique qualities of mateship, independence, and resourcefulness set them apart from soldiers of other nationalities, particularly those from the 'old' and presumably decadent nations of Europe.[25] According to Bean, the Anzacs — ordinary fellows flung into war — had completed their duty nobly, despite failing to capture their stated objective. As Gallipoli had proved, the noble nature of their struggle, rather than the attainment of victory, was the key pillar of the Anzac legend.

Unlike on Gallipoli, the Australians' last days on the Somme were not marked by any great victory, humiliating defeat, or defining moment. The survivors simply left, with the struggle for the farm unfinished. The Anzacs had arrived, in the manner of a huge circus, with great fanfare; now the show was over, they quietly packed up and moved on — to the next town, and the next round of fighting.

Earlier that day, Birdie had prepared to shift his headquarters north. He reflected on the momentous events of the last six weeks, writing in his diary:

> We took Mouquet Farm high ground to NE ... at 5 a.m. We can now feel we have fully done our bit. I think we have taken more [prisoners] than any other corps since we started on 23rd ... while our own casualties have been about 24,000, many of them will I hope return soon.[26]

Birdie appeared pleased with his two-mile advance, even though it had cost him the equivalent of two divisions and the farm remained uncaptured.

In the afternoon of 3 September, Birdie and White vacated their Contay headquarters and departed for Ypres, where the 1st, 2nd, and 5th Divisions were now located; Cox followed a couple of days later. Canadian Corps commander Lieutenant-General Julian Byng oversaw the last-gasp efforts of the 4th Division. Gough remained on the Somme, where he continued to plot the downfall of Thiepval. He sent a message to Cox: 'I shall always be pleased to see your division near me in a fight.'[27] It is unclear whether Cox shared the same feeling.

On the same day that Birdie departed for Ypres, Treloar also prepared to shift the Central Registry north. By 9.00 a.m., his clerks had packed away their stacks of records into cases, and loaded them onto lorries. Treloar stayed behind to hand over to the Canadians. At 3.15 p.m., a car arrived to take him north.[28] Yet even though Treloar had left the Somme, it seemed that the Somme had not left him. Somewhere near Doullens, his car stopped to let a hospital train pass. 'In it were many Australians,' he observed, 'some, I suppose, of those who were wounded in the fighting around Mouquet Farm.' It is hard to imagine that Treloar was not saddened as the train passed, particularly as many of his Gallipoli friends and registry-office clerks had fought and died in the battle.

Bean decided to 'see this business through', and remained on the Somme until the Australians ceased fighting. When he walked from the battlefield on 6 September, he remembered feeling lighthearted, not the least that he was turning his back on Pozières for the last time.[29] Bean caught a train from Amiens to Calais and then crossed the English Channel. He welcomed the respite, noting that the war 'seemed to end at the French quayside'.[30] But the strain of long hours had evidently taken its toll. 'I have aged a lot in this war,' he later explained in a letter to his parents. 'Everyone lives three years in one during the war.'[31]

The Canadians relieved the last Australian unit in the line, the 49th Battalion, on 5 September. 'Can you tell me if we have got Mouquet Farm?' asked a worn soldier.[32] The sad answer was 'no'. On 5 September, the Australians' battering operations against Mouquet Farm finally came to an end. The normally restrained *Official History* described the operation as groaning to a halt in front of Mouquet

Farm like some clumsy machine having ground out, through mud and blood, a few yards of almost valueless advance.[33] On the same day, Haig ordered the Reserve Army to give up its attempts to secure Thiepval prior to the mid-September offensive. Haig re-emphasised to Gough the importance of economising his men so that he had fresh reserves ready to exploit any future successes.[34]

On 8 September, the Germans recaptured the toehold that the Australians had gained in Fabeck Graben and had desperately clung on to with the assistance of the Canadians.[35] Ironically, Thiepval, the cause of all this suffering, eventually fell before Mouquet Farm did. Gough later admitted in his memoirs that the final assault that captured Thiepval on 26 September was 'less costly' than many of the other 'preliminary and minor operations' had been.[36]

Charteris continued gathering intelligence, even though rain had turned the battlefield into a quagmire. He teased of an imminent German collapse. But now, even the War Office didn't believe him. A committee set up by the War Office to examine the Germans' available manpower concluded that they had about 750,000 reserves left. Charteris dismissed the figures, saying that morale was the pivotal determinant in the Germans' willingness to fight. The report did, however, force him to admit that there would be no hope of exhausting their reserves in this year's fighting.[37]

The Australians were not celebrating. The earlier successes at Pozières were forgotten. Even Thomas Blamey — hardly the most sensitive soldier — warned prophetically: 'The grief that struck Australia over Gallipoli will be slight compared to the grief that will strike it now.'[38]

CHAPTER SEVENTEEN
Aftermath

'We are not seeing General Birdwood quite so often these days.'
— Lieutenant-General Iven Mackay

The 1916 Somme campaign ground on through September and October and into November. The British inched forward through the bog, but still with no decisive victory in sight. By the time Haig finally closed it down on 18 November, the Allied and German armies had hurled tens of millions of shells at each other and suffered around one million casualties.[1]

The loose ends of that last attack on Mouquet Farm by the Anzacs took years to tidy up. Glasgow's 13th Brigade suffered 1300 casualties in those last few days, and nearly 500 men were listed as missing.[2] Some soldiers had simply disappeared; some were taken prisoner; others remained stranded behind the German lines. Most were dead, their bodies scattered about the shell holes and the ruins of the farm.

Nine days after the attack, three men, badly wounded and suffering from exposure, were found near the south-west corner of the farm. They had survived on the bully beef scavenged from the dead.[3]

Leslie Parsons, wounded and unable to move, had also sheltered in a shell hole, where he wrote a letter before dying. Accounts differ on the letter's contents and its intended recipient. The *Official History* claims that the letter was addressed to Parsons' brother; researcher Derek Woodhead maintains that Parsons wrote the letter in his own blood, detailing in it where his officer and mates were in the area.[4] Parsons' body was later recovered and buried in a shallow grave, but its location was soon forgotten.

Sergeant Luke Ramshaw was taken prisoner. He lay in a shell hole for three days, the wound to his thigh crawling with maggots, before some Germans stretcher-bearers found him.[5] His relatives were initially informed that he was 'missing in action'. Later, word trickled back, via the Red Cross, that he was a prisoner of war, along with Cotter.

There was no word on Bert Clifford, and the uncertainty of his fate was too much for his father to bear. Thomas Clifford died, perhaps of a broken heart, three weeks after his son was listed as missing. In March 1917, Mrs Emma Clifford received notification that her son's death had been reclassified to 'killed in action'.[6] His body was never recovered. 'There's not a day goes by, dear Bert, that we don't think of you,' she wrote on the first anniversary of his death.[7]

Sometime after the battle, Wright Wadsley and his daughters received the last of Len Wadsley's 60 letters. Reading the letters was like having a conversation with a ghost:

> If you receive this I will by then have passed to the Great Beyond ... I would have liked to have got back again but 'twas not meant that I should. Never mind girls, there'll be someone else to take my place. Well Dad goodbye! Goodbye girls! Let the remainder of the family know I think of you all and hope to meet you all again later on. T'is rotten having to write this but *c'est la guerre!*[8]

Wadsley's body was never found.

By the time Haig finally closed down the Somme campaign, 23,000 Australians of I Anzac Corps had been killed or wounded for a two-mile advance. Based on the 1911 Australian census, their losses represented the entire population of the Melbourne suburb of St Kilda or the Sydney suburb of Paddington. Add the 5th Australian Division's 5300 casualties at Fromelles, and it represented the equivalent of Broken Hill, in South Australia, being wiped from the map.[9]

Even the raw casualty numbers didn't tell the whole story. After Pozières, Brigadier-General Brand's 13th Battalion was reinforced back to its full strength of 1028 men. Of these, only 144 had passed through Gallipoli and Pozières. Nearly all those who had enlisted in 1914 and early 1915 had been killed or wounded.[10] 'Gallipoli accounted for many of the finest and bravest lads that ever lived and now the Western Front has completed the work of destruction,' wrote Lance-Corporal Charles Alexander from his hospital bed in Tidworth, England. 'Only here and there will you meet a soldier who has fought on both sides of Europe.'[11] These grim statistics were repeated across many battalions.

John Terraine reasoned in *The Western Front, 1914–1918* that casualties — even large numbers of casualties, such as those suffered by I Anzac Corps on the Somme — can be made bearable 'if they are accompanied by striking achievements'.[12] Did the Somme offensive achieve striking results, such as shortening the war? John Charteris thought so, writing on 24 November that the battle had 'certainly done all, and more, than we hoped for when we began'.[13] If striking results were achieved, as Charteris suggested, at what cost was it to the Anzacs' spirit? The character of the men had been temporarily crushed. Bean noted in his diary that many were subdued and lifeless after coming out of the trenches, most of them thoroughly sick of the punishment they'd endured from the German bombardment. The men yearned for complete rest and looked forward to some solitude to read or write a few letters home. Bean predicted that the soldiers' spirits would not fully recover until the spring.[14]

Pozières changed the Anzacs. Those carefree divisions that Charles Bean and Paul Maze had observed marching, singing, and laughing their way to Pozières in the middle of a glorious French summer were gone forever. Its men now harboured a simmering bitterness toward their generals. 'Evidently the English want to wipe out the Colonials,' wrote Private Reg Telfer of the Australian Medical Corps, 27th Battalion. 'To Hell with them.'[15]

'Ten months ago I was eager to get into the firing line. My eagerness has been well fulfilled and well I know it,' recorded Private Arthur Kilgour.[16]

'As far as I was concerned, I did not get over this experience fully for six months,' wrote Ted Rule. 'Often at night I would wake up, and in a dazed way live some of it all over again.'[17]

'God knows what we went through was hell itself,' read Second-Lieutenant Walter Claridge's letter, written from his hospital bed in England.[18]

Pozières was bad, but the future looked just as bleak. Charles Bean conceded that there was only one way out of the war for an infantryman, and that was on his back: either sick, wounded, or dead. 'They will be put at it to fight and fight and fight — until if not in this battle then in the next each man gets his bullet,' he wrote in his diary immediately after the battle. 'It is a big shock to a man when he realises that.'[19] The facts validated Bean's assessment: two in three men who left Australia's shores were killed or wounded by the war's end.

Some soldiers could not fathom how they got through Pozières unscathed. Many attributed their luck to God's providence. 'The Lord seems to especially look after us doesn't he,' Allan Leane wrote in a letter home. 'It is remarkable the luck we have, lets hope it lasts.'[20] It didn't; Leane died at Bullecourt in 1917.

Like Leane, Kogarah boy Alfred Stewart thanked God for bringing him through Pozières alive. In return, he promised to devote the rest of his life to God's work. The rest of his life was short; he was killed in action in Belgium in September 1917.[21]

Private Jack Condon, a 47-year-old tailor, vividly described the horrors of Pozières in a letter home to his young son, Donald. 'The dead strewn about sometimes for days and weeks as there is not much use burying them as they are rooted up by shells,' he wrote. Then he pleaded, 'I am telling you this son to try and dampen your ardour for the navy that is just as bad.'[22] Condon had already lost one son at Pozières — 20-year-old Richard — and didn't want to lose a second. Condon succeeded in dampening his son's enthusiasm for the war, but he died a year later at the Messines ridge. It was another cruel blow for his wife, Anne, who lived the rest of her life on a war widow's pension.[23]

Some soldiers tried to justify the huge toll at Pozières, believing that some good had to have come from it. They reiterated noble ideals: these 'little mounds in France will be stones — foundation stones — in the world's new temple of the True, the Good, and Beautiful,' wrote Stanley Cocking.[24]

Others didn't buy it. 'Why go to war with one another?' wrote Jack Bourke. 'With these men we have no quarrel.'[25]

What the Anzacs hated most about the Somme were the attacks on narrow fronts, such as those on Mouquet Farm. They channelled their anger toward their commanders, including Birdie. Bean documented a rumour that, during an inspection, troops hooted Birdie and called him a 'butcher'.[26] After hearing one of Birdie's speeches promising more fighting, Reg Telfer wrote: 'Hell! I don't want to come back here and neither do any of the others. Hang these big "pushes."'[27]

Birdie's behaviour after Pozières baffled some Australians; he seemed to display a complete lack of understanding for what they had just been through. Bean recorded one exchange between Birdie and some troops:

'Well, boys, having a good rest, eh?'
'Yes sir.'

'That's right — you deserve it — get all the rest you can, and then you'll be able to come back soon and kill some more Germans.'[28]

Birdie's comments to men who hadn't yet recovered from Pozières were understandably unpopular. Bean thought the general's intent was to avoid falsely raising the troops' hopes that they would have a prolonged rest. A more likely explanation was that Birdie possessed a simplistic understanding of his soldiers' motivations and assumed that they enjoyed killing Germans, when in fact few wanted to fight again.[29] These incidents were almost certainly another example of Birdie lacking the necessary perspective required of a corps commander.

Ted Rule was a little more forgiving of the 'brass heads' like Birdie. 'When we look back today, we can see how little our leaders understood their jobs at that time, simply through lack of experience,' he reasoned in his memoirs. 'At the same time trained German officers were taking advantage of our inexperience.'[30] Battalion histories such as *The Fighting Thirteenth* echoed a similar theme: 'So many of these small advances were attempted that one is compelled to think that our "heads" were nervous about their ability to manage big affairs.'[31]

In 45 days, the 'nervous heads' had launched 19 attacks in response to Haig's edict for 'steady and methodical' attacks. In practice, the Anzac and British officers had executed piecemeal attacks on narrow fronts.

The British were overwhelmed by the number of soldiers killed on the Somme in 1916, and at a loss as to how best to manage their burial. They could not be buried in French churchyards because there was not enough room. By necessity, soldiers who died from their wounds at advanced dressing stations near villages such as Bécourt, Warloy, and Vadencourt were buried in the nearby fields. John Treloar noticed how quickly these temporary graveyards sprung up behind the lines: 'As we walked we noticed through the twilight three mounds with a post on top of each,' he wrote in his diary. Days later, he passed the same graveyard, 'which was a little fuller than last night'.[32]

Would the dead be returned home after the war? Britain had quickly decided against it. Bodies could not be exhumed for hygiene reasons, and the cost was thought to be prohibitive. Australia followed suit, noting that it would be impractical to transport their dead halfway around the world. A grateful French nation willingly granted permanent concession for British cemeteries.

Masses of enquiries flooded the army from families desperately seeking information about their loved ones' grave sites. The British government responded by setting up the Graves Registration Commission in 1915 to record all graves and to notify the next of kin of their location and the nearest railway station.

Unsurprisingly, families wanted to know who would tend their loved one's grave after the war. Would it fall into ruin and disrepair? In 1917, the British government set up the Imperial War Graves Commission, which had the mandate to honour the dead; Andrew Fisher, Australia's high commissioner in London, represented Australia on the commission. It immediately set about resolving sensitive questions such as the type of headstones to be used and the information permitted on them; if varying treatments based on rank, religion, or social status would be permitted; who would be responsible for the upkeep of the cemeteries and graves; and whether the dead would remain where they fell or be interred in one of the designated cemeteries.

After the 3 September attack on Mouquet Farm, many families waited for word on their missing loved ones; occasionally their remains were discovered and reburied. For many months, Hilda Ekin-Smyth waited patiently for news about her missing husband, Ralph, but little came. Then, a year later, 'out of the blue', she received a parcel. It contained her husband's prized Kodak camera.

Seven years of silence followed, and then, in 1923, Hilda received an unexpected letter. It explained that the Imperial War Graves Commission had discovered Ralph Ekin-Smyth's remains, along with those of 18 others, in a large crater just beyond the farm. The contents in his badly deteriorated wallet had helped to identify him. Hilda requested that it be returned so that her sons, Raymond, Walter, and Kenneth would have something to remember their father by.[33] For these young boys, the perished wallet and that old Kodak camera would be their equivalent of the vast panels listing the missing at Villers-Bretonneux: a personal connection to a father they perhaps never really knew. Ekin-Smyth's remains were reburied in a small military cemetery just west of Albert.

Ninety-five years later, the wallet is in the possession of Margaret Lee, the granddaughter of Ralph. For Margaret, the wallet signifies terrible sadness. In an interview, she recounted that, during the Somme offensive, Ralph, perhaps sensing the 'hopelessness' of the situation, sent a letter to Raymond. In it, he implored his eldest son, who was still at primary school, to care for his mother and siblings should he not return home. According to Margaret, Raymond dutifully accepted this responsibility, no doubt a terrible burden for one so young. Margaret has memories of Hilda's life after Ralph's death: her financial struggles, her custom of always wearing navy to mourn her husband, her torment when sons Walter and Kenneth marched off to battle in the Second World War, and her foreboding during those years whenever the telegram boy rode past the house. Margaret plans to entrust Ralph's wallet to her son, Justin.[34]

In 2004, Margaret's cousin, Michael Ekin-Smyth, visited Ralph's grave. Michael remembered that seeing his family name on a headstone produced a sensation difficult to describe. He wondered how and why the Great War could have enticed so many young men to give up their lives for so little, concluding that there was no possible answer to his question.[35] It was as Bean had predicted: a scrap piece of iron flung at random had followed its course right through to the furthest end of the world, and impacted upon families — in this case, three generations of the Ekin-Smyths.

Daniel McCallum's and Ernest Smythe's bodies were discovered in the same crater as Ralph Ekin-Smyth's. Mrs Edith Smythe, thankful for the discovery of her son's remains and the return of his 'sacred' personal belongings, requested that the following inscription be engraved upon his headstone: 'A beautiful life closed; he lived and died for others'.[36]

Howard Williams' family read in the newspapers that Australian remains had been discovered near the farm, and wondered if Howard was there as well. 'I have waited for any information possible relative to him and would consider it a very great favour if you could forward to me any matter that may have reached you,' wrote his sister to the minister for defence.[37] There was no news to give; unfortunately, Howard's body was not one of the 19 found in the crater. His name is etched among the missing at the Villers-Bretonneux memorial.

More bodies were found in 1927, including Leslie Parsons'. 'It is a great gratification to us all in the family to know that his poor remains have been recovered after 11 years,' wrote his mother to Base Records upon hearing the news. She later received Leslie's perished identity discs in the mail.[38]

The Anzac legend found its roots on Gallipoli, where journalists such as Ellis Ashmead-Bartlett cultivated a romantic image of the Anzacs based on the values of independence, mateship, equality, and a healthy disregard for authority. Pozières was different from Gallipoli — it was darker and uglier. Even though the horror of Pozières filtered back to Australians through telegrams, letters, and casualty lists, the battle added another dimension to the Anzac legend. Emerging themes, such as the Diggers' needless sacrifice due to incompetent leadership and their perseverance in the face of overwhelming odds, became particularly meaningful to Australians, who sought a society free of class distinction and were perhaps keen to erase the stain of their convict past.[39]

Perhaps, in this context, it is unsurprising that Margaret Lee paused when asked whether her grandmother, Hilda, felt resentful that the Great War had snatched her husband away. Margaret suggested that Hilda's resentment was overshadowed by a belief that Ralph had nobly performed his duty for a young country that sought to forge its own path and step away from the societal strictures cast by the old country.[40]

And why do later generations of Australians cling tightly to the Anzac themes that originated at Pozières? Perhaps questioning these premises weakens the foundations of the all-important Anzac legend.

Although Gallipoli remains Australia's chosen and most visible symbol of the Anzac legend, almost certainly the lesser-known Pozières battle casts its own gloom over the myth and, consequently, the national identity.

From a military perspective, Haig had set three objectives for the Somme offensive — the capture of ground, the wearing down of the German army, and relieving the French army at Verdun. Were they achieved?

The final advance totalled, at best, seven miles. The cost of capturing these few miles was unsustainable, and in any case the Germans still had to be thrust back another 150 to 200 miles to reinstate pre-war boundaries. The cost of capturing objectives such as Mouquet Farm was simply too expensive. According to Robin Prior and Trevor Wilson's calculations in their book *The Somme*, it took seven Australian, British, and Canadian divisions and a staggering 18,200 casualties to advance one mile to capture the farm's ruins.[41] As one battalion history noted poignantly, Mouquet Farm smashed some of the finest fighting battalions ever known in history, without anything like commensurate gain in land or enemy losses.[42]

As for the success of the brutal strategy of war by attrition, the scorecard read 623,000 Allied casualties and an estimated 420,000 German casualties. The German army was probably best placed to

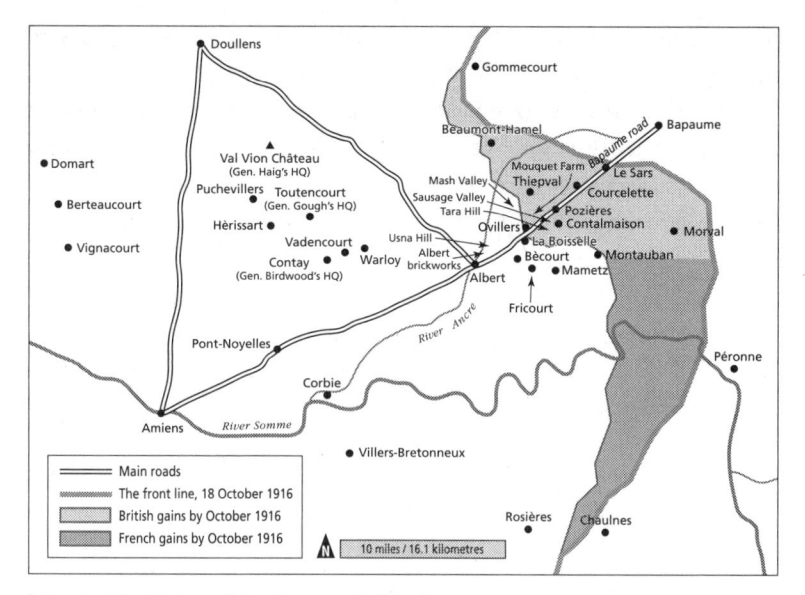

Map 7. The Gains of the Somme Offensive

judge the impact of the Somme offensive. Captain von Hentig, a staff officer with the Guard Reserve Division, said it was 'the muddy grave of the German field army'.[43] In some ways, they helped to dig their own grave — General Erich von Falkenhayn's decree that any ground lost should be retaken by 'immediate counterattack', even to the 'last man', unnecessarily wasted reserves and drained his army.[44] Equally, one is left wondering what it cost the Allies to deliver this blow — the collapse of the French army a year later suggests a high cost. The Somme appeared to be a pyrrhic victory, although its architect, Haig, saw things differently: 'If the whole operations of the ... war are regarded in correct perspective, the summer and autumn victories of 1918 will be seen to be directly dependent upon the two years of stubborn fighting that preceded them.'[45] Haig rightly calculated that the Allies' armies could absorb the losses on the Somme and subsequent battles marginally better than the German army. Haig's view was supported by his adversary, General Erich Ludendorff, who reflected in his memoirs that the strain of 1916 completely exhausted his army on the Western Front.[46]

A young officer perhaps best summed up the prevailing mood of all soldiers. 'In 1916 English, French, and Germans alike saw victory within their grasp, and expected it after every local advantage,' wrote Charles Edmonds. 'In 1917 the war seemed likely to go on forever.'[47]

CHAPTER EIGHTEEN

War-weariness

> 'I have returned to these:
> The farm and the kindly Bush, and the young calves lowing
> But all that my mind sees
> Is the quaking bog in the mist — stark, snapped trees
> And the dark Somme flowing.'
> — Vance Palmer, 'The Farmer Remembers the Somme'

The Great War lurched through the autumn and winter months of 1916 as if it would never end. According to Manning Clark, stories got back to Australia about what had happened at Pozières. Siblings such as Lennon Raws heard how their beloved relatives had been blown to pieces; mothers such as Hester Allen received a knock on the door from a clergyman, or those such as Annie Bennison read letters written by their disfigured sons. Yet 'patriots wanted the war to go on', as Clark noted in his *History of Australia*, 'but the number of doubters had increased.'[1] The political ramifications of the Somme offensive would be felt across Australia and Britain.

Billy Hughes returned to a divided Australia. The prime minister, who had vigorously championed compulsory military service since 1902, was convinced that conscription was the only option. Hughes did not reveal his hand immediately, as he knew his party did not support it. He held a series of meetings all over Australia to gauge the public's mood on the issue, after which his political instincts sensed they were ripe for it. He lobbied his party to put the issue to the people in the form of a referendum vote, and the bill was passed in September.

From that moment, Hughes showed his colours, becoming the most vehement proponent for the 'yes' vote. 'For myself, I say that I am going into this referendum campaign as if it were the only thing for which I lived,' he told parliament.[2] According to Ernest Scott's tome, *Australia During the War*, the Irish-born Roman Catholic archbishop Dr Daniel Mannix became the voice for the 'no' vote. Mannix, with his dark, brooding eyes, hollow cheeks, and pallbearer's demeanour, asked how Irish-Australians could provide unbridled support for Britain's war effort when the nation had persecuted the Irish. The Sinn Fein Easter Rising in Dublin in April, which had resulted in 300 deaths, further sharpened the divide. Trade unions were generally against it, believing that no one could compel a man to kill another against his will.

Even soldiers had mixed feelings. After Pozières, many weren't keen to drag unwilling men into the war. One soldier warned his brother never to take any part in trying to persuade others to enlist, as 'they who are too thick-skinned to come away are in the end the luckiest. After seeing what I have seen in the few short weeks I have been in the trenches, I would not drive a dog of mine into them.'[3]

Others, like Sergeant Daniel Scanlon of the 49th Battalion, supported a 'yes' vote. 'About conscription men are needed at the front badly if they don't come I am afraid that very few of us here will ever return to Australia,' he wrote in a letter home.[4]

Still others weren't sure. 'We are preparing to give our votes on the conscription question,' wrote Pozières veteran Stanley Cocking. 'It's giving me some hard thinking.'[5]

In the end, the troops voted for conscription in a slight majority. In Australia, just under 80,000 votes defeated the referendum. It was a staggering blow for the conscription supporters, particularly as other dominions to which they constantly compared themselves, such as New Zealand, had already introduced it. How would Australia make its mark upon the world if its people weren't prepared to unite toward the war? Hughes, in a humiliating backdown, telegraphed the Army Council, indicating that his cable of 31 August required amendment: 'Not possible now to provide the 20,000 reinforcements promised.'[6]

The 'no' vote reflected the growing feeling among Australians that Australia was not under threat; they were supporting Britain in a war of Europe's making. 'If Australia had really been in danger of invasion, there would be no need to conscript me,' wrote Henry Booth, the editor of the left-leaning paper *The Worker*. 'I would have fought there myself.'[7]

The conscription vote created a political crisis and the Labor Party split. On 14 November, Hughes and 23 other ministers walked out of the party room and formed a new government, with the support of the Liberals, called the Nationalists. Its objective was simply stated as 'winning the war'.[8]

Soldiers had mixed views on the vote's outcome. 'The lads are nearly all glad conscription was not carried,' wrote Stanley Cocking. 'They did not want to fight along conscripts, but we do want more willing men to come over and help us.'[9] Yet they didn't come; voluntary enlistments had dried up. By December, the recruitment offices could only raise 2617 recruits.[10] Undeterred, Hughes held another referendum, in September 1917, but it was again defeated, with the margin almost exactly the same as the first vote.

In the end, the conscription debate tore apart a young nation. It inflamed hatred between Protestants and Catholics, destroyed the Labor government, and left lasting divisions within the nation. 'The riff has never since been quite closed,' admitted Charles Bean in 1957.[11]

The Somme offensive also contributed to the downfall of Britain's Asquith government in December 1916. The new prime minister, David Lloyd George, thought that the Somme offensive had been a bloody and disastrous failure, and wasn't willing to repeat it the following year.[12] At an Anglo–French conference in Boulogne in October 1916, he had said that the time had come for the Allies to distinguish between the illusions and realities of the struggle. 'In 1914–15–16 we could afford to blunder without throwing away the final chance of victory. If we take the wrong turning in 1917, I do not believe that our fortunes can be retrieved,' he advised the conference.

Lloyd George said that whatever the Allies did, it had to mark a distinct break with the methods and conceptions of the past.[13] But, in 1917, the bloody battles fought at Bullecourt, Flanders, Aisne, Arras, and Ypres demonstrated that there were no such 'new methods' to quicken the war's end against Germany. The enemy nation had enacted the Hindenburg Program in 1916, which granted the military absolute control of the economy, so as to better wage total war.[14] Lloyd George had no plausible option other than to persist with the detested war of attrition. As Bean predicted, the Anzacs who survived the Somme would be condemned to more battles, to fight and fight and fight.

The Great War ground on through 1917 and 1918 without an end in sight. The Anzacs continued fighting along the Western Front at Passchendaele, Le Hamel, Villers-Bretonneux, and Mont St Quentin. Gradually, empires, nations, kingdoms, and armies wilted under the all-consuming demands of industrialised war. At five o'clock in the morning of 11 November 1918, the German delegation at Compiègne signed the armistice; at 11.00 a.m., the fighting and dying on the Western Front ceased. Correlli Barnett's book *The Great War* recorded that after 11.00 a.m. soldiers stood upright in unaccustomed safety, listening to the birdsong, marvelling that they had survived, and mourning the dead.[15] Australian troops accepted the news with singular calm. It took days for the men to realise that the bloodshed was over; only then could their thoughts 'be confidently turned towards home'.[16] But what did 'home' hold for the veterans — could they settle back in to society? Would their sacrifices at Pozières be remembered, or would they fade from the nation's mind?

Many Pozières veterans never lived to see Armistice Day. Even senior officers died. A stray shell struck William Holmes, the 'spit and polish' commander of the 5th Brigade, in the chest in July 1917. Taken to the nearest aid post, he died soon after. A shell also wounded Duncan Glasfurd, the plucky Scottish commander of the 12th Brigade, in November 1916. After an agonising ten-hour journey through the mud by stretcher, he died at a casualty clearing station. Third Battalion commander Owen Howell-Price was shot through the brain while checking a machine-gun emplacement in November 1916. He lingered on for two days before dying. Howell-Price symbolised all the promise of a 'new' Australia: bright and energetic, but with a touch of youthful awkwardness. The Great War matured him, but just as quickly snuffed him out. For every soldier who achieved great things after the war, there were many more Owen Howell-Prices, with the same promise left on the battlefields of France.

Other commanders survived the war but were permanently scarred by it. Seventh Brigade commander John Paton wept as his broken battalions returned from the failed attack on the OG lines. He was wounded in November 1916, and later relinquished his command, unable to cope with the strain. The quiet 2nd Brigade commander, John Forsyth, was relieved, exhausted after the heavy shelling at Pozières. After hospitalisation, he assumed command of a training centre in England; however, his health failed again. After doctors assessed him as unfit for active service, he returned to Australia a broken man.[17] Fourth Division commander Herbert Cox suffered another nervous breakdown in January 1917, and was relieved of his command. The 'bloody business' on the Somme also affected 6th Brigade commander, Jack Gellibrand. After a wasteful and ill-planned attack at Bullecourt in 1917, a disgusted Gellibrand, with his 'health broken', walked away from his command. And, after Pozières, sleep was never easy for 3rd Brigade commander Ewan Sinclair-MacLagan — his granddaughter said that after the war he rarely spoke of Gallipoli or France, but he could often be heard shouting out orders in his sleep.[18]

Some of the soldiers whose letters and diaries feature in this book died in later battles. Frederick Callaway, who wrote of sparing a German Red Cross prisoner, died on 5 September 1916 — the day that the last Australian unit was relieved at Mouquet Farm. A *Minenwerfer* exploded in his dugout in Ypres, killing him instantly.[19] Collins Street tailor Arthur Thomas, who described the awe-inspiring sight of columns of Anzacs marching through the French countryside in July 1916, died on a stretcher in February 1917 after an exploding shell cut him to pieces.[20]

Others survived the wearing battles, but evidently lost their will to live. Lieutenant-Colonel Leslie Mather was awarded a Distinguished Service Order for gallantry at Pozières, but was also seriously wounded when a bullet grazed his spine. It left him in terrible pain. 'It must have smashed a bunch of nerves controlling the left arm as I have had almost continuous agony in the shoulder,' he explained in a letter to his friend Geoffrey Drake-Brockman.[21] Maher shot himself on 24 January 1919. According to his suicide note, his 'deliberate and premeditated act' was due to intense worry and ill health, both physical and mental. A court of enquiry concluded that 30-year-old Mather had committed suicide while 'temporarily insane'.[22]

The Pozières veterans returning to Australia had been away for over three years. One veteran accurately predicted that it was 'going to be as hard to demobilise as it was to beat Fritz'.[23] The battalion came home in instalments, never to assemble again, said Ted Rule, with a touch of regret. 'The AIF was slowly dissolving and becoming a mere memory,' he wrote in his war memoirs.[24] It faded from memory, perhaps, but not from sight. Patsy Adam-Smith wrote in *The Anzacs*:

We [now] lived in a world where men were called 'Hoppy', 'Wingy', 'Shifty', 'Gunner', 'Stumpy', 'Deafy', 'Hooky' according to whether they lost a leg, an arm (or part of one), an eye, their hearing, or had a disfigured face drawn by rough surgery into a leer.[25]

The Repatriation Department eased the returning soldiers back into civilian life. It helped thousands to find jobs, vocational training, and, for a few, university courses.[26] Some sought soldier settlement blocks at cheap interest rates. Pozières veteran John Edey took up a lot in the Mallee, while Donovan Joynt ran some cattle in Berwick. Like many of their neighbours, they hardly knew how to milk a cow or mend a fence.[27]

Although John Edey persevered with his selection, the Soldier Settlement Scheme didn't prove to be the utopia that everyone expected. Veterans were often allocated barren land unsuitable for farming, and many did not have the skills to make a go of it. Donovan Joynt was one of many who laboured under a mounting burden of debt. 'After paying my farm employees, little remained in the way of revenue from the land … I walked off it broke after ten years of hard work and the loss of my capital and war savings,' he wrote in his autobiography.[28] Thousands, including Joynt, simply walked away, sometimes only leaving behind a note and a set of keys. In the midst of the Depression, it was a national catastrophe. 'It killed many,' claimed Joynt.

The Australian government provided war-damaged soldiers with a pension. Arthur Foxcroft was one recipient. In 1917, he was seriously wounded a second time, shot through the thigh, which left him with 'drop foot'. His mother, Amelia, pleaded with authorities for his return so he could 'properly mend' himself. He returned in late 1917, recording in his diary on 21 November, while anchored off Williamstown, that he saw his 'first sunrise in Australia for two years'. Unable to raise much more than a shuffle, Foxcroft moved in with his parents in Coburg, Victoria, surviving on a meagre pension of 15 shillings per week.[29] Foxcroft's diary reveals that, upon returning home, he adopted a mundane routine of seeking treatment, occasionally visiting friends, and completing everyday chores. It contrasted starkly with the exhilarating highs and plummeting lows he had experienced during the Great War. Did this adjustment to the normality of civilian life present its own challenges? Foxcroft's diary doesn't disclose the answer, petering out in early 1918.

By June 1921, the government was paying out a quarter of a million war pensions to men like Foxcroft; but soon after, the number decreased, as short-term pensions ended.[30] The statistics hid the melancholy felt by many returning soldiers. Some called it war-weariness. The generous repatriation scheme could never relieve the chronic pain of old wounds, or ease the psychological scars of battle. 'Though most settled back into the community, many were unwell, not only due to their mental scars, but also crippling wounds and severe lung damage from gas,' recounted one battalion history.[31] Doctors found that the soldiers, compared to their civilian counterparts, suffered chronic and advanced stages of disease much earlier in life. These diseases included chronic lung conditions caused by gas poisoning, kidney disease caused by trench nephritis, and mental illness exacerbated by severe shell shock.[32] By 1931, the number of war pensions had increased 27 per cent on the 1921 figure. In *Dinkum Diggers*, Dale Blair traced 1st Battalion soldiers throughout the war; he found that those who relied on pensions were sometimes consumed by guilt, feeling they had betrayed the spirit of those who had died.[33] Some who deserved pensions never bothered to claim them, choosing to suffer in silence.

The 'nervy' men, such as John Harris, who had suffered shell shock at Pozières and returned to Australia in 1918, found it difficult to ease back into civilian life. Their condition was little understood, and administrators treated their pension claims inconsistently. 'Unless you had an arm off or a leg off or a hand off or something like that, it was almost as hard to get a pension as it would be to win Tatts,' remembered Fred Farrall with excusable exaggeration. 'I had neurosis that was not recognised in those days, and so we just had it. You put up with it.'[34] It was speculated among some quarters that the condition was linked to some inherent character defect which exacerbated their plight. Some ended up in lunatic asylums and would have rotted there, had it not been for the soldier associations that pressured medical organisations to take a more enlightened approach to their treatment.

Harris's repatriation medical files indicate that he never sought treatment for shell shock after the war. This is unsurprising, considering that post-traumatic stress disorder was not recognised as a war-induced ailment until the 1980s.[35] Harris most probably felt embarrassed and stigmatised by his inexplicable 'bouts of nerves'. Perhaps he couldn't reconcile his braveness on the one hand with his 'nerves' on the other. Harris conceivably felt that he had disappointed his troops, some of them past students, who still affectionately called him 'Dad'.[36]

Records of other shell-shock victims provide some insight into what Harris may have experienced. Neighbours might have thought he was a bit queer, a little nervous, sometimes tense and jumpy. Fronting a classroom again would have been difficult. Perhaps sometimes his heart would thump against his chest for apparently no reason. The slamming of a door or the back firing of a car would have, most likely, startled him.

Harris didn't talk much about the war. It seemed best forgotten. He did, however, write about his experience at Pozières. The piece, written with a shaky hand and on thin writing paper, might have helped him a bit, but it was more about times, events, and places rather than his personal feelings and experiences. The lasting effect of the 'tremendous bombardment' upon Harris was revealed in a letter he sent to Charles Bean in 1926: he explained that his recollections of Pozières were very 'vague and shadowy' owing to 'shellshock'. 'I lost my memory in regard to numerous things which happened, of which I was informed afterwards by others,' he wrote in the letter.[37]

Harris taught throughout Australia until 1951. He then applied for a pension, claiming that he suffered from arthritis due to exposure to severe weather conditions at Ypres in 1917. In his letter to the deputy commissioner of the repatriation department, Harris wrote that he found it difficult to get and retain a decent position, as headmasters did not want to employ a cripple. His claim was approved. His health declined in later years. Confined to a bed, he died at Bodington Hospital in New South Wales in 1960, aged 82.[38]

Fred Farrall claimed it was hard to get a pension unless you had an arm or leg off, but Robert Smith's plight suggested that it was even a tricky proposition for an amputee. Smith was discharged from the Australian Imperial Force in February 1918. He was initially granted a full pension, but it was reduced to 75 per cent in 1919, after he got a job as a jeweller with Dunklings. Although considered a 'conscientious, diligent' worker, Smith was frequently absent due to chronic stomach trouble. In 1924, he lost his job because of a trade depression. In 1926, he applied to the Repatriation Commission for a living allowance. Although he had not worked for the last 22 months, the commission rejected his application, believing that he was capable of getting a job as a boot repairer. In 1932, Smith's pension was reduced under the Financial Emergency Act.

Smith 'led a quiet and reserved life' and joined the Limbless Soldiers' Association of Queensland. He required constant treatment for his stomach complaint, which doctors attributed, in part, to his incessant worrying.

Smith's health gradually deteriorated. In 1929, he suffered the first of many nerve storms in his stump, which he compared to the pain of an auger boring into his foot. In 1949, he experienced severe back and leg pain due to his artificial leg being inches shorter than his good leg. In 1950, Smith ceased working as a boot maker at the Limb Factory because he was unable to stand for long periods due to his shaky right knee. In 1959, Smith abandoned his peg leg and began to use crutches, as the prosthesis chafed the skin on his scarred stump. Life proved a struggle for Smith: repeated bouts of unemployment, menial jobs, frequent illness, and fluctuating financial circumstances. It was a life that an adventurous 22-year-old soldier, who had enjoyed the pleasures of good French champagne and cheap beer in the months before Pozières, could never have anticipated. Smith died in 1977.[39]

The post-war malaise did not discriminate between officers and soldiers. Gordon Legge's melancholic mood possibly reached its lowest ebb in 1918 when his eldest son, George, died on the Western Front. George's death most likely compounded the disillusionment Legge felt in early 1917, when Birdie relieved him of his 2nd Division command after he fell ill with the 'flu, although Legge claimed that he felt perfectly well. Legge's opinionated and abrasive personality had sealed his fate. Had he worked more collaboratively with fellow officers, he may well have kept his command.[40]

Legge returned to Australia and filled his old pre-war role of chief of the general staff. After the war, he was unceremoniously shoved out of the role in favour of White. History did not treat him kindly, blaming him, along with Gough, for the 2nd Division's failed attack upon the OG lines, even though White and Gellibrand suggested that he had been made a scapegoat: 'Every senior officer in the Corps knew of Gough's constant insistence upon haste.'[41] Bean concluded that Legge's judgement was sometimes defective and that his lack of experience prevented him, despite his intelligence, from being a good leader in battle. Legge seemed to develop a certain inevitability — perhaps resignation — toward his place in history. He elected not to comment publicly on Bean's assessment and chose to spend his remaining years as a semi-recluse on his farm at Weetangera, near Canberra, reluctant to participate in reunions or official ceremonies.[42]

A letter that Legge wrote to Bean in 1928, explaining that his recall to Australia in 1917 was due to the 'higher powers' playing a trick on him, confirmed that he still harboured some bitterness toward his perceived enemies. He also intimated that his divisional papers had mysteriously disappeared: 'It would have been inconvenient for some people if I had been able to refer to them.'⁴³

In Legge's twilight years, a cold reserve gradually replaced his talkativeness. Did he brood on his troubled past? His biography described how, on the odd occasion, while sitting quietly at his homestead, he would reminisce about those days in France — recalling how his troops, even when wet and tired, kept up their spirits by singing marching songs.

When Legge died in 1947, his funeral was a private affair. There was no headstone or memorial placed upon his grave, and his private papers were destroyed.⁴⁴ Today, there is no enduring monument or memorial to him. It seemed that Legge's last forlorn wish was to be expunged from the history books altogether, rather than being damned for his failure at Pozières.

Others weren't going to risk history damning them. They realised that if history was to treat them kindly, they must write it themselves. In the 1920s and 1930s, Gough, Birdie, Monash, Churchill, Lloyd George, and Charteris all recorded their own version of events, justifying their decisions, celebrating their victories, and blaming others for their failures. Yet writing his own version of events didn't prevent history from damning Gough. The brilliant young general and former protégé of Haig was sacked in 1918, blamed for the Fifth British Army's (formerly the Reserve Army) disorganised retreat in the wake of the Germans' final offensive. Hooky Walker's post-war verdict on Gough was scathing: he claimed that Gough had exhibited the worst generalship of the whole campaign.⁴⁵ Gough took his fall from grace badly — he took potshots at his rivals, most of whom he outlived, labelling them as 'crawlers', 'funks', and 'indecisive'. Gough never accepted responsibility for the costly attacks launched upon Mouquet Farm. In his autobiography, he claimed that corps and divisional commanders such as Birdie had pleaded with him to carry out these 'hopeless' attacks and that he had 'reluctantly consented' to do so.[46] In the end, Gough's greatest failing was that he was never able to make the transition from leading a small brigade to managing the logistics of a massive army.

Birdie escaped the post-war malaise and lived a charmed life. What he lacked in intellect he made up for in nonchalance. One general believed that Birdie's way was to shake hands with everyone so that, by the time anyone had found him out, 'thousands more had been won by handshakes in arithmetic progression'.[47] He never achieved his ambition of becoming governor-general: Australians came to their senses and appointed one of their own. While history condemned Legge and Gough for their perceived failings at Pozières, Birdie escaped with his reputation intact. One suspects that his so-called special relationship with the Anzacs dulled people's awareness of his shortcomings. It seemed to be a relationship of unequals: in Birdie's world, there were English Christian gentlemen and then there were the rest. Birdie's imperialist vanities meant that he considered the colonial Australians as little more than tools to further his own mediocre career — Birdie was for Birdie and no one else. For too long, Birdie's patronising praise seduced Australians and blinded them to his limitations, which were laid bare at Pozières.

White never came out from behind Birdie's shadow, even though Haig told him privately in July 1917 that he should command I Anzac Corps. White responded that Birdie should never be removed, as he was an 'imperial asset'.[48] Monash succeeded Birdie as the Australian corps commander in 1918, after Birdie replaced Gough as the Fifth British Army commander.

Upon his transfer to the Fifth Army, Birdie immediately appointed White as his chief-of-staff, no doubt assuring him that it would be good for his career. White was loyal to a fault, which Birdie skilfully exploited. His views on imperialism, at a time when Australia wanted to assert itself, were more suited to 1914 than 1918. He remained captive to the British tradition, still believing that the Australian force was an instrument of the British Imperial Army. What can never be questioned is White's contribution to I Anzac Corps in the first years of the war, particularly at Pozières, when the Australian divisions were inexperienced and the Germans at their strongest.

When the Depression hit in the 1930s, capital-works programs were slashed, leaving many Pozières veterans jobless. In addition, the Financial Emergency Act of 1932 cut back those eligible for pensions. Some veterans, down on their luck, took to hawking cigarettes and bootlaces door to door. Fellow comrades often invited them in for a cup of tea and offered them some discarded clothing or a few spare pennies, no matter how tough their own circumstances were — it was the Anzac way. Ironically, during this crisis the Australian government continued to honour its repayments to British bondholders, who had financed Australia's involvement in the war. It seemed, according to Gerald Stone in his book *1932*, that veterans were once again being asked to make sacrifices while British bondholders got paid every penny in full.[49]

Gellibrand and Haig devoted themselves to the cause of returned soldiers. Gellibrand established the Legacy movement in Tasmania, which aimed to protect the interests of veterans and the needs of their widows and children. The movement quickly spread throughout Australia, and continues to thrive today. Occasionally, Gellibrand led the Anzac Day march down Swanston Street in Melbourne and, true to form, was admonished for wearing the incorrect uniform.

Haig worked tirelessly for veteran organisations after the war. His cool demeanour gradually gave way to concern and empathy. He flatly refused any honours or rewards until the prime minister fixed allowances for disabled officers and ranks.[50] In 1920, with his army commitments fulfilled, he withdrew from public life, but never wavered in championing the cause of returned soldiers. He died suddenly in 1928. One wonders if the ghosts of the Somme ever haunted him. He did not live to see the tide of public opinion turn savagely against him in the late 1920s and early 1930s. It did not soften over time — Patrick Cook of *The Bulletin* wrote of Haig in 2006: 'From first to last, from top to bottom, slice him where you like, Haig was a dense, impermeable, incompetent shit.'[51]

Haig's burden was that his Somme victory was so expensive it became indistinguishable from defeat. The battle is rarely viewed in its full context, that of being a necessary precursor to the victories of late 1918. This viewpoint, which Haig, unsurprisingly, subscribed to, contends that, after the initial manoeuvring for position in 1914, a 'welter of slaughter' was inevitable in 1916 as two opposing forces of equal strength struggled against each other. At some point, one of the belligerents would have had to weaken.[52] Conclusive battles of history, from Carthage to Stalingrad, suggest that this phase of slow slaughter was unavoidable. This viewpoint adds gravity to the words attributed to a Roman general after conquering Carthage: 'Another such victory will destroy us.'[53] On page 946 of the *Official History*, Bean concluded similarly of the Somme offensive.

Billy Hughes tried to exercise his newfound political clout at the Paris Peace Conference in 1919. 'Australia has suffered 90,000 casualties in this war and lost 60,000 killed,' he announced at the conference.[54] But Hughes's voice was drowned out by those of other nations and ethnic groups — the Polish, Chinese, Jews, Arabs, Czechs, Slovaks — that flocked to Paris seeking long-awaited justice. Australia successfully secured a mandate over New Guinea and helped to defeat Japan's attempts to have a racial-equity clause inserted in the League of Nations covenant, but failed to secure reparations from Germany. It's doubtful if the ghosts of Pozières and Mouquet Farm, their graves unmarked, their bodies ploughed into the soil, would have rested any easier knowing that their deaths had extracted such a meagre return.

After the Paris Peace Conference, the French held a victory march, symbolically led by their *grands mutilés*, that legion of men left limbless, armless, blind, crippled, and broken by the Great War. The message was subtle but jolting: this war hadn't been won, but survived.

CHAPTER NINETEEN

The Missing

'It is only the dead who have seen the end of war.'
— attributed to Plato

While politicians redrew the world's boundaries, back in Australia thousands of families continued their painful search for lost relatives. Four thousand Australians soldiers were posted as missing at Pozières, their bodies never recovered — or, if found, never identified. It was as if they had simply vanished. A cold telegram or a clergyman's visit delivered the sad news. Patsy Adam-Smith noted, in *Australian Women at War*, that 'some women wouldn't open their doors to a clergyman during the first war'.[1] They received little beyond the bare facts, forcing families to write to the Base Records Office, the Red Cross Society, fellow soldiers, or anyone else who might shed some greater light on their loved one's fate. It seemed, according to historians Bruce Scates and Raelene Francis, that they had entered a twilight world somewhere between life and death.[2]

While on leave in Edinburgh visiting a bereaved family, Ted Rule witnessed the overwhelming anguish that the simple word 'missing' inflicted. Rule saw the heartache as, day after day, the mother of a missing soldier betrayed her thoughts: '"The missing did very often show up again, didn't they? ... Probably he was a prisoner-of-war. Maybe he had lost his memory and was in some hospital" ... What could I say? I felt justified in telling lies.'[3]

Numerous agencies were set up to deal with the 'missing'. In 1915, the Australian government established a department dedicated to answering the flood of enquiries that came from distraught families. The Australian Red Cross Society created the Wounded and Missing Enquiry Bureau to identify, investigate, and respond to enquiries made regarding the fate of Australian personnel. The Australian Imperial Force conducted its own court of enquiry in the field to ascertain the fate of missing soldiers.

How was a soldier registered as missing, and what investigations were conducted into his disappearance? Who notified his family that he was unaccounted for? Could his relatives achieve emotional closure as long as 'missing' was stamped in his personnel file? The stories of Sergeant Philip Browne and privates George Drosen, Robert Allen, and Stephen Allen provide some insight into these questions.

Private George Drosen, a 36-year-old stevedore from the Melbourne bayside suburb of Williamstown, had apparently disappeared without a trace on 10 August near Mouquet Farm. According to the Red Cross enquiry, he was with a party of 46th Battalion men withdrawing from the front-line trench at about 10.30 p.m. when a shell exploded; in the confusion and darkness, they scattered. Most managed to work their way back to safety, but Drosen did not answer at rollcall.

The 48th Battalion held an enquiry into Drosen's fate in May 1917, nine months after he had disappeared. Witness Sergeant Leonard Coulson testified that he went back to search for Drosen, but all he could find was the warm and quivering trunk of a man. He could not find any identification papers on the body. When the court asked what had happened to the body, Coulson explained that it was buried quickly; however, he reassured the officers that the trunk seemed to be Drosen, as it had a similar build to him. With no identification papers, no body to examine, and reliant on the sketchy identification of a severed torso in the darkness, the court concluded on 2 May 1917 that shellfire had killed Drosen.

The Red Cross also sought information from soldiers on Drosen's disappearance, and their evidence conflicted with the court of enquiry findings. One soldier said that Drosen was evacuated to a casualty clearing station, where he later died from his wounds. Another claimed he was blown to bits.[4] Only one thing seemed certain: he was dead. A telegram informed Drosen's mother, Eliza, of her son's death. Weeks earlier, her younger son, Ernest, had been wounded at Pozières. It is hard to know how she came to terms with George's death so soon afterward. The family's *in memoriam* notice in *The Argus* in 1917 — 'Soldiers yes, and heroes too; forget them, no, we never will' — provides few clues.[5] As a schoolboy in the 1930s, George's nephew Colin Drosen watched Great War veterans march by the Williamstown cenotaph each Anzac Day, oblivious to his uncle's fate. 'It wasn't much talked about,' he remembered. Colin was in his eighties before he discovered, on the internet, the details of George's death. The internet filled the silences that he had experienced as a child: both his father and mother had lost family members in the Great War.[6]

Privates Robert and Stephen Allen of the 13th Battalion had disappeared during their unit's failed attack upon Mouquet Farm on 14 August. The evidence of their fate, presented at the court of enquiry in January 1917, was scant. Sergeant Albert Assenhein told the court that he had heard secondhand that Robert had died on the way to the front line, killed by the heavy German bombardment that had fallen for most of the day. On 23 January 1917, the words 'killed in action' were stamped in blue ink on Robert's file, and the family was duly informed. Although their mother, Hester, later received a parcel containing their personal belongings — a few coins, a purse, and a disc — precious little other information was forthcoming.

The shroud of silence lifted when Hester received a letter from her sons' company commander, Captain Theodore Wells, in March 1917.

He apologised for not having written earlier. He explained, as best he could, the circumstances of the boys' deaths that night. He wrote:

> It was one of the glorious charges in which the Australians have participated ... Our lads got right across but their losses were very heavy and as the regiments on our flanks failed we had to retire ... If you have not yet received information that they are in German hands I think you must make up your mind that they fell gallantly while rushing forward in that glorious charge.[7]

Captain Wells, it seemed, had written many such letters. He finished kindly, 'They were well liked by all ranks and were good soldiers and willing fighters. Although they have given up their lives they did their duty nobly and well. Please accept my deepest sympathy.'

The letter at least gave Hester and her daughters, Florrie and Minnie, a more bearable memory of Robert and Stephen to cling to. According to Wells, they died fulfilling their noble duty in the Great War for civilisation. Yet what good came from Hester eventually knowing the crushing truth: that her beloved sons were blown to bits while sheltering in a shallow trench; that their remains were quickly thrown over the parapet; and that they were later buried in a shallow unmarked grave, along with three other soldiers, which could no longer be located?

The Red Cross enquiry into the boys' disappearance — somewhat delayed because of a backlog of work in the reports department — uncovered more details.

'Your two poor brothers were between my brother and I. When the shell exploded I knew by the screams that someone had caught it,' wrote Private Will Hale in response to the Red Cross's enquiry.

'They came across with me and were very decent chaps,' wrote Private Eric McFarlane.[8] Hale's and McFarlane's letters helped the Red Cross respond to the Allen family's enquiries into Stephen and Robert's fate.

Hester placed a simple *in memoriam* notice in *The Sydney Morning Herald* on the first anniversary of their death. She appeared to believe that this double tragedy could only have been God's will: 'The Lord gave and the Lord hath taken away. Blessed be the name of the Lord.' In later years, Hester's notice simply read: 'In death they were not divided.'[9]

Sporadic official correspondence continued. Hester was informed in February 1917 that she would be entitled to a fortnightly pension of four pounds. Through 1922 and 1923, she received a Memorial Plaque, a Memorial Scroll, and a Victory Medal for each son, as well as a pamphlet entitled *Where the Australians Rest*, which aimed to inform families of the location of prominent cemeteries and the care taken to maintain them. The scroll, signed by King George V, contained the perhaps comforting words that they had given up their own lives that others might live in freedom.

James Browne, from Milton, Queensland, also searched for the truth about his son, Sergeant Philip Browne of the 9th Battalion, who had died on 22 July while trying to help some wounded soldiers. He was buried in a makeshift grave, the location of which was later lost in the confusion of battle. James repeatedly wrote to the Base Records Office in search of information about Philip's disappearance: 'Any particulars as to his last moments will be greatly appreciated,' read one handwritten letter dated October 1916.[10] The replies from the overworked clerks always seemed the same: 'No details are available. They will be furnished at first opportunity.'

In January 1917, Philip's belongings — including his lucky boomerang charm, his prayer book, and his New Testament bible — were returned to James and Jessie. In the same month, they received the letter from Philip's friend and fellow soldier Freddie Barbour, which explained the circumstances of his death.[11] Curiously, they also received a letter from the minister for defence, Senator George Pearce, who sympathised with their loss. The letter concluded: 'I trust that your remaining sons at the Front will go through this terrible ordeal unscathed and return to you safe and sound.'[12]

Despite the small consolations of Philip's kit being returned and receiving Freddie Barbour's letter, James's continuing search for details about the circumstances of his son's death and final resting place continued to be fruitless. 'We are very anxious indeed to find out how he died, whether any friends were with him or any message left,' James wrote to the Base Records Office in October 1916. 'What I want is to be advised is as to the best way, if there is any way to get this information.'[13] No news came.

'It is now six months since he was killed and there is no further information received beyond the bare facts that he was killed,' pleaded James in another letter in January 1917. 'We are still anxious for further particulars as to where he was buried.'

On 22 May 1917, Toowoomba Grammar School officially unveiled its 'magnificent' bronze-and-copper War Honour Board to those old boys, like Philip Browne, who had served in the Great War. If James and Jessie had attended the opening they would have heard former head of the school the Honourable Littleton Ernest Groom express his 'mingled feelings of sorrow, of sympathy, of admiration, of pride' in unveiling the memorial.[14]

A few months after the unveiling, on 21 July 1917, James and Jessie placed a simple *in memoriam* notice for Philip in *The Brisbane Courier*. It was conspicuous among the other notices that day in that it contained no poetry or verse. It simply read: 'In loving memory Sergeant Philip Gerald Browne, killed in action in France, July 22 1916, age 21.'[15]

James's correspondence with the Base Records Office continued. He maintained a dignified and respectful tone in the nine letters he sent them between 1916 and 1922, despite the anguish and frustration he must have felt. How could the Australian Imperial Force simply lose Philip? No doubt James and Jessie must have contemplated why they had signed Philip's consent forms back in May 1915. One can imagine their feelings as they awoke each morning wondering whether there would be any fresh news about what had happened to their son.

James continued writing to Base Records well into the 1920s, his focus shifting from searching for details about his son's death to making sure he was suitably commemorated, even though he had no known grave. He wrote on November 1922, 'As I understand that the grave of my son has not been found will you let me know if anything has been done or is being done by way of a head stone and inscription to keep his name on record same as those whose grave has been found.'[16] James even furnished details as to where his son's unmarked grave might be found, enclosing a sketch he had been given by a returned soldier. 'We have had so many disappointments that we are not placing much reliance on same,' he wrote wearily. Needless to say, his endeavours again bore little fruit.

Eventually, the Australian Graves Detachment and the British Labour Corps, responsible for scouring the battlefields and locating, burying, and re-burying the Australian and British dead, disbanded. This was traumatic for the thousands of families whose sons, husbands, brothers, and fathers were still missing. In 1921, *The Sydney Morning Herald* reported that a Mr Windeyer of Sydney proposed a meeting of influential Australians in London to protest against the cessation of exhumation of war graves and to urge that systematic work be continued in those sectors — including Pozières — where the dead were known to be predominantly Australian.[17] The Australian government discussed alternative arrangements, such as paying a bounty to French farmers who uncovered any remains on their farms; wisely, they didn't pursue the plan.

It is hard to imagine how parents such as Browne's must have felt in their fruitless search for information about their missing sons, although Ted Rule's encounter with John Newton Wanliss, the father of a missing soldier, perhaps provides some insight. The convalescing Rule vividly described the visit, which occurred in 1918 in a hospital in Britain, in *Jacka's Mob*: 'I'd heard of the old man, a splendid old Victorian gentleman, and how he had followed his only boy across from Australia; settling down in London, he counted the days until the boy's leave period brought them together again.'[18] Unfortunately, they never reunited, as Wanliss's son died in 1917. Rule remembered that Wanliss was dazed with grief; he thought and dreamt of nothing else but his boy. Rule recounted:

> Afterward he haunted the hospital to interview each wounded man coming from the battalion. He asked the same questions a hundred times, he heard the same answers and was never satisfied. Seated by my bed, he no sooner introduced himself than he asked: 'When did you see Harold last?'

Parents such as Wanliss would have read with anguish the intermittent newspaper reports of missing soldiers' remains being uncovered. In 1937, another soldier's remains were discovered near Pozières; a tarnished aluminium disc was found on the body, which helped identity it as the remains of James Connelly of the 52nd Battalion.[19] The officer in charge of Base Records forwarded the disc to Connelly's family, suggesting that it would be 'valued on account of its former intimate association with the deceased'. James's brother, William, replied a few weeks later: 'Myself and the rest of the family can now say we have something personal belonging to him which he had at the end.'[20]

Yet the discovery of items such as rings and watches on a soldier's remains didn't always guarantee their identification. In 1937, the bodies of two Australian soldiers were unearthed in a shallow grave near Pozières. A nine-carat gold ring engraved 'T.R. to A.R.' was found in the pocket of one soldier's tunic, so the Imperial War Graves Commission instigated a search in Australia through the Base Records Office to identify the soldier. Based on the burial location and the ring's inscription, veteran Leslie Styles believed the remains were of his mate, John Rowan, whom he helped to bury in July 1916.[21] Based on Styles' claim, Base Records contacted Rowan's widow, Margaret, seeking further help, but their enquiries proved inconclusive.[22] In the same year, another Australian soldier's remains were exhumed near Pozières. A wristwatch engraved 'From M.P. to C.P.' provided Base Records with some clues to assist their investigation; however, by the end of that year the soldier's identity still remained a mystery.[23] There are no records indicating whether the soldiers' remains were ever identified.

Ninety-odd years on, there is little that connects us with George Drosen, Robert and Stephen Allen, or Philip Browne beyond their names chiselled on the Portland limestone memorial panels to the missing located at the Australian National Memorial, on a quiet hill just outside Villers-Bretonneux. By reaching up and running one's fingertips over the coarse panels, the etched letters of each man's name, the visitor achieves, at best, a fleeting connection to the lives and hopes of these young men who left their sunburnt country generations earlier with high ideals, only to die horribly in a foreign land. There are 10,700 names etched on these vast panels, which are located only a few miles from Pozières. Add to this the 6176 Australian names etched on the walls of the Menin Gate at Ypres, Belgium, and the tragic magnitude of Australia's missing on the Western Front hits home.

Families yearned to express their grief for lost ones, but the traditional practice of visiting a grave was rarely possible. Travelling to France was beyond the means of most, especially widows such as Eliza Drosen and Hester Allen. They sought alternatives, such as visiting shrines and memorials, which became quiet places to reflect. Communities formed committees, raised money, and selected sites for these memorials. Within ten years, there were about 1500 memorials located in virtually every town and suburb in Australia.[24]

In 1917, the Australian government endorsed Charles Bean's idea of creating a national museum to commemorate the dead of the Great War. He wished to affirm the identity of each dead man not as a soldier but as a citizen of Australia, as his own family and friends knew him. The agreed response was to etch each man's name into panels contained within a Hall of Memory. It took another 12 years before the design was agreed. Finally, in 1941, in the midst of another world crisis, a permanent war memorial opened.

Memorials were constructed on the Pozières battlefield. In September 1917, Birdie unveiled one dedicated to the 1st Australian Division at Pozières, located near the pillbox at Gibraltar. Another was erected at the highest point of the Pozières ridge, where the old windmill once stood. Charles Bean composed the words on the memorial plaque, which explained that this sacred acre 'was captured on August 4th by Australian troops who fell more thickly on this ridge than any other battlefield of the war'.[25]

The Sydney Morning Herald reported in 1920 that French authorities were 'genuinely anxious' to assist Australia to secure the land it desired for memorials, while French notaries sometimes refused to accept payment for professional work relating to Australian soldiers. One of the few times authorities refused permission was when Australia sought to purchase a six-acre site near Gibraltar, which locals pointed out would obliterate part of the road from Pozières to Thiepval and encompass part of the village. Locals compromised and agreed on a one-acre site. The memorial park was established after an Australian officer searched out and negotiated the purchase with many owners, some whom submitted inordinate claims for their land value.[26]

Not all memorials in France were of bricks and mortar. In 1918, the Bishop of Amiens promised all Australians that his dioceses would piously keep the tombs of its heroes.[27] The promise was kept. Many French villagers adopted the graves of fallen soldiers as if they were their own sons. Twice a year, they visited each military cemetery in their dioceses to honour those who had travelled from all parts of the world to fight on their soil.

According to Jay Winter in *Sites of Memory, Sites of Mourning*, for some widows, the thought of commemorating the dead was a distant second to feeding a family that had lost its main provider. 'I think it would be more fitting to put the money to better use for those that are living and finding it hard to live these days,' wrote Mrs Hinds, after she was asked to provide her dead husband's particulars for the country's honour roll. 'Why worry over the dead, I'm sure that they would not wish for it, if they only knew how we who are left are treated.'[28]

'I appreciate my husband's name being erected on the "Hall of Memory" immensely but what about those left behind,' wrote another.

Mary McNeil, the widow of Pozières veteran Percy Blythe, was one of those left behind. Percy desired, should he be killed, that she live with his parents. Instead, she moved in with another man, Leslie Thomas. It bitterly upset Percy's mother. In her eyes, Mary was an adulteress, betraying the last wishes of her beloved son. She wrote to Base Records in 1922, claiming that Mary didn't deserve Percy's Memorial Plaque.[29] Not that Mary would most likely have cared — what could she do with it? In an era when few women of her class worked, having a family provider mattered more.

The naming of places or landmarks was another way of honouring those who died at Pozières. As soldier settlements sprung up around the country, some streets were named Pozières, Amiens, Albert, or Birdwood. There's even a town in rural Queensland called Pozières. Returned soldier Arthur Watkinson established a small four-hectare farm in northern Queensland and called it Mouquet Farm. He never told anyone why; in fact, he never talked about the war. Years later, some of his farmland was converted into a public park and, fittingly, a large sign explained the significance of the name. For Arthur, it was a quiet tribute to his 15th Battalion mates who died while trying to take the farm in August 1916.

First Battalion veterans formed their own association, and from 1935 commemorated Pozières Day every year, with a memorial service on a Sunday in July.[30]

Battalion histories published in the 1920s and 1930s paid tribute to deceased comrades. One senses that the passage of time did little to dull the veterans' painful memories. 'It is not easy to write the story of Pozières, the bloodiest and most costly battle in which the Battalion was ever engaged,' opened one account.[31]

Veteran Donovan Joynt returned to the Somme battlefields in 1956 to pay his respects. He stood under the famous Albert basilica from which the statue of the Virgin Mary had once hung precariously.[32] Near there, 40 years earlier, he'd watched the high-spirited Anzacs march, joking and singing, toward Pozières. It seemed like yesterday.

Reverend John Raws also visited the Somme in the 1920s and 1930s, wandering its fields in a vain search for the graves of his sons Goldy and Alec.[33] Fred Hocking, who was wounded at Pozières on the same day that Goldy Raws disappeared, returned to the Somme to commemorate the 75th anniversary of Anzac Day. While congregating at the Australian National Memorial, near Villers-Bretonneux, a *Sydney Morning Herald* reporter asked him if he had known a certain soldier killed at Pozières. Standing among rows of uniform headstones that converged into the distance, Hocking replied in the only way he could: 'There were so many killed at Pozières.'[34]

In memoriam notices in newspapers provide the most intimate glimpse of the grief that consumed many families. On anniversaries of heavy fighting, such as 23 July or 4 August, *in memoriam* notices covered the front page of newspapers. Society dictated that parents, brothers, sisters, and wives had to bear their loss stoically. Australians were supposed to have all the 'self control of a ruling race and they will not let their private sufferings dim their eyes to the glory of wounds and death,' preached *The Argus* to its readers.[35] Unsurprisingly, emotionally laden language was avoided in the notices, with poems and verse preferred:

> *You fell at the Battle of Pozières;*
> *We know that you fought brave and true;*
> *You fought for your King and Country;*
> *And the flag of the red, white and blue.*[36]

While repressed emotion was regarded as a sign of inner strength, this veneer occasionally slipped. In the privacy of home, behind drawn curtains, many seemed to buckle under the weight of their overwhelming grief, as this notice inserted for William Johnstone suggests:

We mourn for you, dear Willie;
No eyes can see us weep;
But many a silent tear we shed;
While many are asleep.

The true feelings of Clarence Woolcock's family were unmasked in this notice:

His unknown grave is the bitterest blow;
That none but our sobbing hearts can know.

And the passage of time did little to dull the grief. Thomas Lillie's family wrote in 1921:

Five years have passed and, oh, how we miss him;
Some may think the wound has healed;
But little they know of the sorrow;
That oft' beneath a smile concealed.[37]

Over the years, the Anzac legend, propagated by the likes of Charles Bean, flourished. Many Australians identified with the legend. It was what they wanted to be: bred in the bush, strong, resourceful, and independent. The legend was one-dimensional, but attractive in its simplicity.

It did not have much to do with Ernie Lee. Runaway Lee did not fight at Pozières, as *The Herald* article written in 1919 suggested. He did, however, eventually rejoin the 5th Battalion at Ypres in 1916.

Within weeks of returning, he clashed with his corporal, Charles Woodham. According to court-martial proceedings contained within his personnel dossier, while Lee was performing sentry duty, Woodham told him to stop reading a trench paper and return to his post.

'I'm fucked if I will,' replied Lee.

Woodham snatched the paper from him. Lee apparently had his father's temper — he reached for his rifle, shoved a cartridge into its breech, and pulled the bolt back. 'I'll shoot a bastard like you.'

Woodham wrestled the rifle from him and placed him under close arrest. Lee was charged with offering violence to his superior officer, tried by court martial, found guilty, and sentenced to ten years' penal servitude. Gradually, word spread that he was only 15 years old. Eventually, the Australian minister for defence intervened, suspending the sentence and sending Lee back to Australia.

Lee arrived back in Australia in April 1917. He re-enlisted six months later. And he didn't re-enlist to redeem himself — within a month, he'd been charged with using obscene language, refusing to obey an order, being absent without leave, and being improperly dressed. And that was before he had even left Australia's shores. Lee returned to Europe just before Christmas 1917.

Lee's disappearance added to his parents' worries. Their eldest son, Jack, a quietly spoken boy who had just turned 19, enlisted in April 1917, destined for France. With a constant eye on the casualty lists, Herman and Mary Lee would have realised that the odds of both sons returning home safely were low. Mary, a devout Catholic, lit two candles rather than one at the little Bruthen church each Sunday.

Lee's personnel dossier tells us that, upon disembarking in Italy in early 1918, he was charged with using threatening language against an officer. In April, he went absent again. He was jailed for ten days, only to escape from custody twice. In November, he went absent again, desperately trying to meet up with his brother Jack, who had just arrived in France. They never met up. Jack came down with a mild bout of influenza, and he was evacuated to No. 3 Australian General Hospital in Abbeville, France, where the influenza took a turn for the worse. He died of bronchial pneumonia only a few weeks before the war ended. His grave at the Abbeville Communal Cemetery, Plot 4, Row H, No. 22, received no visitors for the next 90 years.[38]

Military police eventually caught Ernie Lee in Paris. Finally — and undoubtedly with great relief to all those in the Australian Imperial Force — he was discharged in May 1919.

After the war, Lee tried his hand at farming. 'I will settle down now,' he told his father, 'and get a piece of land.'[39] After securing a selection through the Repatriation Committee, his interest quickly waned. On the afternoon of 22 May 1919, while hunting ducks on a swamp, he shot two birds. He stripped off everything except his trousers, leggings, and boots and swam toward them. He started to struggle, and then disappeared from sight.

That afternoon, the parish priest, Reverend Father Buckley, and Constable Howard knocked on Greville Farm's door. Ernie's younger sister Essie answered. They delivered the sad news that Ernie had drowned. It was less than a month since he had returned home.

On the following Saturday, a hearse transported his body to the Bruthen Cemetery. His comrades fired a three-shot volley, and the Last Post sounded as his coffin descended into the ground. His teenage fiancée, Mabel Baade, stood silently by.

Lee's death was widely reported. The evening *Herald* ran the headline: 'Youngest AIF soldier, enlisting at fourteen, lad fights at Pozières'.[40] A local newspaper finished his obituary with the words, 'this splendid specimen of Australia's young manhood is to sleep his last long sleep in his native land on the hillside of the Bruthen Township'.[41] The newspapers didn't mention his colourful past.

Lee's death reveals much about the Anzac legend. Whatever way you look at it, he was a common criminal with a record more like that of hardened criminals twice his age. But Lee had enlisted, left his family, and served overseas in a deadly war. For this, he was permitted to wear the cloak of the legend. The unwritten social covenant that the correspondents, soldiers, soldiers' families, public, and politicians were unconsciously party to allowed him to be referred to evermore in glowing terms as a 'splendid specimen of Australia's young manhood', those who 'with their fine physiques fought for the Empire'.

What was the purpose of this social covenant? Perhaps it rewarded the labourers, farmhands, and clerks who had enlisted and risked their lives for their country with a mythological status that they could never have hoped to achieve in civilian life. Perhaps it softened the blow felt by families, particularly mothers, of the dead. Even though their sons had been blown to bits, mothers could be comforted by the anaesthetising words that their sons had given up their lives gallantly and that their deeds would live forever — their sons were immortalised as Anzac legends. Perhaps this was what Henry Lawson meant when he said that their deeds would be remembered for the next thousand years.

And who would begrudge the Lees the comfort of the legend? Herman and Mary Lee did not have a lot to celebrate. According to the *Herald* article, they were poor and had struggled against bushfire and drought to maintain their large family. The strain of farming a barren selection had broken Herman's health. They had lost their house and all their possessions to fire. They had lost their eldest son, Jack, to pneumonia on the Western Front. At least they could be proud, even if it was just for a moment, that their son Ernie had served the Empire as a hallowed Anzac. These honours were beyond their grasp in normal life.

Is anything gained by stripping Ernie of the Anzac cloak? Is there any justification in revealing the unflattering truth about him? Charles Bean said a historian's obligation was to write the truest history possible. Perhaps the wound of brutal disclosure is the price paid for writing the truth.

It was left to Bean to record that fragile, fleeting, and sometimes ungraspable thing called history. He selected the old station homestead of Tuggeranong as his headquarters from which to draft it, as it was free from distractions and located in the bush he loved so much.

Denis Winter's book, *Making the Legend*, which details the research and drafting of the *Official History*, records that Bean began setting down the history of Pozières and the Great War on Armistice Day, 1919, working from 9.00 a.m. to 11.00 p.m. seven days a week and hardly ever taking a break. And every day that passed, he knew that 'history' was slowly slipping away from him, like grains of sand through outstretched fingers. 'There is only a limited time during which events can be fixed. Men's memories fade. The chief actors die,' explained Bean. Effie Bean quietly watched as her husband spent the 1920s and 1930s absorbed in his memories and documents of the war.[42]

For Bean, there was not one absolute truth that could be wrestled from the piles of manuscripts and records he sifted through. Besides the baldest of facts — the day, the place, the recorded word — everything else seemed open to interpretation. There was even randomness in the way he came across evidence. One day, by chance, he spoke to an electrician, Apcar de Vine, rewiring his office at Victoria Barracks and found out that he had kept a detailed diary during the war; Apcar de Vine's writings were to feature heavily in Bean's Pozières account. Bean also drew from the unit diaries — a massive resource of over 20 million sheets — that John Treloar had carefully catalogued. By including the rich information gained from these sources, Bean turned a roughly three-year undertaking into a mission lasting almost a quarter of a century. In 1926, he wrote a letter to his friend, Major Phillips of the Australian war graves section in London, about their arduous undertaking: 'You and I are some of the few Australians still at work on the war. I expect to reach a declaration of peace somewhere about 1935!'[43]

Occasionally, Bean was asked to explain why the publication of the *Official History* was delayed. 'No one feels more keenly than I the fact that the official history is taking much longer to produce than was originally estimated,' wrote Bean in response to such a request from prime minister Stanley Bruce in 1927. Bean explained that if Australians only wanted a simple narrative of events, it could be produced in six months. But if the people wanted to know the answers to the questions that had puzzled them, it would take longer. For example: What was the real reason for the terrible struggle at Pozières? What happened on the German side of the line? 'If this knowledge is required there is no short cut,' explained an unrepentant Bean. 'It is being obtained by patient labour.'[44]

By chance, Bean also stumbled across Alec Raws's vivid letters describing the horrors of Pozières. Should they be included in the *Official History* — was Alec Raws's dark view, when coming out the trenches, of being 'lousy, stinking, unshaven and sleepless' the dominant emotion experienced by others at Pozières? Bean sought advice from his close friend White, who had read nearly every draft of his history. He responded: 'I saw many of the men as they came out but I am not prepared to agree that all were in the condition you describe so vividly.'[45] Bean drafted another one of the 10,000 letters he wrote to validate facts, sending it to Raws's company commander, Captain Lionel Short, asking his opinion. Of Raws's quote, Short wrote:

> He says with such pathos, 'We were lousy, stinking, unshaven, sleepless.' Now, I remember halting at a cooker as we came out of the line and enjoying some hot tea. I suppose I was lousy, stinking, unshaven and sleepless but I didn't feel those things as a tragedy; rather with exhilaration that one had been through such an experience. Does it all merely lie in the point of view?[46]

And maybe that was the only absolute truth: that it all lay in one's own point of view. Perhaps there was no uniform set of facts; maybe it was impossible to distil the diverse experiences of tens of thousands of men into one definitive document.

When Bean published his final volume in 1942, he had produced one of the most comprehensive histories ever written. He detailed 6550 soldiers in it.[47] Despite White's misgivings, he quoted extensively from Raws's letters, although omitting his most vehement comments.

Bean's *Official History* was largely a concise tome of facts, figures, names, and places. It was, without doubt, true to its title of 'official'. Bean's real literary masterpiece was his diary: fresh and full of unguarded opinions and observations. After the war, Bean, perhaps uncomfortable with his candour, affixed to the inside cover of each volume a typed note with official red lettering that cautioned future readers that his notes were often jotted in the midst of battle, when he was very tired or almost asleep, and typically captured what was utmost on his mind. Despite Bean's half-apology, it is these factors that make his diary a timeless piece of war writing.

White did not live to see the final volumes of the *Official History* published. His tenure as chief of the general staff was cut short in 1940 when the plane he was travelling in, along with three federal ministers, crashed near the Canberra aerodrome, killing all on board. Bean was devastated. 'For me a light went out that was never relit,' he wrote.[48]

In his *Official History*, Bean successfully provided a memorial to those men who fought in the Great War, but had he been 'true' to himself? Much of the horror of war and his unfiltered opinions about it never made it into the *Official History*. Perhaps this troubled him, for later in life, he began what he called his 'unofficial history'. Having fulfilled his official obligations, he set about testing what he had believed to be the truth. But he was 78 years old and his hand was weak and shaky; it soon became apparent that the book that he felt compelled to write was beyond his mortal grasp. He never got beyond his rough draft of the Gallipoli campaign.[49]

In 1952, Bean made possibly his last visit to Pozières. Although grass, stubble, beet trees, and hedges had replaced mud, craters, and lines of ragged stumps, he wrote, 'For me it was as though I had left it yesterday.'[50]

In 1964, he was admitted to the Concord Repatriation Hospital in Sydney, and he spent his last years among comrades from Gallipoli and the Somme. He died in August 1968. There was probably never an Australian who held higher hopes and aspirations for his country than Charles Bean.

Bean predicted that Pozières would become a place of 'eternal pilgrimage' for future generations of Australians.[51] Despite his prediction, Pozières has gradually faded from our memories. Besides battalion reunions and a few church services, the tenth anniversary of Pozières passed without notice. Newspapers seemed more concerned about the pending Ashes Test and whether Clarrie Grimmett or Arthur Mailey would be selected. On the 50th anniversary, only one reference to Pozières appeared in newspapers. In 2004, it finally passed from the edges of our memory into history when Marcel Caux, the last surviving Australian Pozières veteran, passed away, aged 105.[52]

Despite fading memories, the fields of Pozières still disengorge reminders of the past. In 1998, a farmer's plough caught on something. Upon investigating, the farmer found human remains. A special team that excavated the site found a skeleton, part of a uniform, a weapon, some ammunition, and, most importantly, a badly corroded identity disc. It was Australian Russell Bosisto of the 27th Battalion, who had disappeared on 4 August 1916.

Eighty-two years on, with hundreds crowded into the Courcelette Military Cemetery, including four Great War veterans, and with a pipe band playing in the background, Bosisto was finally laid to rest. With the burial came some irony — even though Bosisto's remains have been identified, he lies with 1177 other men who remain unknown. Many are Australians.

In recent years, there has been a resurgence of interest in the Somme battle and Pozières. Australians are increasingly curious about their past. Battalions of Australians visit the Somme each year. These individuals come as tourists, walking the battlefields and exploring the cemeteries, rather than as soldiers.

The visitors find that while many things have changed on the Somme, some have remained the same. The faint whiff of manure still hangs in the air, but now massive caterpillar tractors, rather than peasant's carts and marching troops, tread it into the roads. Albert's war economy continues to flourish. Ninety-five years ago, peasants sold fruit and eggs to troops at exorbitant prices. Now they sell tickets to the war museum, beneath the rebuilt basilica, or brass shell casings with intricate carvings to those visiting the battlefields. The farms of Pozières have retained their traditional quadrangle shape, but are now constructed of brick, rather than yellow clay slapped over wooden frames. The church and cemetery were reconstructed. The windmill was not.

After the war, the surrounding fields were thought to be so contaminated that nothing would ever grow there again. Slowly, the peasants cleared them. Within a few years, they had cleansed the fields and hidden Pozières's scars beneath 'crops of grain and nodding poppies'.[53]

Visitors now lose themselves in these fields. Out among the vegetable fields or up dirt tracks, they try to figure out from their bundles of maps where the German or British front lines once were. Occasionally, they stumble upon a spent cartridge or a lump of jagged iron. The French farmers leave them be as long as they don't disturb the crops. The relationship is, at times, symbiotic. Visitors will follow the path of the farmer's ploughs in the hope of unearthing some relic from the past; the farmers are happy to have their fields cleared before sowing.

Monsieur Vandendriessche, Mouquet Farm's tenant, returned to his ruined farm after the war. He rebuilt the homestead and cleansed the fields of its iron harvest. The farm remains in the family, and his grandson Jose now runs it. Occasionally, Jose notices a solitary figure standing quietly on the edge of his farm. It is often an Australian whose grandfather or great-uncle was killed in his fields. 'It's normal, it's memory,' he explained.[54] Vandendriessche takes the time to describe what happened all those years ago, showing them the pile of shells, grenades, and rifles that he finds in the fields.

Grandchildren and great-grandnephews and -nieces of soldiers killed on the Somme research the location of their graves and pay their respects. There are 242 military cemeteries, or, as Kipling called them, 'Silent Cities', dotted around the Somme region.[55] Some are in the middle of ripening vegetable fields; some are located down back lanes; some are in the folds of valleys or on the brow of hills; some are in small woods shaded by trees; and others, adjacent to motorways. Where the fighting was most intense, around Thiepval, Pozières, and Beaumont-Hamel, the cemeteries are more concentrated and contain thousands of graves. Those dirt mounds with temporary white crosses that John Treloar had seen scattered among the fields on his evening walks were transformed into beautiful and immaculately maintained cemeteries. Uniform rows of Portland limestone headstones replaced the temporary wooden crosses. Lush green lawns replaced the stooked hay and poppy fields. Brick and sandstone walls, bordered by beautiful rose gardens, replaced the temporary picket fences. Today, it is difficult to reconcile the fact that such a terrible war spawned these cemeteries, so serene and peaceful, dotted in the middle of fields of maize. Although separated by generations, visitors still feel a personal connection with a long-lost relative. Their handwritten notes are scribbled in the green visitors' books located at each cemetery. 'At last to see where my grandfather lies; thank you for caring for this special place,' reads one.

Another simply says, 'Please never again.'

The gnarly concrete footings of the old Pozières windmill still remain, and standing on its stumps allows visitors an eerie appreciation of the magnificent views that the Germans had from the OG lines. Some visitors leave laminated postcards at the base of the windmill. One, a faded and grainy picture of Private William Tynan, commemorates his death, not far from there, on 4 August 1916. His mate remembered him being carted away on a stretcher. 'I've got a "blighty"', he said. He was never seen again.[56]

At the Pozières roadside café, Le Tommy, you can pay a few euros to visit its backyard museum. It's a mishmash of old weapons, piles of mud-crusted shells, rolls of rusted barbed wire, and store mannequins dressed in weathered uniforms. Otherwise, you can enjoy the eclectic mix of war artefacts adorning its walls, separated by the occasional fly strip.

Outside the café, on the narrow pavement adjacent to the rebuilt Bapaume road, are a few plastic tables and chairs. B-double trucks occasionally thunder by, swirling loose papers and napkins up in their wake. They roar through Pozières, into the distance, grinding through the gears, passing by the old windmill footings, over the Pozières ridge, and out of sight.

Bécourt Château, which served as a dressing station, was rebuilt and converted, fittingly, into a community centre. Instead of its halls being crowded with broken soldiers, they are now filled with laughing children.

Behind the old front line at Contay, you can still get a beer at the *estaminet*, near the old church, where Australian staff officers were billeted. Rickety wooden floors, a rotund madame pouring beers, and a farm dog resting at the feet of a few local drinkers gives a feeling of yesteryear. The majestic Contay Château remains unchanged, although John Treloar's tent offices are long gone.

The most striking thing about the battlefields is their eerie stillness. It's as if the Great War has drained them of noise forever. Only the corn rippling in the breeze breaks the silence; only the occasional hare or startled deer disturbs the stillness. Standing in the open fields, you cannot help but wonder whether it was all worth it. What would Alec Raws, Leo Butler, or George Drosen think? What about their mothers?

Veteran John Edey reflected on the Pozières legacy whenever he examined old photos of past comrades. While studying the character of their faces, he considered the children. They were different from their parents. 'Whereas their forebears believed that Australia was a country worth dying for, these youngsters will prove that Australia is a country worth working for, and living for,' he said.[57]

And maybe that's the legacy of Pozières. It's one of which Alec Raws would have been proud.

Abbreviations

Conversions

1 inch	2.54 centimetres
1 foot	0.3 metres
1 yard	0.91 metres
1 mile	1.6 kilometres
1 acre	0.4 hectares

Formations in the British Expeditionary Force

Body	*Commanded by*	*Approximate Infantry Number*
Army	General	100,000 to 150,000
Corps	Lieutenant-General	50,000
Division	Major-General	12,000
Brigade	Brigadier-General	4,000
Battalion	Lieutenant-Colonel	1,000
Company	Captain	250
Platoon	Second-Lieutenant	60
Section	Lance-Corporal	15

Divisions of the Australian Imperial Force, Western Front, July 1916

For operations on the Somme in 1916, I Anzac Corps consisted of the 1st, 2nd, and 4th Australian divisions. For operations at Fromelles in July 1916, the 5th Australian Division was part of XI British Corps.

1st Australian Division
Major-General Harold Walker
1st (New South Wales) Brigade
(Brigadier-General Nevill Smyth)
    1st Battalion
    2nd Battalion
    3rd Battalion
    4th Battalion
2nd (Victoria) Brigade
(Brigadier-General John Forsyth)
    5th Battalion
    6th Battalion
    7th Battalion
    8th Battalion
3rd Brigade (Brigadier-General Ewen Sinclair-MacLagan)
    9th (Queensland) Battalion
    10th (South Australia) Battalion
    11th (Western Australia) Battalion
    12th (South and Western Australia, and Tasmania) Battalion
Pioneers
    1st Australian Pioneer Battalion
1st Division Artillery
1st Division Engineers
1st Divisional Medical Services
1st Divisional Train
1st Mobile Veterinary Section
1st Sanitary Section

2nd Australian Division
Major-General James Gordon Legge
5th (New South Wales) Brigade
(Brigadier-General William Holmes)
    17th Battalion
    18th Battalion
    19th Battalion
    20th Battalion
6th (Victoria) Brigade
(Brigadier-General John Gellibrand)
    21st Battalion
    22nd Battalion
    23rd Battalion
    24th Battalion
7th Brigade (Brigadier-General John Paton)
    25th (Queensland) Battalion
    26th (Queensland, Tasmania) Battalion
    27th (South Australia) Battalion
    28th (Western Australia) Battalion
Pioneers
    2nd Australian Pioneer Battalion
2nd Division Artillery
2nd Division Engineers
2nd Division Medical Services
2nd Divisional Train
2nd Mobile Veterinary Section
2nd Sanitary Section

4th Australian Division
Major-General Sir Herbert Cox
4th Brigade (Brigadier-General Charles Brand)
    13th (New South Wales) Battalion
    14th (Victoria) Battalion
    15th (Queensland, Tasmania) Battalion
    16th (South and Western Australia) Battalion
12th Brigade (Brigadier-General Duncan Glasfurd)
    45th (New South Wales) Battalion
    46th (Victoria) Battalion
    47th (Queensland, Tasmania) Battalion
    48th (South and Western Australia) Battalion
13th Brigade (Brigadier-General Thomas Glasgow)
    49th (Queensland) Battalion
    50th (South Australia) Battalion
    51st (Western Australia) Battalion
    52nd (South and Western Australia, Tasmania) Battalion
Pioneers
    4th Australian Pioneer Battalion
4th Division Artillery
4th Division Engineers
4th Division Medical Services
4th Divisional Train
4th Mobile Veterinary Section
4th Divisional Sanitary Section

5th Australian Division
Major-General James McCay
8th Brigade (Brigadier-General Edwin Tivey)
    29th (Victoria) Battalion
    30th (New South Wales) Battalion
    31st (Queensland, Victoria) Battalion
    32nd (South and Western Australia) Battalion
14th (New South Wales) Brigade (Brigadier-General Harold Pope)
    53rd Battalion
    54th Battalion
    55th Battalion
    56th Battalion
15th (Victoria) Brigade (Brigadier-General Harold Elliott)
    57th Battalion
    58th Battalion
    59th Battalion
    60th Battalion
Pioneers
    5th Australian Pioneer Battalion
5th Division Artillery
12th Light Horse Regiment
5th Division Cyclist
5th Division Engineers
5th Division Medical Services
5th Divisional Train
5th Mobile Veterinary Section
5th Divisional Sanitary Section

References

Archives
Australian War Memorial, Canberra
AWM 4, Australian Imperial Force unit war diaries, 1914–18 War
    1st Infantry Brigade, 23/1/12, July 1916
    3rd Infantry Brigade, 23/3/9, July 1916
    5th Infantry Brigade, 23/5/14, August 1916
    4th Infantry Battalion, 23/21/17, July 1916
    4th Infantry Brigade, 23/4/11, August 1916
    6th Infantry Brigade, 23/6/12, August 1916
    7th Infantry Battalion, 23/24/17, July 1916
    15th Infantry Brigade, 23/15/5, July 1916
    20th Infantry Battalion, 23/37/12, July 1916
    23rd Infantry Battalion, 23/40/10, July 1916
    51st Infantry Battalion, 23/68/7, September 1916
    52nd Infantry Battalion, 23/69/6, September 1916
    Administrative Staff, Headquarters, 1st Australian Division, 1/43/18, July 1916
    General Staff, Headquarters, I Anzac Corps, 1/29/6, July 1916
    General Staff, Headquarters, 1st Australian Division, 1/42/18, July 1916
    General Staff, Headquarters, 2nd Australian Division, 1/44/12, July 1916
    General Staff, Headquarters, 4th Australian Division, 1/48/4, July 1916
    General Staff, Headquarters, 4th Australian Division, 1/48/5, August 1916
    Intelligence, Headquarters, I Anzac Corps, 1/30/6, July 1916
AWM 8, Unit embarkation nominal roll, 1914–18 War
AWM 9, Nominal rolls, 1914–18 War
AWM 38, Papers of Charles Bean

3DRL/606, war diaries, folders, and notebooks
AWM 131, Roll of Honour Circulars

Private records
PR87/215 7th Battalion AIF Association
2DRL/0007 Matthew Abson
1DRL/0013 James Aitken
1DRL/0053 Harold Armitage
PR85/111 Edith Florence Avenell
3DRL/3376 William Riddell Birdwood
1DRL/0139 John Bourke
2DRL/0619 Philip Browne
PR87/237 Frederick Callaway
2DRL/0512 Ben Champion
2DRL/0240 Walter Claridge
3DRL/2578 Thomas Cleary
2DRL/0204 John Cohen
2DRL/0209 John Denis Condon
2DRL/0948 Frank Robertson Corney
1DRL/0227 Herbert Crowle
1DRL/0237 Charles Dawkins
PR01054 Kenneth Day
1DRL/0240 Apcar Leslie de Vine
2DRL/0209 Leonard Elvin
3DRL/0895 Richard Gee
1DRL/0337 Hubert Richard Joseph Harris
1DRL/0338 John Harris
PR88/161 Fred Hocking
1DRL/0359 Douglas Horton
1DRL/0411 Allan Leane
2DRL/0001 Harold Malpas
1DRL/0428 Lewis Winchester Marshall
1DRL/0455 Albert McLeod
1DRL/0463 Archibald Joseph (Joe) McSparron
3DRL/7253 Eric Moorhead
PR03407 Henry Palmer
1DRL/0540 Leslie Parsons

PR90105 Daniel Scanlon
PR00626 Frank Shoobridge
PR88/058 Robert Smith
3DRL/2206 Arthur Thomas

Australian Red Cross Society Wounded and Missing Enquiry Bureau files, 1914–18 War, 1DRL/0428
Note, officer files do not contain numbers.
3003 Private Robert Beattie Allen
3002 Private Stephen Charles Allen
1880 Sergeant David Gibson Jude Badger
Captain Francis William Samuel Bailey
Captain Francis Maxwell Barton
Second-Lieutenant Alexander Beatty
3270A Sergeant Philip Gerald Browne
Lieutenant Frederick William Berni Callaway
Captain Norman David Cumming
4173 Private George Drosen
Captain Ralph Ratnevelu Raymond Ekin-Smyth
Second-Lieutenant Alfred John Hearps
Lieutenant Walter Joseph Host
119 Sergeant Lewis Winchester Marshall
Captain Daniel McCullum
Lieutenant Robert Goldthorpe Raws
1995 Private Noel George Sainsbury
1781 Private Wisbey Harrington Sinclair
Second-Lieutenant Ernest George Smythe
6567 Private Arthur Thomas
3601 Private William Patrick Tynan
Lieutenant Lennard Lewis Wadsley

Mitchell Library, State Library of New South Wales, Sydney
Battalion Newsletter, 1918
MSS 1493/1 Archie Barwick

National Archives of Australia
Series B2455 First Australian Imperial Force Personnel Dossiers, 1914–1920, Canberra
Note, officer files do not contain numbers.
3002 Stephen Allen
Francis Maxwell Barton
Lieutenant Percy Blythe
3270A Philip Gerald Browne
Lieutenant William Percy Clemenger
Lieutenant Albert George Clifford
4762 John Condon
3806 James Connelly
3815 John Cotter
Second Lieutenant Herbert Walter Crowle
4173 George Droser [sic]
79 Henry Eggington
3090 Arthur John Foxcroft
Major John Harris
739 William Hatcher
Second Lieutenant Alfred John Hearps
5715 4863 Ernest Victor Lee *aka* Ernest John Jefferies
Lieutenant-Colonel Leslie Francis Strong Mather
1168 Leslie Parsons
1441 John Pearce *aka* Alexander Taylor Pearce
2358 John Thomas Rowan
Lieutenant Ernest George Smythe
8232 Sydney Alfred Stredwick
2219 John Arthur Charles Stuart
Lieutenant George Robert Stewart Walters
Captain Howard de Nyst Williams

Series J34 Department of Veterans' Affairs First World War Pension Case Files, Brisbane
Robert Smith

Series C138/1 Personal Case Files, 1914–1918, Repatriation Department, Sydney
John Redford Oberlin Harris

State Library of Victoria, Melbourne
MS 10434 William Shaw Clayton
MS 10345 Albert E. Coates
MS 10167 Stanley Cocking
MS 10511 John F. Edey
MS 9613 Arthur Foxcroft
MS 9640 Vic Graham
MS 1565 Harold Morris

Articles and journals

Bean, Charles, 'The Reasons for Fromelles', *Reveille*, 30 June 1931, p. 20.
——, 'The Reasons for Pozières', *Reveille*, 20 June 1931, p. 21.
Carlyon, Patrick, 'Who are the Anzacs "known unto God" in a Flanders field?', *The Age*, 21 April 2007, p. 5.
Coulthard-Clark, C.D., 'Legge, James Gordon (1863–1947)', *Australian Dictionary of Biography*, vol. 10, Melbourne University Press, Carlton, 1986, pp. 63–65.
Ekins, Ashley, 'The Battle of Fromelles', *Wartime*, Australian War Memorial, issue 44, 2008, pp. 18–23.
Hitchens, Christopher, 'The Pity of War', *The Atlantic*, November 2009, at www.theatlantic.com/magazine/archive/2009/11/the-pity-of-war/7703.
Londey, Peter, 'If I Die at any Rate I Will Have Tried', *Wartime*, issue 7, 1999, Australian War Memorial, pp. 30–32.
Pedersen, Peter, 'Reflections on a Battlefield', *Wartime*, issue 44, 2008, Australian War Memorial, pp. 24–29.
Perry, Warren, 'Lieutenant-General James Gordon Legge: Australia's first wartime chief of the general staff', *The Victorian Historical Journal*, vol. 48, issue 3, August 1977, p. 209.
Preston, Harry, 'John Leak's V.C.', *Reveille*, vol. 8, issue 12, p. 30–31.
Thomson, Alistair, '"Steadfast until Death?" C.E.W. Bean and the representation of Australian military manhood', *Australian Historical Studies*, vol. 23, issue 93, October 1989, pp. 462–78.
Wadsley, John, 'Dear Everybody at Home: A Tasmanian's letters from the Great War', *The Journal of the Military Historical Society of Australia*, 2005–4, pp. 11–14.

Books and monographs

Adam-Smith, Patsy, *Australian Women at War*, Nelson, Melbourne, 1986.

——, *The Anzacs*, Thomas Nelson Australia, West Melbourne, 1978.

Alomes, Stephen and Jones, Catherine, *Australian Nationalism: a documentary history*, Collins/Angus and Robertson, North Ryde, 1991.

Andrews, E.R., *The Anzac Illusion*, Cambridge University Press, Cambridge and New York, 1993.

Austin, Ron, *As Rough as Bags: the history of the 6th Battalion, 1st AIF, 1914–1919*, Slouch Hat Productions, McCrae, 2005.

——, *The Fighting Fourth: a history of Sydney's 4th Battalion, 1914–1919*, Slouch Hat Productions, McCrae, 2007.

——, *Forward Undeterred: the history of the 23rd Battalion, 1915–1919*, Slouch Hat Publications, Rosebud, 1998.

——, *Our Dear Old Battalion: the story of the 7th Battalion, AIF, 1914–1919*, Slouch Hat Publications, Rosebud, 2004.

Barker, Theo, *Signals: the history of the Royal Australian Corps of Signals 1788–1947*, Royal Australian Corps of Signals Committee, Canberra, 1987.

Barnett, Correlli, *The Great War*, BBC Worldwide Limited, London, 2003.

Barrett, John, *Falling In: Australians and 'boy conscription' 1911–1915*, Hale & Ironmonger, Sydney, 1979.

Bassett, Jan, *Guns and Brooches: Australian Army nursing from the Boer War to the Gulf War*, Oxford University Press, Melbourne, 1997.

Bean, C.E.W., *Anzac to Amiens: a shorter history of the Australian fighting services in the First World War*, Australian War Memorial, Canberra, 1946.

——, *Letters from France*, Cassell, London, 1917.

——, *Official History of Australia in the War of 1914–1918*, vols. 1–2, *The Story of Anzac*, Angus and Robertson, Sydney, 11th edn, 1941.

——, *Official History of Australia in the War of 1914–1918*, vol. 3, *The AIF in France, 1916*, Angus and Robertson, Sydney, 1929.

——, *Two Men I Knew: William Bridges and Brudenell White, founders of the AIF*, Angus and Robertson, Sydney, 1957.

Beaumont, Joan (ed.), *Australia's War, 1914–18*, Allen and Unwin, Sydney, 1995.

Belford, Walter, *Legs-eleven: being the story of the 11th Batallion (AIF) in the Great War of 1914–1918*, Imperial Printing Company, Perth, 1940.

Birdwood, Baron William Riddell, *Khaki and Gown: an autobiography*, Ward, Lock & Company, London and Melbourne, 1941.

Blainey, Geoffrey, *Our Side of the Country: the story of Victoria*, Methuen Haynes, North Ryde, 1984.

Blair, Dale, *Dinkum Diggers: an Australian battalion at war*, Melbourne University Press, Carlton, 2001.

Brown, Ian, *British Logistics on the Western Front, 1914–1919*, Praeger, Westport, 1996.

Brown, Malcolm, *The Imperial War Museum Book of the Somme*, Sidgwick & Jackson, London, 1996.

Browning, Neville, *The 52nd Battalion: the history of the 52nd Battalion AIF 1916–1918*, self-published, Huntingdale, 2005.

——, *The Blue & White Diamond: the history of the 28th Battalion 1915–1919*, self-published, Ballajura, 2003.

——, *Fix Bayonets: the history of the 51st Battalion, AIF*, self-published, Bayswater, 2000.

Butler, A.G., *The Official History of the Australian Army Medical Service in the War of 1914–18*, vol. 2, *The Western Front*, Australian War Memorial, Canberra, 1940.

——, *The Official History of the Australian Army Medical Service in the War of 1914–18*, vol. 3, *Special Problems and Services*, Australian War Memorial, Canberra, 1943.

Carne, W.A., *In Good Company: an account of the 6th Machine Gun Company*, 6th Machine Gun Company (AIF) Association, Melbourne, 1937.

Carthew, Noel, *Voices from the Trenches: letters to home*, New Holland Publishing, Frenchs Forest, 2002.

Chapman, Ivan, *Iven G. Mackay: citizen and soldier*, Melway Publishing, Melbourne, 1975.

Charteris, John, *At GHQ*, Cassell, London, 1931.

——, *Field Marshal Earl Haig*, Cassell, London, 1929.

Churchill, W.S., *The World Crisis*, Thornton Butterworth, London, 1927.

Clark, Manning, *A History of Australia*, vol. 6, *The Old Dead Tree and the Young Tree Green*, Melbourne University Press, Carlton, 1987.

Coates, Albert and Rosenthal, Newman, *The Albert Coates Story: the will that found the way*, Hyland House, South Yarra, 1977.

Corfield, Robin S., *Don't Forget Me, Cobber: the battle of Fromelles*, The Miegunyah Press/Melbourne University Publishing, Carlton, 2009.

Corrigan, Gordon, *Mud, Blood and Poppycock: Britain and the Great War*, Cassell, London, 2003.

Coulthard-Clark, C. D., *No Australian Need Apply: the troubled career of Lieutenant-General Gordon Legge*, Sydney, Allen & Unwin, 1988.
De Groot, Gerard J., *Douglas Haig, 1861–1928*, Unwin Hyman, London, 1988.
Denny, Captain W.J., *A Digger at Home and Abroad*, Popular Publications, Melbourne, 1941.
Department of Veterans' Affairs, *Simply Hell Let Loose: stories of Australians at war*, ABC Books, Sydney, 2002.
Derham, Rosemary, *The Silent Ruse: escape from Gallipoli*, Cliffe Books, Armidale, 1998.
Devine, W., *The Story of a Battalion*, Melville & Mullen, Melbourne, 1919.
Drake-Brockman, Geoffrey, *The Turning Wheel*, Paterson Brokensha, Perth, 1960.
Duffy, Christopher, *Through German Eyes: the British and the Somme 1916*, Weidenfeld & Nicolson, London, 2006.
Ellis, Captain A.D., *The Story of the Fifth Australian Division: being an authoritative account of the division's doings in Egypt, France, and Belgium*, Hodder and Stoughton, London, 1919.
Farrar, Martin J., *News from the Front: war correspondents on the Western Front 1914–18*, Sutton Publishing, Gloucestershire, 1993.
Farrar-Hockley, Anthony, *Goughie: the life of General Sir Hubert Gough*, Hart-David/MacGibbon, London, 1975.
Ferguson, Niall, *The Pity of War*, Allen Lane, London, 1998.
Ferro, Marc, *The Great War: 1914–1918*, (trans. Stone, Nicole), Routledge & Kegan Paul, London, 1973.
Fewster, Kevin (ed.), *Bean's Gallipoli: the diaries of Australia's official war correspondent*, Allen and Unwin, Crows Nest, 3rd ed., 2007.
——, *Gallipoli Correspondent: the frontline diary of C.E.W. Bean*, George Allen and Unwin, Sydney, 1983.
Firkins, Peter, *The Australians in Nine Wars: Waikato to Long Tan*, Pan Books, London, 1971.
Fitzhardinge, L.F., *William Morris Hughes: a political biography,* vol. 2, *The Little Digger, 1914–1952*, Angus and Robertson Publishing, Sydney, 1979.
Freeman, R.R., *Hurcombe's Hungry Half Hundred: a memorial history of the 50th Battalion AIF 1916–1919*, Peacock Publications, Norwood, 1991.
Gammage, Bill, *The Broken Years: Australian soldiers in the Great War*, Australian National University Press, Canberra, 1974.
Gherardin, Walter, *Against the Odds: Albert Coates, a heroic life*, Albert Coates Memorial Trust, Bakery Hill, 2009.

Gibbs, Philip, *The Battles of the Somme*, Heinemann, London, 1917.

Gilbert, Martin, *The Somme: heroism and horror in the First World War*, Henry Holt and Company, New York, 2006.

Gliddon, Gerald, *Somme 1916: a battlefield companion*, The History Press, Gloucestershire, 2009.

Goodman, Rupert, *Our War Nurses: the history of the Royal Australian Army Nursing Corps 1902–1988*, Boolarong Publications, Bowen Hills, 1988.

Gorman, E., *With the Twenty-second: a history of the Twenty-second Battalion, AIF*, H.H. Champion, Melbourne, 1919.

Gough, Hubert, *The Fifth Army*, Hodder and Stoughton, London, 1931.

——, *Soldiering On: being the memoirs of General Sir Hubert Gough*, Arthur Barker, London, 1954.

Green, F.C., *The Fortieth: a record of the 40th Battalion, AIF*, Government Press, Hobart, 1922.

Griffith, Paddy, *Battle Tactics of the Western Front: the British army's art of attack 1916–1918*, Yale University Press, New Haven, 1994.

Griffith, Paddy (ed.), *British Fighting Methods in the Great War*, Frank Cass, London and Portland, 1996.

Hart, Peter, *The Somme*, Weidenfeld & Nicolson, London, 2005.

Harvey, Norman K., *From Anzac to the Hindenburg Line: the history of the 9th Battalion, AIF*, 9th Battalion AIF Association, Brisbane, 1941.

Hetherington, John, *Blamey, Controversial Soldier: a biography of Field Marshal Sir Thomas Blamey, GBE, KCB, CMG, DSO, ED*, Australian War Memorial and the Australian Government Publishing Service, Canberra, 1973.

Hinckfuss, Harold, *Memories of a Signaller: the First World War, 1914–1919*, self-published, Queensland, 1982.

Horne, Alistair, *The Price of Glory: Verdun 1916*, Penguin Books, London, 1993.

Horne, Donald, *Billy Hughes: prime minister of Australia 1915–1923*, Black Inc, Melbourne, 1983.

Horner, David, *The Gunners: a history of Australian artillery*, Allen and Unwin, St Leonards, 1995.

Hudson, W. J., *Billy Hughes in Paris: the birth of Australian diplomacy*, Thomas Nelson Australia, in association with the Australian Institute for International Affairs, West Melbourne, 1978.

Hughes, Robert, *The Fatal Shore: the epic of Australia's founding*, Vintage Books, New York, 1988.

Inglis, K.S., *Anzac Remembered: selected writings of K.S. Inglis* (ed. Lack, John),

University of Melbourne, Parkville, 1998.

———, *Observing Australia 1959–1999* (ed. Wilcox, Craig), Melbourne University Press, Carlton South, 1999.

———, *Sacred Places: war memorials in the Australian landscape*, The Miegunyah Press/Melbourne University Publishing, Carlton, 1998.

Joynt, W.D., *Breaking the Road for the Rest*, Hyland House, Melbourne, 1979.

Kearney, Robert, *Silent Voices: the story of the 10th Battalion AIF in Australia, Egypt, Gallipoli, France and Belgium during the Great War 1914–1918*, Frenchs Forest, New Holland, 2005.

Keech, Graham, *Pozières*, Leo Cooper, South Yorkshire, 1998.

Keegan, John, *The First World War*, Pimlico, London, 1999.

Keown, A.W., *Forward with the Fifth: the story of five years' war service, Fifth Inf. Battalion, AIF*, Speciality Press, Melbourne, 1921.

Knyvett, R. Hugh., *'Over There' with the Australians*, Charles Scribner's Sons, New York, 1918.

Leese, Peter, *Shell Shock: traumatic neurosis and the British soldiers of the First World War*, Palgrave Macmillan, New York, 2002.

Legg, Frank, *The Gordon Bennett Story: from Gallipoli to Singapore*, Angus and Robertson, Sydney, 1965.

Lewis, Brian, *Our War: Australia during World War I*, Melbourne University Press, Carlton, 1980.

Lindsay, Patrick, *Fromelles: Australia's darkest day and the dramatic discovery of our fallen World War One Diggers*, Hardie Grant Books, Prahran, 2008.

Lloyd, Clem and Rees, Jacqui, *The Last Shilling: a history of repatriation in Australia*, Melbourne University Press, Carlton, 1994.

Lloyd George, David, *War Memoirs*, Odhams Press, London, 1938.

Longmore, C., *The Old Sixteenth: being a record of the 16th Battalion, AIF during the Great War, 1914–1918,* History Committee of the 16th Battalion Association, Perth, 1929.

Macdonald, Lyn, *Somme*, Penguin Books, London, 1993.

Mackenzie, K.W., *The Story of the Seventeenth Battalion AIF in the Great War, 1914–1918*, Shipping Newspapers, Sydney, 1946.

Mandle, W.F., *Going it Alone: Australia's national identity in the twentieth century*, Allen Lane, Ringwood, 1978.

Manning, Frederic, *The Middle Parts of Fortune*, The Text Publishing Company, Melbourne, 2000.

Mant, Gilbert. (ed.), *Soldier Boy: the letters of Gunner W.J. Duffell, 1915–18*,

Kangaroo Press, Kenthurst, 1992.
Masefield, John, *The Battle of the Somme*, William Heinemann, London, 1919.
——, *Gallipoli*, William Heinemann, London, 1916.
——, *The Old Front Line*, William Heinemann, London, 1917.
Matthews, Tony, *Australian Soldiers in the Great War 1914–18*, Boolarong, Bowen Hills, 1987, pp. 60–61.
Maze, Paul, *A Frenchman in Khaki*, Heinemann, London, 1941.
McCarthy, Chris, *The Somme: the day-by-day account*, Arms and Armour Press, London, 1993.
McCarthy, Dudley, *Gallipoli to the Somme: the story of C.E.W. Bean*, John Ferguson, Sydney, 2000.
McKernan, Michael, *The Australian People and the Great War*, Collins, Sydney, 1984.
McMullin, Ross, *Pompey Elliott*, Scribe Publications, Carlton North, 2002.
Millman, Brock, *Pessimism and British War Policy 1916–18*, Frank Cass, London, 2001.
Nairn, Bede and Serle, Geoffrey (ed.), *Australian Dictionary of Biography*, vol. 9, *1891–1939*, Melbourne University Press, Melbourne, 1966.
Newton, L.M., *The Story of the Twelfth: a record of the 12th Battalion, AIF during the Great War of 1914–1918*, John Burridge Military Antiques, Swanbourne, 2000.
Oates, Lynette, *With the Big Guns: an Australian artilleryman in the Great War*, Australian Military History Publications, Loftus, 2006.
O'Neil, Lloyd (ed.), *The Poetical Works of Henry Lawson*, Currey O'Neil, South Yarra, 1982.
Partridge, Eric, *Frank Honywood, Private: a personal record of the 1914–1918 war*, Melbourne University Press, Carlton, 1987.
Perry, Roland, *Monash: the outsider who won a war: a biography of Australia's greatest military commander*, Random House, Milsons Point, 2004.
Philpott, William, *Bloody Victory: the sacrifice on the Somme and the making of the twentieth century*, Little, Brown, London, 2009.
Polanski, Ian Leonard, *We were the 46th: the history of the 46th Battalion in the Great War of 1914–18*, self-published, Queensland, 1999.
Pope, Stephen and Wheal, Elizabeth-Anne, *The Macmillan Dictionary of the First World War*, Macmillan, London, 1995.
Prior, Robin and Wilson, Trevor, *Command on the Western Front: the military career of Sir Henry Rawlinson 1914–1918*, Pen and Sword Books, South Yorkshire, 2004.

——, *The Somme*, UNSW Press, Sydney, 2005.
Robbins, Simon, *British Generalship on the Western Front 1914–1918: defeat to victory*, Frank Cass, Oxon, 2005.
Ross, Jane, *The Myth of the Digger: the Australian soldier in two world wars*, Hale & Iremonger, Sydney, 1985.
Rule, Edgar, *Jacka's Mob*, Angus and Robertson, Sydney, 1933.
Sadler, Peter, *The Paladin: a life of Major-General Sir John Gellibrand*, Oxford University Press, Melbourne, 2000.
Scates, Bruce and Francis, Raelene, *Women and the Great War*, Cambridge University Press, Cambridge and New York, 1997.
Scott, Ernest, *Official History of Australia in the war of 1914–1918*, vol. 11, *Australia During the War*, Angus and Robertson, Sydney, 1941.
Seal, Graham, *Inventing ANZAC: the Digger and national mythology*, University of Queensland Press, St Lucia, 2004.
Seely, John, *Adventure*, William Heinmann, London, 1930.
Serle, Geoffrey, *Monash: a biography*, Melbourne University Press, Carlton, 2002.
Sheffield, Gary, *The Somme*, London, Cassell, 2004.
Sheffield, Gary and Bourne, John (eds), *Douglas Haig: war diaries and letters, 1914–1918*, Weidenfeld and Nicolson, London, 2005.
Sheffield, Gary and Todman, Dan (eds), *Command and Control on the Western Front: the British army's experience 1914–18*, The History Press, Gloucestershire, 2004.
Sheldon, Jack, *The German Army on the Somme 1914–1916*, Pen and Sword Books, South Yorkshire, 2007.
Silver, Lynette Ramsey, *Marcel Caux: a life unravelled*, John Wiley & Sons Australia, Milton, 2006.
Souter, Gavin, *Lion and Kangaroo: the initiation of Australia*, The Text Publishing Company, Melbourne, 2001.
Speed, F.W. (ed.), *Esprit de Corps: the history of the Victorian Scottish Regiment and the 5th Infantry Battalion*, Allen and Unwin, Sydney, 1988.
Stedman, Michael, *Thiepval*, Pen and Sword Books, South Yorkshire, 2005.
Stone, Gerald, *1932: a hell of a year*, Pan Macmillan, Sydney, 2005.
Taylor, F.W. and Cusack, T.A., *Nulli Secundus: a history of the Second Battalion, AIF 1914–1919*, New Century Press, Sydney, 1942.
Terraine, John, *Douglas Haig: the educated soldier*, Cassell, London, 2005.
——, *The Western Front 1914–1918*, Pen and Sword Books, South Yorkshire, 2003.

Todman, Dan, *The Great War: myth and memory*, Hambledon Continuum, London, 2005.

Travers, Tim, *The Killing Ground: the British Army, the Western Front, and the emergence of modern warfare, 1900–1918*, Allen and Unwin, London, 1987.

Treloar, Alan (ed.), *An ANZAC Diary*, self-published, Armidale, 1993.

Tuchman, Barbara W., *The Guns of August*, Robinson, London, 2000.

Walker, Jonathan, *The Blood Tub: General Gough and the battle of Bullecourt, 1917*, The History Press, Gloucestershire, 1998.

Warner, Philip, *Field Marshal Earl Haig*, Cassell, London, 2001.

White, Richard and Russell, Penny (eds), *Memories and Dreams: reflection on 20th century Australia*, Allen and Unwin, St Leonards, 1997.

White, T.A., *The Fighting Thirteenth: the history of the Thirteenth Battalion, AIF*, Tyrell's, Sydney, 1924.

Wiest, Andrew A., *Haig: the evolution of a commander*, Potomac Books, Washington D.C., 2005.

Williams, John F., *Anzacs, the Media and the Great War*, UNSW Press, Sydney, 1999.

Winn, John Keeble, *Still Playing the Game: a history of Toowoomba Grammar School, 1875–2000*, Playright Publishing, Caringbah, 2000.

Winter, Denis, *Haig's Command: a reassessment*, Penguin, London, 2001.

—— (ed.), *Making the Legend: the war writings of C.E.W. Bean*, University of Queensland Press, St Lucia, 1992.

Winter, Jay, *Sites of Memory, Sites of Mourning: the Great War in European cultural history*, Cambridge University Press, Cambridge and New York, 1995.

Whyte, W. Farmer, *William Morris Hughes: his life and times*, Angus and Robertson, Sydney, 1957.

Wren, Eric, *Randwick to Hargicourt: history of the 3rd Battalion, AIF*, Ronald G. McDonald, Sydney, 1935.

Youell, Duncan and Edgell, David, *The Somme: ninety years on — a visual history*, Dorling Kindersley, London, 2006.

Young, Margaret and Gammage, Bill (eds), *Hail and Farewell: letters from two brothers killed in France in 1916, Alec and Goldy Raws*, Kangaroo Press, Kenthurst, 1995.

Ziino, Bart, *A Distant Grief: Australians, war graves and the Great War*, University of Western Australia Press, Crawley, 2007.

Field work
Somme, 2003, 2005, 2007
Verdun, 2005

Interviews
Colin Drosen, telephone interview, 16 August 2010.
Jane Ekin-Smyth, telephone interview, 17 August 2010.
Margaret Lee, telephone interview, 30 November 2010.

Unpublished sources
Breed, Florence, 'From France with Love 1916–1918', 1995.
Miller, John Dermot, 'A Study in the Limitations of Command: General Sir William Birdwood and the AIF, 1914–1918', Manuscript 1459, Australian War Memorial, 1993.
Raws, John (ed.), 'Records of an Australian Lieutenant: a story of bravery, devotion, and self sacrifice 1915–1916', 1931.
Taplin, Claire (ed.), 'Dad's War Diaries 1915–1919: Reg Telfer, Australian Medical Corps, 27th Battalion', 1996.
Urban, Frank, 'Somme Anzac Digger', 2000.
Willmington, Margaret (ed.), 'Diaries of an Unsung Hero: Alfred Robert Morrison Stewart', 1995.

Notes

The following organisations have been abbreviated: Australian War Memorial (AWM), National Archives of Australia (NAA), and State Library of Victoria (SLV).

Introduction

1. Foxcroft, MS 9613, SLV. An example of the fabric patch worn by 1st Division soldiers at Pozières is on display at the Australian War Memorial, ID Number RELAWM07976.
2. The activity behind the front line is described in Gee, 3DRL/0895, AWM and Newton, *The Story of the Twelfth*, p. 97. The French peasants working the fields is described in Treloar, *An ANZAC Diary*, pp. 281, 284 and their 'state of mind' in Manning, *The Middle Parts of Fortune*, p. 128.
3. Foxcroft, MS 9613, SLV.
4. 4th Infantry Battalion, 23/21/17, AWM.
5. Harris, 1DRL/0338, AWM and Partridge, *Frank Honywood, Private*, p. 74.
6. Bean, *The AIF in France, 1916*, p. 306. The actual numbers Bean quoted were 63,013 divisional and 4579 corps troops. The New Zealand Division was part of II Anzac Corps.
7. Upon transferring to France in March 1916, I Anzac Corps comprised the 1st and 2nd Australian infantry divisions and a New Zealand division. When the corps transferred to the Somme region in July 1916, it comprised the 1st, 2nd, and 4th Australian infantry divisions. Bean indicated that upon the opening of the Somme offensive, the Allies had over 30 attacking, support, and reserve divisions, and the Germans 12. With approximately 20,000 men per division as well as corps staff, there was in the vicinity of one million men embroiled in battle at any one time. See Bean, *The AIF in France, 1916*, p. 310.
8. Fourth British Army commander General Sir Henry Rawlinson believed that Pozières was the key to the area. Quoted in Bean, *The AIF in France, 1916*, p. 455.

9   Masefield, *The Battle of the Somme*, p. 63. Different sources refer to the road that runs through Pozières as the Bapaume road, Albert road, Pozières road, and Albert–Bapaume road. For consistency purposes, 'the Bapaume road' has been used throughout, as this term is most used in division, brigade, and battalion war diaries.
10 See Macdonald, *Somme*, p. 115; Sheffield and Bourne, *Douglas Haig*, p. 211; Bean, 'The Reasons for Pozières', p. 21; and Masefield, *The Battle of the Somme*, p. 63.
11 British war correspondent John Masefield described the Anzacs as 'the finest body of young men ever brought together in modern times. For physical beauty and nobility of bearing they surpassed any men I have ever seen … they were the flower of the world's manhood, and died as they had lived, owning no master on this earth.' See Masefield, *Gallipoli*.
12 *The Sydney Morning Herald*, 24 July 1917, p. 6.
13 Quoted in Ferguson, *The Pity of War*, p. 213.
14 *The Herald*, 24 July, p. 10; 27 July, p. 7; and 8 August 1916, p. 12, and *The Sydney Morning Herald*, 28 July, p. 7; 8 August, p. 7; and 21 August, p. 7.
15 *The Age*, 12 August 1916, p. 12.
16 *The Herald*, 3 June 1919, p. 12.

Chapter 1: The Road to Pozières

1   Barnett, *The Great War*, pp. 35–37.
2   Bean, *The AIF in France, 1916*, p. 1.
3   Bean, *Anzac to Amiens*, p. 183.
4   ibid., p. 185.
5   Foxcroft, MS 9613, SLV.
6   ibid.
7   Quoted in Winter, *Making the Legend*, p. 10. Bean also wrote that his duty was 'to record the plain and absolute truth so far as it was within his limited power to compass it'. See Bean, *The Story of Anzac*, p. xxx.
8   McCarthy noted that Bean's sense of what was right was unbending, 'sometime disproportionately so'. He cited the example of Bean seeking a small 'sniper' car because it would cost his government less. See McCarthy, *Gallipoli to the Somme*, p. 231. Bean's commitment to the truth and ethical standards are also described in Winter, *Making the Legend*, pp. 1–18.
9   See Bean, *The Story of Anzac*, p. 46.
10 Bean, 38-3DRL/606/2/1, AWM, p. 102.
11 Bean, 38-3DRL/606/1/1, AWM, p. 97.
12 The figure of 286 volumes includes diaries, notebooks, and folders kept by Bean during and after the war.

13 Seal, *Inventing Anzac*, p. 8.
14 '40 men, eight horses'. Description in Chapman, *Iven G. Mackay*, p. 70 and Joynt, *Breaking the Road for the Rest*, p. 70.
15 Drake-Brockman, *The Turning Wheel*, p. 99. Subsequent quotations ibid., pp. 100, 101.
16 Coates, MS 10345, SLV.
17 Foxcroft, MS 9613, SLV.
18 Bean, *Anzac to Amiens*, pp. 202–04.
19 Bean, *Letters from France*, p. 18.
20 Estimates vary on the divisions involved and the attack frontage on the first day. Bean's estimates are in Bean, *The AIF in France, 1916*, p. 232.
21 Ramage and Hanbury-Sparrow quoted in Youell and Edgel, *The Somme*, pp. 70–72.
22 Charteris, *At GHQ*, p. 152.
23 Haig's notification and Birdie's orders are discussed in Bean, *Anzac to Amiens*, pp. 216, 219.
24 Quoted in Chapman, *Iven G. Mackay*, p. 73.
25 Ellis, *The Story of the Fifth Australian Division*. Chapter 1 indicates the composition and functions of an Australian division on the Western Front.
26 'Brass heads' or 'heads' was a term popular with the Anzacs to describe staff officers. See Breed, 'From France with Love 1916–1918', pp. 68–69.
27 Browne, 2DRL/0619, AWM.
28 Thomas, 3DRL/2206, AWM.
29 Maze, *A Frenchman in Khaki*, p. 149.
30 1st Infantry Brigade, 23/1/12, AWM.
31 The following sources describe the hard marching: Coates, MS 10345, SLV; Belford, *Legs-eleven*, pp. 262–64; Taylor and Cusack, *Nulli Secundus*, p. 176; and Newton, *The Story of the Twelfth*, p. 95.
32 Quoted in Willmington, 'Diaries of an Unsung Hero', p. 124.
33 Coates, MS 10345, SLV.
34 Bean, *Letters from France*, p. 26, and Bean, 38-3DRL/606/42/1, AWM, p. 26.
35 Quoted in Chapman, *Iven G. Mackay*, p. 72.
36 Harris, 1DRL/0338, AWM.
37 Drake-Brockman, *The Turning Wheel*, p. 103.
38 McSparron, 1DRL/0463, AWM.
39 de Vine, 1DRL/0240, AWM.
40 McSparron, 1DRL/0463 and Harris, 1DRL/0338, both AWM.
41 Bean's description in Bean, *The AIF in France, 1916*, p. 471; story of soldier weeping in Wren, *Randwick to Hargicourt*, p. 155.
42 Diary entry in Terraine, *Douglas Haig*, pp. 214–15; letter in Sheffield and Bourne, *Douglas Haig*, p. 86.

43 Chapman, *Iven G. Mackay*, p. 70.
44 Bean, *The AIF in France, 1916*, p. 47.
45 General Staff, I Anzac Corps, 1/29/6, AWM.
46 Quoted in Bean, *Two Men I Knew*, p. 134.
47 Sheffield, 'An Army Commander on the Somme' in Sheffield and Todman, *Command and Control on the Western Front*, pp. 76–77.
48 Farrar-Hockley, *Goughie*, p. 190.
49 Quoted in Bean, *The AIF in France, 1916*, p. 455.
50 Bean, *Two Men I Knew*, p. 134.
51 Drake-Brockman, *The Turning Wheel*, p. 104.
52 Fewster, *Gallipoli Correspondent*, p. 154.
53 Drake-Brockman, *The Turning Wheel*, p. 103.
54 Administrative Staff, 1st Australian Division, 1/43/18, AWM.
55 Sheffield and Todman, 'An Army Commander on the Somme', p. 76.
56 General Staff, I Anzac Corps, 1/29/6, AWM.
57 Bean, *The AIF in France, 1916*, pp. 482–85.
58 Rutledge, *Australian Dictionary of Biography*, vol. 8, Melbourne University Press, Carlton, 1981, pp. 555–56.
59 Quoted in Bean, 38-3DRL/606/237/1, AWM.
60 Bean, *The AIF in France, 1916*, pp. 43–46.
61 Andrews, *The Anzac Illusion*, p. 113.
62 Birdie quoted in Bean, 38-3DRL/606/237/1, AWM. Bean wrote of the politics of officer appointments in the AIF in 38-3DRL/606/40/1, AWM, pp. 38–55.
63 Masefield, *The Battle of the Somme*, p. 63.
64 Bean, *The AIF in France, 1916*, p. 457.
65 Keech, *Pozières*, p. 17.
66 Bean, *Anzac to Amiens*, p. 238.
67 ibid., pp. 454, 465 and Bean, *The AIF in France, 1916*, p. 467.
68 Horton, 1DRL/0359, AWM.

Chapter 2: Foreboding

1 Contay Château is described in Treloar, *An ANZAC Diary*, pp. 267–69 and *The Herald*, 7 August 1916, p. 1. *The Times* proprietor Lord Northcliffe wrote the article that appeared in *The Herald*. As an early example of myth-making, he referred to the two Australians guarding the château as 'giants'.
2 White's work habits are described in Derham, *The Silent Ruse*, p. 56.
3 ibid., p. 41. Subsequent quotations ibid., pp. 40, 49.
4 Belford, *Legs-eleven*, p. 258.
5 Birdwood, 3DRL/3376, AWM.

6   Chapman, *Iven G. Mackay*, p. 69.
7   In his autobiography, Birdie referred to those he admired as 'English Christian gentlemen'. See Birdwood, *Khaki and Gown*, p. 25.
8   Letter by Monash dated 1915. Quoted in Serle, *John Monash*, pp. 205–07.
9   Hamilton in a letter to Churchill dated 2 March 1915, quoted in Martin, Gilbert, *Documents*, vol. 3 of *Winston S. Churchill*, 1972.
10 Bean, *Two Men I Knew*, p. 96.
11 Cited in Derham, *The Silent Ruse*, p. 44. Subsequent quotations and discussion of anxiety ibid., pp. 39, 38, 231, 124–7 and Bean, *Two Men I Knew*, p. 81.
12 White's time at the British Staff College and desire for Gough's approval described in Derham, *The Silent Ruse*, pp. 188–91.
13 Bean, *Two Men I Knew*, p. 225. Subsequent quotations pp. 141, 131.
14 Albert and the 'Stooping Virgin' described in Wren, *Randwick to Hargicourt*, p. 156; Chapman, *Iven G. Mackay*, p. 73; Joynt, *Breaking the Road for the Rest*, p. 82; and Maze, *A Frenchman in Khaki*, p. 142.
15 Foxcroft, MS 9613, SLV and de Vine, 1DRL/0240, AWM.
16 The *Official History* notes that when White discovered that the proposed line of the British barrage would fall across the attacking infantry, he communicated, on the afternoon of 21 July, a further 24-hour postponement to the brigadiers. See Bean, *The AIF in France, 1916*, pp. 484–85.
17 Foxcroft, MS 9613, SLV.
18 Maze, *A Frenchman in Khaki*, p. 154.
19 Foxcroft, MS 9613, SLV.
20 Chapman, *Iven G. Mackay*, p. 73.
21 Harris, 1DRL/0338, AWM.
22 General Staff, 1st Australian Division, 1/42/18, AWM.
23 Claridge, 2DRL/0240, AWM.
24 Harris, 1DRL/0338, AWM.
25 Bean, *The AIF in France, 1916*, p. 489.
26 Browne, 2DRL/0619, AWM.
27 Browne's story based on events described in Browne, 1DRL/0428, AWM.
28 Browne, 2DRL/0619, AWM.
29 Correspondence between James Browne and the Base Records Office is archived in series B2455, Philip Gerald Browne, NAA. It includes the letter of consent signed by Philip's parents, permitting him to enlist in the expeditionary force.

Chapter 3: Fromelles

1   Haig's warnings, and concern over Australians' tasks, in Sheffield and Bourne, *Douglas Haig*, p. 208.
2   Quoted in McMullin, *Pompey Elliott*, p. 208.

3   The difficulties confronting both divisions are well documented. See for example Bean, *Anzac to Amiens*, pp. 226–28 and the summary of Pompey Elliott's 1930 lecture in Corfield, *Don't Forget Me, Cobber*, p. 404.
4   Haig's despatch to Munro is quoted in Bean, 'The Reasons for Fromelles' and Bean, *The AIF in France, 1916*, p. 350.
5   Macdonald, *Somme*, p. 176 and Keown, *Forward with the Fifth*, p. 163.
6   Toll's report on operations at Fleurbaix written on 21 July 1916 and reproduced in Bean, 38-3DRL/606/243a/1, AWM.
7   Quoted in Bean, *The AIF in France, 1916*, p. 358.
8   Bean, *Anzac to Amiens*, p. 230 and Bean, 38-3DRL/606/243a/1, AWM.
9   15th Infantry Brigade, 23/15/5, AWM.
10 Bean, *Anzac to Amiens*, p. 230.
11 Colonel Cass described the 8th Brigade retiring 'in what appeared to be a panic'. See Bean, 38-3DRL/606/243a/1, AWM.
12 Bean's actions, including visiting brigade commanders, in Bean, 38-3DRL/606/52/1, AWM.
13 Bean, 38-3DRL/606/237/1, AWM. Pope vehemently denied to McCay and Birdie that he was drunk; he claimed he was asleep.
14 Knyvett, *'Over There' with the Australians*, p. 155.
15 Barbour in a letter to Bean dated 1926. See Bean, 38-3DRL/606/243b/1, AWM.
16 Bean, 38-3DRL/606/52/1, AWM.
17 Bean, 38-3DRL/606/49/1, AWM, p. 61.
18 Bean, 38-3DRL/606/243a/1, AWM.
19 *The Argus*, 10 April 1920, p. 7.
20 See Ekins, 'The Battle of Fromelles' and Pedersen, 'Reflections on a Battlefield', pp. 18–29.
21 Pedersen, 'Reflections on a Battlefield', p. 25.
22 Bean, 38-3DRL/606/52/1, AWM.

Chapter 4: Lurid Clouds of War

1   Scene and sketches in Bean, 38-3DRL/606/52/1, AWM, pp. 37, 45–48.
2   Quoted in Austin, *The Fighting Fourth*, p. 107.
3   Joynt, *Breaking the Road for the Rest*, p. 81. Subsequent quotation ibid.
4   Horton, 1DRL/0359, AWM.
5   The following sources, written by Bean, describe how the troops occupied themselves: *The AIF in France, 1916*, p. 493; 38-3DRL/606/52/1, AWM; and *Letters from France*, p. 104. Also, Belford, *Legs-eleven*, p. 274.
6   Newton, *The Story of the Twelfth*, p. 98.
7   There are numerous examples of Anzacs keeping newspaper articles or poetic works in their dairies. See Coates, MS 10345; Cocking, MS 10167; and

Clayton, MS 10434, all SLV.
8   O'Neil, *The Poetical Works of Henry Lawson*, pp. 2–3.
9   Malpas, 2DRL/0001, AWM.
10 Foxcroft, MS 9613, SLV.
11 Thomas, 3DRL/2206, AWM.
12 Londey, 'If I Die at any Rate I Will Have Tried', p. 30.
13 Joynt, *Breaking the Road for the Rest*, pp. 81–82. The Gallipoli veterans' demeanour and their influence upon the 'cleanskins' is also described on p. 80 and in Urban, 'Somme Anzac Digger', p. 3.
14 Scene described in Belford, *Legs-eleven*, pp. 274–75; Newton, *The Story of the Twelfth*, p. 98; and Maze, *A Frenchman in Khaki*, p. 158.
15 Quoted in Derham, *The Silent Ruse*, pp. 49–50.
16 Treloar, *An ANZAC Diary*, pp. 266, 273.
17 Maze, *A Frenchman in Khaki*, p. 157.
18 Bean recorded the concerns in his diary. See Bean, 38-3DRL/606/52/1, AWM.
19 Thomas Blamey in a letter to James Blamey in Hetherington, *Blamey*, p. 39.
20 Bean's journey to the dugout, and his thoughts during it, are described in Bean, 38-3DRL/606/52/1, pp. 31–38 and 38-3DRL/606/54/1, pp. 53–61, both AWM.
21 Scott, *Australia During the War*, vol. 11, p. 2.
22 Quoted in ibid., p. 6.
23 *The Argus*, 5 August 1914, p. 6.
24 Scott, *Australia During the War*, pp. 13–14.
25 Harry S. Gullet's article, 'United Empire', appeared in the *Journal of the Royal Colonial Institute* in October 1914. Quoted in Alomes and Jones, *Australian Nationalism*, p. 166.
26 Souter, *Lion and Kangaroo*, p. 190.
27 Joynt, *Breaking the Road for the Rest*, p. 3.
28 Andrews, *The Anzac Illusion*, p. 12.
29 Quoted in Scott, *Australia During the War*, p. 859.
30 *The Sydney Morning Herald*, 6 August 1914, p. 5.
31 See Foxcroft, MS 9613, SLV; Joynt, *Breaking the Road for the Rest*, p. 56; Belford, *Legs-eleven*, pp. 1–2; and Chapman, *Iven G. Mackay*, p. 9.
32 Scott, *Australia During the War*, p. 1. Robson's statistics in appendix 3.
33 Hughes, *The Fatal Shore*, p. 14.
34 O'Neil, *The Poetical Works of Henry Lawson*, p. 4.
35 Hughes, *The Fatal Shore*, p. xiv and Bean, *The Story of Anzac*, p. xlvii.
36 Series B2455, Ernest Victor Lee *aka* Ernest John Jefferies, NAA. 'Boy–soldier' was the term used to describe underage soldiers such as Lee in an article in *Every Week*, 22 May 1919, p. 1.

Chapter 5: Storming Pozières

1   Battle plans in Maze, *A Frenchman in Khaki*, p. 496; Wren, *Randwick to Hargicourt*, p. 159; and Bean, *The AIF in France, 1916*, pp. 476–77, 494.
2   The events of that night, and Maze's role in them, are described in *A Frenchman in Khaki*, p. 158–9 and Bean, *Anzac to Amiens*, pp. 158, 241.
3   Quoted in Bean, ibid., p. 159.
4   Maze, *A Frenchman in Khaki*, p. 159.
5   The German side of the narrative, including the order not to abandon one inch of ground, is described in Bean, *The AIF in France, 1916*, pp. 519–24. Bean's sources included official German histories, regimental histories, prisoner interviews, mémoires, and captured documents.
6   Von Below's order is quoted in Sheffield, *The Somme*, p. 88.
7   *The Times*, 12 August 1916.
8   ibid., 19 August 1916, p. 5.
9   Intelligence, I Anzac Corps, 1/30/6, AWM.
10 The German barrage and disorientation of the Australians described in Bean, *The AIF in France, 1916*, p. 495; Wren, *Randwick to Hargicourt*, p. 162; Newton, *The Story of the Twelfth*, p. 98; and Harris, 1DRL/0338, AWM. The description of the gas shell also contained in Harris.
11 Atmosphere in the trenches awaiting the Allied barrage described in Bean, *Anzacs to Amiens*, p. 239 and Maze, *A Frenchman in Khaki*, p. 160.
12 Champion, 2DRL/0512, AWM.
13 Barrage described in Bean, *The AIF in France, 1916*, p. 496, 522 and Horton, 1DRL/0359, AWM. Australian, British, and French divisions contributed.
14 Quoted in Mant, *Soldier Boy*, p. 53.
15 Bean, *The AIF in France, 1916*, p. 498. Subsequent quotation ibid.
16 Bean, *Letters from France*, p. 104.
17 Maze, *A Frenchman in Khaki*, p. 161.
18 Preston, 'John Leak's V.C', p. 30.
19 Foxcroft, MS 9613, SLV.
20 Maze, *A Frenchman in Khaki*, p. 161 and Preston, 'John Leak's V.C', p. 30.
21 Maze, *A Frenchman in Khaki*, p. 161. Rough ground described in Keown, *Forward with the Fifth*, p. 167.
22 Foxcroft, MS 9613, SLV.
23 Series B2455, William Percy Clemenger, NAA. Dossier contains 'Army Form A45: Proceedings of a Medical Board'. Clemenger later returned to his battalion but was killed in Belgium in 1918.
24 Estimate of 2000 is based on the 1st, 2nd, 11th, and 12th battalions each supplying two companies of roughly 250 men to capture the first objective.

25 Foxcroft, MS 9613, SLV.
26 Quoted in Taylor and Cusack, *Nulli Secundus*, p. 190.
27 Horton, 1DRL/0359, AWM.
28 Chapman, *Iven G. Mackay*, p. 75.
29 Quoted in Kearney, *Silent Voices*, p. 189.
30 Maze, *A Frenchman in Khaki*, p. 162.
31 Bean's accounts of his ordeal and the situation in the dugout in Bean, 38-3DRL/606/52/1, pp. 31–38 and 38-3DRL/606/54/1, pp. 53–61, both AWM.
32 Preston, 'John Leak's V.C.', p. 31.
33 Scene described in Harvey, *From Anzac to the Hindenburg Line*, p. 129 and Bean, *The AIF in France, 1916*, pp. 501–04.
34 Quoted in Belford, *Legs-eleven*, p. 278.
35 Preston, 'John Leak's V.C.', p. 31.
36 Bean, *The AIF in France, 1916*, p. 505.
37 See ibid., pp. 504–05; Harris, 1DRL/0338, AWM; and Wren, *Randwick to Hargicourt*, p. 163.
38 Maze, *A Frenchman in Khaki*, p. 162. Subsequent quotations ibid.
39 General Staff, 1st Australian Division, 1/42/18, Part 2, AWM.
40 Bean, *The AIF in France, 1916*, pp. 519–24.
41 Drake-Brockman, *The Turning Wheel*, p. 104.
42 Shoobridge, PR00626, AWM.
43 General Staff, 1st Australian Division, 1/42/18, AWM.
44 Quoted in Butler, *The Western Front*, p. 58.
45 Belford, *Legs-eleven*, p. 282.
46 Quoted in Taylor and Cusack, *Nulli Secundus*, p. 181.
47 Quoted in Butler, *The Western Front*, p. 58.
48 Drake-Brockman, *The Turning Wheel*, p. 105.
49 Shoobridge, PR00626, AWM.
50 Series B2455, Sydney Alfred Stredwick, NAA.
51 Coates, MS 10345, SLV.
52 Bean, *The AIF in France, 1916*, pp. 526.
53 Masefield, *The Battle of the Somme*, p. 85.

Chapter 6: Consolidation
1 Maze, *A Frenchman in Khaki*, pp. 164–65.
2 Bean, *The AIF in France, 1916*, pp. 516–17. Donovan Joynt indicated that a nucleus of officers and non-commissioned officers was kept at the brickworks to replenish units suffering heavy casualties. See Joynt, *Breaking the Road for the Rest*, p. 81.

3   Maze, *A Frenchman in Khaki*, p. 165; Wren, *Randwick to Hargicourt*, p. 167; Foxcroft, MS 9613, SLV; and Bean, *The AIF in France, 1916*, p. 532.
4   Foxcroft, MS 9613, SLV.
5   Horton, 1DRL/0359, AWM.
6   Chapman, *Iven G. Mackay*, p. 75.
7   Maze, *A Frenchman in Khaki*, p. 165.
8   Bean, *The AIF in France, 1916*, p. 514.
9   Wren, *Randwick to Hargicourt*, p. 167.
10 ibid.
11 Harris, 1DRL/0338, AWM.
12 Quoted in Taylor and Cusack, *Nulli Secundus*, p. 190.
13 Foxcroft, MS 9613, SLV.
14 Laing in a letter dated 30 July 1916, quoted in Bean, 38-3DRL/606/244/1, AWM.
15 See Terraine, *Douglas Haig*, p. 215; Bean, *The AIF in France, 1916*, p. 526; and Sheffield and Bourne, *Douglas Haig*, p. 208.
16 Bean, *The AIF in France, 1916*, p. 527.
17 Haig's routine is sourced from Charteris, *Field Marshal Earl Haig*, pp. 193, 196, 205–09.
18 Tim Travers speculated that Haig's personality revolved around an almost obsessive need for order. See Travers, *The Killing Ground*, p. 103.
19 Quoted in Sheffield and Bourne, *Douglas Haig*, p. 211.
20 Clark, *The Old Dead Tree and the Young Tree Green*, pp. 24, 28.
21 Hughes's strident views are documented in Charteris, *At GHQ*, p. 145; Fitzhardinge, *The Little Digger 1914–1952*, pp. xiii, xiv; Hudson, *Billy Hughes in Paris*, pp. 1–2; and Bean, *Anzac to Amiens*, p. 290.
22 Hughes' popularity discussed in Bean, *Anzac to Amiens*, p. 291. Hughes's character discussed in Charteris, *At GHQ*, p. 145; Fitzhardinge, *The Little Digger 1914–1952*, p. xiv; and Horne, *Billy Hughes*, pp. 115–16.
23 Quoted in Whyte, *William Morris Hughes*, p. 209.
24 Hughes expressed concern about the British cabinet's apparent lack of set policy in managing the war. See Bean, *Anzac to Amiens*, p. 291 and Andrews, *The Anzac Illusion*, pp. 73–74. Britain finally established a war cabinet in December 1916; its purpose was to formulate British war strategy.
25 Hughes' visit is outlined in Bean, *Anzac to Amiens*, pp. 291–92 (quotation p. 291); Hudson, *Billy Hughes in Paris*, p. 2; and Whyte, *William Morris Hughes*, part three.
26 Bean, *Anzac to Amiens*, p. 291 and Whyte, *William Morris Hughes*, p. 247.
27 Whyte, *William Morris Hughes*, p. 193 and Charteris, *At GHQ*, p. 145.
28 Fitzhardinge, *The Little Digger 1914–1952*, p. 115 and Charteris, *At GHQ*, p. 145. Charteris recorded that dinner was memorable because Hughes

committed the unforgivable offence of arriving late. To Charteris's surprise, Haig waited patiently.
29 Fitzhardinge, *The Little Digger 1914–1952*, p. 116.
30 Chapman, *Iven G. Mackay*, p. 68.
31 Bean, *The AIF in France, 1916*, p. 47.
32 Chapman, *Iven G. Mackay*, pp. 13, 71.
33 Quoted in ibid., pp. 3, 76.
34 Information about Howell-Price in Wren, *Randwick to Hargicourt*, pp. 195, 167; Bean, *The AIF in France, 1916*, p. 60; and Nairn and Searle, *Australian Dictionary of Biography 1891–1939*, vol. 9, p. 382.
35 Preston, 'John Leak's V.C', p. 31.
36 *The Herald*, 27 July 1916, p. 7.
37 Maze, *A Frenchman in Khaki*, p. 165.
38 Bean, *The AIF in France, 1916*, p. 516.
39 The moniker's origins can be found in Easterly, *Belgian Rattlesnake*, Collector Grade Publications, Ontario, 1998. The gun's tactical importance and design is outlined in Griffith, *British Fighting Methods in the Great War*, pp. 128–34.
40 Bean, *The AIF in France, 1916*, p. 546.
41 Bean refers to Haig's bulldog spirit in Bean, *Anzac to Amiens*, p. 243.
42 Sheffield and Bourne, *Douglas Haig*, p. 209.
43 Charteris wrote that the army held Haig in 'veneration'; see Charteris, *Field Marshal Earl Haig*, p. 388. Lewis explained that the public trusted leaders such as Lord Horatio Kitchener as they trusted God; see Lewis, *Our War*, p. 210. For a newspaper article lauding Haig, see *The Times*, 5 August 1916, p. 7.
44 See Sheffield and Bourne, *Douglas Haig*. On 29 July 1916, Field-Marshal Sir William Robertson sent Haig a letter wanting to know whether the Somme losses would be offset by commensurate gains (p. 213); Haig described how French general Joseph Joffre exploded in rage on 3 July when Haig refused to renew an attack upon Thiepval after the initial failed attack (p. 198).
45 Bean, *The AIF in France, 1916*, p. 527.
46 Haig's character is described in Travers, *The Killing Ground*, pp. 101–18; *The Herald*, 29 August 1916, p. 1; and Wiest, *Haig*, p. 62. Haig's objective of enduring to the 'victorious end' is quoted in Charteris, *Field Marshal Earl Haig*, p. 213.
47 Bean, *The AIF in France, 1916*, p. 529.
48 Quoted in Sheffield and Bourne, *Douglas Haig*, p. 212.
49 Horne, *The Price of Glory*, p. 32. Horne cited von Falkenhayn calling off the offensive against the Russians at Tannenberg in 1914, even though the Germans were on the cusp of victory, as another example of his overly cautious nature.

50 See De Groot, *Douglas Haig, 1861–1928*, p. 166 and Wiest, *Haig*, p. 62. De Groot and Wiest speculated that this incident influenced Haig to persevere with offensives long after the hope of victory had passed.
51 Charteris, *At GHQ*, p. 151.
52 Bean, *The AIF in France, 1916*, pp. 529–30.
53 The German shelling and reaction of the Australians in Harvey, *From Anzac to the Hindenburg Line*, p. 130; Bean, *The AIF in France, 1916*, pp. 517–18; Maze, *A Frenchman in Khaki*, p. 165; and Wren, *Randwick to Hargicourt*, p. 168.
54 Bean, *The AIF in France, 1916*, p. 518. Subsequent quotations p. 514.
55 Documents recounting the soldier's surrender, including Callaway's letter, in Callaway, PR87/237, AWM.
56 Bean, *The AIF in France, 1916*, p. 541.
57 Laing in Bean, 38-3DRL/606/244/1, AWM.
58 Article 23 of the 1907 Hague Convention forbade combatants to kill or wound an enemy who had surrendered.
59 Ferro, *The Great War*, p. 123.
60 Bean, 38-3DRL/606/244/1, AWM.
61 Taylor and Cusack, *Nulli Secundus*, p. 180.
62 Host, 1DRL/0428, AWM.
63 Walter Elkington's diary described the conditioning training at Étaples. See Urban, 'Somme Anzac Digger', p. 35.
64 Breed, 'From France with Love 1916–1918', p. 84.
65 Bean, *The AIF in France, 1916*, p. 541.
66 Callaway, PR 87/237, AWM.
67 Quoted in Chapman, *Iven G. Mackay*, p. 75.
68 Thomson, 'Steadfast until Death?', pp. 464–65.
69 Bean, 38-3DRL/606/244/1, AWM.
70 Ferro, *The Great War*, p. 123.
71 Foxcroft, MS 9613, SLV.
72 General Staff, 1st Australian Division, 1/42/18, Part 1, AWM.
73 Chapman, *Iven G. Mackay*, p. 75; Coates, MS 10345 and Foxcroft, MS 9613, both SLV; and Wren, *Randwick to Hargicourt*, p. 167.
74 Foxcroft, MS 9613, SLV. Foxcroft donated the photographs, along with his diary, letters, and papers, to the library.
75 Bean, *The AIF in France, 1916*, p. 249.
76 Treloar, *An ANZAC Diary*, p. 278.
77 *The Herald*, 27 July 1916, p. 7.
78 Bean, 38-3DRL/606/52/1, AWM.
79 See Bean, 38-3DRL/606/17/1, AWM, pp. 21–34. Information about Ashmead-Bartlett in *The Mercury*, 8 May 1915, p. 5.

80 *The Times*, 22 June 1916, p. 7.
81 Bean, *The AIF in France, 1916*, p. 530.
82 Maze's story in Maze, *A Frenchman in Khaki*, p. 167–69.
83 General Staff, 1st Australian Division, 1/42/18, AWM.
84 Bean, *The AIF in France, 1916*, p. 534.
85 Belford, *Legs-eleven*, p. 283.
86 Bean, *The AIF in France, 1916*, p. 538 and Wren, *Randwick to Hargicourt*, p. 169.
87 Bean, *The AIF in France, 1916*, p. 541.
88 Belford, *Legs-eleven*, p. 284.
89 Series B2455, George Robert Stewart Walters, NAA.
90 Foxcroft, MS 9613, SLV.

Chapter 7: The Pozières Ridge

1   Quoted in Hetherington, *Blamey*, p. 39.
2   Bean, *The AIF in France, 1916*, pp. 549–50.
3   ibid., pp. 349, 551.
4   See 'Lessons Drawn from the Battle of the Somme' in Bean, 38-3DRL/606/244/1, AWM. Page 4 indicated that British prisoners were surprised that so many German machine guns were operational after the seven-day bombardment that preceded that 1 July attack.
5   Intelligence, I Anzac Corps, 1/30/6, AWM.
6   Browning, *The 52nd Battalion*, p. 44. Masefield wrote that men became dizzy and sick from the noise of hammering machines guns combined with the deafening explosion of shells. See Masefield, *The Old Front Line*, p. 127.
7   See 'Experience of the German 1st Army in the Battle of the Somme' in Bean, 38-3DRL/606/244/1, AWM.
8   Foxcroft, MS 9613, SLV.
9   Preston, 'John Leak's V.C', p. 31.
10 Belford, *Legs-eleven*, p. 289.
11 Bean, *The AIF in France 1916*, p. 552.
12 Bombardment of 24 July described in Bean, *The AIF in France 1916*, p. 352; Foxcroft, MS 9613, SLV; Harris, 1DRL/0338, AWM; and Belford, *Legs-eleven*, p. 283, 286. Position of German guns in Intelligence, I Anzac Corps, 1/30/6; for description of shelling see Keown, *Forward with the Fifth*, p. 174.
13 Quoted in Bean, 38-3DRL/606/244/1, AWM. Subsequent quotation ibid.
14 ibid.
15 Wren, *Randwick to Hargicourt*, p. 170. Subsequent quotation ibid., p. 171.
16 Quoted in Chapman, *Iven G. Mackay*, p. 75.
17 Taylor and Cusack, *Nulli Secundus*, p. 191.

18 Coates, MS 10345, SLV. Subsequent quotation ibid.
19 Rations reduction in Wren, *Randwick to Hargicourt*, p. 170; reliance on pigeons in General Staff, 1st Australian Division, 1/42/18 and 1st Infantry Brigade, 23/1/12, both AWM; Dead Man's Road in Bean, *Anzac to Amiens*, p. 245.
20 Quoted in Bean, *The AIF in France, 1916*, p. 553.
21 ibid., p. 555.
22 Wren, *Randwick to Hargicourt*, p. 171.
23 Foxcroft, MS 9613, SLV.
24 Bean, 38-3DRL/606/244/1, AWM.
25 Belford, *Legs-eleven*, p. 292.
26 Bean, *The AIF in France, 1916*, p. 558.
27 ibid., p. 560.
28 Keown, *Forward with the Fifth*, p. 169.
29 Bean, *The AIF in France 1916*, pp. 560–61.
30 Quoted in Austin, *Our Dear Old Battalion*, p. 139.
31 Londey, 'If I Die at any Rate I Will Have Tried', p. 30. Subsequent quotation ibid.
32 7th Battalion AIF Association, PR87/215, AWM.
33 Moorhead, 3DRL/7253, AWM. Subsequent quotation ibid.
34 Londey, 'If I Die at any Rate I Will Have Tried', p. 30. Subsequent quotations ibid., p. 31.
35 Bean, *The AIF in France 1916*, p. 565.
36 ibid., pp. 568–69.
37 This incident recounted in Belford, *Legs-eleven*, p. 285.
38 Bean, *The AIF in France, 1916*, p. 570.
39 1st Division Order Number 37 reads, in type, that the attack date was 'on the morning of the 26th'. A faint pencil mark added sometime afterward crosses out '26th', replacing it with '25th'. A copy of the order is in General Staff, 1st Australian Division, 1/42/18, AWM.
40 Chapman, *Iven G. Mackay*, p. 75.
41 de Vine, 1DRL/0240, AWM.
42 Smyth's troops experiences in K Trench in Bean, *The AIF in France 1916*, p. 570.
43 Theo Barker provides an excellent account of the communication difficulties faced by the Anzacs on the Somme. See *Signals*, pp. 68–73.
44 Bean, *The AIF in France, 1916*, p. 584.
45 General Staff, 1st Australian Division, 1/42/18, AWM.
46 Elvin, 2DRL/0209, AWM.
47 Foxcroft, MS 9613, SLV.
48 Bean, *The AIF in France, 1916*, pp. 579-80.
49 Quotations and account of Bennett's experience taken from Legg, *The Gordon Bennett Story*, p. 105.

50 Quoted in Austin, *As Rough as Bags*, p. 162.
51 Series B2455, Henry Eggington, NAA.
52 Abson, 2DRL/0007, AWM.
53 Legg, *The Gordon Bennett Story*, p. 106.
54 A review of 3rd Battalion soldiers' files in Series B2455 shows some attended the Church of England Grammar School in Sydney and perhaps knew of or were taught by Harris.
55 1st Infantry Brigade, 23/1/12, AWM.
56 Wren, *Randwick to Hargicourt*, p. 169.
57 Harris's experience based on Wren, *Randwick to Hargicourt*, pp. 167–71 and Harris, 1DRL/0338, AWM.
58 Butler, *Special Problems and Services*, p. 103.
59 1st Infantry Brigade, 23/1/12, AWM.
60 Statistics from Butler, *Special Problems and Services*, p. 72, 101.
61 Harris, 1DRL/0337, AWM.
62 Butler, *Special Problems and Services*, pp. 105–06.
63 Harris, 1DRL/0338, AWM.
64 Butler, *Special Problems and Services*, p. 65.
65 Chapman, *Iven G. Mackay*, p. 75.
66 Freeman, *Hurcombe's Hungry Half Hundred*, p. 71.
67 *The Torch-Bearer*, October 1917, p. 40. Harris's letter is dated 8 May 1917.
68 Correspondence between medical officers and Harris's commanding officers about his two breakdowns is archived in Series B2455, John Harris, NAA.
69 Figure in Bean, *The AIF in France, 1916*, pp. 586, 593.
70 Quoted in Oates, *With the Big Guns*, p. 139.
71 Bean, *Letters from France*, p. 109.
72 Bean, *The AIF in France, 1916*, p. 582.
73 Quoted in Horner, *The Gunners*, p. 130.
74 Ammunition columns discussed in Breed, 'From France with Love 1916–1918', pp. 63–64. Statistics in Horner, *The Gunners*, p. 134.
75 Quoted in Sheffield and Bourne, *Douglas Haig*, p. 209. Subsequent quotation ibid.
76 Bean, 38-3DRL/606/44/1, AWM.
77 Bean, *Letters from France*, p. 108.
78 Bean, *The AIF in France 1916*, p. 589.
79 ibid., p. 589.
80 Situation recounted in Bean, *The AIF in France 1916*, pp. 580, 590–91.
81 ibid., p. 590.
82 Quoted in Chapman, *Iven G. Mackay*, p. 76.
83 Quoted in Bean, *The AIF in France, 1916*, p. 591.

84 The situation at Sinclair-MacLagan's headquarters described in Bean, *The AIF in France, 1916*, p. 590.
85 ibid., p. 581.

Chapter 8: The Price of Glory

1 Bean, 38-3DRL/606/53/1 and General Staff, 2nd Division, 1/44/12, Part 1, both AWM.
2 Joynt, *Breaking the Road for the Rest*, p. 88.
3 Breed, 'From France with Love 1916–1918', p. 62.
4 Sinclair-MacLagan's experiences in Bean, 38-3DRL/606/126/1, AWM, pp. 57–60. The 3rd Brigade diary suggested that Sinclair-MacLagan's headquarters was relieved by the 5th Brigade on 26 July.
5 Austin, *The Fighting Fourth*, p. 112.
6 General Staff, 2nd Australian Division, 1/44/12, AWM.
7 Bean, 38-3DRL/606/53/1, AWM.
8 Taylor and Cusack, *Nulli Secundus*, p. 191 and Bean, *The AIF in France, 1916*, p. 661.
9 de Vine, 1DRL/0240, AWM.
10 Horton, 1DRL/0359, AWM.
11 Taylor and Cusack, *Nulli Secondus*, p. 192; Callaway, PR87/237, AWM; and Foxcroft, MS 9613, SLV.
12 Bean, *The AIF in France, 1916*, p. 593.
13 Butler, *Special Problems and Services*, p. 72 and Bean, *The AIF in France, 1916*, p. 593.
14 Cohen, 1DRL/0204, AWM.
15 Quoted in Chapman, *Iven G. Mackay*, p. 76.
16 Moorhead, 3DRL/7253, AWM.
17 Keown, *Forward with the Fifth*, p. 169.
18 Bean, *The AIF in France, 1916*, pp. 639–40.
19 Quoted in Derham, *The Silent Ruse*, p. 105.
20 *The Sydney Morning Herald*, 27 July 1916, p. 9.
21 Rule, *Jacka's Mob*, p. 61.
22 Bean, *Anzac to Amiens*, p. 249 and *The AIF in France, 1916*, p. 599.
23 Quoted in Hetherington, *Blamey*, p. 39.
24 General Staff, 1st Australian Division, 1/42/18, AWM.
25 Bean, 38-3DRL/606/40/1, AWM.
26 Belford, *Legs-eleven*, pp. 294, 295–96. The history claimed that of the 20 officers who led the battalion into action, only three came out unwounded.
27 Bean, *The AIF in France, 1916*, pp. 442, 593.
28 ibid., p. 869.

29 Drake-Brockman, *The Turning Wheel*, p. 108.
30 Manning, *The Middle Parts of Fortune*, p. 94. Subsequent quotation ibid.
31 Hocking, PR88/161, AWM.
32 Graham, MS 9640, SLV. Many soldiers, including Graham, wrote French words phonetically.
33 Mackenzie, *The Story of the Seventeenth Battalion AIF in the Great War 1914–1918*, p. 114.
34 Clayton, MS 10434, SLV.
35 Quoted in Breed, 'From France with Love 1916–1918', p. 62.
36 Raws, 'Records of an Australian Lieutenant', p. 12.
37 23rd Infantry Battalion, 23/40/10, AWM.
38 Information about Alec and Goldy Raws, including quotations, drawn from Young and Gammage, *Hail and Farewell*, pp. 103, 162–66, appendices and Raws, 'Records of an Australian Lieutenant', p. 12.
39 Legge was born and initially educated in England, yet considered himself Australian.
40 General Staff, 2nd Australian Division, 1/44/12, Part 2, AWM.
41 Bean, *The AIF in France, 1916*, p. 607 and Coulthard-Clark, *No Australian Need Apply*, p. 206.
42 Birdie recorded his key meetings with Gough and Legge in Birdwood, 3DRL/3376, AWM.
43 Bean, *The AIF in France, 1916*, pp. 604, 610–13.
44 Coulthard-Clark, 'Legge, James Gordon (1863–1947)', pp. 63–65 and Barrett, *Falling In*, p. 42. Coulthard-Clark suggests that Legge's intellectual arrogance threatened fellow officers. See *No Australian Need Apply*, pp. 74–79.
45 Coulthard-Clark, 'Legge, James Gordon (1863–1947)', p. 98 and Perry, 'Lieutenant-General James Gordon Legge', p. 206.
46 Coulthard-Clark suggests that Birdwood censured Legge for bypassing British authorities, instead communicating directly to Australian authorities the poor state of training facilities in Cairo in June 1915. See *No Australian Need Apply*, p. 106.
47 Perry, 'Lieutenant-General James Gordon Legge', p. 206.
48 Coulthard-Clark, *No Australian Need Apply*, p. 87.
49 Bean thought Legge was inclined to 'cry out Australia for the Australians' with very small provocation. See Bean, 38-3DRL/606/40/1, AWM, pp. 46–47.
50 Coulthard-Clark, *No Australian Need Apply*, p. 138.
51 ibid., p. 131.
52 Quoted in Breed, 'From France with Love 1916–1918', p. 64.
53 Bean, *The AIF in France, 1916*, p. 618.
54 Quoted in Breed, 'From France with Love 1916–1918', p. 64.

55 Difficulties preparing described in Bean, *The AIF in France, 1916*, pp. 619–21 and *Anzac to Amiens*, p. 251.
56 Fewster, *Gallipoli Diaries*, p. 122.
57 Bean referred to Legge as having elements of genius in Bean, *Two Men I Knew*, p. xiii.
58 Gellibrand's views in Sadler, *The Paladin*, p. 93; Bean's views as recorded in his diary, where he wrote that the 7th Brigade never had the discipline or spirit of the other brigades.
59 ibid., p. 94.
60 Bean recorded Birdwood's reservations about Gellibrand's outspokenness and unconventional dress in his diary. Quoted in ibid., p. 78.
61 ibid., p. 77.
62 ibid., p. 63.
63 Sadler wrote that Gellibrand's appointment to brigade command was an 'adventurous' gamble. See ibid., p. 77.

Chapter 9: Legge's Reckoning

1 The prevailing mood among the 2nd Division staff was described in Bean, *The AIF in France, 1916*, p. 619.
2 Urban, 'Somme Anzac Digger', p. 44.
3 Quoted in Browning, *The Blue & White Diamond*, p. 148.
4 Bean, 38-3DRL/606/54/1, AWM, p. 6.
5 Sadler, *The Paladin*, p. 95.
6 Bean, 38-3DRL/606/54/1, AWM, p. 6.
7 Bean, *The AIF in France, 1916*, p. 624.
8 Griffith, *Battle Tactics of the Western Front*, ch. 8.
9 Bean, *The AIF in France, 1916*, pp. 624–25.
10 Bean, 38-3DRL/606/244/1, AWM.
11 Sheffield and Bourne, *Douglas Haig*, p. 210.
12 Quoted in Austin, *Forward Undeterred*, p. 78.
13 Hocking, PR88/161, AWM.
14 Quoted in Browning, *The Blue & White Diamond*, p. 149. Quotation from Mauger ibid., p. 150.
15 Bean, *The AIF in France, 1916*, p. 640.
16 Bean described events in dugout in Bean, 38-3DRL/606/54/1, AWM, pp. 13–16.
17 Bean, *The AIF in France, 1916*, p. 629.
18 Urban, 'Somme Anzac Digger', p. 45.
19 5th Infantry Brigade, 23/5/14, AWM.
20 20th Infantry Battalion, 23/37/12, AWM.
21 Bean, *The AIF in France, 1916*, p. 630.

22 See Bean's notes on conversations with German officers who were in action on 28 and 29 July in Bean, 38-3DRL/606/244/1, AWM.
23 Quoted in Browning, *The Blue & White Diamond*, p. 154. Bean's notebook records conversations with German officers who spotted the Australian advance.
24 The Australian entanglement in German trenches described in Bean, *The AIF in France, 1916*, pp. 627, 631–32, and 38-3DRL/606/54/1 and 38-3DRL/606/244/1, both AWM. Symthe's story in Browning, *The Blue & White Diamond*, p. 166.
25 Series B2455, John Arthur Charles Stuart, NAA.
26 Quoted in Browning, *The Blue & White Diamond*, p. 157. Subsequent quotation from Mauger ibid., p. 158.
27 Bean, *The AIF in France, 1916*, p. 628.
28 Quoted in Matthews, *Australian Soldiers in the Great War 1914–18*, pp. 60–61.
29 Hocking, PR88/161, AWM.
30 Goldy Raws's actions are reconstructed from the evidence Private John McGuire provided to the court of enquiry, held on 12 August 1916. See Bean, 38-3DRL/606/244/1, AWM.
31 Hocking, PR88/161, AWM.
32 Bean, 38-3DRL/606/54/1, AWM.
33 See 'Messages and Signals' for description of events, appendixed in 7th Infantry Brigade, 23/7/11, AWM.
34 Lewis Winchester Marshall, 1DRL/0428, AWM.
35 Carne, *In Good Company*, p. 84.
36 Urban, 'Somme Anzac Digger', p. 45.
37 The activity in Gellibrand's dugout that night is described in Bean, 38-3DRL/606/54/1, AWM, p. 16 and *The AIF in France, 1916*, p. 626.
38 Quoted in Duffy, *Through German Eyes*, p. 189.
39 Quoted in Browning, *The Blue & White Diamond*, p. 169. Also see Sinclair, 1DRL/0428, AWM.
40 Marshall, 1DRL/0428, AWM.
41 Bean, *The AIF in France, 1916*, p. 640.
42 Quoted in Sheldon, *The German Army on the Somme 1914–1916*, p. 230.
43 Sainsbury, 1DRL/0428, AWM.
44 Hocking, PR88/161, AWM.
45 Browning, *The Blue & White Diamond*, p. 169.
46 Lieutenant Robert Goldthorpe Raws, 1DRL/0428, AWM.
47 Young and Gammage, *Hail and Farewell*, p. 141.
48 Bean, *The AIF in France, 1916*, p. 643.
49 Quoted in Browning, *The Blue & White Diamond*, p. 169.

Chapter 10: Promised Land

1. General Staff, 2nd Division, 1/44/12, AWM.
2. Bean, 38-3DRL/606/54/1, AWM, p. 22.
3. The *Official History* suggests that the information supplied to Haig about Legge's failure on 29 July was 'wholly inaccurate'. This picture was likely to have been provided by senior general staff officer Major-General Neill Malcolm, of Gough's Reserve Army. See Sheffield and Bourne, *Douglas Haig*, p. 211 and Bean, *The AIF in France, 1916*, p. 619.
4. Gellibrand is quoted as referring to Legge's chief-of-staff, Colonel Arthur Bridges, as 'a swine'. He often agitated for his removal. See Sadler, *The Paladin*, ch. 13.
5. Legge wrote to Bean in 1934 that any haste for attacks should have been ascribed to the daily pressures of the Reserve Army commander. Quoted in Coulthard-Clark, *No Australian Need Apply*, p. 206.
6. Farrar-Hockley, *Goughie*, p. 138.
7. Bean, *The AIF in France, 1916*, p. 619.
8. Bean, 38-3DRL/606/54/1, AWM, p. 118.
9. Sheffield and Bourne, *Douglas Haig*, pp. 210–11.
10. ibid., p. 497.
11. Charteris, *Field Marshal Earl Haig*, p. 196.
12. Bean's handwritten notes on the meeting in ibid.
13. Account of meeting based on the following sources: White's letter to Bean, May 1928, in Bean, 38-3DRL/606/244/1, AWM; Bean's handwritten notes in Bean, 38-3DRL/606/244/1, AWM and *The AIF in France, 1916*, p. 644 and *Two Men I Knew*, p. 137; Sheffield and Bourne, *Douglas Haig*, p. 211; and Charteris, *Field Marshal Earl Haig*, p. 209.
14. Quotations from Derham, *The Silent Ruse*, pp. 51–53.
15. Charteris, *At GHQ*, p. 159.
16. General Staff, 2nd Australian Division, 1/44/12, AWM.
17. Bean, *The AIF in France, 1916*, p. 649.
18. ibid., pp. 650, 651, 654–65. Bean indicated the morale of the 7th Brigade plummeted after the first attack on the OG lines in Bean, 38-3DRL/606/54/1, AWM. Holmes's preference for a daylight attack in 5th Infantry Brigade, 23/5/14.
19. Bean, *The AIF in France, 1916*, pp. 658–59 and Young and Gammage, *Hail and Farewell*, pp. 146–47.
20. Quoted in Willmington, 'Diaries of an Unsung Hero', pp. 133–34.
21. Bean, *Letters from France*, p. 113.
22. ibid., p. 114.
23. Bean, 38-3DRL/606/54/1, AWM, pp. 48–49.

24 McCarthy, *Gallipoli to the Somme*, p. 237.
25 Bean, 38-3DRL/606/54/1, AWM, p. 47.
26 Bean, *Letters from France*, p. 114.
27 Bean painted a romantic picture of the men rushing to enlist in the 1st Division in 1914 and how their bush skills prepared them for war. See Bean, *The Story of Anzac*, p. 46.
28 Williams contends that, even though Bean was appalled by the loss of life on the Somme, he continued to write despatches that glorified the Anzacs' eagerness for battle. See Williams, *Anzacs, the Media and the Great War*, p. 148.
29 Bean alluded to the wide powers of the censors, who were responsible for enforcing the War Precautions Act, in 38-3DRL/606/54/1, AWM, p. 36.
30 In December 1917 Bean advised his assistant of the official correspondent's duty. See 'Position of the Assistant Correspondent AIF and Duties of the Australian War Correspondent', 12 December 1917, Bean Papers, folder 268, AWM.
31 Bean, *The AIF in France, 1916*, p. 529 and Sheffield and Bourne, *Douglas Haig*, p. 213. Churchill's critique in *World Crisis*, pp. 187–92.
32 Sheffield and Bourne, *Douglas Haig*, pp. 213, 214. Subsequent quotation ibid., p. 214.
33 Todman, *The Great War*, ch. 5; Philpott, *Bloody Victory*, p. 189; and Hitchens, 'The Pity of War'.
34 Bean, *The AIF in France, 1916*, p. 663–65.
35 ibid., pp. 664, 665 and Bean, 38-3DRL/606/54/1, AWM, pp. 118–19.
36 Sheffield and Bourne, *Douglas Haig*, p. 215.
37 Breed, 'From France with Love 1916–1918', p. 68.
38 Bean, *The AIF in France, 1916*, pp. 659, 674.
39 Sheffield and Bourne, *Douglas Haig*, p. 214.
40 Quoted in Terraine, *Douglas Haig*, p. xii.
41 Lloyd George, *War Memoirs*, pp. 2038–42.
42 French's fluctuating moods in the first months of the war are described in Tuchman, *The Guns of August*.
43 Seely, *Adventure*, pp. 150–51.
44 Charteris, *At GHQ*, pp. 208–09.
45 Corrigan summarises the British Expeditionary Force's rapid expansion throughout the war and the pressures it placed upon commanders. See Corrigan, *Mud, Blood and Poppycock*, pp. 192–98.
46 Lloyd George, *War Memoirs*, p. 2042.
47 Charteris commented on 29 July 1916 that many divisional and corps commanders on the Somme were presently 'inexperienced in their new commands'. See Charteris, *At GHQ*, p. 159.
48 Gough, *The Fifth Army*, p. 135.

49 Brown, *British Logistics on the Western Front, 1914–1919*, p. 126.
50 Sheffield and Bourne, *Douglas Haig*, p. 248.
51 Charteris, *Field Marshal Earl Haig*, p. 199.
52 Quoted in Terraine, *Douglas Haig*, 1963, p. 173.
53 Mackenzie, *The Story of the Seventeenth Battalion, AIF, in the Great War 1914–1918*, p. 126.
54 Lord Northcliffe noted that Birdie always gave this advice in *The Herald*, 7 August 1916, p. 1. Subsequent quotation ibid.
55 Devine, *The Story of a Battalion*, p. 51 and Mackenzie, *The Story of the Seventeenth Battalion, AIF, in the Great War 1914–1918*, p. 126.
56 These critical corps-planning responsibilities are defined in Prior and Wilson, *Command on the Western Front*, p. 20.
57 Corrigan notes that in the tiny pre-war British army, few commanders had any experience handling anything larger than a brigade in the field. See Corrigan, *Mud, Blood and Poppycock*, p. 190.
58 Prior and Wilson, *Command on the Western Front*, p. 20.
59 Bean, 38-3DRL/606/113/1, AWM, p. 11.
60 Quotation in Birdwood, *Khaki and Gown*, p. 271 and comment about Pozières trenches in *The Herald*, 7 August 1916, p. 1.
61 Birdwood in a letter to Lord Derby, 15 Aug 1916. Quoted in Miller, John, 'A Study in the Limitations of Command: General Sir William Birdwood and the AIF, 1914–1918', Manuscript 1459, 1993, AWM, p. 145.
62 Birdwood Papers, Imperial War Museum, quoted in ibid.
63 Quoted in Breed, 'From France with Love 1916–1918', p. 69.
64 Intelligence, I Anzac Corps, 1/30/7, Part 1, AWM.
65 Although Haig's formal attack, to which von Gallwitz was alluding, would not occur until September, the Germans would have no doubt been anticipating it. See Sheldon, *The German Army on the Somme 1914–1916*, p. 222.
66 Bean, *The AIF in France, 1916*, p. 688. Subsequent quotation ibid., p. 682.
67 6th Infantry Brigade, 23/6/12, AWM.
68 Author Eric Partridge participated in the attack. Although his book, like other classics such as Robert Graves's *Goodbye to All That* (1960) and Siegfried Sassoon's *Memories of an Infantry Officer* (2000), featured fictional characters, the description of events was based on personal experience. See Partridge, *Frank Honywood, Private*, p. 89.
69 Quoted in Urban, 'Somme Anzac Digger', p. 47. Subsequent quotation ibid., p. 48.
70 Treloar, *An ANZAC Diary*, p. 271.
71 Bean, 38-3DRL/606/54/1, AWM, p. 84.

72 Urban, 'Somme Anzac Digger', p. 48.
73 Quoted in Browning, *The Blue & White Diamond*, p. 177.
74 Description of Australian attack in Bean, *The AIF in France, 1916*, pp. 673, 680, 689–90 and General Staff, I Anzac Corps, 1/29/7, Part 1, both AWM.
75 Quoted in Browning, *The Blue & White Diamond*, p. 180.
76 Corney, 2DRL/0948, AWM.
77 Description of German counterattack in Bean, *The AIF in France, 1916*, pp. 693–96. For a description of the soldiers' view from the ridge, see ibid., pp. 699–700; Gibbs, *The Battles of the Somme*, pp. 169–70; and Masefield, *The Battle of the Somme*, pp. 89–90. The biblical phrase 'the promised land' featured in each account.
78 Urban, 'Somme Anzac Digger', p. 48.
79 Intelligence, I Anzac Corps, 1/30/7, Part 1, AWM.
80 Bean, *The AIF in France, 1916*, p. 700. Subsequent quotation ibid., p. 874.
81 Intelligence, I Anzac Corps, 1/30/7, Part 1, AWM.
82 Quoted in Bean, *The AIF in France, 1916*, p. 874 and 38-3DRL/606/54/1, AWM.
83 Bean, *The AIF in France, 1916*, p. 874.
84 Urban, 'Somme Anzac Digger', p. 48.
85 Browning, *The Blue & White Diamond*, p. 183.
86 Quoted in Breed, 'From France with Love 1916–1918', p. 74.
87 Quoted in Browning, *The Blue & White Diamond*, p. 185.
88 Series B2455, Ernest Norgard, Frank Corney, and Edgar Morrow, NAA and Lewis Marshall, 1DRL/0428, AWM.
89 Quoted in Department of Veterans' Affairs, *Simply Hell Let Loose*, pp. 51–52.
90 Series B2455, William Hatcher, NAA.
91 Quoted in Young and Gammage, *Hail and Farewell*, p. 145.
92 Bean, *The AIF in France, 1916*, p. 699; Haig quoted in Sheffield and Bourne, *Douglas Haig*, p. 215.
93 Charteris, *At GHQ*, p. 163.
94 Treloar, *An ANZAC Diary*, p. 271.
95 Bean, 38-3DRL/606/54/1, AWM, pp. 118–19.
96 Letter from Birdwood to Pearce dated 14 August 1916. See Bean, 38–3DRL/606/237/1, AWM, p. 30.
97 Sheffield and Bourne, *Douglas Haig*, p. 216.
98 Bean, 38-3DRL/606/57/1, AWM, pp. 9–15; Lloyd George, *War Memoirs*, p. 2042; Weist, *Haig*, p. 67; and Terraine, *Douglas Haig*, p. 178.
99 Terraine, *Douglas Haig*, p. 179.
100 Corrigan, *Mud, Blood and Poppycock*, p. 195.
101 ibid., p. 205.
102 Quoted in Horne, *The Price of Glory*, p. 22.

103 Todman, *The Great War*, p. 83.
104 Lloyd George, *War Memoirs*, p. 2036.
105 For an extract of Kitchener's instructions to Haig on 28 December 1915, see Sheffield and Bourne, *Douglas Haig*, appendix 2.
106 Philpott, *Bloody Victory*, pp. 596–600.
107 Charteris, *At GHQ*, p. 134.
108 ibid.
109 Transcript of German wireless dated 25 November in Bean, 38-3DRL/606/66/1, AWM, p. 72.
110 Carthew, *Voices from the Trenches*, p. 169.
111 Haig's supposed inarticulate nature is cited in Winter, *Haig's Command*, pp. 12–13; Wiest, *Haig*, p. 4; Gilbert, *The Somme*, pp. 220–22; and Todman, *The Great War*, p. 83.
112 Bean, *The AIF in France, 1916*, p. 464.
113 Terraine, *Douglas Haig*, p. xii.
114 Lloyd George, *War Memoirs*, p. 2042.
115 Quoted in Breed, 'From France with Love 1916–1918', p. 88.
116 Quoted in Urban, 'Somme Anzac Digger', p. 48.
117 Masefield, *The Battle of the Somme*, p. 93.
118 Quoted in Breed, 'From France with Love 1916–1918', p. 70.
119 Intelligence, I Anzac Corps, 1/30/7, Part 1, AWM.
120 Quoted in Derham, *The Silent Ruse*, p. 50.
121 Bean, *The AIF in France, 1916*, pp. 701, 705.
122 Intelligence, I Anzac Corps, 1/30/7, Part 1, AWM.

Chapter 11: Folly

1   Bean, *The AIF in France, 1916*, p. 724.
2   Quoted in Sadler, *The Paladin*, p. 99.
3   Reference to shaking like aspen leaves in Bean, *The AIF in France, 1916*, p. 724.
4   Quoted in Willmington, 'Diaries of an Unsung Hero', pp. 133–37. Subsequent quotations ibid.
5   Quoted in Young and Gammage, *Hail and Farewell*, pp. 153–54.
6   Quoted in Bean, 38-3DRL/606/244/1, AWM.
7   Carne, *In Good Company*, p. 86.
8   Treloar, *An ANZAC Diary*, p. 273.
9   Quoted in Breed, 'From France with Love 1916–1918', pp. 74–75.
10 Bean, 38-3DRL/606/54/1, AWM.
11 Quoted in Duffy, *Through German Eyes*, p. 190.
12 Bean, *The AIF in France, 1916*, p. 706.
13 Barwick, MLMSS 1493/Box 1, Mitchell Library and Freeman, *Hurcombe's*

Hungry Half Hundred, p. 4.
14 General Staff, 4th Division, 1/48/4, Part 2, AWM; Bean, *The AIF in France, 1916*, pp. 706–07; and Devine, *The Story of a Battalion*, p. 30.
15 Rule, *Jacka's Mob*, p. 57.
16 Browning, *Fix Bayonets*, p. 27.
17 General Staff, 4th Australian Division, 1/48/4, Part 2, AWM.
18 Haig's comments to Cox contained in Sheffield and Bourne, *Douglas Haig*, p. 211; march discipline in General Staff, 4th Division, 1/48/4, Part 2, AWM and discussed in Devine, *The Story of a Battalion*, p. 31.
19 Palmer, PR03407, AWM.
20 Devine, *The Story of a Battalion*, pp. 31–32.
21 Longmore, *The Old Sixteenth AIF*, p. 114 and Devine, *The Story of a Battalion*, p. 31.
22 Bean cited conversations with British staff officers who criticised the Australians' 'dirty and untidy' presentation. See Bean, 38-3DRL/606/50/1, pp. 17–21 (subsequent quotation ibid. p. 22) and 38-3DRL/606/40/1, pp. 13–21, both AWM. John Treloar explained in his diary the Anzacs' reluctance to wear English uniforms in *An ANZAC Diary*, p. 273.
23 Denny, *A Digger at Home and Abroad*, p. 31. Eric Andrews suggests that harsher discipline perhaps prevented British soldiers from showing the independence of spirit the Anzacs sometimes displayed in battle. See Andrews, *The Anzac Illusion*, p. 151.
24 Andrews, *The Anzac Illusion*, pp. 149–51. Alec Raws provided an interesting account of the social differences between British and Australian officers. See Raws, 'Records of an Australian Lieutenant', pp. 42, 54–56.
25 Bean, 38-3DRL/606/50/1, AWM, p. 19 and *The AIF in France, 1916*, p. 53.
26 Wren, *Randwick to Hargicourt*, p. 154.
27 Perry, *Monash*, pp. 246–47.
28 Quoted in Browning, *Fix Bayonets*, p. 30.
29 Frequently, when interviewing German prisoners, Bean eagerly questioned them on the fighting qualities of Australians. See example in Bean, 38-3DRL/606/66/1, AWM, pp. 36–38. Graham Seal asserts that the Anzacs' supposed traditions of irreverence and anti-authoritarianism were propagated after the war by veteran organisations and official institutions in *Inventing Anzac*, pp. 4–6. Jane Ross outlines the unique tenets of the Digger myth that flourished after the war in *The Myth of the Digger*, p. 12.
30 Andrews, *The Anzac Illusion*, p. 151.
31 Leane in a letter to Bean in 1923. See Bean, 38-3DRL/606/244/1, AWM, pp. 54–56.
32 For a colourful sketch of Leane, see Bean, *The AIF in France, 1916*, p. 708.
33 White, *The Fighting Thirteenth*, p. 64.

34 Rule, *Jacka's Mob*, p. 59. Subsequent quotation ibid., p. 63.
35 Bean, *The AIF in France, 1916*, p. 709.
36 Bean, 38-3DRL/606/244/1, AWM, pp. 54–56.
37 Leane's letter to Bean in 1923. See Bean, 38-3DRL/606/244/1, AWM, pp. 54–56.
38 Devine, *The Story of a Battalion*, p. 40.
39 Rule, *Jacka's Mob*, p. 65. Subsequent quotations ibid., pp. 65, 67.
40 Events of the afternoon described in Bean, *The AIF in France, 1916*, pp. 712–15.
41 Foxcroft, MS 9613, SLV.
42 McSparron, 1DRL/0463, AWM. Subsequent quotations ibid.
43 Von Below's orders incorrectly referred to the plateau as Hill 60 rather than its correct name, Hill 160.
44 Bean, *The AIF in France, 1916*, p. 699.
45 Intelligence, I Anzac Corps, 1/30/7, Part 1.
46 Rule, *Jacka's Mob*, p. 69.
47 Bean, *The AIF in France, 1916*, pp. 716 (quotation), 722, and Bean, 38-3DRL/606/54/1, AWM, p. 128.
48 Bean, 38-3DRL/606/244/1, AWM, pp. 54–56.
49 Duffy, *Through German Eyes*, p. 189.
50 Bean, 38-3DRL/606/244/1, AWM, pp. 54–56.
51 Quoted in Bean, *The AIF in France, 1916*, p. 720.
52 Rule, *Jacka's Mob*, pp. 75–78.
53 Duffy, *Through German Eyes*, p. 190.
54 Bean, *The AIF in France, 1916*, p. 723.

Chapter 12: *La Ferme Du Mouquet*
1 Masefield, *The Battle of the Somme*, p. 91.
2 Bean, *The AIF in France, 1916*, p. 728.
3 Stedman, *Thiepval*, pp. 35–39.
4 Bean, *The AIF in France, 1916*, pp. 732–33.
5 Leane, 1DRL/0411, AWM.
6 The challenges confronting the advancing Australians are drawn from Bean, *The AIF in France, 1916*, pp. 728–33.
7 Butler, *Special Problems and Services*, pp. 60–61.
8 For a description of a typical soldier's routine in the trenches, see Green, *The Fortieth*, pp. 15–16.
9 Bean, *The AIF in France, 1916*, p. 735 and 38-3DRL/606/50/1, AWM, p. 151.
10 According to Bean, one officer and 80 men were responsible for supplying rations to each battalion twice daily. See Bean, 38-3DRL/606/54/1, AWM.
11 Leane, 1 DRL/0411, AWM; description of a shell falling among troops crowded around a cooker in Devine, *The Story of a Battalion*, p. 42.

12 Butler, *The Western Front*, pp. 62–63.
13 Edey, MS 10511, SLV.
14 Bean, *The AIF in France, 1916*, p. 730.
15 Barker, *Signals*, p. 73.
16 Kearney, *Silent Voices*, p. 187.
17 For description of communication using pigeons, see Barker, *Signals*, p. 68.
18 Chapman, *Iven G. Mackay*, p. 75 and Bean, *The AIF in France, 1916*, p. 537.
19 White, *The Fighting Thirteenth*, p. 64.
20 Bean, *The AIF in France, 1916*, p. 663.
21 Gary Sheffield notes that narrow-front, 'battering ram' attacks were also conducted by Gough's II British Corps, and the 12th, 48th, and 49th British divisions. Sheffield, *The Somme*, p. 101.
22 Quoted in Bean, *The AIF in France, 1916*, p. 871.
23 Prior and Wilson, *The Somme*, pp. 273–75.
24 Sheffield, *The Somme*, p. 99.
25 Bean, *The AIF in France, 1916*, pp. 726–27.
26 McLeod, 1DRL/0455, AWM.
27 4th Infantry Brigade, 23/4/11, AWM.
28 Bean, 38-3DRL/606/54/1, AWM, pp. 168–69.
29 Bean's and Simkins's opinions from Sheffield, *The Somme*, p. 98 and McCarthy, *The Somme*, p. 10.
30 General Staff, 4th Division, 1/48/5, Part 1, AWM. Subsequent quotation, from Birdie ibid.
31 Sheffield, 'An Army Commander on the Somme', in Sheffield and Todman, *Command and Control on the Western Front*, p. 87.
32 See White's opinions in Bean, 38-3DRL/606/50/1, AWM. Butler also commented that the Mouquet Farm operations were marked by a more sombre and futile approach. See Butler, *The Western Front*, p. 61.
33 Bean, *The AIF in France, 1916*, p. 731.
34 ibid., p. 701.
35 Quoted in Farrar-Hockley, *Goughie*, p. 190.
36 Gough, *Soldiering On*, p. 131.
37 Farrar-Hockley, *Goughie*, p. 190.
38 Sheffield, 'An Army Commander on the Somme', in Sheffield and Todman, *Command and Control on the Western Front*, p. 81.
39 Sheffield and Bourne, *Douglas Haig*, p. 214.
40 Gilbert, *The Somme*, p. 147.
41 *The Herald*, 3 July 1916, p. 7.
42 ibid., 3 July 1916, p. 7 and 25 July 1916, p. 12.
43 *The Sydney Morning Herald*, 16 August 1916, p. 11.

44 *The Herald*, 13 July 1916, p. 8.
45 ibid., 7 August 1916, p. 5.
46 ibid., 26 July 1916, p. 5.
47 *The Mercury*, 26 July 1916, p. 5.
48 *The Herald*, 27 July 1916, p. 7.
49 ibid., 26 July 1916, p. 5.
50 ibid., 3 August 1916, p. 7.
51 ibid., 7 August, 1916, p. 1.
52 Beaumont, *Australia's War 1914–18*, pp. 162–63 and Williams, *Anzacs, the Media and the Great War*, p. 145.
53 Clark, *The Old Dead Tree and the Young Tree Green*, p. 21 and Inglis, *Observing Australia 1959–1999*, ch. 3.
54 Scott, *Australia During the War*, p. 64.
55 Bean, *Letters from France*, pp. 19–20.
56 Scott, *Australia During the War*, pp. 64–65.
57 Bean, 38-3DRL/606/54/1, AWM, p. 36.
58 Bean, *The AIF in France, 1916*, p. 470.
59 Charteris, *At GHQ*, pp. 149, 155.
60 Information on the censor's role and quotations drawn from Bean, 38-3DRL/606/55/1, AWM, pp. 81–86.
61 *The Herald*, 16 August 1916, p. 5.
62 Quoted in Brown, *The Imperial War Museum Book of the Somme*, p. 162.
63 Treloar, *An ANZAC Diary*, p. 283.
64 See *The Herald*, 25 July, p. 12; 27 July, p. 7; 28 July, p. 7; 7 August, p. 5; and 8 August, p. 12, all 1916; *The Mercury*, 26 July 1916, p. 5; and *Brisbane Courier*, 26 July 1916, p. 7.
65 *The Age*, 12 August 1916, p. 12 and *The Herald*, 29 August 1916, p. 12.
66 Quoted in Lewis, *Our War*, p. 216.
67 Sister Cunningham's letter is contained in Smith, PR88/058, AWM.
68 Bean, *The AIF in France, 1916*, p. 618.
69 Smith, PR88/058, AWM.
70 Series B2455, Stephen Allen, AWM.
71 Quoted in Williams, *Anzacs, the Media and the Great War*, p. 121.
72 Charteris, *At GHQ*, p. 144.
73 Farrer, *News from the Front*, p. 220.
74 ibid., p. 121.
75 See *The Mercury*, 26 July, p. 5; *The Mercury*, 28 July 1916, p. 5; and *The Advertiser*, 26 July 1916, p. 7.
76 Quoted in McKernan, *The Australian People and the Great War*, p. 122.
77 Gherardin, *Against the Odds*, p. 30.

78 Bean, *The AIF in France, 1916*, p. 470.
79 Quoted in Ferguson, *The Pity of War*, p. 213.
80 *The Herald*, 8 August 1916, p. 1.
81 Clayton, MS 10434, SLV.
82 Cocking, MS 10167, SLV.
83 Transcript of German wireless dated 25 November in Bean, 38-3DRL/606/66/1, AWM, p. 72.
84 Quoted in Ferguson, *The Pity of War*, p. 246.
85 Andrews, *The Anzac Illusion*, p. 134.
86 *The Argus*, 1 June 1917, p. 9.

Chapter 13: Kicking in the Back Door

1   Morris, MS 1565, SLV.
2   White, *The Fighting Thirteenth*, pp. 65, 66.
3   Gibbs, *The Battles of the Somme*, pp. 175–76.
4   Armitage, 1DRL/0053, AWM.
5   Bean, *The AIF in France, 1916*, p. 757.
6   Heavy shelling and Ross's note in Bean, *The AIF in France, 1916*, pp. 760–61, 763.
7   Armitage, 1DRL/0053, AWM.
8   White, *The Fighting Thirteenth*, p. 67.
9   Bean, *The AIF in France, 1916*, p. 770.
10 General Staff, 4th Division, 1/48/5, Part 3, AWM.
11 Bean, *The AIF in France, 1916*, p. 763.
12 Barton, 1DRL/0428, AWM.
13 White, *The Fighting Thirteenth*, p. 66.
14 Barton, 1DRL/0428, AWM.
15 Series B2455, Francis Maxwell Barton, NAA.
16 Quoted in Freeman, *Hurcombe's Hungry Half Hundred*, p. 239.
17 Armitage, 1DRL/0053, AWM.
18 Freeman, *Hurcombe's Hungry Half Hundred*, p. 65.
19 Bean, 38-3DRL/606/55/1, AWM, p. 145.
20 Bean, *The AIF in France, 1916*, p. 762.
21 Quoted in Souter, *Lion and Kangaroo*, p. 301.
22 Charteris, *At GHQ*, p. 162.
23 Robbins, *British Generalship on the Western Front 1914–1918*, pp. 68–73 and Sheffield and Todman, *Command and Control on the Western Front*, p. 52.
24 Treloar, *An ANZAC Diary*, p. 279. Subsequent quotations ibid., pp. 280, 282.
25 The scene behind the lines is described in Wren, *Randwick to Hargicourt*, p. 175 and Belford, *Legs-eleven*, pp. 299, 302.

26 Coates, MS 10345, SLV.
27 Treloar, *An ANZAC Diary*, p. 275.
28 Belford, *Legs-eleven*, p. 304.
29 Graham, MS 9640, SLV.
30 Coates, MS10345, SLV.
31 Carne, *In Good Company*, p. 79.
32 Belford, *Legs-eleven*, pp. 294, 296 and Taylor and Cusack, *Nulli Secundus*, p. 193. According to Bean, Birdie casually assumed that the Australians wanted to get back at the Germans. See Bean, 38-3DRL/606/60/1, AWM, p. 5.
33 Court of enquiry transcripts contained in Bean, 38-3DRL/606/244/1, AWM.
34 Quoted in Young and Gammage, *Hail and Farewell*, p. 152.
35 *The Herald*, 22 August 1916, p. 1.
36 ibid., 10 August 1916, p. 6.
37 Scott, *Australia During the War*, p. 338. Bean believed that Hughes colluded with Lloyd George to threaten the break-up of the 3rd Division in order to use this as a lever for conscription. See Bean, 38-3DRL/606/59/1, AWM, pp. 11–15.
38 Scott indicated that a reinforcement of 32,500 would be required immediately, and 16,500 for each of the three months following. See Scott, *Australia During the War*, p. 338.
39 ibid., pp. 338, 871.
40 Smith, PR8858, AWM. Subsequent quotation ibid.
41 Quoted in Goodman, *Our War Nurses*, p. 54.
42 Quoted in Bassett, *Guns and Brooches*, p. 71.
43 Quoted in Goodman, *Our War Nurses*, p. 54. See Avenell, PR85/111, AWM.
44 Griffith, *British Fighting Methods in the Great War*, p. 91.
45 Quoted in Breed, 'From France with Love 1916–1918', p. 87. Subsequent quotation ibid.
46 Smith, PR88/058, AWM.
47 Gibbs, *The Battles of the Somme*, p. 176.
48 Bean, *The AIF in France, 1916*, p. 770.
49 Freeman, *Hurcombe's Hungry Half Hundred*, p. 65.
50 Champion, 2DRL/0512, AWM. Subsequent quotations ibid.
51 Bean, *The AIF in France, 1916*, p. 771.
52 The *Official History* provides a breakdown of losses for all divisions on the Somme. The losses of the 1st, 2nd, and 4th Australian Divisions were marginally higher than those of the British divisions. See ibid., p. 862.
53 See Bean, 38-3DRL/606/40/1, AWM.
54 Chapman, *Iven G. Mackay*, p. 77.

Chapter 14: Second Stunt

1. The scene is described in Harvey, *From Anzac to the Hindenburg Line*, p. 137 and de Vine, 1DRL/0240, AWM.
2. Bean, *The AIF in France, 1916*, p. 771.
3. ibid., p. 772.
4. Bean described the approaches that the troops followed to the firing line in Bean, 38-3DRL/606/55/1, AWM.
5. Thomas, 3DRL/2206, AWM.
6. Abson, 2DRL/0007, AWM and Foxcroft, MS 9613, SLV.
7. Moorhead, 3DRL/7253, AWM.
8. Bean, 38-3DRL/606/55/1, AWM, p. 32.
9. Chapman, *Iven G. Mackay*, p. 78.
10. Harvey, *From Anzac to the Hindenburg Line*, p. 138.
11. Bean, *The AIF in France, 1916*, p. 777 and 38-3DRL/606/55/1, AWM, p. 43.
12. General Staff, 1st Australian Division, 4/1/42, Part 2, AWM.
13. Bean, *The AIF in France, 1916*, p. 778.
14. ibid. Also see Bean, 38-3DRL/606/55/1, AWM, p. 43.
15. Foxcroft, MS 9613, SLV.
16. Edey, MS 10511, SLV.
17. Londey, 'If I Die at any Rate I Will Have Tried', p. 32. Subsequent quotation ibid.
18. Edey, MS 10511, SLV. Subsequent quotation ibid.
19. Moorhead, 3DRL/7253, AWM. Subsequent quotations ibid.
20. Chapman, *Iven G. Mackay*, p. 78. Subsequent quotation and discussion of deserting soldier ibid., p. 79.
21. Treloar, *An ANZAC Diary*, p. 275.
22. The *Official History* stated that the Australian Defence Act allowed no death penalty except for men found guilty of mutiny, or desertion to, or treacherous dealings with, the enemy. See Bean, *The AIF in France, 1916*, pp. 870–71.
23. Bean, 38-3DRL/606/55/1, AWM, pp. 58–59.
24. For more detail on the attacks, see Bean, *The AIF in France, 1916*, pp. 780–91.
25. Bean, 38-3DRL/606/55/1, AWM, p. 87.
26. Prior and Wilson, *The Somme*, p. 167.
27. Bean, *The AIF in France, 1916*, p. 791.
28. Duffy, *Through German Eyes*, pp. 190–91.
29. General Staff, 1st Australian Division, 1/42/19, Part 4, AWM.
30. Bean, *The AIF in France, 1916*, p. 793.
31. General Staff, 1st Australian Division, 1/42/19, Part 2, AWM.
32. Foxcroft's experiences described in Foxcroft, MS 9613, SLV.
33. Quoted in Young and Gammage, *Hail and Farewell*, p. 156. Subsequent quotations ibid., pp. 155, 156.

34 For Howard and Nicholson's story, see Carne, *In Good Company*, pp. 101–06.
35 Series B2455, Ernest Victor Lee, NAA.
36 ibid. Lee's statement of service suggests that he was located at Étaples when the 5th Battalion completed its two stunts at Pozières.
37 Eric Andrews noted that, of the 182 absent-without-leave cases reported on the Western Front in December 1916, 130 were Australian. See Andrews, *The Anzac Illusion*, p. 105.
38 Bean, *The AIF in France, 1916*, p. 787.
39 Austin, *As Rough as Bags*, p. 174.
40 Bean, 38-3DRL/606/55/1, AWM, p. 87.
41 Bean, *The AIF in France, 1916*, p. 795, 797.
42 Series B2455, Herbert Walter Crowle, NAA.
43 The key contributor to shell shock, exposure to prolonged artillery shelling, was much less prevalent on Gallipoli, compared to the Somme.
44 Series B2455, Alfred John Hearps, NAA.
45 Newton, *The Story of the Twelfth*, p. 103.
46 The *Official History* recorded that the 10th Battalion troops were naturally shaken after passing through the German bombardment to reach the front line. See Bean, *The AIF in France 1916*, p. 797.
47 3rd Infantry Brigade, 23/3/10, AWM.
48 Kearney, *Silent Voices*, p. 194.
49 Bean, *The AIF in France, 1916*, p. 799.
50 Hearps, 1DRL/0428, AWM.
51 Bean, *The AIF in France, 1916*, p. 801.
52 Belford, *Legs-eleven*, p. 318.
53 Badger, 1DRL/0428, AWM.
54 Crowle, 1DRL/0227, AWM. Subsequent quotations ibid.
55 Casualty figure taken from Bean, *The AIF in France, 1916*, p. 802.
56 Belford, *Legs-eleven*, pp. 319–24.
57 For more on the aftermath of Crowle's, Badger's, and Hearps's deaths, see Series B2455, Personnel Dossiers, NAA and 1DRL/0428, AWM.
58 Badger, 1DRL/0428, AWM.
59 *The Sydney Morning Herald*, 4 April 1925, p. 16.
60 Quoted in Fewster, *Gallipoli Correspondent*, p. 14.
61 Bean, *Letters From France*, p. 123.
62 Bean, 38-3DRL/606/55/1, AWM, pp. 39–42.
63 ibid, p. 138.
64 Bean, 38-3DRL/606/56/1, AWM, p. 28.
65 ibid., p. 30.
66 Bean, 38-3DRL/606/55/1, AWM, pp. 145A–145H.

67 Bean, 38-3DRL/606/56/1, AWM, p. 52. Subsequent quotation ibid., p. 32.
68 Bean, *The AIF in France, 1916*, p. 802.
69 Chapman, *Iven G. Mackay*, p. 78.
70 Harvey, *From Anzac to the Hindenburg Line*, p. 143.
71 Speed, *Esprit de Corps*, p. 76.
72 Joynt, *Breaking the Road for the Rest*, p. 93.
73 Chapman, *Iven G. Mackay*, p. 79.

Chapter 15: Battering Ram

1 Bean, 38-3DRL/606/55/1, AWM, pp. 84–86, 87. Bean suspected that the censors deliberately withheld stories that credited the Australians' efforts in the battle.
2 Bean, *The AIF in France, 1916*, p. 802.
3 Quoted in Sheldon, *The German Army on the Somme 1914–1916*, p. 243.
4 Bean, *The AIF in France, 1916*, p. 873.
5 Gilbert, *The Somme*, p. 160.
6 Bean, *The AIF in France, 1916*, p. 805.
7 Sadler, *The Paladin*, p. 99 (quotation from Gellibrand ibid.) and Bean, *The AIF in France, 1916*, p. 807.
8 Quoted in Breed, 'From France with Love 1916–1918', p. 105.
9 Birdwood's view of Gellibrand is contained in letters to Senator George Pearce. See Bean, 38-3DRL/606/237/1, AWM, pp. 42, 53.
10 Bean, 38-3DRL/606/244/1, AWM, pp. 88–90.
11 Derham, *The Silent Ruse*, pp. 52–53; Bean, 38-3DRL/606/244/1, pp. 88–90 and 38-3DRL/606/55/1, p. 113, both AWM; Bean, *The AIF in France, 1916*, p. 798; and Sadler, *The Paladin*, p. 90, ch. 13.
12 According to his biographer, Gough removed 11 British officers of the rank of major or above prior to the Somme offensive, as he considered them unfit for command. Gough, with Haig's blessing, also sacked X British Corps commander Lieutenant-General Sir Thomas Morland, who disagreed with his approach of attacking the Germans repeatedly to prevent them from rebuilding their defences. See Farrar-Hockley, *Goughie*, pp. 183, 190.
13 Sadler, *The Paladin*, pp. 88, 99, 100.
14 Bean, *The AIF in France, 1916*, p. 809.
15 Sheldon, *The German Army on the Somme 1914–1916*, p. 244.
16 Breed, 'From France with Love 1916–1918', p. 105 and Gorman, *With the Twenty-second*, p. 40.
17 Sadler, *The Paladin*, p. 89.
18 Bean, *The AIF in France, 1916*, p. 810, 821 and 38-3DRL/606/56/1, AWM, p. 3.
19 Beatty, 1DRL/0428, AWM.

20 Bean, *The AIF in France, 1916*, pp. 821 and Cumming, 1DRL/0428, AWM.
21 Bean, 38-3DRL/606/56/1, AWM, p. 60.
22 Figures from Bean, *The AIF in France, 1916*, p. 821.
23 Short in a letter to Bean dated 7 May 1928, in Bean, 38-3DRL/606/244/1, AWM.
24 Quoted in Young and Gammage, *Hail and Farewell*, p. 159.
25 Rule, *Jacka's Mob*, p. 88.
26 White, *The Fighting Thirteenth*, p. 72.
27 Bean, *The AIF in France, 1916*, p. 828.
28 General Staff, 4th Division, 1/48/5, Part 3, AWM and White, *The Fighting Thirteenth*, p. 73.
29 Stedman, *Thiepval*, pp. 35–36.
30 See notes on interrogations on 5, 7, and 8 August. Intelligence, I Anzac Corps, 1/30/7, Part 1, AWM.
31 Treloar, *An ANZAC Diary*, p. 287.
32 Intelligence, I Anzac Corps, 1/30/7, Part 1, AWM, p. 90.
33 *The Times*, 31 August 1916, p. 7.
34 Quoted in Bean, *The AIF in France, 1916*, p. 887.
35 Gilbert, *The Somme*, pp. 162–63.
36 Quoted in Breed, 'From France with Love 1916–1918', p. 91.
37 White, *The Fighting Thirteenth*, p. 72.
38 Quoted in Bean, *The AIF in France, 1916*, p. 829.
39 Bean, *The AIF in France 1916*, p. 831; Bean, 38-3DRL/606/57/1, AWM, pp. 1–2; and White, *The Fighting Thirteenth*, p. 74.
40 Bean, 38-3DRL/606/57/1, AWM, p. 5 and *The AIF in France, 1916*, p. 832.
41 Bean, 38-3DRL/606/57/1, AWM, pp. 6–7.
42 Longmore, *The Old Sixteenth*, p. 118 and White, *The Fighting Thirteenth*, p. 72.
43 Rule, *Jacka's Mob*, p. 109.
44 Bean, 38-3DRL/606/57/1, AWM, p. 9. Subsequent quotations ibid., pp. 8, 9–15.
45 Story of the Raws family in Young and Gammage, *Hail and Farewell*, introduction, pp. 165, 172.
46 Foxcroft, MS 9613, SLV.
47 Bean, 38-3DRL/606/55/1, AWM, pp. 110–11.
48 General Staff, 4th Australian Division, 1/48/5, Part 3.
49 Quoted in Urban, 'Somme Anzac Digger', p. 53.
50 There are numerous references to the dead lying about the battlefield. For examples see Moorhead, 3DRL/7253 and Condon, 1DRL/0209, both AWM; and Morris, MS 1565 and Foxcroft, MS 9613, both SLV.
51 Bean, 38-3DRL/606/54/1, AWM, p. 48.
52 Carlyon, 'Who are the Anzacs "known unto God" in a Flanders field?', p. 5.
53 Bean, *The AIF in France, 1916*, p. 661.

54 Quoted in Polanski, *We Were the 46th*, p. 17.
55 Hinckfuss, *Memories of a Signaller*, p. 73.
56 Rule, *Jacka's Mob*, p. 82. Subsequent quotation ibid., p. 81.
57 Series B2455, Alexander Taylor Pearce (alias John Pearce), NAA.
58 Quoted in Austin, *Our Dear Old Battalion*, p. 147.
59 Quoted in 'Families Discover Link 17 Years Later', Australians at War, 2001, australiansatwar.gov.au.

Chapter 16: Graveyard or Glory

1 Treloar, *An ANZAC Diary*, pp. 287–88.
2 Bean, *The AIF in France, 1916*, p. 837–38.
3 General Staff, 4th Division, 1/48/16, Part 1, AWM.
4 Dawkins, 1DRL/0237, AWM.
5 Wadsley, 'Dear Everybody at Home', pp. 11–14. Subsequent quotations ibid.
6 Series B2455, Howard de Nyst Williams, NAA.
7 Quoted in Duffy, *Through German Eyes*, p. 202.
8 Statement by repatriated prisoner contained in Series B2455, John Cotter, NAA. Subsequent quotation ibid.
9 Wadsley, 'Dear Everybody at Home', pp. 11–14. Troops in Fabeck Graben described in Bean, *The AIF in France, 1916*, pp. 846–54; Bean, 38-3DRL/606/58/1, AWM, p. 17; and Wadsley, 1DRL/0428, AWM.
10 Ekin-Smyth, 1DRL/0428, AWM.
11 Bean, *The AIF in France, 1916*, pp. 845–46 and *Letters from France*, p. 161.
12 Message in Bean, *The AIF in France, 1916*, p. 845 and quotation from Morris, MS 1565, SLV.
13 Bean, 38-3DRL/606/58/1, AWM, pp. 11–12.
14 McCallum, 1DRL/0428, AWM.
15 Events described in, and quotations from, Bean, *The AIF in France, 1916*, p. 852. Subsequent quotation ibid., p. 851.
16 Bailey, 1DRL/0428 and Bean, 38-3DRL/606/244/1, p. 69, both AWM.
17 Williams, 1DRL/0428, AWM.
18 Quoted in Browning, *Fix Bayonets*, p. 52.
19 Smythe, 1DRL/0428, AWM.
20 Series B2455, John Cotter, NAA.
21 Bean, 38-3DRL/606/58/1, AWM, p. 13.
22 General Staff, 4th Division, 1/48/6, Part 1, AWM.
23 Bean, *The AIF in France, 1916*, p. 856.
24 Bean, *The AIF in France, 1916*, p. 854; Gough, *The Fifth Army*, entry dated 3 September; and Gilbert, *The Somme*, p. 174.
25 Ross, *The Myth of the Digger*, p. 16.

26 Birkwood, 3DRL/3376, AWM.
27 General Staff, 4th Division, 1/48/6, Part 1, AWM.
28 Treloar, *An ANZAC Diary*, p. 290. Subsequent quotation ibid.
29 Bean, 38-3DRL/606/58/1, AWM, p. 40.
30 Bean, *Letters from France*, p. 175.
31 Quoted in Winter, *Making the Legend*, p. 11.
32 Quoted in Bean, *Letters from France*, p. 173.
33 Bean, *The AIF in France, 1916*, p. 874.
34 ibid., p. 860 and Sheffield and Bourne, *Douglas Haig*, p. 227.
35 Bean, *The AIF in France, 1916*, p. 860.
36 Gough, *The Fifth Army*, p. 148.
37 Charteris, *At GHQ*, p. 162.
38 Quoted in Hetherington, *Blamey*, p. 39.

Chapter 17: Aftermath

1 The actual casualties incurred during the conflict on the Somme remain controversial, partly because each army used its own method for calculating them. The figures quoted by Gerald Gliddon are: British, 419,000; French, 204,000; German, 420,000. See Gliddon, *Somme 1916*, pp. 454–55.
2 Bean, *The AIF in France, 1916*, p. 858.
3 ibid., p. 852.
4 ibid., p. 852 and Woodhead, 'Families Discover Link 17 Years Later'.
5 Sergeant Ramshaw's notes in Bean, 38-3DRL/606/244/1, AWM, p. 70.
6 Series B2455, Albert Clifford, NAA.
7 *The West Australian*, 3 September 1917, p. 1.
8 Wadsley, 'Dear Everybody at Home', pp. 11–14.
9 Population and casualty comparisons based on 1911 Australian census conducted by Commonwealth Bureau of Census and Statistics.
10 White, *The Fighting Thirteenth*, p. 79.
11 Quoted in Breed, 'From France with Love 1916–1918', p. 79.
12 Terraine, *The Western Front 1914–1918*, p. 15.
13 Charteris, *At GHQ*, p. 179.
14 Bean, 38-3DRL/606/60/1, AWM, pp. 2–6.
15 Quoted in Taplin, 'Dad's War Diaries 1915–1919', p. 20.
16 Quoted in Gammage, *The Broken Years*, pp. 169–70.
17 Rule, *Jacka's Mob*, p. 110.
18 Claridge, 2DRL/0240, AWM.
19 Bean, 38-3DRL/606/60/1, AWM, p. 7.
20 Leane, 1DRL/0411, AWM.
21 Willmington, 'Diaries of an Unsung Hero', p. 137.

22 Condon, 1DRL/0209, AWM.
23 Series B2455, John Condon, NAA.
24 Cocking, MS 10167, SLV.
25 Bourke, 1DRL/0139, AWM.
26 Bean thought it was a lie, but believed it reflected the prevailing feeling toward Birdwood. See Bean, 38-3DRL/606/60/1, AWM, p. 2.
27 Quoted in Taplin, 'Dad's War Diaries 1915–1919', p. 21.
28 Quoted in Bean, 38-3DRL/606/60/1, AWM, p. 5.
29 ibid., pp. 5–6.
30 Rule, *Jacka's Mob*, pp. 109–10.
31 White, *The Fighting Thirteenth*, p. 75.
32 Treloar, *An ANZAC Diary*, pp. 285–86.
33 Series B2455, Ralph Ratnevelu Raymond Ekin-Smyth, NAA.
34 Interview with Margaret Lee, 30 November 2010.
35 See Ekin-Smyth, Michael, 'Anzac Day 2004', wordsmythltd.blogspot.com.
36 Series B2455, Ernest George Smythe, NAA.
37 Series B2455, Howard de Nyst Williams, NAA.
38 Series B2455, Leslie Parsons, NAA.
39 Mandle, *Going it Alone*, ch. 1; Ross, *The Myth of the Digger*, introduction and ch. 1; and Beaumont, *Australia's War 1914–18*, pp. 152–77.
40 Interview with Margaret Lee, 30 November 2010.
41 Prior and Wilson, *The Somme*, p. 184.
42 White, *The Fighting Thirteenth*, p. 75.
43 Quoted in Sheffield, *The Somme*, p. 155.
44 ibid., 88.
45 For an extract of Douglas Haig's final despatch on 21 March 1919, see Sheffield and Bourne, *Douglas Haig*, appendix 4.
46 Charteris, *Field Marshal Earl Haig*, p. 226.
47 Quoted in Gilbert, *The Somme*, p. 243.

Chapter 18: War-weariness
1 Information from Clark, *The Old Dead Tree and the Young Tree Green*; Smith, PR88/058, AWM; and Series B2455, Stephen Allen, NAA.
2 Quoted in Scott, *Australia During the War*, p. 348.
3 Quoted in Matthews, *Australian Soldiers in the Great War 1914–18*, p. 59.
4 Scanlon, PR90/105, AWM.
5 Cocking, MS 10167, SLV.
6 Quoted in Scott, *Australia During the War*, p. 359.
7 Quoted in Bean, *Anzac to Amiens*, p. 293.
8 Scott, *Australia During the War*, p. 370.

9   Cocking, MS 10167, SLV.
10 For monthly enlistments see Scott, *Australia During the War*, p. 871.
11 Bean, *Two Men I Knew*, p. 145.
12 Terraine, *The Western Front 1914–1918*, p. 81.
13 Millman, *Pessimism and British War Policy 1916–18*, pp. 32, 33.
14 Pope and Wheal, *The Macmillan Dictionary of the First World War*, pp. 230–31.
15 Barnett, *The Great War*, p. 209.
16 Gorman, *With the Twenty-second*, p. 103.
17 Birdie's letter to Senator Pearce, which explains Forsyth's condition, dated 12 November 1916. Bean, 38-3DRL/606/237/1, AWM, p. 36.
18 See Maclean, 'Australia's Military Hero', www.activeboard.com.
19 Callaway, 1DRL/0428, AWM.
20 Thomas, 1DRL/0428, AWM.
21 Drake-Brockman, *The Turning Wheel*, p. 107.
22 Series B2455, Leslie Francis Strong Mather, NAA.
23 Battalion newsletter, 1918, Mitchell Library.
24 Rule, *Jacka's Mob*, p. 340.
25 Adam-Smith, *The Anzacs*, p. 2.
26 Scott, *Australia During the War*, p. 835.
27 Blainey, *Our Side of the Country*, p. 178.
28 Joynt, *Breaking the Road for the Rest*, p. 169. Subsequent quotation ibid.
29 Series B2455, Arthur Foxcroft, NAA and Foxcroft, MS 9613, SLV.
30 Scott, *Australia During the War*, p. 888.
31 Freeman, *Hurcombe's Hungry Half Hundred*, p. 264.
32 Lloyd and Rees, *The Last Shilling*, p. 227.
33 Blair, *Dinkum Diggers*, p. 168.
34 Quoted in White and Russell, *Memories and Dreams*, pp. 62–67.
35 Leese, *Shell Shock*, p. 171.
36 See *The Torch-Bearer*, 29 August 1929, pp. 72–73.
37 Bean, 38-3DRL/606/244/1, AWM, p. 103.
38 Series C138, John Harris, NAA.
39 Information on Robert Smith drawn from Series J34, Robert Smith, NAA and Smith, PR88/058, AWM.
40 Coulthard-Clark argues that Birdie's irritation toward Legge's Australianist outlook, rather than failings in his exercise of command, were behind his decision to send him back to Australia. See *No Australian Need Apply*, p. xi.
41 Andrews, *The Anzac Illusion*, p. 99.
42 Coulthard-Clark, *No Australian Need Apply*, pp. 160, 205.
43 Legge in a letter to Bean dated 9 January 1928. See Bean, 38-3DRL/606/244/1, AWM, p. 103.

44 Coulthard-Clark, *No Australian Need Apply*, p. 209, 211.
45 Hooky Walker's note to Bean dated 13 August 1928. Quoted in Sheffield and Todman, 'An Army Commander on the Somme', in *Command and Control on the Western Front*, p. 71. Subsequent quotation ibid., p. 75.
46 Gough, *The Fifth Army*, p. 143.
47 Winter, *Haig's Command*, p. 265.
48 Derham, *The Silent Ruse*, p. 74.
49 Stone, *1932*, p. 17.
50 Wiest, *Haig*, p. 113.
51 Cook, 'In the Realm of the Senseless', *The Bulletin*, November 2006, p. 42.
52 Viewpoint contained in Douglas Haig's final despatch on 21 March 1919. See Sheffield and Bourne, *Douglas Haig*, appendix 4.
53 Firkins, *The Australians in Nine Wars*, p. 94.
54 Hudson, *Billy Hughes in Paris*, p. 20.

Chapter 19: The Missing

1 Adam-Smith, *Australian Women at War*, pp. 73–74.
2 Scates and Francis, *Women and the Great War*, p. 104.
3 Rule, *Jacka's Mob*, p. 337.
4 Drosen, 1DRL/0428, AWM.
5 ibid. and Series B2455, Private George Droser [sic], NAA.
6 Interview with Colin Drosen, 16 August 2010.
7 Captain Theodore Wells's letter of condolence written to Hester Allen on 1 March 1917, at www.awm.gov.au/encyclopedia/memorial_scroll/letter5.asp. Subsequent quotation ibid.
8 1DRL/0428 Private Stephen Charles Allen and Allen, 1DRL/0428, both AWM.
9 *The Sydney Morning Herald*, 14 August 1917, p. 6 and 14 August 1919, p. 8.
10 Series B2455, Philip Gerald Browne, NAA. Subsequent quotation ibid.
11 Browne, 2DRL/0619, AWM.
12 *The Brisbane Courier*, 28 November 1916, p. 8.
13 Series B2455, Philip Gerald Browne, NAA. Subsequent quotation ibid.
14 Quoted in Winn, *Still Playing the Game*, pp. 8, 196.
15 *The Brisbane Courier*, 21 July 1917, p. 4.
16 Series B2455, Philip Browne, NAA. Subsequent quotation ibid.
17 *The Sydney Morning Herald*, 27 September 1921, p. 9.
18 Rule, *Jacka's Mob*, 1933, p. 338. Subsequent quotation ibid.
19 *The Sydney Morning Herald*, 29 November 1937, p. 13.
20 Series B2455, James Connelly, NAA.
21 *The Argus*, 28 October 1937, p. 1 and *The Canberra Times*, 27 October 1937, p. 3.
22 Series B2455, John Thomas Rowan, NAA.

23 *The Argus*, 29 January 1938, p. 4.
24 Inglis, *Sacred Places*, p. 485.
25 Quoted in Keech, *Pozières*, p. 118.
26 *The Sydney Morning Herald*, 4 August 1920, p. 12.
27 'Address in Memory of Australian Dead', Bishop of Amiens in the Church of Long, Somme, 4 Nov 1918, Mitchell Library, State Library of New South Wales.
28 Quoted in Winter, *Sites of Memory, Sites of Mourning*, p. 50. Subsequent quotation ibid.
29 Series B2455, Percy Blythe, NAA.
30 Blair, *Dinkum Diggers*, p. 177.
31 Gorman, *With the Twenty-second*, p. 33.
32 Joynt, *Breaking the Road for the Rest*, p. 194.
33 Raws, 'Records of an Australian Lieutenant', p. 9.
34 Inglis, *Anzac Remembered*, p. 163.
35 *The Argus*, 3 May 1915, p. 6.
36 *The Sydney Morning Herald*, 24 July 1917, p. 6. Subsequent verses ibid., pp. 5, 6.
37 *The Brisbane Courier*, 23 July 1921, p. 6.
38 Lee's story from Series B2455, Ernest Victor Lee *aka* Ernest John Jefferies, NAA.
39 *Every Week*, 19 May 1919, p. 1.
40 *The Herald*, 3 June 1919, p. 12.
41 *Every Week*, 19 May 1919, p. 1. Subsequent quotation ibid.
42 Winter, *Making the Legend*, pp. 14, 18.
43 Bean, 38-3DRL/606/244/1, AWM.
44 *The Brisbane Courier*, 17 September 1927, p. 12.
45 White in a letter to Bean dated 19 September 1927. Quoted in Winter, *Making the Legend*, 1992, p. 157.
46 Short in a letter to Bean dated 19 July 1928. See Bean, 38-3DRL/606/244/1, AWM.
47 Winter, *Making the Legend*, p. 1.
48 Quoted in McCarthy, *Gallipoli to the Somme*, p. 388.
49 McCarthy, *Gallipoli to the Somme*, p. 387.
50 *The Sydney Morning Herald*, 26 January 1952, p. 6.
51 *The Argus*, September 1917, p. 7.
52 For Caux's biography, see Silver, *Marcel Caux*.
53 *The Sydney Morning Herald*, 25 November 1927, p. 8.
54 *The Age*, 22 April 2006, pp. 1, 9.
55 Sheffield, *The Somme*, 2004, p. 164.
56 Tynan, 1DRL/0428, AWM.
57 Edey, MS 10511, SLV.

Acknowledgements

My principal debt is to two individuals who said yes — Lyn Tranter of Australian Literary Management and Henry Rosenbloom of Scribe Publications. It would have perhaps been safer for both to say no to a first-time Australian author; instead, they took a punt and backed me unwaveringly. I hope their approach encourages all unpublished authors to persevere.

I am forever indebted to my partner, Alex, and daughters, Isabella and Amelia, for their patience, particularly as this project lasted longer than the Great War and resulted in me being office-bound for most sunny weekends. I promise you that our next family holiday will be somewhere other than northern France.

In researching *Pozières*, I have relied heavily on the following institutions: Australian War Memorial, Imperial War Museum, National Archives of Australia, National Library of Australia, State Library of Victoria, and State Library of New South Wales. I am staggered by the number and diversity of records retained by these institutions and the unfettered access that researchers such as myself have to them. Many recently digitised records — personnel dossiers at the National Archives of Australia; Charles Bean's diaries and notebooks, unit diaries, official histories, and soldiers' records at the Australian War Memorial; and copies of Australian newspapers at the National Library of Australia — have been critical to this project.

They have allowed me to complete large swathes of research on the internet rather than repeatedly visiting each site to view the original records, which is challenging when juggling other priorities, such as work and family. I firmly believe that the digitisation of records at sites such as the Australian War Memorial is an important step toward the democratisation of our history.

Behind each great institution is a team of dedicated professionals, who always surprised me with their willingness to assist in this project: Penny Hyde and David McGill of the Research Centre at the Australian War Memorial; Simeon Barlow, Cheryl McNamara, and Fiona Burn of the National Archives of Australia; and Ranald Leask of the Commonwealth War Graves Commission. Archivists Denise Miller, of Toowoomba Grammar School, and Welwyn Peterson, of Sydney Church of England Grammar School, also provided invaluable assistance.

Thank you to Paul Matton, James Bennett, Roger Coupe, and Robert Hadler for providing feedback and encouragement on a raw manuscript; Tom Flood of Flood Manuscripts for his incisive reviews; and Dr Peter Stanley, who, with a generosity rarely encountered among others, reviewed the entire manuscript and provided critical feedback and ongoing encouragement throughout the project.

Finally, a big thank you to the Scribe team who guided me — initially Nicola Redhouse, who helped to articulate what the book was about and then worked patiently through the early chapters; and later Julia Carlomagno, for her encouragement, thoughtful editing, and commitment to telling the soldiers' story. I feel privileged to have worked with you both.

And to those men who left Australia's shores almost 100 years ago, who fought, died, and were buried in unmarked graves on the Somme — I hope this book imparts later generations with an understanding of your lives, motivations, and hopes.

Index

I Anzac Corps *see also* 1st Australian Division; 2nd Australian Division; 4th Australian Division
  advance on Mouquet Farm, 195
  allocated to Reserve Army, 14–16
  casualties at Pozières, xii, xiv–xv, xvi, 33–34, 99–100, 112, 276–77
  casualty clearing stations, 111
  Central Registry, 46, 213–14, 273
  complement, x–xi, 4, 9
  Contay Château headquarters, 22, 262, 272, 325
  failure of Intelligence, 251–2
  formation, 3–4
  introduction to trench warfare, 7
  march to staging villages, 11
  prepare for battle, 43–45
  railway timetables, 194
  supply lines, 190–91
  transfer to the Somme, 9–10
  transferred to Ypres, 262
  underpreparedness, 13–14
  water, 191
1st Australian Division
  1st Brigade, 17–18, 91, 225
  2nd Battalion, 119
  2nd Brigade, 18, 91, 92, 107, 112, 223, 234
  3rd Battalion, 98, 225
  3rd Brigade, 18, 47, 116, 223, 234, 238
  4th Battalion, ix, x, 27, 105, 118–19
  5th Battalion, 100–3, 224, 226
  6th Battalion, 107–8, 224, 234
  7th Battalion, 100, 103
  9th Battalion, 103, 224–25, 307
  11th Battalion, 103–4, 121, 238
  ammunition columns, 113–14
  attack Fabeck Graben Trench, 229–30
  attack intersection of Pozières Trench and OG lines, 31–34
  casualties, 119, 121, 227–28, 238, 241
  engineers, 100
  entrain to Ypres, 241–42
  formation, 50
  Fromelles, 35–36
  Gallipoli campaign, 126–27
  howitzer batteries, 113
  infantry battalions, 29
  Lewis gun crews, 78–79
  march to firing line, 27–28
  ordered to attack Pozières, 14–15, 42
  placed under British command, 14
  Pozières Day, 313
  Pozières Ridge, 94–95
  Pozières Ridge, first attack, 100–3
  Pozières Ridge, second attack, 103–4
  Pozières Trench, capture, 63–64, 69
  'prospecting', 86
  'ratting', 83–84
  reinforcements, 228–29, 243
  relieve British Army, 28
  relieved by 2nd Division, 114–15, 116, 117, 119–22, 234

387

relieved by 4th Division, 181
return to the line, 220–21, 222, 224–25
sail to France, 4
Sanitary Hygiene Section, 215
in staging villages, 214–15
transfer to Somme, 9
Vignacourt, 11
war memorials, 312
Ypres, 272–73
II Anzac Corps, 3–4
2nd Australian Auxiliary Hospital, 218–19
2nd Australian Division
  5th Brigade, 117, 118, 125, 126, 129, 132, 171, 234, 244
  6th Brigade, 117, 125, 126, 129, 130, 150, 152, 244–45
  6th Brigade Machine-gun Company, 174
  7th Brigade, 117, 125, 126, 129, 131, 132, 143, 153, 244
  10th Battalion, 234, 235, 246
  12th Battalion, 130, 235, 236
  14th Battalion, 248–49
  18th Battalion, 126
  20th Battalion, 132, 134–36, 139, 160
  21st Battalion, 246–49
  22nd Battalion, 130, 160, 161, 203–4, 247
  23rd Battalion, 124, 130, 133–34, 138, 141, 143, 174, 215–16, 245, 247, 249
  24th Battalion, 123, 130
  25th Battalion, 132, 137, 142, 161
  26th Battalion, 132, 137, 138, 142, 161, 162
  28th Battalion, 132, 134, 136–37, 142, 182
  Amiens, 11–12
  casualties, 132, 143, 173, 244, 249
  complement, 125
  Fabeck Graben Trench, attack, 234, 235–37
  formation, 127
  Legge commands, 19
  Mouquet Farm, advance on, 244–49
  OG lines, advance on, *135*, 297
  OG lines, follow-up attack on, 158–64

  relieve 1st Division, 114, 116, 117, 122–23, 234
  relieved by 4th Division, 173–74, 249–50
  return to the line, 231–32, 234, 244
  sail to France, 4
  transfer to Somme, 9
  Ypres, 272–73
3rd Australian Division, 217
4th Australian Division
  4th Brigade, 175, 180
  12th Brigade, 175, 180
  13th Battalion, 208–9, 209–10, 250–51, 253–56, 277, 280, 305
  13th Brigade, 175–76, 180, 262, 268, 271, 275
  15th Battalion, 194, 196, 313
  16th Battalion, 196, 250–51, 253–56
  27th Battalion, 181, 322
  45th Battalion, 186
  48th Battalion, 176, 180, 181–82, 186, 191, 304
  49th Battalion, 262, 265–66, 267, 288
  50th Battalion, 211
  51st Battalion, 209–10, 262, 264–65, 266, 267–68, 271
  52nd Battalion, 262, 264, 266–67, 271
  advance on Mouquet Farm, 208, 253–56, 258, 261, 262–72, *263*, 305
  bombardment of, 181–83
  casualties, 186, 220, 275
  in Egypt, 4
  encounter 1st Division, 181
  Fabeck Graben Trench, 210
  Germans attempt to retake Hill 60, 185–87
  lack of battle experience, 175
  march to Pozières, 37
  march to the Somme, 175–76
  relieve 2nd Division, 173–74, 249–50
  relieved by 1st Division, 219–20, 224–25
  Thiepval, 188
  transfer to Somme, 9, 11
5th Australian Division
  15th Brigade, 37
  casualties, 40, 121, 277

in Egypt, 4
Fromelles, 36, 38–39, 40
Ypres, 272–73

absent without leave, 232–33
Abson, Lieutenant Matthew, 108, 224
aid posts, 67, 191–92
AIF (Australian Imperial Force) *see also* Anzac Corps
  Bean, 5, 13
  disciplinary problems, 233–34
  divisional commands, 18–19
  enquiry into missing, 304
  penal servitude in, 228
  promotion in, 178, 179
Aitken, Sister, 164–65
Albert (France), 27–28, 323
alcohol abuse, 120
Alexander, Lance-Corporal Charles, 277
Allen, Hester, xiv, 204, 305–7
Allen, Private Robert, 204, 304, 305–7
Allen, Private Stephen, 204, 304, 305–7
Alliston, Sergeant James, 215–16
Amiens (France), 11–12, 312
Amiens–Doullens Road, 10–11
amputees, 218–19, 296–97
Anzac Corps *see also* I Anzac Corps; II Anzac Corps
  ANZAC (acronym), x
  battle kit, x
  Birdwood commands, 24, 156–58
  British divisional commands, 18–19
  in British tunics, 177
  formation, x–xi, 3–4
  from Gallipoli, 3
  Memorial Scroll, 307
  metallic discs, 137, 158
  missing, 303–18
  post-war diseases, 294
  troops vote for conscription, 288
  veterans, 292–94, 300–1, 313, 322
Anzac Day, xv
Anzac legend, xiii, 85, 179, 200, 272, 283–84, 315, 317–18
Armentières (France), 6–7, 90
Armistice Day, 290–91
Armitage, Captain Harold, 209, 210, 211

artillery management, 132–33
Ashmead-Bartlett, Ellis, 89–90
Asquith, Herbert, 52, 72, 74, 151, 289
Assenhein, Sergeant Albert, 305
Auld, Captain Pat, 211
Australia
  British demand manpower from, 217
  censorship laws, 200–1, 205–7
  conscription, xvi, 217, 287–89
  constitutional ties to Britain, 49
  economic dependence on Britain, 50
  enlistments, 3, 76, 289
  importance of Gallipoli, 51–53
  recruitment, 216
  status as an ally, 75
Australian Army Council, 217
Australian Base Records Office, 165, 204, 307
Australian Comforts Fund, 119
Australian Graves Detachment, 309
Australian Journalists' Association, 124
Australian Labor Party, 289
Australian National Memorial, 283, 311, 314
Australian Naval and Military Expeditionary Force, 127
Australian Red Cross Society, 304–6
Australian Repatriation Commission, 293, 296, 317
Australian War Memorial, 30, 179, 311–12
Avenell, Sister Edith, 218

Baden-Powell, Robert, 17
Badger, Sergeant Dave, 234–38
Bailey, Lieutenant Francis, 269–70
bandsmen, 191
Bapaume (France), 162
Barbour, Sergeant Freddie, 33, 307
Barbour, Captain Thomas, 40
Barton, Cecilia, 211
Barton, Captain Francis ('Toby'), 210–11
battles of attrition, 168–70, 285, 301
Bean, Private Arthur, 236
Bean, Charles
  1st Australian Division, 120

AIF, 5, 13
attitude towards Australian soldiers, 4–6, 85, 272
Australian Outback, 5
Australian War Memorial, 311–12
British, 20
censorship, xv, 201
Contalmaison, 47
the dead, 259
death of, 322
despatches from Pozières, xii, 88–90, 150–51, 207
Fromelles, 39, 40
honorary rank in army, 205
Legge, 297–98
Leo Butler, 239–41, 249
letters from parents, 212
Official History of Australia in the War of 1914–18, 6, 319–21
as official war correspondent, xv, 2, 202
Park Lane Trench, 196
personal diary, 5–6, 246, 248–49, 277, 321
private assessment, 243–44, 278
Sinclair-MacLagan, 62–63
Somme, 273
'unofficial history', 321
visits Pozières, 43, 149–51, 239, 249, 321–22
White, 3, 25, 26, 42, 256, 320
working methods, 238–39
Beatty, Second-Lieutenant Alexander, 248
Beck, Private Alfred, 236
Bécourt Château (France), 150, 280, 325
Belford, Captain Walter, 104
Belgium, 2, 49 *see also* Ypres
Below, General Fritz von, 57, 184–6, 244, 252
Bennett, Lieutenant-Colonel Alfred, 76
Bennett, Lieutenant-Colonel Gordon, 107–8, 115, 234
Bennison, Mrs Annie, 204
Berteaucourt (France), 11
Biggs, Lieutenant Frederick, 31, 32
Birch, Brigadier-General James, 133

Birdwood, Lieutenant-General Sir William ('Birdie')
autobiography, 298
commands Anzac Corps, 3–4, 9
commands of AIF, 18–19
Cox, 273
the dead, 261
Gallipoli campaign, 157
Gellibrand, 130, 144
Gough, 14, 17, 172
Haig, 24, 114, 145
I Anzac Corps, 22, 23–25, 193
Legge, 125, 127–28, 147
medal distribution, 220–21
Mouquet Farm, 272
relations with troops, 156–58, 279–80
reputation, 299
request for manpower, 217
Walker, 16, 19, 47, 121, 225
war memorials, 312
White, 3, 146–47, 299–300
Ypres, 272–73
Black, Sergeant Allan, 266–67
Black, Major Percy, 254
Blamey, Lieutenant-Colonel Thomas, 16, 29, 30–31, 47, 91, 94, 117, 121, 274
Blythe, Corporal Percy, 134, 137, 161, 164, 313
Booth, Henry, 289
Bosisto, Russell, 322
Bourke, Private John, 87, 279
Brand, Brigadier-General Charles ('Digger'), 180, 194, 196, 246, 277
breakdown, 235
Bridges, Colonel Arthur Holroyd, 148, 153, 246
Bridges, Major-General William, 24, 50, 126, 130
Britain
British bondholders, 300
burials, 280–81
class distinctions, 177–78
Gallipoli campaign, 52
British 7th Suffolk Battalion, 194, 196
British 12th Division, 209
British 36th (Ulster) Division, 197
British Army Council, 289

British Committee of Imperial Defence, 48
British Expeditionary Force, 1, 155–56
  artillery, 17, 29, 99, 113, 186, 256
British Fifth Army *see* British Reserve Army
British First Army, 36, 37
British Fourth Army
  attack on Guillemont, 229, 264
  early attempts to capture Pozières, 20–21, 47
  II Corps, 209
  III Corps, 82
  lack of co-ordination, 194
  Rawlinson commands, 14
  relieved by 1st Australian Division, 28
  southern Pozières, 17, 56, 60, 68, 71
  Thiepval, 15
British Graves Registration Commission, 281
British Imperial General Staff, 125
British Imperial War Graves Commission, 281, 282, 310
British Labour Corps, 309
British Reserve Army, 14, 15–16, 17, 21, 42, 71, 194, 197, 264, 274, 298
British Second Army, 7
British Staff College (Camberley), 26–27
British War Council, 151, 154, 217, 244
British War Office, 201, 274
Brookes, Norman, 48
Brown, Lieutenant Arnold, 164
Browne, James, 307–9
Browne, Sergeant Philip, 11, 31–34, 304, 307–9
Brownell, Sergeant Raymond, 60
Bruce, Stanley, 320
Buckley, Reverend Father, 317
burials *see* war graves
Butler, Angus, 240
Butler, Leo, 239–41, 249
Byng, Lieutenant-General Julian, 273

Callaway, Second-Lieutenant Fred, 83, 85, 119, 292
Campbell, Mrs, 216
Canadian corps, 262, 273

carrier pigeons, 192
Carvick, Lieutenant James, 174
Casey, Lieutenant Richard, 130
casualties
  1st Australian Division at Pozières, 119, 121, 227–28, 238, 241
  2nd Australian Division at Pozières, 132, 142, 143, 173, 244, 249
  4th Australian Division at Pozières, 186, 220, 275
  5th Australian Division at Fromelles, 40, 121, 277
  Allied, 284
  Anzacs in Gallipoli campaign, 51, 277
  British, 1, 8
  French, 1, 8
  German, 58, 284
  I Anzac Corps at Pozières, xii, xiv–xv, xvi, 33–34, 99–100, 112, 276–77
  Russian, 8
  Somme, 275
Caux, Marcel, 322
censorship, 150, 200–1, 205–7
Champion, Lance-Corporal Ben, 59, 220–21
Charteris, Brigadier-General John, 81, 167, 202, 205, 277, 298
  chief-of-intelligence, 8, 165, 213, 251–52, 274
Churchill, Winston, 25, 52, 151, 166, 169–70, 298
Claridge, Lieutenant Walter, 31, 278
Clayton, Private William, 122–23, 206
Clemenger, Lieutenant William, x, 61
Clifford, Private Arthur, 123, 128, 153, 158, 171, 174, 245, 247, 268–69, 270
Clifford, Lieutenant Bert, 265, 266, 276
Clifford, Thomas and Emma, 276
Coates, Albert, 7, 12, 67, 99, 205, 214, 215
Cocking, Captain Stanley, 206, 279, 288, 289
Combles (France), 264
communications, 105–6, 163–64, 192, 259
Condon, Private Jack, 279
Condon, Richard, 279

Connelly, James, 310
conscription, xvi, 217, 287–89
Contalmaison (France), 47
Contay Château (France), 22, 262, 272, 325
Cook, Joseph, 48
Cook, Patrick, 301
Corney, Captain Frank, 161, 163
corps commanders, 157
Cotter, Private John, 266, 270, 276
Coulson, Sergeant Leonard, 304
Courcelette (France), 162–63, 256, 266, 322
Cowans, William, 216
Cox, Major-General Sir Herbert Birdwood, 273
   commands 4th Division, 175–76, 291
   Mouquet Farm, 193–94, 196
   promotions by, 178–80
   takes control front line, 250, 264
Croft, Brigadier-General Sir Henry Page, 21
Crowle, Mrs Beatrice, 238
Crowle, Lieutenant Bert, 234–38
Cumming, Lieutenant Norman, 248
Cunliffe-Owen, Brigadier-General Charles, 114, 169
Cunningham, Sister, 203–4

Dawkins, Captain Charles, 264–65
the dead *see* war graves
Dean, Lieutenant Archibald, 261
desertion, 228, 232
Dexter, Chaplain Walter, 119, 259
discipline, 175–77, 233–34
Domart (France), 11
Dowling, Private Claude, 92
Drake-Brockman, Lieutenant-Colonel Edmund, 196
Drake-Brockman, Captain Geoffrey, 6–7, 12, 16, 66, 67, 122
Drayton, Sergeant Bruce, 140
Drosen, Colin, 305
Drosen, Ernest, 305
Drosen, Private George, 304–5
Durack, Fanny, 28

Edey, Sergeant John, 191–92, 226, 227, 293, 325–26
Edmonds, Charles, 286
Eggington, Second-Lieutenant Henry, 107
Ekin-Smyth, Michael, 282
Ekin-Smyth, Captain Ralph, 267, 281–82, 284
Elkington, Private Walter, 131, 139, 159, 160, 162, 163, 170, 259
Elliott, Lieutenant Colonel, 116
Elliott, Brigadier-General Harold ('Pompey'), 37–41
Elliott, Mrs Helen, 261
Elvin, Sergeant Leonard, 107

Fabeck, Major Hans von, 189
Falkenhayn, General Erich von, 81, 169, 250, 252, 285
Farrall, Fred, 294–95
fatigue parties, 237
Fayolle, General Marie Émile, 194
Ferdinand, Archduke Franz, 47
Ferguson, Mr Justice, 207
Ferguson, Private Robin, 170
Ferguson, Sir Ronald Munro, 24, 127–28
First World War *see* Great War
Fisher, Andrew, 24, 281
Foch, Marshal Ferdinand, 169
Forsyth, Brigadier-General John, 18, 91, 107, 115, 230, 291
Foxcroft, Private Arthur
   4th Battalion, ix, 226
   attitude towards Germans, 86–87
   the dead, 258–59
   diary, 7, 29, 30, 45, 119, 183
   enlists, x, 3–4, 50
   Pozières Ridge, 224
   Pozières Trench, 59–60, 70
   war pension, 293–94
   wounded, 230–31
France
   army collapses, 285
   Australian war memorials, 312
   concession for British cemeteries, 281
   grands mutilés march, 301–2
   Sixth Army, 194, 264

French, General Sir John, 154, 166
Fromelles (France), 36–42
front line, 2, *2*, 3

Gallipoli campaign
  Birdwood, 25, 157
  British deploy Anzacs, 75
  British view of, 52
  casualties, 277
  evacuation, 3, 13–14
  importance for Australia, xiii, xvi, 51–52
  Legge, 126–27
  Lone Pine, 183–84
  Tivey, 39
  veterans, 45
  Walker, 16
Gallwitz, General Max von, 158, 186, 229, 252
Gellibrand, Brigadier-General John ('Jack'), 125, 129, 130, 132, 139, 144, 163, 173, 244–47, 291–92, 300
George V, King, 13, 72, 74, 307
Germans
  artillery bombardments, 7, 8, 14, 82, 95–96, 107, 112–13, 116, 128–29, 181–83, 208
  attempt to retake Hill 60, 184–87
  casualties, 58, 284
  change command structure, 250, 252–53
  the dead, 261
  defense of Mouquet Farm, 243–44, 250
  Hindenburg Program, 290
  howitzers, 97–100
  intelligence, 57, 140, 165–66, 175
  manpower, 274
  Minenwerfer, 269
  'no retreat' doctrine, 250, 252–53
  precarious defences, 229
  prisoners, 84–86
  propaganda machine, 206
  recapture Fabeck Graben Trench, 274
  recapture Skyline Trench, 209
  snipers, 71
  treatment of wounded, 139–40

Glasfurd, Brigadier-General Duncan, 180–81, 291
Glasgow, Brigadier-General Thomas ('Bill'), 180, 210, 255, 262, 270–71, 275
Godley, General Sir Alexander, 4
Goodwin, Sergeant-Major Frank, 105
Gough, General Sir Hubert
  2nd Australian Division, 125, 142, 145, 153, 165
  4th Australian Division, 142, 193
  Bean, 234, 256
  Birdwood, 14, 17, 172
  commands I Anzac Corps, 68, 91, 297
  commands Reserve Army, 14–15
  the dead, 260
  dismissal of officers, 246
  Guillemont, 223
  Haig, 35–36
  Legge, 244
  Maze, 46, 65
  Mouquet Farm, 188–90, 209, 271, 298
  Thiepval strategy, 194, 197–98, 271, 273, 274
  Walker, 16, 17, 47, 91–92, 121, 229, 298–99
  White, 17, 25, 27
Graham, Private Vic, 122, 215
Graham, Sergeant Wally, 64
Grandcourt (France), 266
Graves, Robert, 152
Great Depression (1930s), 300
Great War, xi, xvii, 1, 48, 278, 290–91
Green, Lance-Corporal Ernest, 267
Groom, Littleton Ernest, 308
Guillemont (France), 223, 229, 264

Haig, General Sir Douglas
  2nd Australian Division, 133, 144–46, 165
  attitude towards Anzacs, 13, 169–70
  battles of attrition, 168–70, 285, 301
  Birdwood, 24, 114, 145
  capture of Pozières, 15–16, 21, 71
  Charteris, 8
  commander-in-chief British Expeditionary Force, xii, 155–56
  daily schedule, 71–72

dismissal of officers, 246
Fromelles, 35–36, 37–38, 41
Gough, 35–36
Hughes, 75
instructions, 169
Legge, 146
limitations, 170
manner, 73, 145
orders local actions, 81–82
Somme objectives, 284
Somme strategy, 79–81, 151–52, 167, 252, 275, 285
Thiepval, 274
veterans, 300–1
White, 146
Ypres, 81
Haking, Lieutenant-General Sir Richard, 36–37, 40–41
Hale, Private Will, 306
Halvorsen, Lieutenant William, 270
Hamilton, Lieutenant, 114
Hamilton, General Sir Ian, 24, 25, 52, 241
Hanbury-Sparrow, Captain Alan, 8
Harris, Captain Hubert, 110
Harris, Captain John, xv, 12, 13, 30, 31, 64, 99, 108–12, 294–96
Harrison, Lance-Corporal Ivan, 253
Harwood, Captain Ross, 254
Hatcher, Lance-Corporal William, 161, 164–65
Hearps, Mrs, 238
Hearps, Lieutenant Alfred, 235–37, 238
Hentig, Captain von, 285
High Wood (France), 229
Hinckfuss, Private Harold, 192, 260
Hindenburg, Field-Marshal Paul von, 250, 252–53
Hindenburg Program, 290
Hinds, Mrs, 313
Hoban, Lieutenant, 114
Hocking, Private Fred, 122, 134, 138, 141, 314
Holmes, Lieutenant Ernest, 113
Holmes, Brigadier-General William, 125, 171, 234, 291
Horton, Lance-Corporal Douglas, 44, 59, 62, 70, 119

Host, Lieutenant Walter ('Tiny'), 84
Howard, Signaller Denis, 232–33
Howell-Price, Lieutenant-Colonel, 75–78, 98, 99, 108, 225, 239, 291
Hughes, William Morris, xv, 73–75, 217, 287–88, 289, 301
Hunter-Weston, Lieutenant-General Aylmer, 47
hysteria, 235

In memoriam notices, 314–15
Ireland, 288

Jackson, Private Thomas, 138
Jacob, Private Gilbert, 220
Japan, 301
Jess, Lieutenant-Colonel Carl, 100–1, 115
Joffre, General Joseph, 9, 72, 194
Johnstone, William, 315
Joynt, Captain William Donovan, 44, 50–51, 117, 241, 293, 314

Keane, Private Vincent, 101
Kellerman, Annette, 28
Kiggell, Brigadier-General Launcelot, 24, 126
Kilgour, Private Arthur, 278
Kitchener, Lord Horatio, 3, 24–25, 126, 168
Knyvett, Lieutenant Hugh, 40

La Boisselle (France), 29–30
Laing, Lieutenant Elmer, 71, 83–84, 98
Lawson, Henry, 44, 51–52
Le Maistre, Lieutenant-Colonel Frank, 100–1
Le Nay, Lieutenant Louis, 104
Le Sars (France), 162
League of Nations, 301
Leane, Captain Allan, 191, 278
Leane, Lieutenant-Colonel Ray ('Bull'), 180–82, 185, 186
Lee, Ernie, xvi, 52–53, 233, 315–18
Lee, Herman and Mary, xvi–xvii, 52, 233, 316, 318
Lee, Jack, xvii, 316–17
Lee, Margaret, 282, 284

Legacy, 300
Legge, George, 297
Legge, Major-General James Gordon
   attack on OG trenches, 128–29, 131–33, 143–44
   Bean, 297–98
   Birdwood, 125, 127–28, 147
   commands 2nd Division, 19, 27, 117, 125
   follow-up attack on OG lines, 147–48, 166–67
   Gallipoli campaign, 126–27
   Haig, 146
   military career, 126, 297–98
Lillie, Captain Cyril, 102
Lillie, Thomas, 315
Lloyd George, David, xv, 72, 152, 154, 155, 166, 168, 170, 206, 216, 289, 298
Londey, Private George, 45, 101, 102, 103, 226–27
Loos, Battle of, 167
Ludendorff, General Erich, 252, 285–86

McCallum, Captain Daniel, 264–65, 266, 268–69, 283
McCay, Major-General James, 37, 39, 126–27
McFarlane, Private Eric, 306
McGuire, Private John, 215
Mackay, Lieutenant-Colonel Iven Bean, 239
   biography, 85
   Birdwood, 24
   commands 4th Battalion, 6, 9, 12, 13, 31, 75–78, 118–19, 227–28
   enlists, 50
   K Trench, 105
   La Boisselle, 30
   nickname, 77
   observations of shell shock, 111
   return to the line, 221, 224
McNeil, Mary, 313
McPherson, Corporal John, 211
McSparron, Bill, 183–84
McSparron, Mrs Jane, 184
McSparron, Private Joe, 12–13, 183–84
Malcolm, General Neil, 145

Malpas, Lieutenant Harold, 45
Manifold, Colonel Courtenay, 260
Manning, Frederic, 121
Manning, Major Charlie, 174
Mannix, Dr Daniel, 288
maps, 193
Marseilles (France), 6
Marshall, Sergeant Lewis, 138, 140, 164
Masefield, John, xii, 19, 68, 72, 170, 188
Mather, Lieutenant-Colonel Leslie, 67, 292
Mauger, Corporal Francis, 134, 137
Maxwell, Lieutenant Duncan ('Big'), 264, 266–67, 271
May, John, 226
Maze, Paul, 11, 28, 29, 46, 56–57, 61, 65, 69, 70, 90–91
media *see* newspapers
Mediterranean Expeditionary Force, 3, 25, 52
Menin Gate (Ypres), 311
missing *see* war graves
Mobbs, Private Herbert, 62
Moltke, Helmuth von, 154
Monash, Brigadier-General John, 25, 126–27, 217, 298
Monteath, Lieutenant Charles, 31, 32
Moore, Lieutenant-Colonel Donald, 112
Moorhead, Private Eric, 102, 120, 224, 227
Morgan, Lance-Corporal Roger, 66
Morland, Lieutenant-General Sir Thomas, 144
Morris, Harold, 268
Morrison, Private Alfred, 12
Morrow, Private Edgar, 141, 142, 163–64
Munro, General Sir Charles, 37–38
Murdoch, Keith, 24, 199
Murray, General Sir Archibald, 4

Napier, Brigadier-General William, 114
New Guinea, 127, 301
New Zealand, 289
New Zealand Division *see* I Anzac Corps
newspapers, xv–xvi, 6, 47–48, 199–200, 202–3, 216 *see also* war correspondents

censorship, 200–1, 205–7
In memoriam notices, 314–15
Nicholson, Private Tod, 232–33
Norgard, Private Ernest, 131, 163
Northcliffe, Lord Alfred, 72, 156–57

O'Brien, Private Dan, 219
Official History of Australia in the War of 1914–18, 6, 319–21
Owens, Private Jack, 184

Palmer, Sergeant Henry, 176
Paris (France), 232–33
Paris Peace Conference (1919), xv, 301
Parsons, Sergeant Leslie, 261, 275–76, 283
Paton, Brigadier-General John, 125, 139, 149, 291
Peach, Private William, 102
Pearce, Senator George, 24, 203, 307
Pearce, Jack, 260–61
Perry, Private Percy, 137
personal effects, 260
Phillips, Major, 319
Plant, Captain Harold, 174
politicians, 206
Pollard, Sergeant Roy, 267
Polygon Wood (Belgium), 112
Pope, Brigadier-General Harold, 39
Pozières 1916 (Charlton), xvii
Pozières, Battle of
  Allied bombardment, 58–59
  Anzacs, xii–xiii
  assembly trenches, 58–59
  Bapaume Road, 64–65
  battle plans, 54–56, 82, 132, 147–48, 153–54, 222–43, 245, 250
  battlefield, 55
  capture plan, 17
  Centre Way, 185
  Chalk Pit, 30, 222
  Chalk Pit Road, 259
  clay soils, 253
  Dead Man's Road, 99
  Death Valley, 224
  early British attempts to capture, 20–21

Fabeck Graben Trench, 190, 210, 212, 223, 229–30, 234, 235–37, 250, 254, 255, 263, 265–67, 268
First Avenue Trench, 223–24
Gibraltar (German blockhouse), 19
Hill 60, 184–87
jumping-off trenches, 148–49
K Trench, 19, 104–5, 128
Kollmann Trench, 265
light railway, 65
Mash Valley, 192
military value of Pozières, xi
Mouquet Farm, 182, 186–87, 188–90, 220, 244
Mouquet Farm, 2nd Division advance on, 244–49
Mouquet Farm, 4th Division advance on, 208, 253–56, 258, 261, 262–72, *263*
Mouquet Farm fortification, 250–51
Mouquet Farm, I Anzac Corps advance on, *195*
OG (old German) trench lines, 18, 20, 64, 65, 68, 78–79, 125–26
OG (Old German) trench lines, attack on, 128–29
OG (Old German) trench lines, capture of part of, 172
OG (Old German) trench lines, follow-up attack on, 158–64
Park Lane Trench, 189–90, 193–6, 208
Pozières Ridge, 94–116, 223
Pozières today, xii, 323–25
Pozières Trench, 19, 43, 59–60, 63–64
Pozières Trench and OG lines intersection, 31–34
Quarry, 225
Skyline Trench, 189–90, 209
Tom's Cut, 185
villagers of Pozières, 19–20, 261, 323–24
war memorials, 312
Windmill, 181
wire, 136–37
Zigzag Trench, 245, 247
Preston, Sergeant Harry, 60, 61, 63, 64, 78, 97

Price Weir, Lieutenant-Colonel Stanley, 246
Pugh, Lieutenant George, 118

RAAF (7 Squadron Royal Flying Corps), 193
Ramage, Private, 8
Ramshaw, Sergeant Luke, 276
Rawlinson, General Sir Henry, 14, 15, 229
Raws, Lieutenant Alec ('Little Raws'), 123–24, 141, 149, 165, 215–16, 231–32, 249, 256–58, 320
Raws, Reverend John, 123, 124, 256–58, 314
Raws, Lennon, 257–58
Raws, Lieutenant Robert Goldthorpe ('Goldy'), 123, 124, 138, 141, 215–16, 231–32, 256
Red Cross, 304–6
Redburg, Major George, 246
Reith, Private William, 269
Remarque, Reich Maria, 152
Repington, Colonel Charles, 166–67
Riordan, Annie, 211
Riordan, Sergeant John, 211
Robertson, Field-Marshal Sir William, 151–52, 154, 166
Roper, Lieutenant Osmund, 236
Ross, Lieutenant-Colonel Arthur, 209
Rowan, John, 310
Rowlands, Major Verner, 109
Ruggles, Private Charles, 102–3
Rule, Sergeant Ted, 278, 280, 292, 303–4
  14th Battalion, 120, 175, 182, 185, 186, 250, 256
  background, 181
  Jack Pearce, 260–61
  John Newton Wanliss, 309–10
runners, 192–93

Sainsbury, Private Noel, 140
Sale, Captain Fred, 247
Samsonov, Alexander, 154
Sassoon, Siegfried, 152
Scanlon, Sergeant Daniel, 288
Sedgman, Private Stan, 248

Selmes, Captain Jeremiah, 113
shell shock, xv, 108–12, 235, 295–96
  burial by shells, 226–27
  shell design, 218–19
Shoobridge, Private Frank, 66, 67
Short, Captain Lionel, 174, 249, 320
signallers, 192
Sinclair-MacLagan, Brigadier-General Ewen, 18, 29, 31, 47, 62–63, 68, 103, 115–16, 118, 234, 292
Sinclair, Private Wisbey, 139–40
Sinn Fein Easter Rising, 288
Smith, Private Peter, 61–2, 71, 98, 118
Smith, Private Robert ('Roy'), xv, 203–4, 218, 296–97
Smyth, Brigadier-General Neville, 17–18, 68, 91, 104, 221, 225
Smythe, Lieutenant Ernie, 269, 270, 283
Snodgrass, Private Peter, 66
Soldier Settlement Scheme, 293, 313
Somme, Battle of the, xi, 7–9, 9, 12, 42, 275, 284, *285*
  military cemeteries, 323, 324
South, Paddy, ix, 231
Stewart, Private Alfred, 149, 173–74, 278
Stredwick, Sydney, 67
stretcher-bearers, 66–67, 191, 237–38
Stuart, Private John, 137
Styles, Leslie, 310
support logistics, 10
Sutherland, Lieutenant, 114

Tara Hill (France), 271
Tara Valley (France), 117
Tatnall, Captain William, 174
Telfer, Private Reg, 278, 279
Thiepval (France), xi, 15–16, 163, 188, 264, 274
  Gough's strategy, 194, 197–98, 271, 273, 274
Thomas, Corporal Arthur, 11, 45, 224, 292
Thomas, Leslie, 313
Thompson, Lieutenant-Colonel Astley, 76
Tivey, Brigadier-General Edwin, 39
Toll, Lieutenant-Colonel Frederick, 38

Toowoomba Grammar School, 308
Touzel, Rollie, 260
Treloar, Lieutenant John
   Anzac Corps Central Registry, 46, 87–88, 165, 213–14, 273
   diary, 160, 174, 202, 228, 252, 262, 280–81
   unit diaries, 319
Tschoeltsch, Lieutenant, 247
Turner, Charles, 133–34
Tynan, Private William, 324–25

Vadencourt Wood (France), 120, 280
Vandendriessche, Monsieur, 189, 323–24
veterans, 292–94, 300–1, 313, 322
Victoria Cross, xiv
Vignacourt (France), 11
Villers-Bretonneux (France), 283, 311, 314
Vine, Corporal Apcar de, 13, 28, 105, 119, 319

Wadsley, Lieutenant Len, 264, 267, 276
Walker, Major-General Harold ('Hooky')
   Birdwood, 16, 19, 47, 121, 225
   commands 1st Division, 14, 27, 46–47, 65, 115, 223, 225, 228–30
   Gough, 16, 17, 47, 91–92, 121, 229, 298–99
   Legge, 117, 127
   Pozières Ridge, 94–95, 106
   relations with troops, 179–80
   White, 42
Walters, Lieutenant George, 92
Wanliss, Harold, 310
Wanliss, John Newton, 309–10
war correspondents, xv, 4, 80, 89–90, 200–2 *see also* newspapers
   accreditation, 201–2
   complicity with army, 205–7
   reporting, 203, 207
war graves
   burial by shells, 226–27
   burial parties, 259–60
   burials, 280–81, 309
   the dead, 258–61
   missing, 303–18
   Somme military cemetaries, 323, 324
   war memorials in Australia, 311
war pensions, 293–94
Warloy (France), ix, 280
Watkinson, Arthur, 313
Wells, Captain Theodore, 204, 305–6
Western Front, 3
White, Brigadier-General Cyril Brudenell
   on alcohol abuse, 120
   battle plans, 245, 250
   Bean, 3, 25, 26, 42, 256, 320
   Birdwood, 3, 146–47, 299–300
   chief-of-staff, 3
   death in plane crash, 321
   Fromelles, 40, 42
   Gellibrand, 130
   Gough, 17, 25, 27
   Haig, 146
   health, 246
   I Anzac Corps, 22–23, 25–27, 46, 193–94
   Legge, 127, 147, 153, 297
   Mouquet Farm, 250–51
   request for manpower, 217
   Ypres, 272–73
White, Ethel, 23, 171
Williams, Captain Howard, 265, 266, 267–68, 270, 283
Wilson, Colonel Hutton, 201
Wilson, Roy ('Bluey'), ix, 226
Windeyer, Mr, 309
Woodham, Corporal Charles, 316
Woolcock, Clarence, 315
Wright, Lieutenant, 114
Wright, Private Walter, 43–44

Young, Private Tom, 136
Ypres (Belgium), 81, 241–42, 250, 272–73, 311